# Broadway Musicals

## SHOW BY SHOW
### THIRD EDITION

**Other Books By Stanley Green**

The World of Musical Comedy

The Great Clowns of Broadway

Encyclopaedia of the Musical Theatre

Encyclopaedia of the Musical Film

Broadway Musicals of the 30s (Ring Bells! Sing Songs!)

Starring Fred Astaire

The Rodgers and Hammerstein Story

Rodgers and Hammerstein Fact Book (editor)

# Broadway Musicals

## SHOW BY SHOW
### THIRD EDITION

## by Stanley Green

070102

**Hal Leonard Publishing Corporation**

Published by HAL LEONARD PUBLISHING CORP.
P.O. Box 13819, 7777 W. Bluemound Road
Milwaukee, WI 53213 U.S.A.

First edition, 1985
Second edition, 1987

**Library of Congress Cataloging-in-Publication Data**

Green, Stanley.
    Broadway musicals, show by show / by Stanley Green. — 3rd ed.
       p.     cm.

Includes index.
ISBN 0-88188-761-7 :   $16.95
1. Musical revue, comedy, etc.—United States.   I. Title.
ML1711.G735   1987
782.81'0973—dc19                                   90-17372

# Contents

## Show by Show

(For a complete alphabetical listing of the
shows included in this book, see page 279.)

# Contents

# Contents

# Contents

## Contents

# Indexes

# Preface

*Broadway Musicals Show by Show* is a combination history, guide, fact book, and photograph album of the most memorable productions presented both on and off Broadway from *The Black Crook* in 1866 right up to the present. There are over 300 entries, including 22 adaptations of foreign works and 16 revivals, comprising musical comedies, musical dramas, operettas (or comic operas), revues, two retrospective "catalogue" shows (*Ain't Misbehavin'* and *Sophisticated Ladies*), one all-dancing show (*Dancin'*), one gospel show (*Don't Bother Me, I Can't Cope*), and one celebration of a director's work (*Jerome Robbins' Broadway*). Among criteria for selection were length of run (all book musicals remaining over 500 performances are here), seminal importance, people involved, uniqueness of approach or subject matter, quality of the score, and general acceptance as a significant work in the field. Broadway revivals were included if they ran longer than the original productions, if they were notable in their own right, or if they were part of extended tours.

In the section devoted to a show's credits, I have included names in parentheses of writers, producers, directors, and choreographers who made major contributions to a production, but — for whatever reason — did not receive official credit. Cast listings contain the names of only principal actors (except when a future well-known performer had a bit part or was in the chorus). Song listings are usually only of the best-known musical numbers.

Reference books occasionally differ as to number of performances and, in general, I have followed the listings in *The Best Plays* yearbooks, currently edited by Otis Guernsey, Jr. and Jeffrey Sweet. Continuous runs have been credited to productions that went directly from off to on Broadway and those that may have been temporarily closed for vacations or other reasons. Return visits following a tour, however, have not been included under the original engagements. (The 1954 *Threepenny Opera,* which reopened 15 months after its initial Off-Broadway run, is a special case.)

Since shows today need to play much longer to succeed than in the past, I have cited the five longest running musicals of each decade to give a more accurate indication of their success.

Whenever a theatre is mentioned for the first time, I have noted its location, whether it is still in use, and, if so, whether it has changed its name. (Note that the Majestic Theatre that once stood on Columbus Circle is different from the one still in use, which is on West 44th Street.)

The symbols following most entries indicate if the show has been recorded, published in book form, or licensed for amateur and professional use. An original-cast recording is abbreviated by OC, a studio-cast recording by SC, and a subsequent original-cast recording contains the year that the new production was offered on Broadway. In most cases, the record company listed is the one under whose label the album is currently available. A musical whose text and lyrics (and occasionally songs) have been published as a trade book bears the name of the publisher and the year of publication. An asterisk indicates a softcover acting edition. In some cases, the musical's text is published in an anthology. Performing rights organizations that license musicals are represented by the following abbreviations: TW for Tams-Witmark (757 3rd Avenue, New York 10017); SF for Samuel French (25 West 45th Street, New York 10036); MTI for Music Theatre International (49 East 52nd Street, New York 10022); R&H for Rodgers & Hammerstein (598 Madison Avenue, New York, 10022); DPC for Dramatic Publishing Co. (4150 North Milwaukee Avenue, Chicago 60641); SO for Shubert Organization (234 West 44th Street, New York 10036); and TM for Theatre Maximus (1650 Broadway, New York 10019).

The following books were used to check facts: *Songs of the Theatre* by Richard Lewine and Alfred Simon (H. W. Wilson); *The City and the Theatre* by Mary C. Henderson (Preston); *The Collector's Guide to the American Musical Theatre* by David Hummel (Scarecrow); *At This Theatre* by Louis Botto (Dodd, Mead); *Musicals!* ("Directory of Musical Properties Available for Production") by Richard Chigley Lynch (American Library Assn.); *The American Musical Theatre* by Gerald Bordman (Oxford); *Show Music on Record* by Jack Raymond (Frederick Ungar); *American Song* ("The Complete Musical Theatre Companion") by Ken Bloom (Facts on File).

I am particularly grateful to my Hal Leonard associates — Keith Mardak (who first proposed that I write this book), Glenda Herro, and Mary Bultman — for their interest, cooperation, and support. My wife, Kay, as always, was indispensable in checking the manuscript, selecting photographs, and offering many helpful suggestions, and Susan Green and Rudy Green, as always, were available for welcome comments.

Stanley Green
Brooklyn, New York

November, 1989

# Foreword

With its glitter, its imagination, and its rhythmic beat, the Broadway musical has become a distinctive commodity, recognized and admired throughout the world, even though the form itself derived from many sources. The earliest example of musical comedy is generally cited as John Gay's *The Beggar's Opera,* first performed in London in 1728. Labeled a "ballad-opera," it used popular songs of the day as part of a story that satirized both corrupt political leaders and florid Italianate opera, best exemplified by the works of Handel. Later precursors include the English comic operas of Gilbert and Sullivan, the French *opéra bouffe* of Offenbach, and the Viennese operettas of Strauss, Lehar, Straus, and others. In fact, the first use of the term "musical comedy" dates back to the productions of George Edwardes at the Gaiety Theatre, London, at the end of the 19th Century.

America saw the first musical comedy in 1750 when a traveling company offered the premiere North American showing of *The Beggar's Opera* (whose most celebrated spinoff was Kurt Weill's *The Threepenny Opera*). Homegrown examples of the form were also on view during Colonial days, but it was not until 1866 when the first long-run musical smash, *The Black Crook,* was unveiled in New York to dazzle theatregoers with its spectacular scenic effects and its bevy of barelimbed coryphées. From then on, plays embellished with songs became a major attraction for seekers of theatrical entertainment along the Great White Way.

Possibly because their contributions distinguished this particular form of theatre and also because of the high quality of their work, composers were more noted than lyricists during the early years of the 20th Century. Victor Herbert, Rudolf Friml, Sigmund Romberg, Jerome Kern, George Gershwin, and Vincent Youmans were the most prominent figures during the first two decades, as well as George M. Cohan and Irving Berlin who, because they wrote the words that went with their music, helped prepare the public for a greater awareness of the importance of lyrics. Due recognition was — eventually — given to the contributions of such practitioners as P. G. Wodehouse, Otto Harbach, Oscar Hammerstein II, Ira Gershwin, and B. G. DeSylva, but it was not until the emergence of Lorenz Hart (who shared equal billing with composer Richard Rodgers) and Cole Porter (who wrote his own music) that lyric-writing was elevated to the same level of public appreciation as that given to music-writing.

It took somewhat longer for the book or libretto (Italian for "little book") to be considered in the same league as music and lyrics, since up through the 1920s it was hardly more than a framework designed to provide opportunities to spotlight the singers, dancers, and comedians. That was also a factor in the popularity of the revue which did away with a story line completely in favor of short farcical or satirical sketches. Florenz Ziegfeld was easily the dominant figure of this kind of entertainment with his elaborate annual *Follies* which he guided through 21 editions. Rival showmen George White and Earl Carroll brought out their own annual *Scandals* and *Vanities,* and this form of musical theatre persisted in popularity through the Forties. Revues should not be confused with vaudeville or variety since they are assembled with a unity of style and can even have a unifying theme or concept. Early masters of the form were such directors as Hassard Short, John Murray Anderson, and Vincente Minnelli, and such writers as Howard Dietz and Arthur Schwartz, E. Y. Harburg, Harold Arlen, and Vernon Duke.

Through the influence of Kern and Hammerstein's *Show Boat,* Broadway's first serious attempt at a modern musical play, creators of musicals began showing greater concern for the stories and the way music and lyrics augmented and embellished them. Because of the country's dire economic condition in the Thirties and the increasing threat of war, musicals began to reflect a more adult and cynical attitude toward the world beyond the footlights, particularly to be seen in works involving George S. Kaufman, Moss Hart, Morrie Ryskind, Marc Blitzstein, and Harold Rome. Beginning in the Forties — largely because of the enormous success of Rodgers and Hammerstein's *Oklahoma!* — the emphasis was now on both the integration of songs, dances and story, and also on the adaptation of works of substance as suitable subject matter in the musical theatre. Plays and novels by Ferenc Molnar, Elmer Rice, Shakespeare, James Michener, Alan Paton, Marcel Pagnol, Bernard Shaw, Voltaire, Eugene O'Neill, Edmond Rostand, T. H. White, Thornton Wilder, Sholom Aleichem, Clifford Odets, Cervantes, Christopher Isherwood, and Nikos Kazantzakis — as well as the Bible — provided the bases for some of the most distinguished productions.

Once the library shelves were exhausted, the manner of telling a story through a particular staging device or personal viewpoint became of increasing concern. These so-called concept musicals developed through the emerging influence of such directors as Gower Champion, Harold Prince, Bob Fosse, Joe Layton, Michael Bennett, and Tommy Tune, and since these men — except for Prince — were all choreographers, their shows put a greater accent on dancing in communicating the deeper meanings of these frequently metaphorical musicals. Paradoxically, many have avoided the conventional linear story line — with its beginning, middle, and end — in favor of a freer, more episodic structure consisting of individual scenes interspersed with songs and dances. What they had created, of course, is a modern, stylized variation on the supposed outdated revue form.

It comes as no surprise that the amount of money involved in bringing a musical to Broadway has escalated appreciably in recent years. This is due not only to inflated production costs, but also to the increasing necessity of mounting large-scale advertising and promotion campaigns. Because of the enormous expenditure — and since movie sales are so infrequent — shows are rarely able to turn a profit without achieving a run of over 1,000 performances, sending out at least one touring company, and having presentations in foreign countries. That's part of the reason why ticket prices are scaled so high. In 1960, *Camelot* was capitalized at $670,000 and an orchestra seat cost $9.40. In 1971, *Follies* cost $700,000 and had a top weekend ticket price of $15.00. By 1981, *Dreamgirls* had production expenses totalling $3.6 million; two years later *My One and Only* was brought in for over $4 million and *La Cage aux Folles* $5 million. The most recent entries in this book, *The Phantom of the Opera* and *Jerome Robbins' Broadway,* both cost over $8.5 million. In 1989, top ticket prices for most musicals were up to $50.00, $55.00, and even $60.00.

The affluent and the expense-account set have always been able to afford not only top prices but scalper prices for tickets. Those of more modest means, however, are finding that the cheapest seats are proportionately more expensive than the high priced. During the 1958-1959 season, for example, it was possible to see such major attractions as *The Music Man* for $2.50 and *My Fair Lady* for $2.30. By 1989, there were hardly any musicals that could be seen from the last row of the top balcony for less than $30.00, and some were getting over $40.00. Two-fer tickets distributed to neighborhood stores, TKTS booths offering half-price seats, and the even lower priced mail-order tickets available to people in certain professions thorugh TDF (Theatre Development Fund, which also operates the TKTS booths) help somewhat to ease the inflationary burden.

The matter of preserving Broadway musicals — other than on original-cast albums — has been of concern to a number of individuals and organizations. Though schools, community groups, and summer theatres may be relied on to revive the blockbuster hits of the past, other performing centers, such as Michael P. Price's Goodspeed Opera House in East Haddam, Connecticut, are dedicated to pumping new life into the long lost and the barely remembered. Concert versions of vintage shows have also been cropping up throughout the country.

Another hopeful sign is the number of opera companies that have added musical-theatre works to their repertoires. Not only does this help break down artificial artistic barriers, it also creates new audiences for such notable examples as the Kern-Hammerstein *Show Boat*, the Gershwin-Heyward *Porgy and Bess*, the Rodgers-Hammerstein *Carousel* and *South Pacific*, the Lerner and Loewe *Brigadoon*, the Weill-Hughes-Rice *Street Scene*, the Weill-Anderson *Lost in the Stars*, the Bernstein-Sondheim-Laurents *West Side Story*, the Bernstein-Wilbur *Candide*, the Sondheim-Wheeler *Sweeney Todd*, and — almost inevitably — the Sondheim-Lapine *Sunday in the Park With George*.

# Show by Show

**The Black Crook.** Four alluring coryphées.

# THE BLACK CROOK

**Music & lyrics:** Miscellaneous writers
**Book:** Charles M. Barras
**Producers:** William Wheatley & Henry Jarrett
**Directors:** William Wheatley & Leon Vincent
**Choreographer:** David Costa
**Cast:**  Annie Kemp Bowler, Charles Morton, Marie Bonfanti, J.W. Blaisdell, E.B. Holmes, George Boniface
**Songs:** "You Naughty Naughty Men"; "March of the Amazons"; "Dare I Tell?"
**New York run:** Niblo's Garden, September 12, 1866; 475 p.

American plays embellished with songs were being offered in New York as early as Colonial days, but *The Black Crook* was the first long-running musical hit, with a record run that was not overtaken until *Adonis* established a new mark in the late 1880's. It also toured throughout the United States and was revived in New York at least fifteen times.

Although the musical score was partly made up of popular numbers of the day and the grafting of songs, dances and plot was crude, *The Black Crook* claims an important place in theatrical history by introducing such staples of the musical-comedy form as elaborate scenic effects, colorful costumes, and rows of barelimbed dancing girls. The production, however, was something of an accident. A Parisian ballet troupe was booked to appear at the Academy of Music in the fall of 1866, but the theatre burned down the previous May. William Wheatley, the manager of Niblo's Garden, a huge auditorium then at Broadway and Prince Street, had already scheduled a spectacular production of a new work, *The Black Crook*, as his fall attraction. With the ballet company now without a booking, he was persuaded that the play would benefit immeasurably from the addition of one hundred or so immodestly garbed female dancers, since it was obvious that Charles M. Barras's embarrassing script — a preposterous melodrama based on the *Faust* legend — could use all the help it could get. Thus, Henry Jarrett, the ballet company's sponsor, became the co-producer of *The Black Crook*, and the dancers crossed the Atlantic in August to join the production.

In the story, set in, around and even underneath the Harz Mountains of Germany, the year is 1600 and Hertzog, a crook-backed sorcerer (hence the play's title) makes a pact with the Arch Fiend, or Devil, that would allow him to live one extra year for every soul he delivers. The sorcerer's first intended victim is the virtuous Rudolphe, who has been imprisoned by the evil Count Wolfenstein. Rudolphe escapes, discovers a buried treasure, saves the life of Stalacta, the fairy queen, who then reciprocates by saving him from Hertzog's nefarious scheme. At the end, the Black Crook, having failed to deliver on his part of the arrangement, is himself carted off to Hell. (The theme of pact-making with the Devil has since shown up occasionally in the musical theatre, most notably in the 1955 success, *Damn Yankees*.)

But the main attraction was unquestionably the imported dancing girls — used primarily for sequences requiring demons, spirits and water sprites — who proved so alluring to post-Civil War audiences that at a ticket scale of 5¢ to $1.50 they kept flocking to view the spectacle. And it surely did not hurt the boxoffice — nor would it ever — when clergymen and editorial writers turned up their blue noses to denounce the sinful display of bare flesh.

In 1954, *The Girl in Pink Tights*, a Broadway musical with a score by Sigmund Romberg (his last) and Leo Robin, was loosely based on circumstances surrounding the production of *The Black Crook*. The cast was headed by Jeanmaire, Charles Goldner, Brenda Lewis, and David Atkinson, and the show ran for 115 performances.
Applause (1985).

# EVANGELINE

**Music:** Edward E. Rice
**Lyrics & book:** J. Cheever Goodwin
**Producer-director:** Edward E. Rice
**Cast:** Ione Burke, James Dunn, W. H. Crane, J. W. Thoman, Connie Thompson
**Songs:** "Evangeline March"; "Spinning-Wheel Song"; "Thinking, Love, of Thee"; "Sweet Evangeline"
**New York run:** Niblo's Garden, July 27, 1874; 16 p.

*Evangeline* (or *The Belle of Acadia*) was among the first successful musicals to have a score specifically written by one song-writing team. It first opened in New York as an interim booking, then played Boston and toured extensively before returning to New York in 1877 at the Fifth Avenue Theatre (then at 24th Street) in a more elaborate production. After playing two months, it again went on tour, during which it was billed as *Rice's Beautiful Evangeline*. In all, it was revived periodically in New York for almost 30 years, with its most successful engagement being the 251-performance run in 1885 at the 14th Street Theatre.

The "American Opera-Bouffe Extravaganza" came about after its two authors had seen a performance in Boston of Lydia Thompson and her troupe of high-kicking British Blondes. Vowing that they could surely write a more tasteful entertainment that would also feature bare-legged dancers, they chose Longfellow's poem as general inspiration, and they enabled the female members of the cast to show their legs by putting them in tights and casting most of them in male roles. Two other attractions: a two-man dancing heifer and the character of the Lone Fisherman, who spent the evening sitting silently in a corner. In the story, our heroine has a number of comic adventures as she journeys from Acadia to Africa to Arizona in search of her beloved Gabriel.

# THE MULLIGAN GUARD BALL

**Music:** David Braham
**Lyrics & book:** Edward Harrigan
**Producers:** Edward Harrigan & Tony Hart
**Director:** Edward Harrigan
**Cast:** Edward Harrigan, Tony Hart, Nellie Jones, Annie Yeamans, Annie Mack
**Songs:** "The Mulligan Guard"; "The Babies on Our Block"; "Pitcher of Beer"; "Skidmore Fancy Ball"
**New York run:** Theatre Comique, January 13, 1879; 153 p.

Edward "Ned" Harrigan and Tony Hart were the first team to offer plays with music populated by newly arrived immigrants living in the slums of New York. They began their series of shows about the Irish Mulligan Guard in 1878, and in all did seven productions featuring the drinking, brawling members of the social and military club. In this production, their most popular, they were concerned with the rivalry between the Mulligan Guard and a Negro group, the Skidmore Guard, who, through an error, both engage the Harp and Shamrock Ballroom for a social affair on the same night. A compromise of sorts is reached when the Skidmore group is given a room on the second floor right above the ballroom, but their dancing becomes so animated that they crash through the floor and land on top of the celebrating Mulligans. This was the first production to play the Theatre Comique, then located on lower Broadway, and the top ticket price was 75¢. Harrigan's use of working-class Americans as characters in his stories influenced the work of Charles H. Hoyt and George M. Cohan.

# ROBIN HOOD

**Music:** Reginald DeKoven
**Lyrics & book:** Harry B. Smith
**Producer:** The Bostonians
**Director:** Harry Dixon
**Cast:** Tom Karl, Eugene Cowles, Caroline Hamilton, Jessie Bartlett Davis, W.H. MacDonald, Henry Clay Barnabee, George Frothingham
**Songs:** "Song of Brown October Ale"; "Oh, Promise Me!" (lyric: Clement Scott); "Tinkers' Chorus"; "Ah, I Do Love Thee"
**New York run:** Standard Theatre, September 28, 1891; 40 p.

The most celebrated American operetta of the 19th century, *Robin Hood* was produced by a touring company that first presented it in Chicago in June 1890. Though hastily put together at a total cost of $109.50, the musical caught on and was remounted in a more stylish production. It made an auspicious New York bow at the Standard Theatre (then on Broadway at 32nd Street), but its run was cut short because of a prior booking. Eight revivals were shown in the city, the last in 1944.

The story remains faithful to the familiar legend about Robin and his merry band of altruistic outlaws who dwell in Sherwood Forest and take from the have-lots and give to the have-nots. In addition to Robin's beloved Maid Marian, the well-known characters include Little John, Friar Tuck, Will Scarlet, and Alan-a-Dale (a traditionally female part originated by Jessie Bartlett Davis, who scored a hit singing the interpolated "Oh, Promise Me!"). This was the third musical created by the team of Reginald DeKoven and Harry B. Smith, who collaborated on a total of 17, including the unsuccessful sequel, *Maid Marian*.

# A TRIP TO CHINATOWN

**Music:** Percy Gaunt
**Lyrics:** Percy Gaunt & Charles H. Hoyt
**Book:** Charles H. Hoyt
**Producer:** Charles H. Hoyt
**Directors:** Charles H. Hoyt & Julian Mitchell
**Cast:** Anna Boyd, Lloyd Wilson, George Beane Jr., Lillian Barr, Harry Conor
**Songs:** "Reuben and Cynthia"; "The Bowery"; "Push Dem Clouds Away"; "After the Ball" (Charles K. Harris)
**New York run:** Madison Square Theatre, November 9, 1891; 657 p.

In a large American city at the turn of the century, two young couples are encouraged by a coquettish widow to defy a rich merchant by having a merry night on the town at a fashionable restaurant. Complications arise when the merchant also shows up at the restaurant and is stuck with their bill — which he cannot pay because he doesn't have his wallet. If this outline reads like the plot of *Hello, Dolly!*, well it is. It is also the plot of *A Trip to Chinatown*, which came along 73 years earlier and which also set a long-running record for continuous performances. In fact, its tenure at the Madison Square Theatre (formerly the Fifth Avenue) was so extraordinary for its time that the show held the durability record for 28 years.

*A Trip to Chinatown* (though set in San Francisco, no one takes a trip anywhere near Chinatown) was the creation of Charles H. Hoyt, a prolific writer of American farces. It was also the first musical to boast no less than three song hits: "Reuben and Cynthia," "The Bowery," and the interpolated "After the Ball."

Indiana U. Press (1964)

5

# THE FORTUNE TELLER

**Music:** Victor Herbert
**Lyrics & book:** Harry B. Smith
**Producer:** Frank L. Perley
**Director:** Julian Mitchell
**Cast:** Alice Nielsen, Eugene Cowles, Frank Rushworth, Marguerite Silva, Joseph Herbert, Joseph Cawthorn, May Boley
**Songs:** "Always Do as People Say You Should"; "Romany Life"; "Gypsy Love Song"; "Czardas"; "Only in the Play"
**New York run:** Wallack's Theatre, September 26, 1898; 40 p.

Like *Robin Hood, The Fortune Teller* was created for a touring company — in this case the Alice Nielsen Opera Company — which accounted for its brief stay at Wallack's Theatre (then located at Broadway and 30th Street). It was the third and most celebrated of the 13 shows written together by composer Victor Herbert and lyricist-librettist Harry B. Smith (whose total Broadway output was an incredible 123 productions). The musical, which did much to establish Herbert as America's preeminent composer of operetta, makes use of the popular theme of mistaken identity. Hungarian heiress Irma loves a dashing Hussar, but is promised in marriage to a wealthy count. To avoid this unwanted union, Irma gets gypsy fortune teller Musette (both roles being played by Alice Nielsen) to substitute for her. Eventually — somehow aided by a Hungarian military victory — Irma and Musette end up with their appropriate inamoratos. In 1946, a Broadway musical, *Gypsy Lady,* combined this score with that of another Herbert-Smith work, *The Serenade.* The plot, however, was relatively original.

# FLORODORA

**Music:** Leslie Stuart
**Lyrics:** Leslie Stuart, Paul Rubens, Frank Clement
**Book:** Owen Hall
**Producer:** Tom Ryley & John Fisher
**Directors:** Lewis Hopper & Willie Edouin
**Cast:** Edna Wallace Hopper, Fannie Johnston, Willie Edouin, Sydney Deane, R.E. Graham, May Edouin
**Songs:** "The Shade of the Palm" (Stuart); "Tell Me, Pretty Maiden" (Stuart); "When I Leave Town" (Rubens); "I Want to Be a Military Man" (Clement)
**New York run:** Casino Theatre, November 12, 1900; 553 p.

Next to the Gilbert and Sullivan comic operas, *Florodora* was the most successful early British import staged in New York, even exceeding the original London run of 455 performances. The highlight of the show was the appearance of the dainty, parasol-twirling *Florodora* Sextette who, with six male partners, introduced the coquettish number, "Tell Me, Pretty Maiden." In the plotty plot, Florodora is both the name of an island in the Philippines and the locally manufactured perfume. The elderly manufacturer Cyrus Gilfain wants to marry Dolores, whose father had been cheated by Gilfain, but Dolores loves Gilfain's manager, whom Gilfain wants for his own daughter, even though she loves someone else. For some reason, everyone ends up in Wales where the complications get unknotted and the knots get properly tied. The Casino Theatre, which was torn down in 1930, stood at Broadway and 39th Street.

The last Broadway revival of *Florodora* occurred in 1920 and ran for 150 performances. Christie MacDonald, Eleanor Painter, Walter Woolf, and George Hassell were in the cast.
TW.

**Florodora.** Pictured on the sheet music cover are the ladies of the original Sextette: Daisy Greene, Marjorie Relyea, Vaughn Texsmith, Margaret Walker, Agnes Wayburn, and Marie L. Wilson.

# THE WIZARD OF OZ

**Music:** Paul Tietjens, A. Baldwin Sloane
**Lyrics & book:** L. Frank Baum
**Producer:** Fred R. Hamlin
**Director-choreographer:** Julian Mitchell
**Cast:** David Montgomery, Fred Stone, Anna Laughlin, Arthur Hill, Bessie Wynn, Grace Kimball
**Songs:** "Alas for a Man Without Brains" (Tietjens); "When You Love Love Love" (Tietjens); "Sammy" (Edward Hutchinson - James O'Dea); "Hurrah for Baffin's Bay" (Theodore Morse - Vincent Bryan)
**New York run:** Majestic Theatre, January 20, 1903; 293 p.

*The Wizard of Oz* was the premiere attraction at the Majestic Theatre on the west side of Columbus Circle (demolished in 1954), and it also marked the legitimate theatre debut of two vaudeville clowns, Dave Montgomery and Fred Stone, as the Tin Woodman and the Scarecrow. In the spectacular production, which L. Frank Baum adapted from his own fairytale, *The Wonderful Wizard of Oz*, a cyclone blows Dorothy and her pet cow all the way from Kansas to the country of the Munchkins. After meeting the Scarecrow, the Tin Woodman, and the Cowardly Lion, Dorothy takes her three new friends on a number of adventures until they finally meet the Wizard in the Emerald City. The Victor Herbert-Glen MacDonough *Babes in Toyland,* a successor to *The Wizard of Oz,* followed it into the Majestic. In 1939, the classic screen version featured Judy Garland, Frank Morgan, Ray Bolger, Bert Lahr, and Jack Haley, and a new score by Harold Arlen and E.Y. Harburg. *The Wiz,* a contemporary black variation, opened on Broadway in 1975. (See page 241.)
TW (film score).

---

# BABES IN TOYLAND

**Music:** Victor Herbert
**Lyrics & book:** Glen MacDonough
**Producers:** Fred R. Hamlin & Julian Mitchell
**Director-choreographer:** Julian Mitchell
**Cast:** William Norris, Mabel Barrison, George Denham, Bessie Wynn
**Songs:** "I Can't Do the Sum"; "Go to Sleep, Slumber Deep"; "Song of the Poet"; "March of the Toys"; "Toyland"; "Never Mind, Bo-Peep"
**New York run:** Majestic Theatre, October 13, 1903; 192 p.

Because of the popularity of *The Wizard of Oz,* producers Fred R. Hamlin and Julian Mitchell (who was Broadway's most prolific director of musicals with 78 shows to his credit) commissioned Victor Herbert and Glen MacDonough to come up with a successor, if not exactly a sequel, to follow their previous hit into the Majestic Theatre. Once again audiences were delighted with a fantasy about children that included a devastating storm, a frightening journey through the woods, and the eventual arrival at a mythical magical city, in this case substituting Toyland for the Emerald City. The book may have been no more that a serviceable variation, but the score — the second and most successful of the five collaborations between Herbert and MacDonough — was far superior to its predecessor's. Laurel and Hardy appeared in the 1934 screen version, and Ray Bolger and Ed Wynn were in the 1961 version.
MCA SC./Dramatic Publishing Co. (1978)*/DPC.

**Babes in Toyland.** William Norris and Mabel Barrison, as the two babes, lead Mother Hubbard's children in singing "I Can't Do the Sum." (Byron)

# LITTLE JOHNNY JONES

**Music, lyrics & book:** George M. Cohan
**Producer:** Sam H. Harris
**Director:** George M. Cohan
**Cast:** George M. Cohan, Jerry Cohan, Helen Cohan, Donald Brian, Ethel Levey, Tom Lewis
**Songs:** "The Yankee Doodle Boy"; " Give My Regards to Broadway"; "Life's a Funny Proposition After All"
**New York run:** Liberty Theatre, November 7, 1904; 52 p.

George M. Cohan was cocky, straight-shooting, self-assured, quick-witted, fast-moving, naively patriotic — in short, the personification of the American spirit at the beginning of the 20th Century. He was also just about the most multi-talented man ever to hit Broadway, winning fame as an actor, composer, lyricist, librettist, playwright, director, and producer, with an output comprising 21 musicals and 20 plays.

*Little Johnny Jones,* Cohan's third musical and his first hit, had an initial run of less than two months at the Liberty Theatre (now a movie house on 42nd Street west of Times Square). After extensive revisions during the road tour, the show returned to New York twice in 1905 for a total run of 20 weeks. The musical was prompted by a newspaper article about Tod Sloan, an American jockey then in England. In Cohan's story, jockey Johnny Jones has gone to Britain to ride his horse Yankee Doodle in the Derby. Accused of throwing the race, Johnny discovers that he has been framed by an American gambler (played by the author's father, Jerry Cohan). With the help of a private detective, he clears his name and celebrates by singing and dancing "Give My Regards to Broadway" on a Southampton pier. In the third act, with the locale abruptly switched to San Francisco's Chinatown, Johnny discovers that his fiancée, Goldie Gates (played by Ethel Levey, Cohan's wife at the time) has been kidnapped. When the jockey and the private detective apprehend the abductor, he turns out to be the same villain who had framed our hero in England. In 1982, a revival of *Little Johnny Jones* with Donny Osmond tarried but one night on Broadway.

# MLLE. MODISTE

**Music:** Victor Herbert
**Lyrics & book:** Henry Blossom
**Producer:** Charles Dillingham
**Director:** Fred Latham
**Cast:** Fritzi Scheff, Walter Percival, William Pruette, Claude Gillingwater, Josephine Bartlett
**Songs:** "Kiss Me Again"; "The Time, the Place and the Girl"; "I Want What I Want When I Want It"; "The Mascot of the Troop"
**New York run:** Knickerbocker Theatre, December 25, 1905; 202 p.

*Mlle. Modiste* inaugurated the partnership of composer Victor Herbert and librettist-lyricist Henry Blossom (they wrote eight scores together), and was their second in popularity to *The Red Mill.* The operetta was closely identified with prima donna Fritzi Scheff, who would be called upon to sing "Kiss Me Again" for the rest of her life (indeed, Miss Scheff returned to New York in *Mlle. Modiste* on five occasions, the last, when she was 50, in 1929). The musical, which opened at the Knickerbocker (then on Broadway and 38th Street), spins a Cinderella tale of a stagestruck Parisian named Fifi, who works in Mme. Cecile's hat shop on the Rue de la Paix. A wealthy American helps Fifi become a celebrated singer, which also helps smooth the way to her winning the approval of her sweetheart's aristocratic, crotchety uncle.
TW.

**Mlle. Modiste.** Fritzi Scheff in the final scene at the charity bazaar in the gardens of the Château de St. Mar. From the left are Walter Percival (in uniform), William Pruette, and Claude Gillingwater. (Byron)

**Forty-five Minutes from Broadway.** The dramatic will-tearing scene with Victor Moore and Fay Templeton. (Hall)

# FORTY-FIVE MINUTES FROM BROADWAY

**Music, lyrics & book:** George M. Cohan
**Producers:** Marc Klaw & A. L. Erlanger
**Director:** George M. Cohan
**Cast:** Fay Templeton, Victor Moore, Donald Brian, Lois Ewell
**Songs:** "I Want to Be a Popular Millionaire"; "Mary's a Grand Old Name"; "So Long, Mary"; "Forty-five Minutes from Broadway"
**New York run:** New Amsterdam Theatre, January 1, 1906; 90 p.

More of a play with music than a musical comedy — there were only five songs in the score — *Forty-five Minutes from Broadway* was written as a vehicle for Fay Templeton, but it was Victor Moore, in his first leading role on Broadway, who stole everyone's attention. In the story, set in New Rochelle, New York — which is only 45 minutes from Broadway — a nasty millionaire has died leaving a will that no one can find. His nephew (Donald Brian), who has been assigned as his heir, visits his uncle's home with his secretary, Kid Burns (Mr. Moore), and his fiancée. Burns discovers the will — and the fact that everything has been left to housekeeper Mary Jane Jenkins (Miss Templeton). Since the Kid has fallen in love with Mary, his pride won't let him marry his beloved for her money. The only solution: Mary tears up the will. After only a modest run at the New Amsterdam (now a movie house on 42nd Street west of Times Square), the show became a hit on the road, then was revived in 1912 with Cohan himself taking over the Kid Burns part. Moore, however, again played the same character in Cohan's 1907 musical, *The Talk of New York*.
Dramatic Publishing Co. (1978)*/ DPC.

# THE RED MILL

**Music:** Victor Herbert
**Lyrics & book:** Henry Blossom
**Producer:** Charles Dillingham
**Director:** Fred Latham
**Cast:** David Montgomery, Fred Stone, Augusta Greenleaf, Joseph Ratliff, Allene Crater, Edward Begley
**Songs:** "The Isle of Our Dreams"; "When You're Pretty and the World Is Fair"; "Moonbeams"; "Every Day Is Ladies Day With Me"; The Streets of New York"; "Because You're You"
**New York run:** Knickerbocker Theatre, September 24, 1906; 274 p.

*The Red Mill* was closer to being a musical farce than the kind of operetta usually associated with Victor Herbert. There was ample compensation, however, in the fact that it achieved the longest run of any of the composer's 41 book musicals produced during his lifetime. The show, which was typical of many of the period in depicting Americans as innocents abroad, is concerned with the adventures of Kid Conner and Con Kidder (Montgomery and Stone), two impoverished tourists stranded in Katwyk-aan-Zee, Holland. Their comic predicaments force them to don a number of disguises (including Sherlock Holmes and Dr. Watson), and they also manage to rescue a girl from a windmill by perching her precariously on one of the sails.
A 1945 production (see page 128) ran almost twice as long as the original, with Eddie Foy scoring a hit in the Dave Montgomery part. Also associated with the show were Stone's two daughters, co-producer Paula and featured actress Dorothy. The favorable reception that greeted this version sparked revivals of two other vintage shows as vehicles for major comedians: *Sweethearts* with Bobby Clark (1947) and *Sally* with Willie Howard (1948).
Capitol SC; Turnabout SC/ TW.

# FOLLIES OF 1907

**Music & lyrics:** Miscellaneous writers
**Sketches:** Harry B. Smith
**Producer:** Florenz Ziegfeld
**Director:** Herbert Gresham
**Choreographers:** Julian Mitchell, Joe Smith, John O'Neil
**Cast:** Grace LaRue, Mlle. Dazie, Prince Tokio, Emma Carus, Harry Watson Jr., Marion Sunshine & Florence Tempest, George Bickel, Helen Broderick, Nora Bayes (added)
**Songs:** "Budweiser's a Friend of Mine" (Seymour Furth-Vincent Bryan); "I Think I Oughtn't Auto any More" (E. Ray Goetz-Bryan); " Handle Me With Care" (Jean Schwartz-William Jerome); "Miss Ginger from Jamaica" (Billy Gaston); "Bye Bye, Dear Old Broadway" (Gus Edwards - Will Cobb)
**New York run:** Jardin de Paris, July 8, 1907; 70 p.

With the *Follies of 1907,* showman Florenz Ziegfeld inaugurated the most celebrated and durable series of annual revues in the history of the Broadway theatre. From 1907 to 1931, there were 21 such entertainments designated as *Follies* (actually, there should have been 22, but the 1926 edition, due to a legal hassle, was initially called *No Foolin',* then *Ziegfeld American Revue*). The title of the first edition came about through the suggestions of sketch writer Harry B. Smith, who had written a newspaper column called "Follies of the Day," and also because Ziegfeld, whose lucky number was 13, wanted the name to have 13 letters. It was not until 1911 that the impresario's ego triumphed over his superstition and thenceforth the series was known as the *Ziegfeld Follies.*

The idea for the series is credited to Ziegfeld's wife, Anna Held, who suggested that the producer put together a show based on the French revue style of entertainment that took satirical pot-shots at society, the theatre, and politics. The hallmark of the *Follies* was opulent production numbers, decoratively adorned showgirls, farcical and topical sketches, comic personalities, and a generous amount of songs. The first edition, presented on the roof garden of the New York Theatre (then at 45th Street on the east side of Broadway), used the theme of introducing Pocahontas and Capt. John Smith to modern life. Along the way they were enlightened by scenes involving the likes of John D. Rockefeller, Anthony Comstock, Oscar Hammerstein, Teddy Roosevelt, and Enrico Caruso, plus a "Dance of the Seven Veils" takeoff and 64 "Anna Held Girls" beating snare drums while marching up and down the aisles. The total production cost was $13,000, and the top ticket price was $2.50.

Known as "A National Institution Glorifying the American Girl," the *Ziegfeld Follies* was itself glorified through the years by the presence of such notable performers as Fanny Brice, Bert Williams, Ann Pennington, W.C. Fields, Will Rogers, Ray Dooley, Lillian Lorraine, Leon Errol, Eddie Cantor, Nora Bayes, Van and Schenck, John Steel, Ed Wynn, Ina Claire, Marilyn Miller, Ruth Etting, and Eddie Dowling. The *Follies* may not have been the first Broadway revue — that was *The Passing Show* in 1894 — but it was the one that established the model for this type of entertainment, and which spawned such diversified rivals as *George White's Scandals* (13 editions), the Messrs. Shubert's *Passing Shows* (12 editions), the *Earl Carroll Vanities* (11 editions), the *Greenwich Village Follies* (8 editions), and Irving Berlin's *Music Box Revues* (4 editions). There were also four productions of the *Ziegfeld Follies* — in 1934, 1936, 1943, and 1957 — that were presented on Broadway after Ziegfeld's death. For subsequent editions of the *Follies* see pages 20, 29, 31, 34, 38, 85, and 93.

# THE MERRY WIDOW

**Music:** Franz Lehár
**Lyrics:** Adrian Ross
**Book:** (Basil Hood uncredited)
**Producer:** Henry W. Savage
**Director:** George Marion
**Cast:** Ethel Jackson, Donald Brian, Lois Ewell, R.E. Graham, William Weedon, Fred Frear
**Songs:** "A Dutiful Wife"; "In Marsovia"; "Oh, Come Away, Away!"; "Maxim's"; "Vilia"; "Silly, Silly Cavalier"; "I Love You So" ("The Merry Widow Waltz"); "The Girls at Maxim's"; "Love in My Heart"
**New York run:** New Amsterdam Theatre, October 21, 1907; 416 p.

The epitome of the lighthearted, melodious, romantic European operetta, Franz Lehár's *The Merry Widow* first swirled onto the stage in Vienna in 1905 under the title *Die Lustige Witwe*. The original text by Viktor Leon and Leo Stein was adapted for the highly successful London production by Basil Hood who refused program credit to spare the feelings of the original librettist whose work had been rejected. This version was also used in New York where the musical won such acclaim that it not only made celebrities of Ethel Jackson and Donald Brian, as the Widow and the Prince, it also prompted the introduction of Merry Widow hats, gowns, corsets, and cigarettes.

The first theatrical offshoot was a parody, *The Merry Widow Burlesque,* which opened less than three months after the operetta's première and continued for 156 performances. Producer Joe Weber (of Weber and Fields) even managed to get permission to use the Lehár music. A more lasting influence, however, was the rash of imported continental operettas that remained a major part of the Broadway scene until the outbreak of World War I. Among the most popular of these were Oscar Straus's *A Waltz Dream,* Leo Fall's *The Dollar Princess,* Straus's *The Chocolate Soldier,* Heinrich Reinhardt's *The Spring Maid,* Johann Strauss's *The Merry Countess (Die Fledermaus),* Lehár's *The Count of Luxembourg,* Emmerich Kalman's *Sari,* and Edmund Eysler's *The Blue Paradise* (with interpolated songs by Sigmund Romberg).

Based on *L'Attaché d'Ambassade,* a French play by Henri Meilhac, *The Merry Widow* is set in Paris and concerns the efforts of Baron Popoff, the ambassador of the mythical kingdom of Marsovia, to induce his attaché, Prince Danilo, to marry wealthy widow Sonia Sadoya in order to aid the country's dwindling finances. Though the widow is wary of fortune-hunting suitors and the prince is chary of being taken for one, they find themselves falling in love with the seductive strains of "The Merry Widow Waltz." Danilo eventually proposes marriage — but only after Sonia has teasingly confessed that she has no money.

*The Merry Widow* has had five Broadway revivals, the last in 1943. That production, with a libretto coauthored by novelist Sidney Sheldon, had a successful run of 322 performances, then returned in October 1944 for an additional 32. The cast was headed by the husband-wife team of Jan Kiepura and Marta Eggerth. (See page 120.) In 1964, the operetta was mounted by the Music Theatre of Lincoln Center (with Patrice Munsel and Bob Wright), and in 1978 by the New York City Opera (with Beverly Sills and Alan Titus). There have been three Hollywood screen versions: a silent in 1925 directed by Erich Von Stroheim; the Ernst Lubitsch treatment in 1934 with lyrics by Lorenz Hart and starring Maurice Chevalier and Jeanette MacDonald; and a 1952 remake with Lana Turner and Fernando Lamas.

Columbia SC; RCA OC (1964); Angel OC (1978)/ TW.

# THE CHOCOLATE SOLDIER

**Music:** Oscar Straus
**Lyrics & book:** Stanislaus Stange
**Producer:** Fred C. Whitney
**Director:** Stanislaus Stange
**Choreographer:** Al Holbrook
**Cast:** Ida Brooks Hunt, J. E. Gardner, Flavia Arcaro, William Pruette
**Songs:** "My Hero"; "Sympathy"; "Seek the Spy"; "That Would Be Lovely";
  "Falling In Love"; "The Letter Song"; "Thank the Lord the War Is Over"
**New York run:** Lyric Theatre, September 13, 1909; 296 p.

Of all the European operettas imported by Broadway producers in the wake of the spectacular success of *The Merry Widow,* by far the most popular was *The Chocolate Soldier.* Originally presented in Vienna in 1908 as *Der Tapfere Soldat,* the musical was adapted from George Bernard Shaw's play, *Arms and the Man,* though the author always regretted having given his permission. (The next musical treatment of a Shaw play, *My Fair Lady,* came along 47 years later.)

Producer Fred Whitney secured the rights to the English-language version even before the operetta had had its première at the Theater an der Wien, and he opened it in New York at the Lyric Theatre (now a movie house on 42nd Street west of Times Square). The satire on heroes and heroism is set in 1885 during the Serbian invasion of Bulgaria. Lt. Bumerli, the chocolate-eating Swiss soldier serving in the Serb army, is more concerned about saving his neck than displaying valor on the battlefield. He hides in the home of Col. Popoff, a Bulgarian, and soon meets Popoff's daughter, Nadina. Though Nadina's hero is the swaggering Major Alexius Spiridoff, it is not long before she drops him for the peace-loving Bumerli. Other Broadway productions of *The Chocolate Soldier* were offered in 1921, 1930, 1931, 1934, and 1947 (the last in a revised version by Guy Bolton). The 1941 movie with Risë Stevens and Nelson Eddy used a different story. RCA SC.

# MADAME SHERRY

**Music:** Karl Hoschna
**Lyrics & book:** Otto Harbach
**Producers:** A. H. Woods, H. H. Frazee, George Lederer
**Director:** George Lederer
**Cast:** Lina Abarbanell, Ralph Herz, Elizabeth Murray, Jack Gardner, Dorothy Jardon, Frances Demarest
**Songs:** "Every Little Movement"; "The Smile She Meant for Me"; "I Want to Play House With You"; "The Birth of Passion"; "Put Your Arms Around Me Honey" (Albert Von Tilzer - Junie McCree)
**New York run:** New Amsterdam Theatre, August 30, 1910; 231 p.

*Madame Sherry* remains the best remembered of the six productions written by Karl Hoschna and Otto Harbach (who spelled his name Hauerbach until World War I). It was adapted from an English musical of 1903, which had a different score, and which, in turn, had been based on a French musical. Among the reasons for its success were the insinuating number, "Every Little Movement" ("...has a meaning all its own") and the interpolated "Put Your Arms Around Me Honey." In this tangled tale of mistaken identity, Ed Sherry deceives his uncle, wealthy archeologist Theophilus Sherry, into accepting his Irish landlady as his wife and a dancing teacher's pupils as their children. At first Ed is smitten with Lulu, the dancing teacher, but then transfers his affections to Yvonne, his cousin (played by Metropolitan opera diva Lina Abarbanell). Audiences could enjoy matinee performances of *Madame Sherry* for a top ticket price of $1.50.

# NAUGHTY MARIETTA

**Music:** Victor Herbert
**Lyrics & book:** Rida Johnson Young
**Producer:** Oscar Hammerstein
**Director:** Jacques Coini
**Cast:** Emma Trentini, Orville Harrold, Edward Martindel, Marie Duchene, Peggy Wood
**Songs:** "Tramp! Tramp! Tramp!"; "Naughty Marietta"; "'Neath the Southern Moon"; "Italian Street Song"; "Live for Today"; "I'm Falling in Love With Someone"; "Ah! Sweet Mystery of Life"
**New York run:** New York Theatre, November 7, 1910; 136 p.

Victor Herbert's crowning achievement came into being because mounting debts had forced opera impresario Oscar Hammerstein (grandfather of Oscar II) into the area of the more commercial musical theatre. Hammerstein had it staged with all the care of one of his Manhattan Opera productions, with two of his stars, Emma Trentini and Orville Harrold, in the leading roles of Marietta d'Altena and Capt. Dick Warrington.

*Naughty Marietta* takes place in New Orleans in 1780. Marietta is there to escape from an unwanted marriage in France and Capt. Dick is there to lead his Rangers against a pirate gang led by Bras Piqué ("Tattooed Arm"). Though Marietta is first attracted to Etienne Grandet, the son of the lieutenant governor, when he is revealed as the pirate leader she is happy to sing her romantic duets with Capt. Dick. She is, in fact, sure that he is the man for her because he is able to finish the "Dream Melody" ("Ah! Sweet Mystery of Life") that Marietta recalls from childhood. One historical error committed by the authors is that New Orleans is supposed to be a French posession, whereas in the year in which the story takes place the colony belonged to Spain. (This error was also made in *The New Moon* in 1928, which had the same locale and period.) The 1935 movie version co-starred Jeanette MacDonald and Nelson Eddy.
Smithsonian SC/ Weinberger, London (1959)*/ TW.

# THE PINK LADY

**Music:** Ivan Caryll
**Lyrics & book:** C. M. S. McLellan
**Producers:** Marc Klaw & A. L. Erlanger
**Director:** Herbert Gresham
**Choreographer:** Julian Mitchell
**Cast:** Hazel Dawn, Alice Dovey, William Elliott, Frank Lalor, Jed Prouty
**Songs:** "On the Saskatchewan"; "My Beautiful Lady"; "Hide and Seek"; "Donny Did, Donny Didn't"
**New York run:** New Amsterdam Theatre, March 13, 1911; 312 p.

After winning success in London, composer Ivan Caryll indited the scores for 14 Broadway musicals. His most celebrated production was *The Pink Lady*, which contained the durable song "My Beautiful Lady" and gave Hazel Dawn a memorable role that allowed her to play the violin. The story, adapted from a French play, *Le Satyr*, takes place in one day, during which we visit a restaurant in the woods at Compiègne, a furniture shop on the Rue Honoré, and the Ball of the Nymphs and Satyrs. Before settling down to marriage with Angele, Lucien Garidel hopes to enjoy one last fling with Claudine (Miss Dawn), known as the Pink Lady because of her monochromatic wardrobe. When they accidentally meet Angele, Lucien covers his embarrassment by introducing Claudine as the wife of a friend. Following comic complications, the day ends with the involved couples properly sorted.
AEI SC.

# THE FIREFLY

**Music:** Rudolf Friml
**Lyrics & book:** Otto Harbach
**Producer:** Arthur Hammerstein
**Director:** Fred Latham
**Choreographer:** Signor Albertieri, Sammy Lee
**Cast:** Emma Trentini, Craig Campbell, Roy Atwell, Sammy Lee, Audrey Maple, Melville Stewart
**Songs:** "Giannina Mia"; "When a Maid Comes Knocking at Your Heart"; "Love Is Like a Firefly"; "Sympathy"
**New York run:** Lyric Theatre, December 2, 1912; 120 p.

During a performance he was conducting of *Naughty Marietta*, Victor Herbert had a disagreement with the star, Emma Trentini, and stormed off the podium. He also refused to have anything to do with her next vehicle, *The Firefly*, for which he had been contracted. The composer's decision opened the way for Rudolf Friml, who had never written a Broadway score before, to become a leading creator of American operettas. It also began his partnership with librettist-lyricist Otto Harbach, with whom he would be associated on ten musicals. In the Cinderella tale, cut from a similar bolt of cloth as the one used for *Mlle. Modiste*, Nina Corelli, an Italian street singer in New York, disguises herself as a cabin boy to be near Jack Travers, a guest on a yacht sailing for Bermuda. After hearing her sing, a music teacher offers to give her lessons, and within three years she becomes both a renowned prima donna and Mrs. Jack Travers.
TW.

# SWEETHEARTS
**MUSIC:** Victor Herbert
**Lyrics:** Robert B. Smith
**Book:** Harry B. Smith & Fred De Gresac
**Producers:** Louis Werba & Mark Luescher
**Director:** Fred Latham
**Choreographer:** Charles Morgan Jr.
**Cast:** Christie MacDonald, Thomas Conkey, Ethel Du Fre Houston, Edwin Wilson, Tom McNaughton
**Songs:** "Sweethearts"; "Angelus"; "Every Lover Must Meet His Fate"; "Pretty as a Picture"; "Jeannette and Her Little Wooden Shoes"
**New York run:** New Amsterdam Theatre, September 8, 1913; 136 p.

Though allegedly based on the real-life adventures of a 15th Century Neapolitan princess, *Sweethearts* was easily among Broadway's most farfetched musical romances, complete with a mythological country, an abducted princess, and a prince in disguise. To keep her from harm during a war, the infant Princess Sylvia of Zilania has been taken to Bruges where she is brought up believing she is the daughter of a laundress. While traveling incognito, Prince Franz falls in love with Sylvia even before they meet. After their true identities are revealed, they assume the throne as King and Queen of Zilania.

Prompted by the successful 1945 revival of Herbert's *The Red Mill* starring comic Eddie Foy Jr., Herbert's *Sweethearts* was resuscitated for comic Bobby Clark (see page 134). Here the secondary role of political operator Mikel Mikeloviz was retailored to Clark's specifications, and the resourceful clown turned the evening into a self-kidding, hilarious romp. The run was almost twice as long as the original. The 1938 Jeanette MacDonald-Nelson Eddy movie version had a different story.
MMG SC/ TW.

# THE GIRL FROM UTAH
**Music:** Jerome Kern, etc.
**Lyrics:** Harry B. Smith, etc.
**Book:** James T. Tanner, Harry B. Smith
**Producer:** Charles Frohman
**Director:** J. A. E. Malone
**Cast:** Julia Sanderson, Donald Brian, Joseph Cawthorn, Queenie Vassar, Venita Fitzhugh
**Songs:** "Same Sort of Girl"; "They Didn't Believe Me" (lyric: Herbert Reynolds); "Gilbert the Filbert" (Herman Finck - Arthur Wimperis); "Why Don't They Dance the Polka?"; "The Land of Let's Pretend"
**New York run:** Knickerbocker Theatre, August 24, 1914; 120 p.

Based on a 1913 London musical with music by Paul Rubens and Sidney Jones and lyrics by Adrian Ross and Percy Greenbank, *The Girl from Utah* underwent a major sea change by the time it opened on Broadway, with no less than seven songs now credited to Jerome Kern (including his first hit, "They Didn't Believe Me"). Despite the somewhat misleading title, the story is set in London where Una Trance (Julia Sanderson) has fled to avoid marrying a bigamist Mormon. Though the Mormon pursues her, Una eventually finds true love in the arms of Sandy Blair (Donald Brian), a London song-and-dance man. The show was the first musical hit on Broadway following the outbreak of World War I. With its appealing Kern additions (it was the composer's sixth of 39 Broadway shows), the production was a transitional work leading to the soon-to-come American domination of the musical-comedy field.

# WATCH YOUR STEP

**Music & lyrics:** Irving Berlin
**Book:** Harry B. Smith
**Producer:** Charles Dillingham
**Director:** R. H. Burnside
**Cast:** Vernon & Irene Castle, Frank Tinney, Charles King, Elizabeth Brice, Elizabeth Murray, Harry Kelly, Justine Johnstone
**Songs:** "Play a Simple Melody"; "They Always Follow Me Around"; "When I Discovered You"; "Settle Down in a One-Horse Town"; "The Syncopated Walk"
**New York run:** New Amsterdam Theatre, December 8, 1914; 175 p.

In 1911, at the age of 23, Irving Berlin had the entire country ragtime crazy with "Alexander's Ragtime Band." Three years later, he wrote his first Broadway score (out of a total of 21) which was the first to feature ragtime. It also introduced audiences to another Berlin skill in the contrapuntal "Play a Simple Melody." The songs accompanied a vehicle for dancers Vernon and Irene Castle (it would be the couple's last professional appearance together) that was so flimsy the program credit line read, "Plot, if any, by Harry B. Smith." That plot had to do with a will leaving $2 million to anyone who had never been in love, but by the second act the story was discarded and the evening was turned into a facsimile of a Fifth Avenue nightclub floor show. Also discarded was W.C. Fields. Then primarily a juggler, Fields had sailed from Australia to join the cast during the Syracuse tryout, only to be fired after one performance. The reason: producer Dillingham was fearful that Fields would be such a hit that audiences wouldn't pay attention to the Castles.

# ZIEGFELD FOLLIES

**Music:** Louis A. Hirsch
**Lyrics:** Gene Buck
**Sketches:** Gene Buck, Rennold Wolf, Channing Pollock
**Producer:** Florenz Ziegfeld
**Directors:** Julian Mitchell, Leon Errol
**Choreographer:** Julian Mitchell
**Cast:** W.C. Fields, Ed Wynn, Ann Pennington, Mae Murray, Bernard Granville, George White, Bert Williams, Ina Claire, Justine Johnstone, Leon Errol, Carl Randall, Will West, Melville Stewart
**Songs:** "Hello, Frisco!"; "Hold Me in Your Loving Arms"; "I Can't Do Without Girls"; "A Girl For Each Month of the Year" (lyric: Wolf, Pollock)
**New York run:** New Amsterdam Theatre, June 21, 1915; 104 p.

To take the American public's mind off the grave news about World War I (the *Lusitania* had recently been torpedoed), Ziegfeld's ninth annual edition of his *Follies* was the most extravagant and spectacular to date. With its brilliant cast and the equally brilliant scenic designs created by Joseph Urban (his first of 12 *Follies*), this production ushered in an eight year period that is regarded as the pinnacle of the series. Among the show's pleasures: the opening underwater sequence ("The stage setting is the greatest Mr. Ziegfeld has ever presented," according to the program); the first-act finale called "America," with everyone and everything in red, white and blue and Justine Johnstone as the Spirit of Columbia; "The Silver Forest" scene with the girls parading about as months of the year; Ina Claire singing the hit song, "Hello, Frisco!"; the "Gates of Elysium" sequence with real elephants on the stage; and W.C. Fields's comic poolshooting routine (during the road tour Ed Wynn horned in on the act only to have Fields almost knock him unconscious with a cue).

# THE BLUE PARADISE

**Music:** Sigmund Romberg, Edmund Eysler
**Lyrics:** Herbert Reynolds
**Book:** Edgar Smith
**Producers:** Messrs. Shubert
**Director:** J.H. Benrimo
**Choreographer:** Ed Hutchinson
**Cast:** Vivienne Segal, Cecil Lean, Cleo Mayfield, Ted Lorraine, Robert Pitkin,
Frances Demarest, Teddy Webb
**Songs:** "Auf Wiedersehn" (Romberg); "One Step Into Love" (Romberg); "Vienna, Vienna" (Eysler); "A Toast to Woman's Eyes" (Romberg)
**New York run:** Casino Theatre, August 5, 1915; 356 p.

The fourth longest running book musical of the 1910's, *The Blue Paradise* gave Sigmund Romberg his first chance to compose the kind of sentimental, romantic songs with which he would become identified. (His total Broadway output — including shows for which he shared the writing assignment — was a record 57 productions.) Adapted from *Ein Tag im Paradies,* a Viennese operetta by Edmund Eysler, the musical also provided Vivienne Segal with her professional debut when she took over the female lead during the Washington tryout. In the story, Mizzi (Miss Segal), the flower seller at the Blue Paradise, a Viennese garden restaurant, must bid a tearful "Auf Wiedersehn" (Romberg's first song hit) to her sweetheart Rudolphe (Cecil Lean) as he leaves to make his fortune in America. With fortune made, Rudolphe returns many years later, only to discover that time had transformed sweet little Mizzi into a virago.

**The Blue Paradise.** Ted Lorraine and Vivienne Segal come to the aid of Teddy Webb, who has apparently bitten off more than he can swallow. (White)

21

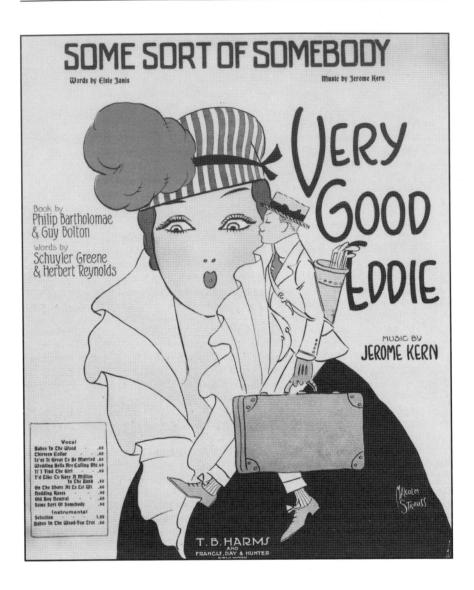

# VERY GOOD EDDIE

**Music:** Jerome Kern
**Lyrics:** Schuyler Greene
**Book:** Philip Bartholomae & Guy Bolton
**Producers:** Elisabeth Marbury & F. Ray Comstock
**Director:** (uncredited)
**Choreographer:** David Bennett
**Cast:** Ernest Truex, Alice Dovey, Oscar Shaw, Helen Raymond, John E. Hazzard, John Willard, Ada Lewis
**Songs:** "Some Sort of Somebody" (lyric: Elsie Janis); "Isn't It Great to Be Married?"; "On the Shore at Le Lei Wi" (music with Henry Kailimai; lyric: Herbert Reynolds); "Thirteen Collar"; "Babes in the Wood" (lyric with Kern); "Old Boy Neutral"; "Nodding Roses" (lyric with Reynolds)
**New York Run:** Princess Theatre, December 23, 1915; 341 p.

When, in 1914, producer F. Ray Comstock was having difficulty filling his 299-seat Princess Theatre (then on 39th Street near 6th Avenue), theatrical and literary agent Elisabeth Marbury suggested that they jointly sponsor a series of modern musical comedies, all with music written by Jerome Kern and librettos by Guy Bolton. The aim was to offer scaled-down shows with casts of no more that 30 (including chorus) and with the action taking place in only two different locations, thus allowing for one set in the first act and another in the second. The stories, all occurring in contemporary America, would have believable if bubbleheaded characters caught in comic situations that evolved naturally out of the action, and the songs would have more than a passing relevance to what was going on in the plot.

The first effort, *Nobody Home,* which opened in April 1915, was something of a compromise since it was based on an English musical, *Mr. Popple of Ippleton,* and it had interpolated numbers. The action, however, took place in New York City, and the story was filled with the same kind of romantic complications and misunderstandings that would be the concern of subsequent shows at the theatre. The second offering did, in fact, indicate greater assurance in fulfilling the goals that the Princess management had initially outlined. *Very Good Eddie* not only adhered to the general plan but also set the style and standard for three subsequent Kern musicals written with Bolton and P.G. Wodehouse — *Oh, Boy!, Leave It to Jane,* and *Oh, Lady! Lady!!* — that formed the seminal quartet known as the Princess Theatre Musicals.

*Very Good Eddie* — no comma in the title since it was an appraisal of character rather than an expression of approval — takes place at first aboard the Hudson River dayliner *Catskill,* which is carrying two honeymooning couples. Eddie Kettle (Ernest Truex) is short and timid and his wife Georgina (Helen Raymond) is tall and domineering, Percy Darling (John Willard) is tall and domineering and *his* wife Elsie (Alice Dovey) is short and timid. Georgina and Percy are accidentally left on shore before the boat sails, thereby resulting in embarrassing predicaments for Eddie and Elsie. Matters get straightened out in the second act at the Rip Van Winkle Inn where Eddie now asserts his authority over his suddenly subservient spouse.

In 1975, the Goodspeed Opera in East Haddam, Connecticut, revived the musical which then had a Broadway run almost as long as the original production. There were some changes in the score, and the final scene — in the renamed Honeymoon Inn — found both couples switching partners according to size and temperament after discovering that the minister who married them had no legal right to perform the ceremony.
DRG OC (1975)/ TW.

# OH, BOY!

**Music:** Jerome Kern
**Lyrics:** P. G. Wodehouse
**Book:** Guy Bolton & P. G. Wodehouse
**Producers:** William Elliott & F. Ray Comstock
**Directors:** Edward Royce, Robert Milton
**Choreographer:** Edward Royce
**Cast:** Marie Carroll, Tom Powers, Anna Wheaton, Hal Forde, Edna May Oliver, Marion Davies, Justine Johnstone, Dorothy Dickson & Carl Hyson
**Songs:** "You Never Knew About Me"; "The Land Where the Good Songs Go"; "An Old-Fashioned Wife"; "A Pal Like You"; "Till the Clouds Roll By"; "Rolled into One"; "Nesting Time in Flatbush"
**New York run:** Princess Theatre, February 20, 1917; 463 p.

For *Oh, Boy!*, their third Princess Theatre Musical and the third longest running book musical of the 1910's, Jerome Kern and Guy Bolton were joined by British humorist P. G. Wodehouse, who helped give the characters the flavor of transplanted silly-ass Englishmen. Again the settings were modern and modest, the songs fitted the story, and the comic tale involved romantic and marital mixups. When George Budd (Tom Powers) arrives home to his Long Island apartment after eloping with Lou Ellen Carter (Marie Carroll), he finds his country club friends having a party in his digs. The newlyweds separate while Lou Ellen prepares her parents for the news of her marriage, and George becomes innocently involved with Jackie Sampson (Anna Wheaton), a madcap actress, who has climbed through his bedroom window to avoid the advances of a lecherous judge. After further complications, during which the judge turns out to be Lou Ellen's father and Jackie is alternately passed off as both George's wife and his Quaker aunt, the couple is reunited at the Meadowsides Country Club.

# MAYTIME

**Music:** Sigmund Romberg
**Lyrics & book:** Rida Johnson Young
**Producers:** Messrs. Shubert
**Director:** Edward Temple
**Choreographer:** Allan K. Foster
**Cast:** Peggy Wood, Charles Purcell, Ralph Herbert, William Norris, Gertrude Vanderbilt
**Songs:** "The Road to Paradise"; "Will You Remember?"; "Jump Jim Crow"; "Dancing Will Keep You Young" (lyric: Cyrus Wood)
**New York run:** Shubert Theatre, August 16, 1917; 492 p.

*Maytime* established Sigmund Romberg as Victor Herbert's successor as the leading creator of sentimental operettas. The musical, with such pieces as "Will You Remember?" and "The Road to Paradise," became New York's most popular attraction during World War I, even though, ironically, it was based on a German operetta, *Wie Einst im Mai*. In Washington Square, New York, in 1840, wealthy Ottilie Van Zandt (Peggy Wood) and poor Richard Wayne (Charles Purcell) are unable to marry because Ottilie's father has other plans for her. Richard becomes rich and Ottilie, fallen upon hard times, must sell her house which is turned into a dress shop. Their grandchildren (played by the same actors) prove that love will find a way — even if it takes 60 years.

The second longest running book musical of the decade, *Maytime* was seen in three New York theatres following its engagement at the Shubert (on 44th Street west of Broadway). During the run, Purcell was succeeded by future Metropolitan Opera tenor John Charles Thomas. The 1937 movie version, with Jeanette MacDonald and Nelson Eddy, changed the story and the score.

**Maytime.** Peggy Wood and Charles Purcell in the romantic climax of Act IV.

070102

# LEAVE IT TO JANE

**Music:** Jerome Kern
**Lyrics:** P. G. Wodehouse
**Book:** Guy Bolton & P. G. Wodehouse
**Producers:** William Elliot, F. Ray Comstock, Morris Gest
**Director-Choreographer:** Edward Royce
**Cast:** Edith Hallor, Robert Pitkin, Oscar Shaw, Georgia O'Ramey
**Songs:** "Wait Till Tomorrow"; "Just You Watch My Step"; "Leave It to Jane";
"The Crickets Are Calling"; "The Siren's Song"; "There It Is Again";
"Cleopatterer"; "The Sun Shines Brighter"; "I'm Going to Find a Girl"
**New York run:** Longacre Theatre, August 28, 1917; 167 p.

Except for the technicality that *Leave It to Jane* never played the Princess Theatre, in every other respect it qualifies as a Princess Theatre Musical. Its score was by Kern and Wodehouse, its book was by Bolton and Wodehouse, and it was presented by the Princess management. In fact, this version of George Ade's 1904 play, *The College Widow*, had been scheduled to follow *Oh, Boy!* into the Princess but that show was doing so well that *Jane* was shifted to a larger house (the Longacre is on 48th Street east of Broadway), with the top ticket price reduced from $3.50 to $2.50. *Leave It to Jane* takes place at good old Atwater College, where everyone is concerned about the Thanksgiving Day football game with rival Bingham. It is left to flirtatious Jane Witherspoon (Edith Hallor), the president's daughter, to induce All-American halfback Billy Bolton (Robert Pitkin), who is to play for Bingham, to switch colleges and play for Atwater under an assumed name. He does and wins both the game and Jane. Over 40 years later, the musical was successfully revived at a Greenwich Village theatre. DRG OC (1959)/ TW.

# OH, LADY! LADY!!

**Music:** Jerome Kern
**Lyrics:** P. G. Wodehouse
**Book:** Guy Bolton & P. G. Wodehouse
**Producers:** William Elliott & F. Ray Comstock
**Directors:** Edward Royce, Robert Milton
**Choreographer:** Edward Royce
**Cast:** Vivienne Segal, Carl Randall, Harry C. Browne, Carroll McComas,
Edward Abeles, Florence Shirley, Margaret Dale, Constance Binney
**Songs:** "Not Yet"; "Do Look at Him"; "I Found You and You Found Me"; "Moon
Song"; "When the Ships Come Home"; "Before I Met You"; "Greenwich
Village"
**New York run:** Princess Theatre, February 1, 1918; 219 p.

Using a minstrel-show catch line for a title, the last Kern-Wodehouse-Bolton Princess Theatre Musical was the exclamatory successor to *Oh, Boy!* In a plot that amounted to virtual self-plagiarism, the characters were again caught up in a series of amatory mixups and misunderstandings. Willoughby "Bill" Finch (Carl Randall) is about to marry Molly Farrington (Vivienne Segal) when May Barber (Carroll McComas), his former fiancee from East Giliad, Ohio, shows up at Molly's Long Island home. Though May is there only to deliver Molly's lingerie, her appearance — and that of a comic jewel thief — cause complications that result in the wedding being called off. In Act II the lovers are reunited at a party in Greenwich Village. Curiously, the best known song written for *Oh, Lady! Lady!!* was never used in the show. The heroine was originally to have sung "Bill," but the lyric did not accurately describe the show's Bill, and "Do Look at Him" was substituted. A slightly altered "Bill," of course, later turned up in *Show Boat.* TW.

**Oh, Lady! Lady!!** Vivienne Segal and Carl Randall. (White)

**Sinbad.** Al Jolson and showgirl. (White)

# SINBAD

**Music:** Sigmund Romberg, etc.
**Lyrics:** Harold Atteridge, etc.
**Book:** Harold Atteridge
**Producers:** Messrs. Shubert
**Director:** J. C. Huffman
**Choreographers:** Jack Mason, Alexis Kosloff
**Cast:** Al Jolson, Kitty Doner, Mabel Withee, Forrest Huff, Grace Washburn, Alexis Kosloff
**Songs:** "Beauty and the Beast"; "Rock-a-Bye Your Baby With a Dixie Melody" (Jean Schwartz-Sam Lewis, Joe Young); "Why Do They All Take the Night Boat to Albany?" (Schwartz-Lewis, Young); " 'N Everything" (B. G. DeSylva-Gus Kahn)
**New York run:** Winter Garden, February 14, 1918; 388 p.

At a time when it was not uncommon for musicals to be built around the talents of one individual, no shows were more vehicular than those created to spotlight the exuberant personality of "Mammy" singer Al Jolson. Though they had large casts, such extravaganzas as *Robinson Crusoe, Jr.* (1916), *Sinbad*, *Bombo* (1921), and *Big Boy* (1925) were virtually one-man shows. All the Jolson entertainments were presented by the Messrs. Shubert, directed by J. C. Huffman, had easily ignored books by Harold Atteridge, were full of interpolated songs, and — except for *Bombo* — played the Winter Garden (on Broadway between 50th and 51st Streets).

In *Sinbad*, in which the star wore his customary black-face makeup, Jolson appeared in ancient Bagdad as a comical chap named Inbad who poses as Sinbad the Sailor. Between adventures, he literally stopped the show to introduce his own musical specialties, including "Avalon" (added after the opening) and George Gershwin's first hit, "Swanee" (added during the road tour).

# ZIEGFELD FOLLIES

**Music & lyrics:** Miscellaneous writers
**Sketches:** Gene Buck, Rennold Wolf
**Producer:** Florenz Ziegfeld
**Director-choreographer:** Ned Wayburn
**Cast:** Marilyn Miller, Eddie Cantor, W. C. Fields, Will Rogers, Harry Kelly, Ann Pennington, Lillian Lorraine, Savoy & Brennan, Fairbanks Twins
**Songs:** "Syncopated Tune" (Louis A. Hirsch-Gene Buck); "Blue Devils of France" (Irving Berlin); "I'm Gonna Pin a Medal on the Girl I Left Behind" (Berlin); "Any Old Time at All" (Hirsch-Buck)
**New York run:** New Amsterdam Theatre, June 18, 1918; 151 p.

The star-filled 1918 *Follies* — the 12th annual edition — put the focus on World War I in most of its sketches, production numbers, and songs. These included a "Yankee Doodle" dance by Marilyn Miller (in her *Follies* debut); Will Rogers' topical monologues; a skit with Eddie Cantor playing a would-be aviator in a recruiting office; a stirring parade of showgirls representing the allied nations; a first-act finale of living statues created by Ben Ali Haggin titled "Forward, Allies"; and a sketch showing women on the home front performing jobs usually done by men (a reassuring note in the program contained the information that all members of the male chorus were rejected for military service). Popular pastimes of the day were covered in W. C. Fields' golf routine and a grand finale with everyone indulging in the current passion for jazz dancing. One of six *Follies* staged by the prolific Ned Wayburn, the revue also had the services of a 19-year-old rehearsal pianist named George Gershwin.

**Ziegfeld Follies (1918).** W.C. Fields, Will Rogers, Eddie Cantor, and Harry Kelly serenade Lillian Lorraine with "Any Old Time at All." (White)

**Ziegfeld Follies (1919).** Showgirls as ingredients in "The Follies Salad" — Spice, Oil, Paprika, Sugar, Lettuce, and Chicken. (White)

# ZIEGFELD FOLLIES

**Music & lyrics:** Irving Berlin, etc.
**Sketches:** Gene Buck, Rennold Wolf
**Producer:** Florenz Ziegfeld
**Director-choreographer:** Ned Wayburn
**Cast:** Marilyn Miller, Eddie Cantor, Bert Williams, Eddie Dowling, Ray Dooley, Johnny Dooley, Delyle Alda, John Steel, Van & Schenck, Mary Hay
**Songs:** "My Baby's Arms" (Harry Tierney-Joseph McCarthy); "Tulip Time" (David Stamper-Gene Buck); "Mandy"; "A Pretty Girl Is Like a Melody"; "You'd Be Surprised"; "You Cannot Make Your Shimmy Shake on Tea" (Berlin-Rennold Wolf)
**New York run:** New Amsterdam Theatre, June 16, 1919; 171 p.

With more song hits than any previous *Follies*, the 13th edition even gave the entire series a theme song in Irving Berlin's "A Pretty Girl Is Like a Melody." Rivalling the 1918 production as the premier revue in the series, it offered showgirls clad as salad ingredients and classical music; Ben Ali Haggin's tableaux depicting the 13th Folly and a scene showing Lady Godiva astride a white horse; and a first-act finale offering a minstrel show with Eddie Cantor and Bert Williams as "Tambo" and "Bones," Marilyn Miller as George Primrose, and a tambourine-banging, high-strutting line of Mandys. The grand finale was a grand tribute to the Salvation Army's morale-boosting contributions to the war. The chief nonmilitary topic was the imminent arrival of Prohibition whose effects were shown in a nightclub scene with showgirls parading around as Coca-Cola, Sarsaparilla, Grape Juice, Lemonade, and Bevo. The production cost was now over $100,000, and the top ticket price was $3.50 at night, $2.00 for matinees. Smithsonian OC.

# GREENWICH VILLAGE FOLLIES

**Music & lyrics:** Miscellaneous writers
**Sketches:** John Murray Anderson, Philip Bartholomae
**Producer:** The Bohemians Inc. (Al Jones & Morris Green)
**Director:** John Murray Anderson
**Cast:** Bessie McCoy Davis, Ted Lewis Orchestra, Cecil Cunningham, Harry K. Morton
**Songs:** "When My Baby Smiles at Me" (Billy Munro-Andrew Sterling); "I Want a Daddy who Will Rock Me to Sleep" (A. Baldwin Sloane-Arthur Swanstrom, John Murray Anderson); "(I'll See You in) C-U-B-A" (Irving Berlin)
**New York run:** Greenwich Village Theatre, July 15, 1919; 232 p.

A stylishly mounted, somewhat less elaborate variation on the *Ziegfeld Follies* format was the *Greenwich Village Follies* (Ziegfeld even threatened to sue over the use of the *Follies* name), which came along in 1919 and lasted through eight editions up to 1928. The guiding light was director John Murray Anderson, who made his professional debut with the first of the series and staged six in all. (Murray's total Broadway credits were 28 musicals.) Despite the title, all editions of the *Greenwich Village Follies* were moved uptown during their runs, with the 1919 production switched to the Nora Bayes Theatre (then on West 44th Street) soon after its Greenwich Village opening. The show, which called itself "A Revusical Comedy of New York's Latin Quarter," took satirical aim at the ballet, free love, Prohibition, and the arts in general. Among the distinguishing characteristics of the series were female impersonations and arty "ballet ballads" based on literary works. In 1925, Hassard Short took over as director (Anderson had replaced *him* at the *Music Box Revue*) and in 1928 it was J. C. Huffman.

31

# IRENE

**Music:** Harry Tierney
**Lyrics:** Joseph McCarthy
**Book:** James Montgomery
**Producers:** Carle Carlton & Joseph McCarthy
**Director-Choreographer:** Edward Royce
**Cast:** Edith Day, Walter Regan, Bobbie Watson, Dorothy Walters, John Litel, Hobart Cavanaugh, Eva Puck
**Songs:** "Alice Blue Gown"; "Castle of Dreams"; "Irene"; "Skyrocket"; "The Last Part of Ev'ry Party"
**New York run:** Vanderbilt Theatre, November 18, 1919; 670 p.

By remaining at the Vanderbilt Theatre (then on 48th Street east of 7th Avenue), for one year eight months — and by running 11 performances longer than *A Trip to Chinatown* — *Irene* set a Broadway endurance record that it held onto for 18 years. What made it such a hit for its day (at one time it claimed 17 road companies) resulted from what critics hailed as its intelligent book, diverting comedy, brisk pacing, melodious songs that fitted logically into the story, and talented performers. The show, in fact, won not only critical applause but also gratitude for relieving what Alexander Woollcott termed "Broadway's desperate plight with only 17 or 18 musical comedies in view." Actually, the plot was little more than another version of the Cinderella tale, which has served as the basis for many other musicals including *Mlle. Modiste, The Firefly, Sally, Sunny, Annie Get Your Gun, My Fair Lady, Annie,* and *42nd Street.*

In this variation, a chatty upholsterer's assistant, Irene O'Dare (Edith Day), is sent to a Long Island mansion to mend some cushions. There she meets the instantly smitten Donald Marshall (Walter Regan), who persuades his friend, a male couturier known as Madame Lucy (Bobbie Watson), to hire Irene to pose as a socialite and show off his latest creations. Even though her humble origin is revealed, Irene makes a hit at an elegant party wearing and singing about her Alice blue gown, and ends in Donald's arms.

The show was designed as a star vehicle for Edith Day (who left the cast after only five months to head the London company) and it was the first — of seven — Broadway musicals with songs by Harry Tierney and Joseph McCarthy. During the New York run, Irene Dunne became the fourth actress to play Irene, and Jeanette MacDonald joined the cast as a Long Island belle. Busby Berkeley played Madame Lucy on the road. As for Miss Day, though she appeared on Broadway in two subsequent musicals, her career flourished mostly in London where she was known as the Queen of Drury Lane.

Prompted by the successful revival of *No, No, Nanette* in 1971, *Irene* was brought back two years later by the same producer, Harry Rigby, who had first thought of bringing back *Nanette.* (See page 238.) The new production was also plagued at the outset by the same kind of problems that had affected the previous show, including the replacement of a major cast member (George S. Irving for Billy DeWolfe as Madame Lucy) and the director (Gower Champion for Sir John Gielgud). Though greeted by mixed reviews in New York, the musical remained a year and a half at the newly built Minskoff Theatre, located on the west side of Broadway between 44th and 45th Streets. Debbie Reynolds, who was succeeded during the run by Jane Powell, made her Broadway debut as Irene. Her occupation, however, was changed to that of a piano tuner so that the title song might be used for a male chorus tapping away on top of four uprights as they sing of the charms of Irene. Only five numbers were retained from the original score, with others either pop tunes of the period (though all had lyrics by Joseph McCarthy) or new songs. A screen version was filmed in 1940 with Anna Neagle and Ray Milland.

M-E London OC (1920); Columbia OC (1973)/ TW.

# SALLY

**Music:** Jerome Kern
**Lyrics:** Clifford Grey, etc.
**Book:** Guy Bolton
**Producer:** Florenz Ziegfeld
**Director-choreographer:** Edward Royce
**Cast:** Marilyn Miller, Leon Errol, Walter Catlett, Irving Fisher, Mary Hay, Stanley Ridges, Dolores
**Songs:** "Look for the Silver Lining" (lyric: B.G. DeSylva); "Sally"; "Wild Rose"; "Whip-Poor-Will"; "The Lorelei" (lyric: Anne Caldwell); "The Church 'Round the Corner" (lyric: P.G. Wodehouse)
**New York run:** New Amsterdam Theatre, December 21, 1920; 570 p.

Just as *Irene* was a Cinderella tale created to show off the talents of singer Edith Day, so *Sally* was a Cinderella tale created to show off the talents of dancer Marilyn Miller (then spelling her first name "Marilynn") in her first starring role. Producer Florenz Ziegfeld commmissioned the Princess Theatre triad of Kern, Bolton and Wodehouse to come up with a suitable vehicle and the team settled on an unproduced musical they had written called *The Little Thing*. Early in the preparations, Wodehouse withdrew from the project, and in the altered script, initially known as *Sally of the Alley,* Sally Green first appears as a dishwashing drudge at the Alley Inn in Groonwich Village dreaming of fame and singing "Look for the Silver Lining." Invited by one of the waiters, really the exiled Duke of Czechogovinia (Leon Errol), Sally goes to an elegant ball in the guise of Mme. Nookerova, a celebrated ballerina. In *Irene* fashion, her true identity is discovered, but here the heroine not only wins the affluent young tenor she is also signed for the *Ziegfeld Follies* and dances a Butterfly Ballet by Victor Herbert. *Sally* was the third longest running Broadway musical of the Twenties. An unsuccessful revival was presented in 1948 with Bambi Linn as Sally and Willie Howard as the duke. Miss Miller was also in the 1929 movie version.
M-E London OC (1921)/ TW.

**Sally.** Marilyn Miller as a Russian ballerina. (White)

# SHUFFLE ALONG

**Music:** Eubie Blake
**Lyrics:** Noble Sissle
**Book:** Flournoy Miller & Aubrey Lyles
**Producer:** Nikko Producing Co. (Al Mayer)
**Director:** Walter Brooks
**Choreographer:** Lawrence Deas
**Cast:** Flournoy Miller, Aubrey Lyles, Noble Sissle, Gertrude Saunders, Roger Matthews, Lottie Gee, Lawrence Deas, Eubie Blake
**Songs:** "I'm Just Wild About Harry"; "Love Will Find a Way"; "Bandana Days"; "If You've Never Been Vamped by a Brownskin"
**New York run:** 63rd St. Music Hall, May 23, 1921; 504 p.

Developed from a vaudeville sketch, *Shuffle Along* became the first successful musical written, directed, and acted by black people. Little money was spent on costumes or scenery, but white audiences were happy to travel a bit north of the theatre district to enjoy the show's earthy humor, fast pacing, spirited dancing, and infectious rhythms. The plot is concerned with the race for mayor of Jimtown, in Dixieland, between the venal Steve Jenkins (Flournoy Miller) and the virtuous Harry Walton (Roger Matthews), about whom, we are repeatedly advised, everyone is just wild. Though Steve wins, Harry eventually has him and his equally corrupt police chief, Sam Peck (Aubrey Lyles), thrown out of office. During the run, Paul Robeson joined the cast briefly as a member of a vocal quartet, and Josephine Baker was added to the touring company as a chorus girl. There were three titular successors to *Shuffle Along: Keep Shufflin'* (1928), *Shuffle Along of 1933* (1932), and another *Shuffle Along* (1952). All of them availeth not. New World OC.

# ZIEGFELD FOLLIES

**Music, lyrics & sketches:** Miscellaneous writers
**Producer:** Florenz Ziegfeld
**Directors:** Edward Royce, George Marion
**Choreographer:** Edward Royce
**Cast:** Fanny Brice, W. C. Fields, Raymond Hitchcock, Ray Dooley, Mary Milburn, Van & Schenck, Florence O'Denishawn, Vera Michelena, Mary Eaton, Channing Pollock, Mary Lewis
**Songs:** "Strut, Miss Lizzie" (Henry Creamer-Turner Layton); "Second Hand Rose" (James Hanley-Grant Clarke); "Sally, Won't You Come Back?" (David Stamper-Gene Buck); "My Man" (Maurice Yvain-Channing Pollock)
**New York run:** Globe Theatre, June 21, 1921; 119 p.

The 15th annual *Ziegfeld Follies* was among the Great Glorifier's most elaborate revues, with another star-filled cast and a number of memorable scenes and songs. It was also the first of two editions to play the Globe Theatre (now the Lunt-Fontanne on 46th Street just west of Broadway), since *Sally* was still packing them in at the New Amsterdam, the *Follies'* customary home. The show got off to an unexpected display of social consciousness with a scene celebrating the arrival of immigrants from all over the world. More accustomed forms of spectacle and spoofing then took over, with an array of chorus girls depicting various types of roses; a takeoff on both the Barrymore clan and *Camille* with Fanny Brice, W. C. Fields, and Raymond Hitchcock; and a W. C. Fields sketch about the frustrations of subway travel. Two of the show's highlights involved Miss Brice alone, first her comic lament "Second Hand Rose," then her masochistic wail, "My Man," which, though a French song, became a personal expression about the singer's recently convicted gangster husband.

**Shuffle Along.** Flournoy Miller and Aubrey Lyles. (White)

**Music Box Revue (1921).** Irving Berlin with ''The Eight Little Notes,'' including Miriam Hopkins at the upper right. (White)

**Music Box Revue (1924).** Oscar Shaw and Grace Moore singing ''All Alone.'' (White)

**Music Box Revue (1924).** Bobby Clark and Fanny Brice as Adam and Eve. (White)

# MUSIC BOX REVUE

**Music & lyrics:** Irving Berlin
**Sketches:** Miscellaneous writers
**Producer:** Sam H. Harris
**Directors:** Hassard Short, William Collier
**Choreographers:** Bert French, I. Tarasoff
**Cast:** William Collier, Wilda Bennett, Paul Frawley, Sam Bernard, Ivy Sawyer, Joseph Santley, Florence Moore, Brox Sisters, Chester Hale, Irving Berlin, Miriam Hopkins
**Songs:** "In a Cozy Kitchenette Apartment"; "My Little Book of Poetry"; "Say It With Music"; "Everybody Step"; "The Schoolhouse Blues"; "They Call It Dancing"; "The Legend of the Pearls"
**New York run:** Music Box, September 22, 1921; 440 p.

The *Music Box Revues* were the only annual revue series to be created with the express purpose of providing a showcase for the songs of just one composer. The project stemmed from Irving Berlin's suggestion to producer Sam H. Harris that the Music Box would be an ideal name for a theatre designed specifically for musicals. Harris and Berlin built the theatre (located on 45th Street west of Broadway) and opened it with the appropriately titled *Music Box Revue*. The initial edition — there would be three more — was an elaborate and colorful show that greatly benefited from the ingenious staging of Hassard Short (whose credits would total 40 Broadway musicals) and a collection of appealing Berlin ballads (including "Say It With Music," sung by Wilda Bennett and Paul Frawley, which was used as a theme for the entire series). Among the visual pleasures were scenes showing chorus girls parading as a pageant of fans, displaying themselves as courses in a restaurant meal, and succumbing to the craze for syncopation in "Everybody Step." Berlin himself appeared in a scene with an octet dubbed "The Eight Little Notes" (the eighth was future film star Miriam Hopkins). As Alexander Woollcott wrote in *The Times*, the show's creators "crowded the stage with such a sumptuous and bespangled revue as cannot possibly earn them anything more substantial than the heart-warming satisfaction of having produced it at all."

None of the subsequent *Music Box Revues* ran as long as the first, yet all were well received. The 1922 edition featured the buffoonery of Bobby Clark and Paul McCullough and the antics of long-legged Charlotte Greenwood, as well as the singing of John Steel ("Lady of the Evening" was his most popular number) and Grace LaRue (who recalled the charms of "Crinoline Days"). The McCarthy Sisters were also on hand to stir things up with "Pack Up Your Sins and Go to the Devil" and "Bring on the Pepper." In 1923, Grace Moore sang "Tell Me a Bedtime Story," "The Waltz of Long Ago," "An Orange Grove in California," and — added during the run — "What'll I Do?" (the last two as duets with John Steel). It was also in this revue that Robert Benchley delivered his classic "Treasurer's Report." For the final edition, in 1924, John Murray Anderson took over as director, with Hassard Short replacing him at the *Greenwich Village Follies*. Clark and McCullough were back, with Clark doing an Adam and Eve sketch with Fanny Brice. On her own Miss Brice was an immigrant pleading "Don't Send Me Back to Petrograd" and a flat-footed gazelle proclaiming "I Want to Be a Ballet Dancer." Grace Moore returned to sing "Tell Her in the Springtime," "Rockabye Baby," and, in a duet with Oscar Shaw, the interpolated "All Alone."

Sam Harris, who produced 32 musicals on Broadway, was also associated with Irving Berlin on *The Cocoanuts, Face the Music,* and *As Thousands Cheer.* Ironically, because of its relatively small size, (1,010 seats), the Music Box is no longer considered economically feasible as a showplace for large-scale musical productions.

# BLOSSOM TIME

**Music:** Sigmund Romberg, based on Franz Schubert
**Lyrics & book:** Dorothy Donnelly
**Producers:** Messrs. Shubert
**Director:** J. C. Huffman
**Choreographer:** F. M. Gillespie
**Cast:** Bertram Peacock, Olga Cook, Howard Marsh, Roy Cropper
**Songs:** "Serenade"; "Three Little Maids"; " Song of Love"; "Tell Me Daisy"
**New York run:** Ambassador Theatre, September 29, 1921; 516 p.

For the first Broadway musical with songs based on themes from classical compositions, Sigmund Romberg was assigned by the producing Shuberts to adapt melodies by the composing Schubert. The fanciful biographical libretto — a variation on a Viennese operetta, *Das Dreimaederlhaus* — deals with the composer's supposed unrequited love for one Mitzi Kranz. When, at Schubert's request, his friend Baron Schober sings the composer's "Song of Love" to Mitzi, she becomes enamored of the baron, and poor Schubert, no longer inspired, is unable to complete his "Unfinished Symphony." Four road companies of *Blossom Time* were sent out soon after the opening at the Ambassador Theatre (on 49th Street west of Broadway), and the operetta had five revivals in New York, the most recent in 1943.

Broadway has also offered musicals with scores derived from works by such composers as Offenbach in *The Love Song* (1925) and *The Happiest Girl in the World* (1961); Tschaikowsky in *Nadja* (1925) and *Music in My Heart* (1947); Chopin in *White Lilacs* (1928) and *Polonaise* (1945); Grieg in *Song of Norway* (1944); Fritz Kreisler in *Rhapsody* (1944); Villa Lobos in *Magdalena* (1948); Borodin in *Kismet* (1953); and Rachmaninoff in *Anya* (1965). SO.

# ZIEGFELD FOLLIES

**Music:** Louis A. Hirsch, David Stamper
**Lyrics:** Gene Buck
**Sketches:** Miscellaneous writers
**Producer:** Florenz Ziegfeld
**Director:** Ned Wayburn
**Choreographers:** Ned Wayburn, Michel Fokine
**Cast:** Will Rogers, Gilda Gray, Gallagher & Shean, Evelyn Law, Andrew Tombes, Florence O'Denishawn, Lulu McConnell, Mary Eaton, Nervo & Knox, Mary Lewis, Alexander Gray, Jack Whiting
**Songs:** "My Rambler Rose"; "Mr. Gallagher and Mr. Shean" (Ed Gallagher-Al Shean, Ernest Ball); " 'Neath the South Sea Moon"; "Oh! Gee, Oh! Gosh, Oh! Golly, I'm in Love" (Ole Olsen-Chic Johnson, Ernest Brewer)
**New York run:** New Amsterdam Theatre, June 5, 1922; 541 p.

Because of a Summer Edition that began June 25, 1923, and followed without a break, the 1922 *Follies* had the longest run of any revue in the series produced during Ziegfeld's lifetime. Now proclaiming itself "A National Institution Glorifying the American Girl," the 16th annual edition ended the eight-year period generally annointed The Great *Follies*. Humorist Will Rogers made his fourth *Follies* appearance in the show, and hits were also scored by shimmy dancer Gilda Gray and the team of Gallagher and Shean. Among the lavish scenes were "Lace Land," with girls parading in lace before lace costumes in front of lace draperies, and a dance featuring Greek statues coming to life in an art museum. Eddie Cantor, Ann Pennington, and Ilse Marvenga joined the Summer Edition cast.

# GEORGE WHITE'S SCANDALS

**Music:** George Gershwin
**Lyrics:** B. G. DeSylva
**Sketches:** George White, Andy Rice
**Producer-director-choreographer:** George White
**Cast:**  W. C. Fields, Winnie Lightner, Paul Whiteman Orchestra, Lester Allen, George White, Jack McGowan, Pearl Regay, Dolores Costello
**Songs:** "Cinderelatives"; "I Found a Four-Leaf Clover"; "I'll Build a Stairway to Paradise" (lyric: DeSylva, Ira Gershwin); "Argentina"; "Blue Monday Blues"
**New York run:** Globe Theatre, August 28, 1922; 88 p.

Of all the revues that enjoyed more than one annual edition, the *George White's Scandals* series was the nearest to the *Ziegfeld Follies* in fame and longevity. Beginning in 1919, George White, who had danced in two *Follies*, turned out 13 editions in 21 years. His series was faster paced, more youthful, less ornately mounted than their model, with a greater emphasis on dancing and new dance steps. They also differed from the *Follies* in having one songwriter or team of songwriters responsible for an entire score, e.g. George Gershwin who, with various lyricists, composed the music for five editions between 1920 and 1924. The 1922 *Scandals* introduced Gershwin's first Broadway hit, "I'll Build a Stairway to Paradise," performed as the first-act finale, and "Blue Monday," an "Opera ala Afro-American." Though it was not well received and was removed after opening night, the work was a forerunner of the composer's later full-length opera, *Porgy and Bess*. For subsequent editions of the *George White's Scandals* see pages 52 and 76.

# POPPY

**Music:** Stephen Jones, Arthur Samuels
**Lyrics:** Dorothy Donnelly, etc.
**Book:** Dorothy Donnelly (Howard Dietz, W. C. Fields uncredited)
**Producer:** Philip Goodman
**Director:** Dorothy Donnelly
**Choreographer:** Julian Alfred
**Cast:**  Madge Kennedy, W. C. Fields, Robert Woolsey, Alan Edwards, Luella Gear
**Songs:** "Two Make a Home"; "Alibi Baby" (music: Samuels; lyric: Howard Dietz); "On Our Honeymoon"; "What Do You Do Sunday, Mary?" (music: Jones; lyric: Irving Caesar)
**New York run:** Apollo Theatre, September 3, 1923; 346 p.

*Poppy* was a tour-de-force for W. C. Fields, though initially he received featured billing while Madge Kennedy, who played the eponymous heroine, was solo starred. Fields, however, won stardom when Miss Kennedy's understudy took over her role, and he was co-starred with Miss Kennedy for the tour. In the part of Professor Eustace McGargle, the bulbous-nosed comedian established the character of the bogusly elegant, ornately speaking conman by which he was identified in his later career. Set in 1874 in a Connecticut town, *Poppy* presented Fields as a carnival grifter, juggler, card shark, and shell-game artist who attempts to pass off his foster daughter, Poppy, as a long-lost heiress — only to discover that she really is an heiress. The Apollo Theatre, where *Poppy* was shown, still stands on 42nd Street west of Broadway. Fields appeared in two film versions of the musical: in 1925 (renamed *Sally of the Sawdust*), a silent directed by D. W. Griffith, and in 1936.

**Poppy.** W. C. Fields demonstrates his latest musical creation, the kadoola-kadoola. (White)

# ANDRE CHARLOT'S REVUE OF 1924

**Music, lyrics & sketches:** Miscellaneous writers
**Producer:** Arch Selwyn
**Director:** Andre Charlot
**Choreographer:** David Bennett
**Cast:** Beatrice Lillie, Gertrude Lawrence, Jack Buchanan, Douglas Furber, Herbert Mundin, Jessie Matthews, Constance Carpenter
**Songs:** "Parisian Pierrot" (Noël Coward); "You Were Meant for Me" (Eubie Blake-Noble Sissle); "Limehouse Blues" (Philip Braham-Douglas Furber); "March With Me!" (Ivor Novello-Furber); "There's Life in the Old Girl Yet" (Coward)
**New York run:** Times Square Theatre, January 9, 1924; 298 p.

London impresario Andre Charlot entered New York's crowded revue field with a sly, sophisticated, witty, intimate show made up of songs, dances, and sketches from his West End revues. He also introduced New York audiences to three performers — Beatrice Lillie, Gertrude Lawrence, and Jack Buchanan — whose careers would flourish on both sides of the Atlantic. The show, which played the Times Square Theatre (now a movie house on 42nd Street west of Times Square), offered such highlights as Miss Lillie as a dignified but disoriented Britannia in "March With Me!," Miss Lawrence crooning "Parisian Pierrot" and "Limehouse Blues," and Jack Buchanan's version of the tired businessman trying to get some peace and quiet at home.

The success of his first endeavor on Broadway prompted Charlot to follow it up with *The Charlot Revue of 1926*, which opened November 10, 1925, at the Selwyn Theatre (right next to the Times Square). The triad of Lillie, Lawrence and Buchanan was again on hand, with Miss Lillie as Wanda Allova in a ballet takeoff, Lillie and Lawrence in a sketch as two precocious babies in their prams, Miss Lawrence singing Noël Coward's moralistic "Poor Little Rich Girl," and Lawrence and Buchanan in a duet of "A Cup of Coffee, a Sandwich and You." A third *Andre Charlot Revue* opened in January 1927 as featured attraction of the "International Edition" of the *Earl Carroll Vanities*. Jessie Matthews and Herbert Mundin headed the cast.

# ROSE-MARIE

**Music:** Rudolf Friml*, Herbert Stothart#
**Lyrics & book:** Otto Harbach & Oscar Hammerstein II
**Producer:** Arthur Hammerstein
**Director:** Paul Dickey
**Choreographer:** David Bennett
**Cast:**  Mary Ellis, Dennis King, William Kent, Dorothy Mackaye, Eduardo
    Ciannelli, Pearl Regay, Arthur Deagon
**Songs:** "Rose-Marie"*; "The Mounties"*#; "Indian Love Call"*; "Why Shouldn't
    We?"#; "Totem Tom-Tom"*#; "The Door of Her Dreams"*
**New York run:** Imperial Theatre, September 2, 1924; 557 p.

With such settings as Saskatchewan, the Kootenay Pass in the Canadian Rockies, and the Chateau Frontenac in Quebec, *Rose-Marie* offered audiences at the
Imperial Theatre (on 44th Street west of Broadway) an entirely new locale for an
opulent, romantic musical. It was, in fact, the idea of doing the first musical with
a Canadian setting that prompted producer Arthur Hammerstein to send nephew
Oscar Hammerstein II and his lyricist-librettist partner, Otto Harbach, to research
a rumored annual ice carnival in Quebec that he felt would make a spectacular
stage background. Though the writers were unable to locate the carnival, they
did devise an original tale that would take advantage of Canadian locales: singer
Rose-Marie La Flamme (Mary Ellis) and fur trapper Jim Kenyon (Dennis King) are
in love, but a jealous suitor tries to pin a false murder rap on Jim. True to tradition,
the Mounties get their man — who turns out to be a woman — and Rose-Marie
and Jim go off into the sunset. The fact that the story deals with a murder was
considered something of a novelty for a musical as was the conscientious effort,
though it was not entirely successful, to integrate the musical pieces into the
story (the program listed only the above five songs that "stand out independent
of their dramatic association").

*Rose-Marie* was composer Rudolf Friml's biggest hit and the fourth longest
running musical of the Twenties. In 1936, Jeanette MacDonald and Nelson Eddy
were seen in a popular — though completely altered — screen version. The second one, with Howard Keel and Ann Blyth, came out in 1954.
RCA SC/ TW.

# LADY, BE GOOD!

**Music:** George Gershwin
**Lyrics:** Ira Gershwin
**Book:** Guy Bolton & Fred Thompson
**Producers:** Alex A. Aarons & Vinton Freedley
**Director:** Felix Edwardes
**Choreographer:** Sammy Lee
**Cast:** Fred & Adele Astaire, Walter Catlett, Cliff Edwards, Alan Edwards, Kathlene Martyn
**Songs:** "Hang on to Me"; "Fascinating Rhythm"; "So Am I"; "Oh, Lady Be Good!"; "The Half of It Dearie Blues"; "Little Jazz Bird"; "Swiss Miss" (lyric with Arthur Jackson)
**New York run:** Liberty Theatre, December 1, 1924; 330 p.

With their first of 14 Broadway musicals written as a team, George and Ira Gershwin established the jazzy, pulsating sound of the Broadway musicals of the Twenties. The show also made Fred and Adele Astaire Broadway's leading song-and-dance team. Originally titled *Black Eyed Susan, Lady, Be Good!* had a simple-minded story about Dick and Suzie Trevor, a carefree vaudeville team who are dispossessed but continue their dancing and singing at the homes of wealthy friends. Along the way Suzie poses as a Spanish heiress to collect a large inheritance but the ruse is found out. Somehow, she and Dick come into money anyway and somehow she saves Dick from a disastrous marriage. As Stark Young wrote in the *Times,* it is "a drama of outcasts, rents, social shining, loving resolutions, and well-ending marital fortunes." Though the score had enough hits — especially "Fascinating Rhythm" and "Oh, Lady Be Good!" — one eventual hit, "The Man I Love," was dropped from the show during the pre-Broadway tryout.
M-E OC; Smithsonian OC/ TW.

**Lady, Be Good!** Fred Astaire surrounded by a dozen ostrich-plumed lovelies. (White)

# THE STUDENT PRINCE IN HEIDELBERG

**Music:** Sigmund Romberg
**Lyrics & book:** Dorothy Donnelly
**Producers:** Messrs. Shubert
**Director:** J. C. Huffman
**Choreographer:** Max Scheck
**Cast:** Howard Marsh, Ilse Marvenga, Greek Evans, George Hassell, Roberta Beatty
**Songs:** "Golden Days"; "To the Inn We're Marching"; "Come Boys, Let's All Be Gay, Boys" ("Students March Song"); "Drinking Song"; "Deep in My Heart, Dear"; "Serenade"; "Just We Two"
**New York run:** Jolson's 59th Street Theatre, December 2, 1924; 608 p.

Bucking the popularity of fast-moving, up-to-date musical comedy and the plotless revue, *The Student Prince in Heidelberg* (the complete title was used throughout the New York run) set the record as the longest running musical of the decade. That fact is all the more impressive since the theatre in which it played, on 59th Street and 7th Avenue, was some distance from the theatre district (the playhouse, later renamed the New Century, was demolished in 1962).

Based on *Old Heidelberg*, a popular turn-of-the-century play which had been adapted from the German *Alt Heidelberg*, the sentimental operetta is set in 1860 in the German university town where Prince Karl Franz (Howard Marsh) has gone with his tutor, Dr. Engel (Greek Evans), to complete his education. There he meets Kathie (Ilse Marvenga), a waitress at the Inn of the Three Golden Apples, and it isn't long before they are professing their love through the melting strains of, "Deep in my heart, dear, I have a dream of you . . ." The prince, however, is soon called away to assume the throne. Two years later, King Karl Franz returns to Heidelberg in a vain effort to recapture the golden days of his youth. *The Student Prince* toured the United States between 1925 and 1933, was revived on Broadway in 1931 and 1943, and joined the repertory of the New York City Opera in 1980. A silent film verson, with Ramon Novarro and Norma Shearer, was made in 1927; a Technicolor version, with Edmund Purdom (using Mario Lanza's singing voice) and Ann Blyth, was made in 1954. A previous Broadway musical, *The Prince of Pilsen* of 1903, also had a Heidelberg student prince as a leading romantic character.

M-E London OC (1926); Odyssey SC/ TW.

**The Student Prince in Heidelberg.** Howard Marsh and Ilse Marvenga. (White)

# THE GARRICK GAIETIES

**Music:** Richard Rodgers
**Lyrics:** Lorenz Hart
**Sketches:** Miscellaneous writers
**Producer:** Theatre Guild
**Director:** Philip Loeb
**Choreographer:** Herbert Fields
**Cast:** Sterling Holloway, Romney Brent, Betty Starbuck, Libby Holman, June
Cochrane, Edith Meiser, Philip Loeb, Sanford Meisner, Lee Strasberg
**Songs:** "April Fool"; "Manhattan"; "Do You Love Me?"; "Sentimental Me"; "On
with the Dance", "Old Fashioned Girl" (lyric: Edith Meiser)
**New York run:** Garrick Theatre, June 8, 1925; 211 p.

The Garrick Gaieties was an impudent, high-spirited modestly mounted revue
created by and featuring young members of the Theatre Guild company to help
raise money for tapestries at the Guild's new Guild Theatre on West 52nd Street.
The entertainment, however, served equally as a showcase for the talents of the
songwriting team of Richard Rodgers and Lorenz Hart, whose score included
their first hit, "Manhattan." This was not their first professional show — that was
Poor Little Ritz Girl in 1919 — but it did provide the stimulus for a partnership that
lasted through 26 Broadway musicals until 1943.

Though originally scheduled for only two performances at the Garrick Theatre (then on 35th Street east of Broadway), the revue caught on and had a successful commercial run. Besides the songs, highlights were satirical jibes at the
theatre in general and the Theatre Guild in particular whose usually pretentious
offerings provided ready targets. A second edition of the Gaieties opened the following year with almost the same cast, and a Rodgers and Hart score that included "Mountain Greenery" and an operetta burlesque called "The Rose of Arizona." A third edition, in 1930, was shown at the Guild Theatre (currently named the
Virginia). The cast included Sterling Holloway, Edith Meiser, and Philip Loeb, plus
newcomers Imogene Coca and Ray Heatherton. A brief return engagement the
same year gave Rosalind Russell her first Broadway assignment.

46

# NO, NO, NANETTE

**Music:** Vincent Youmans
**Lyrics:** Irving Caesar
**Book:** Otto Harbach & Frank Mandel
**Producer-director:** H. H. Frazee
**Choreographer:** Sammy Lee
**Cast:** Louise Groody, Charles Winninger, Josephine Whittell, Wellington Cross, Eleanor Dawn, Georgia O'Ramey, Mary Lawlor, John Barker
**Songs:** "Call of the Sea"; "Too Many Rings Around Rosie"; "I Want to Be Happy"; "No, No, Nanette" (lyric: Otto Harbach); "Tea for Two"; " 'Where Has My Hubby Gone?' Blues"; "You Can Dance With Any Girl at All"
**New York run:** Globe Theatre, September 16, 1925; 321 p.

Thanks to its worldwide reception, *No, No, Nanette* was probably the most popular musical of the Twenties. It was also the quintessential example of the kind of song-and-dance show of that period that was affectionately satirized in Sandy Wilson's spoof, *The Boy Friend.* In the story, based on a 1919 play, *My Lady Friends,* Jimmy Smith (Charles Winninger), a married bible publisher and guardian of the play's doubly admonished heroine (Louise Groody), has been giving financial support to three comely young ladies living in three different cities. When the Smiths and their friends, including Lucille and Billy Early (Josephine Whittell and Wellington Cross) — plus the three recipients of Jimmy's largesse and a sassy housemaid named Pauline (Georgia O'Ramey) — all turn up at the Smiths' Chickadee Cottage in Atlantic City, no end of comical embarrassments ensue.

The musical's initial production underwent a difficult break-in period on the road. When it first opened in Detroit in April 1924, the reviews were encouraging but the attendance wasn't. Producer H.H. Frazee then took drastic steps. He ordered composer Vincent Youmans and lyricist Irving Caesar (who had replaced Otto Harbach for most of the songs) to come up with two hits — and they obliged with "Tea for Two" and "I Want to Be Happy." He also took over the direction himself and replaced most of the principals in the cast. The result was that the show clicked so well in Chicago that it remained for a year. By the time *No, No, Nanette* arrived in New York a second road company had been touring since January 1925 (with Cleo Mayfield, Cecil Lean, Donald Brian, and Ona Munson), and a London facsimile had been running for six months. Three years later, an affirmative successor yclept *Yes, Yes, Yvette,* did not fare so well, despite the contributions by *Nanette* veterans H.H. Frazee, Irving Caesar, Charles Winninger, and choreographer Sammy Lee.

In 1971, a new production of *No, No, Nanette* opened in New York after experiencing an equally difficult tryout tour (see page 231). Harry Rigby, who conceived the idea of the revival, was bought out by his co-producer Cyma Rubin, Burt Shevelove replaced Busby Berkeley as director, and Jack Gilford and Susan Watson took over the roles of Jimmy and Nanette. Once more, however, the production was whipped into proper shape, and — helped by a sudden nostalgia craze — it went on to a lengthy and profitable run. One of the major attractions of this version was the appearance of Ruby Keeler, who returned to Broadway after an absence of over 41 years to play the part of Sue Smith, Jimmy's wife. During the New York engagement, leading roles were assumed by Penny Singleton (Sue), Benny Baker (Jimmy), and Martha Raye (Pauline). The first road company was headed by June Allyson, Dennis Day, and Judy Canova; the second by Evelyn Keyes, Don Ameche, and Ruth Donnelly.

Movie versions of *No, No, Nanette* were made in 1930 and 1940. Bernice Claire and Alexander Grey were in the first, Anna Neagle and Victor Mature were in the second.

Stanyan London OC (1925); Columbia OC (1971)/ TW.

# DEAREST ENEMY

**Music:** Richard Rodgers
**Lyrics:** Lorenz Hart
**Book:** Herbert Fields
**Producer:** George Ford
**Directors:** John Murray Anderson, Charles Sinclair, Harry Ford
**Choreographer:** Carl Hemmer
**Cast:** Helen Ford, Charles Purcell, Flavia Arcaro, Detmar Poppen
**Songs:** "Here in My Arms"; "I Beg Your Pardon"; "Cheerio"; "I'd Like To Hide It";
"Bye and Bye"; "Sweet Peter"; "Old Enough to Love"; "Here's a Kiss"
**New York run:** Knickerbocker Theatre, September 18, 1925; 286 p.

*Dearest Enemy*, the first of eight book musicals written together by songwriters Rodgers and Hart and librettist Herbert Fields, found the trio going back to the unlikely subject of the American Revolution for inspiration. Set in 1776 in the mansion of Mrs. Robert Murray — of the Murray Hill Murrays — the saga tells how the wily patriot and her lady friends manage to divert Gen. Howe's British troops long enough for Gen. Putnam's men to link up with the forces under the command of Gen. Washington. The attraction between Irish-American lass Betsy Burke (Helen Ford) and British Captain Sir John Copeland (Charles Purcell) provides a romantic alliance — cemented by their duet, "Here in My Arms" — that is resumed after the war.

The only previous Broadway musical dealing with the American Revolution was *A Daughter of the Revolution* in 1895. Later works concerned with the conflict were *Virginia* (1937), *Arms and the Girl* (1950), *Ben Franklin in Paris* (1964), and the most successful of all, *1776* (1969).
R&H.


# THE VAGABOND KING

**Music:** Rudolf Friml
**Lyrics:** Brian Hooker
**Book:** Brian Hooker, Russell Janney, W. H. Post
**Producer:** Russell Janney
**Director:** Max Figman
**Choreographer:** Julian Alfred
**Cast:** Dennis King, Carolyn Thomson, Max Figman, Herbert Corthell
**Songs:** "Song of the Vagabonds"; "Some Day"; "Only a Rose"; "Huguette
Waltz"; "Love Me Tonight"; "Love for Sale"; "Nocturne"
**New York run:** Casino Theatre, September 21, 1925; 511 p.

Originally, producer Russell Janney planned this operetta to have a score by the youthful team of Richard Rodgers and Lorenz Hart who had already transformed the venerable novel and play, *If I Were King*, into an amateur musical. When he was unable to get financial backing, however, Janney turned to the more experienced team of Rudolf Friml and Brian Hooker. *The Vagabond King* is concerned with the amours and adventures of the 15th Century outlaw Francois Villon (Dennis King) during the reign of King Louis XI. In this attractively mounted, picaresque tale, the poet-vagabond is appointed King of France for a day (it was a week in the original story) in order to save both his neck and Paris by leading his rabble of low degree against the Duke of Burgundy's forces. As a fitting capper to his successful endeavors, Villon even wins the hand of the aristocratic Katherine de Vaucelles (Carolyn Thomson). There were two screen versions: King and Jeanette MacDonald were co-starred in 1930; Oreste and Kathryn Grayson in 1956.
RCA SC/ Samuel French (1929)*/ SF.

48

**Dearest Enemy.** Discovered swimming in the nude, Helen Ford keeps Charles Purcell at bay with an umbrella as he tries to return her shoe. (White)

**The Vagabond King.** Dennis King leads his followers in the "Song of the Vaga-bonds." (White)

**Sunny.** Esther Howard, Joseph Cawthorn, Dorothy Francis, Clifton Webb, Marilyn Miller, Paul Frawley, Mary Hay, and Jack Donahue. (White)

# SUNNY
**Music:** Jerome Kern
**Lyrics & book:** Otto Harbach & Oscar Hammerstein II
**Producer:** Charles Dillingham
**Director:** Hassard Short
**Choreographers:** Julian Mitchell, David Bennett, Alexis Kosloff, John Tiller, Fred Astaire
**Cast:** Marilyn Miller, Jack Donahue, Clifton Webb, Mary Hay, Joseph Cawthorn, Paul Frawley, Cliff Edwards, Pert Kelton, Moss & Fontana, Esther Howard, Dorothy Francis, George Olsen Orchestra
**Songs:** "Sunny"; "Who?"; "Let's Say Good Night Till It's Morning"; "D'Ye Love Me?"; "Two Little Bluebirds"; "I Might Grow Fond of You"
**New York run:** New Amsterdam Theatre, September 22, 1925; 517 p.

In another variation on the Cinderella story, *Sunny* tells the saga of Sunny Peters (Marilyn Miller), a spirited bareback rider appearing with a circus in Southampton, England, whose heart has been stolen away by Tom Warren (Paul Frawley), an American tourist. In pursuit of this glittering prize, Sunny stows aboard the ocean liner taking him back to the United States. In order to be allowed to land, Sunny weds Tom's friend, Jim Deming (Jack Donahue), but once the agreed-to divorce has been granted Sunny and Tom are happily reunited at a fashionable Southern resort. (In the London version, in which Jim was played by popular star Jack Buchanan, Sunny decided that he was really the man for her. This denouement has also been used in American revivals.)

*Sunny* was the alliterative successor to *Sally*, a musical that also had Marilyn Miller singing and dancing to Jerome Kern melodies. Here, however, the composer was collaborating for the first time with Otto Harbach and Oscar Hammerstein II. Miss Miller repeated her role in the first movie version in 1930; Anna Neagle followed 10 years later.

Stanyan London OC (1926)/ Chappell, London (1926)*/ TW.

**The Cocoanuts.** Groucho Marx auctioning off Florida land assisted by brothers Chico, Zeppo, and Harpo. (White)

# THE COCOANUTS

**Music & lyrics:** Irving Berlin
**Book:** George S. Kaufman (Morrie Ryskind uncredited)
**Producer:** Sam H. Harris
**Director:** Oscar Eagle
**Choreographer:** Sammy Lee
**Cast:** The Marx Brothers, Margaret Dumont, John Barker, Mabel Withee, Frances Williams, Brox Sisters, Basil Ruysdael, George Hale
**Songs:** "Lucky Boy"; "Why Am I a Hit With the Ladies?"; "A Little Bungalow"; "Florida by the Sea"; "The Monkey Doodle-Doo"
**New York run:** Lyric Theatre, December 8, 1925; 276 p.

*The Cocoanuts* was the second of three musicals that the Marx Brothers starred in on Broadway, the others being *I'll Say She Is* and *Animal Crackers*. As might be expected, it offered a gag-filled, loosely constructed spree in which the madcap team was allowed enough room to improvise and add new routines, such as the now classic Groucho-Chico exchange based on the misunderstanding of the word "viaduct" for "Why a duck?" The story is set in Cocoanut Beach, Florida, where Groucho, as Henry W. Schlemmer, runs a hotel and is also a shady real-estate developer trying to cash in on the Florida land boom. Complications arise when jewel thieves posing as hotel guests steal the gems from rich dowager Margaret Dumont, and try to pin the blame on the fiancé of the dowager's daughter. Adding to the mayhem were Chico and Harpo, as hotel guests and Zeppo as a desk clerk. The 1929 screen version of *The Cocoanuts* was the Marx Brothers' first feature-length movie.

    The Marx Brothers were leading characters in two later Broadway musicals: the biographical *Minnie's Boys* (1970) and the second half of the "Musical Double Feature," *A Day in Hollywood/A Night in the Ukraine* (1980). St. Martin's Press (1979).

# TIP-TOES

**Music:** George Gershwin
**Lyrics:** Ira Gershwin
**Book:** Guy Bolton & Fred Thompson
**Producers:** Alex A. Aarons & Vinton Freedley
**Director:** John Harwood
**Choreographer:** Sammy Lee
**Cast:** Queenie Smith, Allen Kearns, Andrew Tombes, Harry Watson Jr., Jeanette MacDonald, Robert Halliday, Gertrude McDonald
**Songs:** "Looking for a Boy"; "When Do We Dance?"; "These Charming People"; "That Certain Feeling"; "Sweet and Low-Down"; "Nice Baby"; "Nightie Night"
**New York run:** Liberty Theatre, December 28, 1925; 194 p.

*Tip-Toes* was something of a creative successor to *Lady, Be Good!*, since it shared the same songwriting team (whose new hit was "That Certain Feeling"), librettists, producers, and choreographer, and it even played the same theatre. There was also a thematic similarity in that the new story was again concerned with down-on-their-luck vaudevillians who become involved with high society. Tip-Toes Kaye (Queenie Smith) and her uncles Al and Harry (Andrew Tombes and Harry Watson Jr.) are stranded in Palm Beach where the uncles try to pass off Tip-Toes as a blueblood to win a rich husband. She falls for glue king Steve Burton (Allen Kearns) and sticks with him even after — as a test, of course — he admits to being penniless. A 1928 screen variation, made in England, featured Dorothy Gish and Will Rogers.
M-E London OC (1926)/ TW.

# GEORGE WHITE'S SCANDALS

**Music:** Ray Henderson
**Lyrics:** B. G. DeSylva & Lew Brown
**Sketches:** George White, William K. Wells
**Producer-director-choreographer:** George White
**Cast:** Willie & Eugene Howard, Frances Williams, Harry Richman, Tom Patricola, Ann Pennington, McCarthy Sisters, Fairbanks Twins, Buster West, Portland Hoffa
**Songs:** "Lucky Day"; "Black Bottom"; "Birth of the Blues"; "St. Louis Blues" (W.C. Handy); "Rhapsody in Blue" (music: George Gershwin); "The Girl Is You and the Boy Is Me"
**New York run:** Apollo Theatre, June 14, 1926; 424 p.

Possibly the foremost edition in the series, the 1926 *Scandals* — the eighth of that title — had by far the longest run. Its attributes included a strong score by DeSylva, Brown and Henderson (the second *Scandals* for the trio), plus a sure-fire combination of mirth (mostly resting on the capable if stooped shoulders of Willie Howard) and production numbers (George White's new dance sensation was the successor to the "Charleston" called the "Black Bottom"). The first-act finale offered a musical debate between the blues and the classics, with such examples of the former as "Birth of the Blues" (sung by Harry Richman), "St. Louis Blues," and the "Rhapsody in Blue" (with lyrics!). The producer was so confident of the show's success that he charged $55.00 per ticket for the first eight rows on opening night (the top price reverted to $5.50 after that).

# COUNTESS MARITZA

**Music:** Emmerich Kalman
**Lyrics & book:** Harry B. Smith
**Producer:** Messrs. Shubert
**Director:** J. C. Huffman
**Choreographers:** Carl Randall, Jack Mason
**Cast:** Yvonne D'Arle, Walter Woolf, Odette Myrtil, Carl Randall, Harry K. Morton, Vivian Hart, George Hassell
**Songs:** "Play, Gypsies — Dance, Gypsies"; "I'll Keep on Dreaming"; "The One I'm Looking For"; "The Call of Love"
**New York run:** Shubert Theatre, September 18, 1926; 321 p.

One of the few transplanted mid-Twenties operettas to retain its original European score, *Countess Maritza* was the last successful show written by Harry B. Smith. It was also his 115th Broadway production! Originally presented as *Grafin Mariza* two and a half years earlier in Vienna, the work has a certain kinship with *The Merry Widow* in that it offers a heroine constantly on her guard against fortune hunters and a hero who is afraid of being considered one. Set in Hungary, the plot finds the impecunious Count Tassilo (Walter Woolf) working under an assumed name as the overseer on the estate of his beloved countess (Yvonne D'Arle), and leading the merry peasants in the stirring strains of "Play, Gypsies — Dance, Gypsies." After he is dismissed when Maritza erroneously pegs him for a gold digger, the countess — too proud to admit her mistake verbally — proposes to Tassilo via a letter.


# OH, KAY!

**Music:** George Gershwin
**Lyrics:** Ira Gershwin
**Book:** Guy Bolton & P. G. Wodehouse
**Producers:** Alex A. Aarons & Vinton Freedley
**Director:** John Harwood
**Choreographer:** Sammy Lee
**Cast:** Gertrude Lawrence, Oscar Shaw, Victor Moore, Harland Dixon, Fairbanks Twins, Gerald Oliver Smith, Betty Compton, Constance Carpenter
**Songs:** "Dear Little Girl"; "Maybe"; "Clap Yo' Hands"; "Do Do Do"; "Someone to Watch Over Me"; "Fidgety Feet"; "Heaven on Earth" (lyric with Howard Dietz); "Oh, Kay!" (lyric with Dietz)
**New York run:** Imperial Theatre, November 8, 1926; 256 p.

Following her Broadway appearances in the *Charlot Revues*, Gertrude Lawrence was besieged with offers to star in an American musical comedy. By accepting the leading role in *Oh, Kay!*, Miss Lawrence became the first British actress to originate a part on Broadway before repeating it in London. The production reunited the Princess Theatre librettists, Guy Bolton and P.G. Wodehouse, whose book for *Oh, Kay!* retained something of the Anglo-American flavor of their previous *Oh, Boy!* and *Oh, Lady! Lady!!* The action takes place at the home of Jimmy Winter (Oscar Shaw) in the imaginary town of Beachampton, Long Island. Jimmy is about to wed when he discovers that he has fallen in love with Kay Denham, who is posing as a cook in his house to be near the hooch that her brother, a titled English bootlegger, has stashed in Jimmy's cellar. Though Kay and Jimmy make their feelings clear in the duet "Maybe," and Kay plaintively pleads for someone to watch over her, the couple must survive obstacles, both legal and matrimonial, before settling down to a life of musical-comedy bliss. A revival of *Oh, Kay!*, somewhat revised, was produced Off Broadway in 1960. Smithsonian part OC; Columbia SC; DRG OC (1960)/ TW.

# THE DESERT SONG

**Music:** Sigmund Romberg
**Lyrics:** Otto Harbach & Oscar Hammerstein II
**Book:** Otto Harbach, Oscar Hammerstein II & Frank Mandel
**Producers:** Laurence Schwab & Frank Mandel
**Director:** Arthur Hurley
**Choreographer:** Bobby Connolly
**Cast:**  Vivienne Segal, Robert Halliday, Eddie Buzzell, Pearl Regay, William O'Neal
**Songs:** "The Riff Song"; "Romance"; "French Military Marching Song"; "I Want a Kiss"; " 'It' "; "The Desert Song"; "Let Love Go"; "One Flower Grows Alone in Your Garden"; "One Alone"
**New York run:** Casino Theatre, November 30, 1926; 471 p.

Possibly the decade's most enduring operetta, *The Desert Song* marked Sigmund Romberg's first association with librettists-lyricists Otto Harbach and Oscar Hammerstein II (Romberg and Hammerstein would do four other musicals together). Though a swashbuckling romance created along familiar lines, the work was equally inspired by such recent events as the Riff uprising in French Morocco, the accomplishments of Lawrence of Arabia, and the sizzling Rudolph Valentino films *The Sheik* and *The Son of the Sheik*. The operetta is primarily concerned with Margot Bonvalet (Vivienne Segal), a French woman who is abducted into the Sahara — to the emotional strains of "The Desert Song" — by the mysterious Red Shadow (Robert Halliday), the masked leader of the rebellious Riffs. To the surprise of all, he turns out to be Pierre Birabeau, the simpering son of the Governor of Morocco (thus providing a variation on the *Naughty Marietta* story). During the out-of-town tryout, when the show was called *Lady Fair,* Miss Segal was rushed in to replace another actress in the leading female role. *The Desert Song* had an unsuccessful New York revival in 1973. Film versions were released in 1929, 1943, and 1953.
M-E London OC (1927); Columbia SC/ SF.

# PEGGY-ANN

**Music:** Richard Rodgers
**Lyrics:** Lorenz Hart
**Book:** Herbert Fields
**Producers:** Lew Fields & Lyle D. Andrews
**Director:** Robert Milton
**Choreographer:** Seymour Felix
**Cast:**  Helen Ford, Lester Cole, Lulu McConnell, Betty Starbuck, Edith Meiser
**Songs:** "A Tree in the Park"; "A Little Birdie Told Me So"; "Where's That Rainbow?"; "Maybe It's Me"
**New York run:** Vanderbilt Theatre, December 27, 1926; 333 p.

A daring work for its day, *Peggy-Ann* was loosely adapted from a 1910 Marie Dressler vehicle, *Tillie's Nightmare.* Most of the show was set in a Freudian dreamworld in which Peggy-Ann of Glens Falls, New York, travels to New York City's Fifth Avenue, takes a trip on a yacht, gets married in her step-ins, is thrown overboard by a mutinous crew, and attends the horse races in Havana. At the end, she awakes happily in the arms of her Glens Falls boyfriend. Among the staging innovations: no songs were sung within the first fifteen minutes, the scenery and costumes were changed in full view of the audience, and the first and last scenes were played in almost total darkness. The show was the fourth of five Rodgers and Hart musicals that were presented on Broadway during 1926; the fifth, *Betsy,* opened just one night after *Peggy-Ann.*

# RIO RITA

**Music:** Harry Tierney
**Lyrics:** Joseph McCarthy
**Book:** Guy Bolton & Fred Thompson
**Producer:** Florenz Ziegfeld
**Director:** John Harwood
**Choreographers:** Sammy Lee, Albertina Rasch
**Cast:** Ethelind Terry, J. Harold Murray, Bert Wheeler, Robert Woolsey, Ada May, Vincent Serrano
**Songs:** "Rio Rita"; "The Rangers' Song"; "The Kinkajou"; "If You're in Love You'll Waltz"; "Following the Sun Around"
**New York run:** Ziegfeld Theatre, February 2, 1927; 494 p.

*Rio Rita* was Florenz Ziegfeld's premiere attraction at his Ziegfeld Theatre, then located on the northwest corner of 6th Avenue and 54th Street. In the spectacular production, Capt. James Stewart (J. Harold Murray) leads his Texas Rangers in the stirring "Rangers' Song" as they chase a bank robber known as the Kinkajou. The pursuit takes Capt. Jim across the Rio Grande into the town of Santa Luca where he falls in love with tempestuous Rita Ferguson (Ethelind Terry), whose name is fluvially linked only in the show's title and in song. Their romance hits a snag when Capt. Jim suspects Rita's brother to be the Kinkajou, but he eventually turns out to be a Mexican general (Vincent Serrano) who also has eyes for Rita. (This was still another variation on the outlaw-in-disguise theme of such previous offerings as *Naughty Marietta* and *The Desert Song*.) The 1929 film version, with Bebe Daniels and John Boles, was the first successful screen adaptation of a Broadway musical.
M-E London OC/ TW.

**Rio Rita.** Ethelind Terry, Vincent Serrano, and J. Harold Murray. (White)

# HIT THE DECK!

**Music:** Vincent Youmans
**Lyrics:** Clifford Grey & Leo Robin
**Book:** Herbert Fields
**Producers:** Lew Fields & Vincent Youmans
**Director:** Alexander Leftwich
**Choreographer:** Seymour Felix
**Cast:** Louise Groody, Charles King, Stella Mayhew, Madeline Cameron, Brian Donlevy, Jack McCauley
**Songs:** "Join the Navy"; "Harbor of My Heart"; "Lucky Bird"; "Looloo"; "Why, Oh Why?"; "Sometimes I'm Happy" (lyric: Irving Caesar); "Hallelujah"
**New York run:** Belasco Theatre, April 25, 1927; 352 p.

Vincent Youmans' *Hit the Deck!* was second only to *No, No, Nanette* as the most popular of the composer's 12 Broadway musicals. Based on the 1922 play *Shore Leave*, the show was about a Newport, Rhode Island, coffee-shop owner known as Looloo (Louise Groody, the previous Nanette), who is so totally smitten with sailor Bilge Smith (Charles King) that she follows him all the way to China and even spends her inheritance to salvage a scow for him after his Navy hitch is over. The production, one of the few musicals to play the Belasco Theatre (on 44th Street east of Broadway), introduced audiences to two enduring songs: "Sometimes I'm Happy" and "Hallelujah." The second of three movie versions, retitled *Follow the Fleet*, and released in 1936, featured Fred Astaire and Ginger Rogers and new songs by Irving Berlin.
TW.

# GOOD NEWS!

**Music:** Ray Henderson
**Lyrics:** B. G. DeSylva & Lew Brown
**Book:** Laurence Schwab & B. G. DeSylva
**Producers:** Laurence Schwab & Frank Mandel
**Director:** Edgar MacGregor
**Choreographer:** Bobby Connolly
**Cast:** Mary Lawlor, John Price Jones, Gus Shy, Inez Courtney, Zelma O'Neal, George Olsen Orchestra
**Songs:** "Just Imagine"; "He's a Ladies Man"; "The Best Things in Life Are Free"; "The Varsity Drag"; "Lucky in Love"; "Good News"
**New York run:** 46th Street Theatre, September 6, 1927; 551 p.

The fifth longest running musical of the Twenties, *Good News!* was the first of a quartet of breezy, youthful DeSylva, Brown and Henderson musical comedies that capitalized on popular sports, fads, occupations, and innovations. (The others: *Hold Everything!*, *Flying High,* and *Follow Thru.*) In this caper about America's flaming youth, the setting is Tait College, where students spend their time dancing "The Varsity Drag," where the burning issue is whether football hero Tom Marlowe will be allowed to lead the team despite his failing grade in astronomy, and where hero can console heroine Connie Laine by assuring her "The Best Things in Life Are Free." Helping to establish the collegiate atmosphere of the entertainment were the members of George Olsen's Orchestra who, before playing the overture, marched down the theatre aisles sporting diamond-pattern sweaters and barking football cheers. In the fall of 1974, Alice Faye and Gene Nelson opened on Broadway in a revival that lasted two weeks. June Allyson and Peter Lawford were in the 1947 screen version.
Samuel French (1932)*/ SF.

**Hit the Deck!** Charles King and Louise Groody. (White)

# A CONNECTICUT YANKEE

**Music:** Richard Rodgers
**Lyrics:** Lorenz Hart
**Book:** Herbert Fields
**Producers:** Lew Fields & Lyle D. Andrews
**Director:** Alexander Leftwich
**Choreographer:** Busby Berkeley
**Cast:** William Gaxton, Constance Carpenter, Nana Bryant, June Cochrane, William Norris, Jack Thompson
**Songs:** "My Heart Stood Still"; "Thou Swell"; "I Feel at Home With You"; "On a Desert Island With Thee"
**New York run:** Vanderbilt Theatre, November 3, 1927; 418 p.

Long before winning notice with their songs for *The Garrick Gaieties*, Rodgers and Hart — along with librettist Herbert Fields — had tried unsuccessfully to interest producers in their version of Mark Twain's *A Connecticut Yankee in King Arthur's Court*. By 1927, however, they had little trouble getting Lew Fields to present it at the Vanderbilt Theatre following the run of the trio's first dream fantasy, *Peggy-Ann*, and it became their biggest hit of the 1920s.

The curtain rises on a hotel room in modern-day Hartford, where Martin (William Gaxton), about to be married, gets bopped on the head by his intended spouse. He dreams of being a stranger at the court of King Arthur, where he sings "Thou Swell" and "My Heart Stood Still" with Dame Alisande (Constance Carpenter), and becomes a confidant of the king by industrializing the realm. Upon awakening Martin realizes that he is marrying the wrong girl and turns to Alisande's modern-day double, Alice Carter. (A more serious approach to the Arthurian legend was Lerner and Loewe's *Camelot* in 1960.)

*A Connecticut Yankee* was revived in 1943 with Dick Foran, Vivienne Segal, Julie Warren, and Vera Ellen. Five of the original songs were retained and six new ones were added, including Miss Segal's showstopper, "To Keep My Love Alive." For the present-day scenes all the characters appeared in military uniforms. This production, which ran 135 performances, opened just five days before Lorenz Hart's death.
AEI OC (1943)/ TW.

**A Connecticut Yankee.** Yankee William Gaxton is frightened by one of King Arthur's knights.

# FUNNY FACE

**Music:** George Gershwin
**Lyrics:** Ira Gershwin
**Book:** Paul Gerard Smith & Fred Thompson
**Producers:** Alex A. Aarons & Vinton Freedley
**Director:** Edgar MacGregor
**Choreographer:** Bobby Connolly
**Cast:** Fred & Adele Astaire, Victor Moore, William Kent, Allen Kearns, Betty Compton, Dorothy Jordan
**Songs:** "Funny Face"; "High Hat"; "He Loves and She Loves"; " 'S Wonderful"; "Let's Kiss and Make Up"; "My One and Only"; "The Babbitt and the Bromide"
**New York run:** Alvin Theatre, November 22, 1927; 244 p.

The second musical the Gershwin brothers wrote for Fred and Adele Astaire, *Funny Face* was another popular lighter-than-air concoction that —like *Lady, Be Good!* —gave the dancing siblings plenty of room for their specialties. In the plot, Frankie Wynne (Adele), the ward of Jimmie Reeve (Fred), persuades aviator Peter Thurston (Allen Kearns), to steal her incriminating diary from Jimmie's wall safe. By mistake, Peter steals a bracelet, which sets off a mad chase that takes the dramatis personae — including two comic burglars — to Lake Wapatog, New Jersey, then on to the Paymore Hotel and the Two-Million Dollar Pier in Atlantic City.

When tried out under the title of *Smarty,* with Robert Benchley as coauthor, the musical was greeted with such disfavor that drastic alterations were quickly made. The name was changed, Benchley was replaced by librettist Paul Gerard Smith, Victor Moore was added as one of the burglars, Allen Kearns took over the male romantic lead, and seven songs were dropped in favor of five new ones (including "He Loves and She Loves," which replaced "How Long Has This Been Going On?"). *Funny Face* became both a hit and the first attraction at the newly built Alvin Theatre (named for the show's producers), which, renamed the Neil Simon, is on 52nd Street west of Broadway.

In 1983, six songs from *Funny Face* were used in the score of *My One and Only,* which had a different book. The 1957 film, *Funny Face,* starring Fred Astaire and Audrey Hepburn, kept four of the original songs but also changed the story.

M-E OC; Smithsonian OC.

**Funny Face.** Fred Astaire leading the boys in the "High Hat" number. (White)

59

# SHOW BOAT

**Music:** Jerome Kern
**Lyrics & book:** Oscar Hammerstein II
**Producer:** Florenz Ziegfeld
**Director:** Zeke Colvan (Oscar Hammerstein II uncredited)
**Choreographer:** Sammy Lee
**Cast:**   Charles Winninger, Norma Terris, Howard Marsh, Helen Morgan, Jules Bledsoe, Edna May Oliver, Eva Puck, Sammy White, Tess Gardella, Charles Ellis, Francis X. Mahoney
**Songs:** "Make Believe"; "Ol' Man River"; "Can't Help Lovin' Dat Man"; "Life Upon the Wicked Stage"; "You Are Love"; "Why Do I Love You?"; "Bill" (lyric with P. G. Wodehouse); "After the Ball" (Charles K. Harris)
**New York run:** Ziegfeld Theatre, December 27, 1927; 572 p.

Both Jerome Kern and Oscar Hammerstein II had felt for some time that the Broadway musical theatre was suffering from too much sameness and tameness. After reading Edna Ferber's sprawling novel of life on the Mississippi, they became convinced that it was the story best suited to help them make the kinds of changes they felt were needed. Their efforts resulted in a recognized landmark in the history of the theatre, one that broke ground in steering a course away from lightweight musical comedy and overweight operetta. Their characters were more three-dimensional, the music was more skillfully integrated into the libretto, and their plot dared to deal with such unaccustomed subjects as unhappy marriages, miscegenation, and the hard life of black stevedores (as expressed through "Ol' Man River").

The saga covers the period from the mid 1880s to the then current 1927, and is primarily concerned with the fortunes of impressionable Magnolia Hawks (Norma Terris) — whose father Cap'n Andy Hawks (Charles Winninger) runs the showboat *Cotton Blossom* — and ne'er-do-well riverboat gambler Gaylord Ravenal (Howard Marsh). Meeting on the Natchez levee, the couple fall in love at first sight (singing "Make Believe"), then become actors on the showboat, marry, and move to Chicago (revealing their devotion in "Why Do I Love You?"). After they separate when Ravenal loses his money gambling, Magnolia has a tearful meeting with her father while singing at the Trocadero on New Year's Eve. She goes on to become a musical-comedy star, as does her daughter Kim, and years later she and Ravenal are reunited aboard the *Cotton Blossom*. A secondary plot involves Magnolia's mulatto friend, the tragic Julie La Verne (Helen Morgan), and her devotion to *her* man, Steve Baker (though the song she sings about him is called "Bill"). *Show Boat* was the second longest running musical of the 1920's. For the 10-month tour, Irene Dunne replaced Norma Terris.

In 1932, Ziegfeld brought the musical back with basically the original cast, except that Howard Marsh was succeeded by Dennis King and Jules Bledsoe by Paul Robeson (for whom the part of the stevedore Joe had originally been intended). The 1946 *Show Boat* was the most successful revival, running 418 performances. The major change was the addition of "Nobody Else but Me" (the last song Kern wrote) in the final scene. (See page 128.) Twenty years later, the musical was remounted by the Music Theatre of Lincoln Center, with Barbara Cook, Stephen Douglass, David Wayne, Constance Towers, and William Warfield. The fourth revival, in 1983, was by the Houston Grand Opera with Donald O'Connor, Sheryl Woods, Ron Raines, Lonette McKee, and Bruce Hubbard.

Three movie versions were filmed: a part-talkie in 1929 with Laura LaPlante and Joseph Schildkraut; the 1936 reproduction with Irene Dunne, Allan Jones, Helen Morgan, Charles Winninger, and Paul Robeson; and the 1951 reconstruction with Kathryn Grayson, Howard Keel, Ava Gardner, Joe E. Brown, and William Warfield.

CSP part OC (1932); Columbia OC (1946); RCA OC (1966); EMI SC/ Chappell, London (1934)*/ R&H.

**Show Boat.** A dramatic scene with Helen Morgan surrounded by Francis X. Mahoney, Charles Ellis, Eva Puck, Norma Terris, Charles Winninger, and Edna May Oliver. (White)

**Show Boat.** Edna May Oliver (right) is unable to stop the wedding of Howard Marsh and Norma Terris. Others in foreground are Charles Winninger, Sammy White, and Eva Puck. (White)

**Rosalie.** Marilyn Miller and ladies of the ensemble. (White)

# ROSALIE

**Music:** George Gershwin, Sigmund Romberg
**Lyrics:** Ira Gershwin, P. G. Wodehouse
**Book:** William Anthony McGuire & Guy Bolton
**Producer:** Florenz Ziegfeld
**Director:** William Anthony McGuire
**Choreographers:** Seymour Felix, Michel Fokine
**Cast:** Marilyn Miller, Jack Donahue, Frank Morgan, Margaret Dale, Bobbe Arnst, Oliver McLennan
**Songs:** "Say So!" (music: Gershwin); "West Point Song" (Romberg - Wodehouse); "Oh Gee! Oh Joy!" (music: Gershwin); "How Long Has This Been Going On?" (Gershwin - Gershwin); "Ev'rybody Knows I Love Somebody" (Gershwin - Gershwin).
**New York run:** New Amsterdam Theatre, January 10, 1928; 335 p.

Although Florenz Ziegfeld is said to have agreed to produce the musical only because it was named after his mother and the score did not represent either Gershwin or Romberg at his best, *Rosalie* became one of the hits of the season — thanks chiefly to twinkling star Marilyn Miller, dancing comedian Jack Donahue, and a stylishly mounted production. The story was "inspired" by two recent events: Lindbergh's solo flight to Paris and the visit of Rumania's Queen Marie and her daughter to the United States. After West Point ace Richard Fay has flown to the mythical kingdom of Romanza to be near the princess he loves, the royal family goes on a state visit to America. Luckily for Richard, he has been appointed leader of the guard of honor; luckily for Richard and Rosalie, the king abdicates so that his daughter might be free to marry a commoner.

The reason the two composers shared the assignment is that Romberg could not undertake it alone because he was then also creating the music for *The New Moon*. Though he was occupied with *Funny Face* at the time, Gershwin agreed to join the project to help relieve the work load. The 1936 movie version, with Eleanor Powell and Nelson Eddy, scrapped all their songs and came up with a new score by Cole Porter.
TW.

# THE THREE MUSKETEERS

**Music:** Rudolf Friml
**Lryics:** Clifford Grey
**Book:** William Anthony McGuire
**Producer:** Florenz Ziegfeld
**Directors:** William Anthony McGuire, Richard Boleslawsky
**Choreographer:** Albertina Rasch
**Cast:** Dennis King, Vivienne Segal, Lester Allen, Vivienne Osborne, Yvonne D'Arle, Reginald Owen, Joseph Macaulay, Harriet Hoctor, Douglass Dumbrille, Detmar Poppen, Clarence Derwent
**Songs:** "March of the Musketeers" (lyric with P.G. Wodehouse); "Ma Belle"; "Your Eyes" (lyric: Wodehouse); "One Kiss"; "My Sword and I"; "Queen of My Heart"
**New York run:** Lyric Theatre, March 13, 1928; 318 p.

Just as *The Vagabond King* had offered Dennis King as the dashing Francois Villon singing Rudolf Friml songs in a tale of adventure and intrigue in the days of Louis XI, so *The Three Musketeers* offered King as the dashing d'Artagnan singing Friml songs in a tale of adventure and intrigue in the days of Louis XIII. In this operetta version of the popular Alexandre Dumas novel, the story covers d'Artagnan's first meeting with Musketeers Athos, Porthos, and Aramis (Douglass Dumbrille, Detmar Poppen, and Joseph Macaulay), his romance with Constance Bonacieux (Vivienne Segal), and his noble efforts to save the honor of Queen Anne (Yvonne D'Arle), whom the wily Cardinal Richelieu (Reginald Owen) tries to blackmail. A revised version of the musical had a brief stay on Broadway in 1984.
M-E London OC (1930)/ Chappell, London (1937)*/ TW.

# BLACKBIRDS OF 1928

**Music:** Jimmy McHugh
**Lyrics:** Dorothy Fields
**Sketches:** (uncredited)
**Producer-director:** Lew Leslie
**Cast:** Adelaide Hall, Bill Robinson, Aida Ward, Tim Moore, Elizabeth Welch, Mantan Moreland, Cecil Mack, Hall Johnson Choir
**Songs:** "Diga Diga Doo"; "I Can't Give You Anything but Love"; "Porgy"; "Doin' the New Low-Down"; "I Must Have That Man"
**New York run:** Liberty Theatre, May 9, 1928; 518 p.

Proclaiming itself "A Distinctive and Unique Entertainment with an All-Star Cast of 100 Colored Artists," *Blackbirds of 1928* was the brainchild of impresario Lew Leslie who had first exhibited a *Blackbirds* revue in London in 1926. Florence Mills scored such a hit in that production that Leslie planned to build a show around her in New York, but she died before rehearsals began. Leslie then secured Adelaide Hall and Bill Robinson (who joined the cast during tryout and had only one number, "Doin' the New Low-Down"), and assigned Jimmy HcHugh and Dorothy Fields to write the songs. Among the musical offerings were their first hit, "I Can't Give You Anything but Love," a spirited jungle number, "Diga Diga Doo," and a capsule version of the play, *Porgy,* thus preceding the Gershwin opera by six years. Leslie sponsored *Blackbirds* revues on Broadway in 1930 (with Ethel Waters and Buck and Bubbles), in 1933 (with Bill Robinson), and in 1939 (with Lena Horne), but none flew very high.
Columbia part OC.

# THE NEW MOON

**Music:** Sigmund Romberg
**Lyrics:** Oscar Hammerstein II
**Book:** Oscar Hammerstein II, Frank Mandel, Laurence Schwab
**Producers:** Laurence Schwab & Frank Mandel
**Director:** (Edgar MacGregor uncredited)
**Choreographer:** Bobby Connolly
**Cast:** Evelyn Herbert, Robert Halliday, Gus Shy, Max Figman, William O'Neal
**Songs:** "Marianne"; "Softly, as in a Morning Sunrise"; "Stouthearted Men";
"One Kiss"; "Wanting You"; "Lover, Come Back to Me"
**New York run:** Imperial Theatre, September 19, 1928, 509 p.

The New Moon had to endure a tryout so disastrous that it was shut down completely while extensive alterations were made to the story, the score, and the cast. (Part of the problem was that both Sigmund Romberg and Oscar Hammerstein had to devote much of their time to other shows then in preparation: Romberg had Rosalie and Hammerstein had Show Boat.) After eight months the new New Moon reopened on the road with such musical pleasures as "Softly, as in a Morning Sunrise" and "Lover, Come Back to Me," and went on to win acclaim in New York.

What kept audiences happy was, in fact, deliberately designed as the successor to the same writers' Desert Song, with a similar improbably heroic tale loosely based on fact accompanied by a lush, pulse-pounding score. The story takes place in New Orleans in 1788, where Robert Misson (Robert Halliday), a French nobleman wanted for murder, serves as a bondsman and recruits stouthearted men in the cause of liberty. After his arrest, Robert is sent back to France on The New Moon, a vessel also carrying his beloved Marianne Beaunoir (Evelyn Herbert). Misson's followers, disguised as pirates, rescue their leader, who takes Marianne with him to establish a colony of free men on the Isle of Pines. The New Moon has something of a kinship with Naughty Marietta since they both dealt with a person of noble birth in disguise, and they were both set in New Orleans at roughly the same time. (They also shared the same historical error of making New Orleans a French colony when at the time it belonged to Spain.) Jeanette MacDonald and Nelson Eddy were in the 1940 movie version.
M-E London OC (1929); Capitol SC/ Chappell, London (1937)*/ TW.

**Hold Everything!** Frank Allworth, Bert Lahr, Victor Moore, Buddy Harak, and Harry Locke. (White)

# HOLD EVERYTHING!

**Music:** Ray Henderson
**Lyrics:** B. G. DeSylva & Lew Brown
**Book:** B. G. DeSylva & John McGowan
**Producers:** Alex A. Aarons & Vinton Freedley
**Director:** (uncredited)
**Choreographers:** Sam Rose, Jack Haskell
**Cast:** Jack Whiting, Ona Munson, Bert Lahr, Betty Compton, Victor Moore, Nina Olivette, Frank Allworth, Gus Schilling
**Songs:** "Don't Hold Everything"; "You're the Cream in My Coffee"; "Too Good to Be True"; "To Know You Is to Love You"
**New York run:** Broadhurst Theatre, October 10, 1928; 413 p.

Bearing a title more applicable to a tale about wrestling, *Hold Everything!* was a saga of the manly art of boxing. In it, we are concerned with the ambitions of Sonny Jim Brooks (Jack Whiting), a welterweight challenger, and his girl, Sue Burke (Ona Munson), who is the cream in his coffee. Sonny Jim becomes temporarily distracted by socialite Norine Lloyd (Betty Compton) and for a while even considers her advice to try using boxing skills rather than slug it out with the champion. But when our hero finds out that the champ has insulted Sue, his killer instincts are aroused and he wins both the crown and his lady. The major attraction of the show turned out to be the uninhibited buffoon, Bert Lahr, as a punch-drunk pug. (When asked in one scene what book he was reading, Bert replied, "Da Woiks, by William Shakespeare.") During the run at the Broadhurst Theatre (on 44th Street west of Broadway), Whiting was succeeded by George Murphy. The film version was released in 1930 with Joe E. Brown and Winnie Lightner.

# WHOOPEE

**Music:** Walter Donaldson
**Lyrics:** Gus Kahn
**Book:** William Anthony McGuire
**Producer:** Florenz Ziegfeld
**Director:** William Anthony McGuire
**Choreographers:** Seymour Felix, Tamara Geva
**Cast:**  Eddie Cantor, Ruth Etting, Ethel Shutta, Paul Gregory, Frances Upton, Tamara Geva, Albert Hackett, George Olsen Orchestra, Buddy Ebsen
**Songs:** "I'm Bringing a Red Red Rose"; "Makin' Whoopee"; "Until You Get Somebody Else"; "Love Me or Leave Me"
**New York run:** New Amsterdam Theatre, December 4, 1928; 379 p.

Eddie Cantor was an eye-popping, bouncing comedian who had appeared in five *Ziegfeld Follies* before starring in this lavish Ziegfeld book musical. In the story, adapted from the 1923 play *The Nervous Wreck,* hypochondriac Henry Williams, in California for his health, becomes unwittingly involved with the daughter of a ranch owner whom he helps escape from marrying the local sheriff. After comic adventures that involve hiding out on an Indian reservation and Henry (in blackface) posing as a singing waiter, the girl is reunited with her true love, an Indian halfbreed who turns out to be white. The score, written by pop songwriters Walter Donaldson and Gus Kahn, produced two hits, "Love Me or Leave Me" and the Cantor specialty, "Makin' Whoopee." During the show's run, Paul Whiteman's Orchestra replaced George Olsen's for two months. A Broadway revival in 1979, originally presented at the Goodspeed Opera House in Connecticut, ran 204 performances. Eddie Cantor also starred in the 1930 film version. Smithsonian OC.

**Whoopee.** Eddie Cantor as Henry Williams.

# FOLLOW THRU

**Music:** Ray Henderson
**Lyrics:** B. G. DeSylva & Lew Brown
**Book:** Laurence Schwab & B. G. DeSylva
**Producers:** Laurence Schwab & Frank Mandel
**Director:** Edgar MacGregor
**Choreographer:** Bobby Connolly
**Cast:** Jack Haley, Zelma O'Neal, Irene Delroy, Eleanor Powell, Madeline Cameron, John Barker
**Songs:** "My Lucky Star"; "Button Up Your Overcoat"; "You Wouldn't Fool Me, Would You?"; "I Want to Be Bad"
**New York run:** 46th Street Theatre, January 9, 1929; 403 p.

After collaborating on musical comedies about football *(Good News!)* and boxing *(Hold Everything!)*, DeSylva, Brown and Henderson followed up with *Follow Thru*, which was about golf. Subtitled "A Musical Slice of Country Club Life," the show was an appropriately fleet-footed successor to the previous sporty musicals, with another catchy score (including "Button Up Your Overcoat"), some comic situations for Jack Haley (in his first major Broadway role), and a negligible plot about female rivalry for both the club championship and the golf pro. Most important, however, was the show's contagious high spirits. As Gilbert Gabriel reported in the *American,* "Wild-faced, free-legged kids shouted catch lines across the footlights that fairly roped and yanked the audience onto the stage." Jack Haley repeated his role in the 1930 movie version, which also featured Nancy Carroll and Buddy Rogers.
TW.

# THE LITTLE SHOW

**Music:** Arthur Schwartz etc.
**Lyrics:** Howard Dietz, etc.
**Sketches:** Howard Dietz, George S. Kaufman, etc.
**Producers:** William A. Brady Jr. & Dwight Deere Wiman
**Directors:** Dwight Deere Wiman, Alexander Leftwich
**Choreographer:** Danny Dare
**Cast:** Clifton Webb, Fred Allen, Libby Holman, Romney Brent, Portland Hoffa, Bettina Hall, Jack McCauley, Peggy Conklin, Constance Cummings
**Songs:** "I've Made a Habit of You"; "Can't We Be Friends?" (Kay Swift-Paul James); "Hammacher-Schlemmer, I Love You"; "A Little Hut in Hoboken" (Herman Hupfeld); "I Guess I'll Have to Change My Plan"; "Moanin' Low" (music: Ralph Rainger)
**New York run:** Music Box, April 30, 1929; 321 p.

*The Little Show* was the first of 11 Broadway musicals to feature songs by the team of Arthur Schwartz and Howard Dietz. In its smartness, style, and intimacy (in 1929 a show with 29 in the cast qualified as little), the revue was something of an American counterpart to the British *Charlot Revues* and *This Year of Grace.* The most dramatic scene was the torrid dance Clifton Webb and Libby Holman performed after Miss Holman moaned "Moanin' Low" in a squalid Harlem tenement. The funniest sketch was George S. Kaufman's "The Still Alarm," about some nonchalant hotel guests, including Webb and Fred Allen, totally impervious to their being in the midst of a blazing fire. There were two subsequent *Little Shows*, neither one a success, though *The Third Little Show,* in 1931, co-starred Beatrice Lillie and Ernest Truex. Miss Lillie introduced Noël Coward's "Mad Dogs and Englishmen" in that one.

# SWEET ADELINE
**Music:** Jerome Kern
**Lyrics & book:** Oscar Hammerstein II
**Producer:** Arthur Hammerstein
**Director:** Reginald Hammerstein
**Choreographer:** Danny Dare
**Cast:** Helen Morgan, Charles Butterworth, Irene Franklin, Robert Chisholm, Violet Carlson, Max Hoffman Jr.
**Songs:** " 'Twas Not So Long Ago"; "Here Am I"; "Why Was I Born?"; "The Sun About to Rise"; "Some Girl Is on Your Mind"; "Don't Ever Leave Me"
**New York run:** Hammerstein's Theatre, September 3, 1929; 234 p.

Because of their admiration for Helen Morgan's performance in *Show Boat,* Jerome Kern and Oscar Hammerstein collaborated on a nostalgic musical designed as a vehicle to show off the singer's talents. Set in and around New York in 1898, the story concerns Addie Schmidt, the daughter of a Hoboken beergarden owner, and her three loves. After Tom Martin has gone to fight in the Spanish-American War, Addie — now known as Adeline Belmont — becomes a Broadway star and falls for wealthy socialite James Day. But his family disapproves and she happily ends up in the arms of composer Sid Barnett. Full of period charm, *Sweet Adeline* was something of a Hammerstein family affair, since it was produced by Oscar's uncle Arthur, directed by his brother Reginald, and played in Arthur's theatre (now a CBS television playhouse on Broadway between 53rd and 54th Streets). Irene Dunne starred in the 1935 movie.
TW.

# BITTER SWEET
**Music, lyrics & book:** Noël Coward
**Producers:** Florenz Ziegfeld & Arch Selwyn
**Director:** Noël Coward
**Choreographer:** Tilly Losch
**Cast:** Evelyn Laye, Gerald Nodin, Max Kirby, Mireille, John Evelyn
**Songs:** "The Call of Life"; "If You Could Come With Me"; "I'll See You Again"; "Ladies of the Town"; "Dear Little Café"; "If Love Were All"; "Tokay"; "Ziguener"
**New York run:** Ziegfeld Theatre, November 5, 1929; 159 p.

Though celebrated for the brittle wit of his revue songs and sketches, as well as his plays, the multitalented Noël Coward was equally at home in the world of operetta. Indeed, no less than six of his eight book musicals were awash in old-fashioned sentiment, elegant period decor, and melodious, emotional ballads. The first of these, *Bitter Sweet,* was written simply because Coward felt that the time was right for a romantic renaissance in the theatre. After Gertrude Lawrence's vocal limitations ruled out her taking the leading role, the part went to the American actress, Peggy Wood, who starred in the London production, and the English actress, Evelyn Laye, who then starred in New York.

Living in Grosvenor Square, the widowed Marchioness of Shayne aids her niece in deciding whether to marry for love or position by recalling that day in 1875 when, as Sarah Millick, she joined music teacher Carl Linden in singing "I'll See You Again" — and promptly eloped with him to Vienna. Five years later, they were poor but happy café entertainers until Carl was killed in a duel. Sarah went on to become the renowned prima donna, Madame Sari Linden, then the wife of the wealthy Marquis of Shayne. Jeanette MacDonald and Nelson Eddy were in the second screen version, released in 1941.
Angel SC/ Heinemann, London (1934)/ TW.

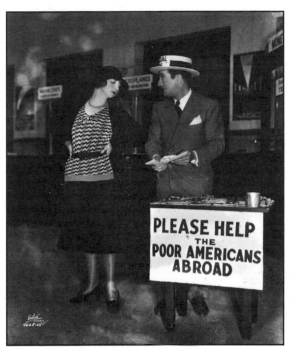

**Fifty Million Frenchmen.** Helen Broderick and William Gaxton. (White)

# FIFTY MILLION FRENCHMEN
**Music & lyrics:** Cole Porter
**Book:** Herbert Fields
**Producer:** E. Ray Goetz
**Director:** Monty Woolley
**Choreographer:** Larry Ceballos
**Cast:** William Gaxton, Genevieve Tobin, Helen Broderick, Betty Compton, Evelyn Hoey, Jack Thompson, Thurston Hall
**Songs:** "You Do Something to Me"; "You've Got That Thing"; "Find Me a Primitive Man"; "The Tale of an Oyster"; "Paree, What Did You Do to Me?"; "You Don't Know Paree"
**New York run:** Lyric Theatre, November 27, 1929; 254 p.

Noted for his throbbing, minor-key melodies and his wordly, highly polished lyrics, Cole Porter was responsible for the scores of 23 Broadway musicals. His first hit — dubbed "A Musical Comedy Tour of Paris" — was a carefree tale concerning wealthy Peter Forbes (William Gaxton) who has a wager with a friend that he and Looloo Carroll (Genevieve Tobin) will be betrothed within a month. This gives Peter the excuse to become an impoverished tour guide so that, in pursuit of his beloved, he can determine if Looloo really loves him — and also so that they might enjoy such landmarks of the city as the Ritz Hotel Bar (where they mutually confess "You Do Something to Me"), the Café de la Paix, the Longchamps Racetrack, the Hotel Claridge, and Les Halles. The 1931 screen version retained the services of William Gaxton and Helen Broderick, but eliminated the songs. TW.

# STRIKE UP THE BAND

**Music:** George Gershwin
**Lyrics:** Ira Gershwin
**Book:** Morrie Ryskind
**Producer:** Edgar Selwyn
**Director:** Alexander Leftwich
**Choreographer:** George Hale
**Cast:** Bobby Clark & Paul McCullough, Blanche Ring, Jerry Goff, Doris Carson, Dudley Clements, Red Nichols Orchestra
**Songs:** "I Mean to Say"; "Soon"; "Strike Up the Band"; "Mademoiselle in New Rochelle"; "I've Got a Crush on You"
**New York run:** Times Square Theatre, January 14, 1930; 191 p.

*Strike Up the Band* was first scheduled for a Broadway opening in 1927, but the original George S. Kaufman book was so uncompromisingly grim in its antiwar sentiment that the show closed on the road. Morrie Ryskind then rewrote the story, putting most of the action in a dream, and the leading roles were given to the zany team of Clark and McCullough. The revised script dealt with a war between the United States and Switzerland over the issue of tariffs on imported Swiss chocolate, with plenty of room for barbs aimed at jingoists, politicians, and White House advisers. Musical-comedy conventions, however, helped make it palatable to 1930 audiences. This was the first of a number of book shows and revues of the Thirties that, influenced by the Depression and the growing threat of another World War, were emboldened to make satirical observations on the problems then besetting the country and the world. Of interest to jazz buffs is that Red Nichols' pit band included such future luminaries as Benny Goodman, Gene Krupa, Glenn Miller, Jimmy Dorsey, and Jack Teagarden.

70

**Flying High.** Bert Lahr and Kate Smith. (Vandamm)

# FLYING HIGH
**Music:** Ray Henderson
**Lyrics:** B. G. DeSylva & Lew Brown
**Book:** John McGowan, B. G. DeSylva & Lew Brown
**Producer:** George White
**Directors:** George White, Edward Clark Lilley
**Choreographer:** Bobby Connolly
**Cast:**   Bert Lahr, Oscar Shaw, Kate Smith, Grace Brinkley, Russ Brown, Pearl Osgood
**Songs:** "I'll Know Him"; "Thank Your Father"; "Good for You — Bad for Me"; "Red Hot Chicago"; "Without Love"
**New York run:** Apollo Theatre, March 3, 1930; 357 p.

With athletic inspiration apparently exhausted, DeSylva, Brown and Henderson followed their musicals about football, boxing, and golf with one dealing with another current obsession, air travel. *Flying High*, however, was still something of a successor to *Hold Everything!* since it again put Bert Lahr in a role that enabled him to play a terrified cluck who must endure torturous preparations before he can triumph in a hazardous occupation. In this show, Lahr appeared as Rusty Krause, an airplane mechanic whose preparations for flight include a hilarious examining-room scene, and whose achievement is setting a record for the number of hours he is able to keep an airplane aloft—because he doesn't have the slightest idea how to get it down. Kate Smith played the comic role of Bert's mail-order fiancée. Lahr repeated his part in the 1931 film version, which also featured Pat O'Brien and Charlotte Greenwood.

# FINE AND DANDY

**Music:** Kay Swift
**Lyrics:** Paul James
**Book:** Donald Ogden Stewart (Joe Cook uncredited)
**Producers:** Morris Green & Lewis Gensler
**Directors:** Morris Green, Frank McCoy
**Choreographers:** David Gould, Tom Nip
**Cast:** Joe Cook, Nell O'Day, Dave Chasen, Eleanor Powell, Alice Boulden, Joe Wagstaff
**Songs:** "Fine and Dandy"; "Can This Be Love?"; "Let's Go Eat Worms in the Garden"; "The Jig Hop"
**New York run:** Erlanger's Theatre, September 23, 1930; 255 p.

Comic Joe Cook was an innocent looking clown with a wide smile whose specialties were non sequitur stories (including his trademark routine about why he would not imitate four Hawaiians), Rube Goldberg-type inventions, and acrobatic and juggling skills. *Fine and Dandy*, a follow-up to his popular vehicle, *Rain or Shine*, not only included the Cook specialties but also featured a superior score (including the durable title song), the tapping of Eleanor Powell, and a tale that found Cook as Joe Squibb, the general manager of the Fordyce Drop Forge and Tool Factory, who ineptly copes with problems of labor and management. Erlanger's Theatre, now the St. James, stands on 44th Street west of Broadway.

# GIRL CRAZY

**Music:** George Gershwin
**Lyrics:** Ira Gershwin
**Book:** Guy Bolton & John McGowan
**Producers:** Alex A. Aarons & Vinton Freedley
**Director:** Alexander Leftwich
**Choreographer:** George Hale
**Cast:** Willie Howard, Allen Kearns, Ginger Rogers, William Kent, Ethel Merman, Antonio & Renee DeMarco, Lew Parker, Roger Edens, Red Nichols Orchestra
**Songs:** "Bidin' My Time"; "Could You Use Me?"; "Embraceable You"; "I Got Rhythm"; "But Not for Me"; "Sam and Delilah"; "Treat Me Rough"
**New York run:** Alvin Theatre, October 14, 1930; 272 p.

Temporarily turning from the satiric world of their recent *Strike Up the Band*, the Gershwin brothers joined their former colleagues, librettist Guy Bolton and producers Aarons and Freedley, to escape to the more innocent world of conventional musical comedy. For *Girl Crazy*, however, they abandoned the East Coast haunts of high society that had been their customary locales in favor of the wide open spaces of Custerville, Arizona. There playboy Danny Churchill (Allen Kearns) has been sent by his wealthy father to manage a ranch in order to keep out of the clutches of predatory females. Arriving by taxi from New York, Danny soon turns the place into a dude ranch where Kate Fothergill (Ethel Merman in her first Broadway role) entertains guests with the undeniable assertion, "I Got Rhythm." Later our hero gets to croon "Embraceable You" with Molly Gray (Ginger Rogers in her second Broadway role), and helps taxi driver-turned-sheriff Gieber Goldfarb (Willie Howard in a part intended for Bert Lahr) apprehend the outlaw who has been threatening his life. Red Nichols' band included the same impressive personnel as in *Strike Up the Band*. Three film adaptations were made of *Girl Crazy*, with Judy Garland and Mickey Rooney co-starred in the 1943 version.
Columbia SC/ TW.

**Three's a Crowd.** Libby Holman singing "Something to Remember You By" as she bids farewell to matelot Fred MacMurray. (Apeda)

# THREE'S A CROWD

**Music:** Arthur Schwartz, etc.
**Lyrics:** Howard Dietz, etc.
**Sketches:** Miscellaneous writers
**Producer:** Max Gordon
**Director:** Hassard Short
**Choreographer:** Albertina Rasch
**Cast:** Clifton Webb, Fred Allen, Libby Holman, Tamara Geva, Portland Hoffa, Earl Oxford, Fred MacMurray
**Songs:** "Something to Remember You By"; "Body and Soul" (Johnny Green-Edward Heyman, Robert Sour); "The Moment I Saw You"; "Forget All Your Books" (music: Burton Lane); "Right at the Start of It"
**New York run:** Selwyn Theatre, October 15, 1930; 272 p.

Once the sponsors of *The Second Little Show* decided that the stars of the first *Little Show* — Clifton Webb, Fred Allen, and Libby Holman — would not be in their new revue, fledgling producer Max Gordon persuaded the trio to appear in his own revue. He further assured that *Three's a Crowd* would be accepted in fact if not in name as the sequel to *The Little Show* by bringing along composer Arthur Schwartz and lyricist Howard Dietz (with Dietz additionally credited with having "conceived and compiled" the new show). The musical standouts of the evening were Miss Holman's masochistic "Body and Soul" and her "Something to Remember You By," a tearful ballad of farewell she sang to a matelot played by Fred MacMurray. Fred Allen won his biggest laughs as explorer Admiral Byrd, who has just returned from the Antarctic to announce his discovery of 500,000 square miles of brand new snow.

# THE NEW YORKERS

**Music & lyrics:** Cole Porter
**Book:** Herbert Fields
**Producer:** E. Ray Goetz
**Director:** Monty Woolley
**Choreographer:** George Hale
**Cast:** Frances Williams, Charles King, Hope Williams, Ann Pennington, Richard Carle, Marie Cahill, Fred Waring Orchestra, Clayton, Jackson and Durante, Kathryn Crawford, Oscar Ragland
**Songs:** "Where Have You Been?"; "Love for Sale"; "Take Me Back to Manhattan"; "Let's Fly Away"; "I Happen to Like New York"
**New York run:** Broadway Theatre, December 8, 1930; 168 p.

The first stage production at the Broadway Theatre (on 53rd Street), *The New Yorkers* was something of a forerunner of *Pal Joey* in its amoral characters, cynical outlook, and flashy nightclub atmosphere. Just as Cole Porter and Herbert Fields' previous *Fifty Million Frenchmen* had offered a musical tour of Paris, so the new outing (with the same producer and director) offered a musical tour of high and low life in Manhattan, stopping off at a Park Avenue apartment, a speakeasy, a bootleg distillery, the Cotton Club in Harlem, and Reuben's Restaurant on Madison Avenue. The surrealistic satire concerns a socialite (Hope Williams) in love with a bootlegger (Charles King) because she is impressed with the way he bumps people off. Other characters include the lady's philandering parents and an irrepressible gangster henchman (Jimmy Durante), who brings the first act to a riotous close with his description of the varied products made from wood. Soon after the show's opening, Elisabeth Welch replaced Kathryn Crawford to sing the torchy invitation of a streetwalker, "Love for Sale."

# THE BAND WAGON

**Music:** Arthur Schwartz
**Lyrics:** Howard Dietz
**Sketches:** George S. Kaufman, Howard Dietz
**Producer:** Max Gordon
**Director:** Hassard Short
**Choreographer:** Albertina Rasch
**Cast:** Fred & Adele Astaire, Frank Morgan, Helen Broderick, Tilly Losch, Philip Loeb, John Barker
**Songs:** "Sweet Music"; "High and Low"; "Hoops"; "Confession"; "New Sun in the Sky"; "I Love Louisa"; "Dancing in the Dark"; "White Heat"
**New York run:** New Amsterdam Theatre, June 3, 1931; 260 p.

Put together by the same creative team that had been responsible for *Three's a Crowd, The Band Wagon* may well have been the most sophisticated, imaginative, and musically distinguished revue ever mounted on Broadway. To assure that the production would have the same homogeneity of style as a book musical, there were no interpolations in the score and only two writers were credited for the sketches. Among the evening's pleasures: Fred and Adele Astaire (in their tenth and last Broadway appearance together) as two French children cavorting to "Hoops"; the principals riding on a Bavarian merry-go-round while singing "I Love Louisa"; Tilly Losch dancing to "Dancing in the Dark" on a slanted, mirrored stage; "The Pride of the Claghornes" sketch spoofing the Southern aristocracy's honor-of-the-family code. *The Band Wagon* was also the first New York production to use a double revolving stage for both its musical numbers and sketches. The 1953 Fred Astaire-Cyd Charisse film retained five songs, added others, and threw in a story line.
RCA OC.; Smithsonian part OC.

Cover designed by John Held, Jr.

**The Band Wagon.** Adele and Fred Astaire singing "Hoops." (Vandamm)

**The Band Wagon.** "The Pride of the Claghornes" sketch with Helen Broderick, Adele Astaire, Frank Morgan, and Fred Astaire. (Vandamm)

# EARL CARROLL VANITIES

**Music:** Burton Lane, etc.
**Lyrics:** Harold Adamson, etc.
**Sketches:** Ralph Spence, Eddie Welch
**Producer-director:** Earl Carroll
**Choreographers:** George Hale, Gluck Sandor
**Cast:** Will Mahoney, Lillian Roth, William Demarest, Mitchell & Durant, Milton Watson
**Songs:** "Have a Heart"; "Heigh Ho, the Gang's All Here"; "Good Night, Sweetheart" (Ray Noble-Jimmy Campbell, Reg Connelly); "Tonight or Never" (Vincent Rose-Ray Klages, Jack Meskill)
**New York run:** Earl Carroll Theatre, August 27, 1931; 278 p.

A major rival to the *Ziegfeld Follies* and the *George White's Scandals* series was the *Earl Carroll Vanities,* which Carroll introduced in 1923. He staged 11 editions of a revue featuring girls even less modestly garbed and production numbers even more overblown than found in similar entertainments then being offered to keep the tired businessman awake. The 1931 edition was the first attraction at the newly built Earl Carroll Theatre at 50th Street and 7th Avenue, situated on the site of the previous theatre of the same name. No longer in existence, the playhouse was as much attraction as the show. Because of its 3,000-seat size, it enabled Carroll to sell orchestra seats at a top price of $3.30, for which theatregoers could enjoy such gaudy delights as a massive "Bolero" ballet accompanied by tom-toms and a "living curtain" of undraped showgirls posing as allegorical figures.

# GEORGE WHITE'S SCANDALS

**Music:** Ray Henderson
**Lyrics:** Lew Brown
**Sketches:** Lew Brown, George White, Irving Caesar
**Producer-director-choreographer:** George White
**Cast:** Rudy Vallee, Ethel Merman, Willie & Eugene Howard, Everett Marshall, Ray Bolger, Ethel Barrymore Colt, Alice Faye
**Songs:** "Life Is Just a Bowl of Cherries"; "The Thrill Is Gone"; "This Is the Missus"; "Ladies and Gentlemen, That's Love"; "That's Why Darkies Were Born"; "My Song"
**New York run:** Apollo Theatre, September 14, 1931; 202 p.

The only challenger to the 1926 *Scandals* (see page 52) as the best of the series was the 11th Edition, which came along in 1931. Ray Henderson and Lew Brown (but minus B. G. DeSylva) were on hand for their fourth and last *Scandals* together with an impressive array of song hits introduced by pop crooner Rudy Vallee, powerhouse belter Ethel Merman (who had joined the cast during the tryout), and robust baritone Everett Marshall. Among the attractions were a celebration of the opening of the Empire State Building with Ray Bolger as a dancing Al Smith (with decor by former Ziegfeld designer Joseph Urban); a chins-up Depression anthem, "Life Is Just a Bowl of Cherries," trumpeted by Miss Merman; Willie and Eugene Howard in their classic comedy sketch "Pay the Two Dollars"; and a bold first-act finale, "That's Why Darkies Were Born," that took a compassionate view of Negro fortitude in the face of injustice.

The Cat and the Fiddle. Georges Metaxa, George Meader, and Bettina Hall. (White)

# THE CAT AND THE FIDDLE

**Music:** Jerome Kern
**Lyrics & book:** Otto Harbach
**Producer:** Max Gordon
**Director:** José Ruben
**Choreographer:** Albertina Rasch
**Cast:** Georges Metaxa, Bettina Hall, Odette Myrtil, Eddie Foy Jr., José Ruben, Lawrence Grossmith, Doris Carson, George Meader
**Songs:** "The Night Was Made for Love"; "I Watch the Love Parade"; "Try to Forget"; "Poor Pierrot"; "She Didn't Say 'Yes' "; "A New Love Is Old"; "One Moment Alone"
**New York run:** Globe Theatre, October 15, 1931; 395 p.

*The Cat and the Fiddle* was a generally successful attempt to put the florid operetta form into a contemporary, intimate setting. In creating the work, Jerome Kern and Otto Harbach did without choruses, spectacles, and dragged-in comedy routines to keep the focus on the main story of what they called "A Musical Romance." Set in modern Brussels, it tells of the attraction between Victor Florescu (Georges Metaxa), a serious-minded Rumanian composer, and Shirley Sheridan (Bettina Hall), a vivacious American composer with a penchant for jazz. Though Victor is furious when a producer tries to lighten his rather heavy operetta, *The Passionate Pilgrim*, with some of Shirley's bright, uptempo numbers, true love eventually has hero and heroine singing in harmony. The true hero of the evening, however, was Jerome Kern whose score was an almost continuous flow of melodic pleasures, with songs well integrated into the story and with a highly advanced use of musical underscoring. In 1934, a film version was released starring Jeanette MacDonald and Ramon Novarro.
Epic (SC)/ TW.

# OF THEE I SING

**Music:** George Gershwin
**Lyrics:** Ira Gershwin
**Book:** George S. Kaufman & Morrie Ryskind
**Producer:** Sam H. Harris
**Director:** George S. Kaufman
**Choreographer:** George Hale
**Cast:** William Gaxton, Victor Moore, Lois Moran, Grace Brinkley, June O'Dea, George Murphy, Dudley Clements, Edward H. Robins, Florenz Ames, Ralph Riggs, George E. Mack
**Songs:** "Wintergreen for President"; "Because, Because"; "Love Is Sweeping the Country"; "Of Thee I Sing, Baby"; "Here's a Kiss for Cinderella"; "Who Cares?"; "Hello, Good Morning"; "The Illegitimate Daughter"
**New York run:** Music Box, December 26, 1931; 441 p.

Constructed more in the style of a Gilbert and Sullivan comic opera than of a Broadway musical comedy, *Of Thee I Sing* was an extension of the satirical approach of the same writers' previous *Strike Up the Band*. Here, however, the technique was surer and the compromises to popular taste less apparent, with songs and story complementing each other and expressing a uniform point of view. Sharply and deftly skewered were such institutions as political conventions and campaigns, beauty pageants, marriage, the Vice Presidency, the Supreme Court, foreign affairs, and motherhood.

The fanciful tale covers the fortunes of the Presidential ticket of John P. Wintergreen and his running mate, Alexander Throttlebottom — abetted by Wintergreen's bride, Mary Turner (Lois Moran) — which, with its campaign song "Of Thee I Sing, Baby," sweeps the country on a platform of Love. Once in office, however, the President is threatened with impeachment because he jilted Diana Devereaux (Grace Brinkley), the Miss America contest winner he had promised to marry. She, it seems, is "the illegitimate daughter of the illegitimate son of an illegitimate nephew of Napoleon," and France is insulted because of this slight. After the First Lady somehow saves the day by giving birth to twins, France's honor is assuaged when Throttlebottom agrees to wed Diana because, according to the Constitution, "When the President of the United States is unable to fulfil his duties, his obligations are assumed by the Vice President."

*Of Thee I Sing,* the third longest running musical of the Thirties, became the first musical ever awarded the Pulitzer Prize for drama (though ironically George Gershwin was not included in the citation since his was a musical contribution and therefore not considered eligible for a literary award). It also established brash, sharp-featured William Gaxton and bumbling, dumpling-shaped Victor Moore, who played Wintergreen and Throttlebottom, as Broadway's leading musical-comedy team. After touring, the show returned to New York for a month-long engagement in May 1933. It then resumed its tour with a cast headed by Oscar Shaw, Donald Meek, and Ann Sothern.

In October 1933, a sequel, *Let 'Em Eat Cake,* written by the same writers and featuring the original leading players, opened on Broadway. Supposedly a satire on dictatorship, the show proved too acerbic and thematically confusing, and it remained only three months. The song "Mine," which was in this production, was added to *Of Thee I Sing* when the musical was revived in 1952. Jack Carson and Victor Moore were signed to play Wintergreen and Throttlebottom, but Moore decided against repeating his original role and the part went to Paul Hartman. George S. Kaufman again directed. In 1987, a concert version was performed with *Let 'Em Eat Cake* at the Brooklyn Academy of Music.
Capitol OC (1952); CBS OC (1987)/ Knopf (1932); Samuel French (1935)*; Chilton (1973)/ SF.

**Of Thee I Sing.** Victor Moore and William Gaxton, surrounded by political advisers, getting ready for the campaign. (Vandamm)

# FACE THE MUSIC
**Music & lyrics:** Irving Berlin
**Book:** Moss Hart
**Producer:** Sam H. Harris
**Directors:** Hassard Short, George S. Kaufman
**Choreographer:** Albertina Rasch
**Cast:** Mary Boland, J. Harold Murray, Andrew Tombes, Hugh O'Connell, Katherine Carrington, David Burns
**Songs:** "Let's Have Another Cup o' Coffee"; "On a Roof in Manhattan"; "Soft Lights and Sweet Music"; "I Say It's Spinach"
**New York run:** New Amsterdam Theatre, February 17, 1932; 165 p.

The mood of cynicism created by the Depression continued to spawn a number of sharply satirical Broadway musicals. The Gershwin brothers, George S. Kaufman, and Morrie Ryskind had led the way with *Strike Up the Band* and *Of Thee I Sing,* and now it was the turn of Irving Berlin and Moss Hart (with Kaufman joining the project as director). In *Face the Music* the concern was with New York politicians and policemen with little tin boxes, the reduced financial circumstances of the city's elite (former wealthy socialites sing "Let's Have Another Cup o' Coffee" in the Automat), and the insane world of the theatre. In the leading role, Mary Boland played Mrs. Martin Van Buren Meshbesher, the wife of a police sergeant "lousy with money," who tries to lose some of it by backing a tasteless Broadway show, *The Rhinestone Girl,* that surprisingly becomes a hit. Despite the Seabury investigation into police corruption (which also figured in the 1959 musical, *Fiorello!*), the boys in blue manage to beat the rap when Mrs. Meshbesher contributes the profits from the show to the city's depleted treasury. Early in 1933 *Face the Music* returned to Broadway for a month-long run.

# FLYING COLORS

**Music:** Arthur Schwartz
**Lyrics & sketches:** Howard Dietz
**Producer:** Max Gordon
**Director:** Howard Dietz
**Choreographer:** Albertina Rasch
**Cast:** Clifton Webb, Charles Butterworth, Tamara Geva, Patsy Kelly, Philip Loeb, Vilma & Buddy Ebsen, Larry Adler, Imogene Coca, Monette Moore
**Songs:** "Two-Faced Woman"; "A Rainy Day"; "A Shine on Your Shoes"; "Alone Together"; "Louisiana Hayride"; "Smokin' Reefers"
**New York run:** Imperial Theatre, September 15, 1932, 188 p.

*Flying Colors* flew in a direct line from *The Little Show, Three's a Crowd,* and *The Band Wagon.* Like all three, it had music by Arthur Schwartz and lyrics by Howard Dietz (though this time Dietz also received credit as sole sketch writer and director). Like the most recent two revues, it was produced by Max Gordon and was choreographed by Albertina Rasch, and it also featured two veterans of the series, Clifton Webb and Tamara Geva. Though too closely patterned after its illustrious predecessors (Brooks Atkinson headed his Sunday *Times* piece, "Flying the Band Wagon Colors"), the show was witty and attractive, and had its share of standout numbers: "A Shine on Your Shoes" presented Vilma and Buddy Ebsen dancing around a shoeshine stand accompanied by Larry Adler's harmonica; "Alone Together" offered Webb and Geva in a dramatic, sinuous dance; and "Louisiana Hayride" brought the first act to a jubilant close. Then there was Charles Butterworth's hilarious soapbox speech, "Harvey Woofter's Five Point Plan," on how to end the Depression. Times were tough for the show, too. After opening it at a $4.40 top, Gordon was soon forced to lower the ticket price to $2.20.

**Flying Colors.** Buddy Ebsen, Monette Moore, Vilma Ebsen, and Larry Adler performing "A Shine on Your Shoes." (White)

# MUSIC IN THE AIR

**Music:** Jerome Kern
**Lyrics & book:** Oscar Hammerstein II
**Producer:** Peggy Fears (A. C. Blumenthal uncredited)
**Directors:** Jerome Kern & Oscar Hammerstein II
**Cast:** Reinald Werrenrath, Natalie Hall, Tullio Carminati, Katherine Carrington, Al Shean, Walter Slezak, Nicholas Joy, Marjorie Main
**Songs:** "I've Told Ev'ry Little Star"; "There's a Hill Beyond a Hill"; "And Love Was Born"; "I'm Alone"; "I Am So Eager"; "One More Dance"; "When the Spring Is in the Air"; "In Egern on the Tegern See"; "The Song Is You"; "We Belong Together"
**New York run:** Alvin Theatre, November 8, 1932; 342 p.

Hailed by Alexander Woollcott in *The New Yorker* as "that endearing refuge, that gracious shelter from a troubled world," the Jerome Kern-Oscar Hammerstein *Music in the Air* continued along the same path as the Jerome Kern-Otto Harbach *Cat and the Fiddle.* The setting was again modern Europe, the story again had to do with the preparations for an operetta, and the songs — among Kern's most memorable — and the underscoring again enhanced the characters and the situations. The plot of this "Musical Adventure" concerns Sieglinde and Karl (Katherine Carrington and Walter Slezak), two Bavarian naifs, who hike from Edendorf to Munich to help Sieglinde's father, Dr. Walther Lessing (Al Shean), interest a music publisher in his new composition, "I've Told Ev'ry Little Star." Soon they become involved with glamorous star Frieda Hatzfeld (Natalie Hall) and her lover, librettist Bruno Mahler (Tullio Carminati), during the rehearsals of Bruno's new work, *Tingle-Tangle.* When the temperamental diva walks out on the production, Sieglinde is given her big chance. Contrary to show-business legend, however, she proves totally inept, and when Frieda comes back Sieglinde sadly returns to her mountain village.

Hammerstein brought *Music in the Air* back to Broadway in 1951, with a cast headed by Jane Pickens (Frieda), Dennis King (Bruno), and Charles Winninger (Lessing). Because of possible anti-German sentiment following World War II, he changed the locale from Munich to Zurich and made everybody Swiss. The show remained less than two months. The 1934 Hollywood version starred Gloria Swanson, John Boles, and Al Shean.
Capitol SC/ Chappell, London (1934)*/ TW.

**Music in the Air.** Katherine Carrington, Al Shean and Walter Slezak. (Vandamm)

# TAKE A CHANCE

**Music:** Richard A. Whiting, Nacio Herb Brown, Vincent Youmans
**Lyrics:** B. G. DeSylva
**Book:** B. G. DeSylva, Laurence Schwab, Sid Silvers
**Producers:** Laurence Schwab & B. G. DeSylva
**Director:** Edgar MacGregor
**Choreographer:** Bobby Connolly
**Cast:** Jack Haley, Ethel Merman, Jack Whiting, Sid Silvers, June Knight, Mitzi Mayfair, Oscar Ragland, Robert Gleckler
**Songs:** "Should I Be Sweet?" (Youmans); "Turn Out the Lights" (Whiting, Brown); "Rise 'n' Shine" (Youmans); "You're an Old Smoothie" (Whiting, Brown); "Eadie Was a Lady" (Whiting; lyric with Roger Edens)
**New York run:** Apollo Theatre, November 26, 1932; 243 p.

In September 1932, a musical titled *Humpty Dumpty* began its tryout tour in Pittsburgh. It involved Lou Holtz, Ethel Merman, and Eddie Foy Jr. in what was basically a revue with songs and sketches dealing with incidents in American history. It was so poorly received that the show closed in five days. Within three weeks, however, the production was totally revised, partly recast (Holtz and Foy were replaced by Jack Whiting and Jack Haley), and had five new songs by Vincent Youmans. Retitled *Take a Chance* — to indicate something of the risks involved — the show was now an old-fashioned book musical concerned with a romance between the leading man and leading lady (Whiting and June Knight) who are appearing in a revue about American history called *Humpty Dumpty*. What turned it into a hit, though, were the comedy and specialty numbers, with Miss Merman given two show stoppers — "Rise 'n' Shine" and "Eadie Was a Lady" — that let her blast her way clear up to the second balcony. During the Broadway run, Haley and Sid Silvers were succeeded by the vaudeville team of Olsen and Johnson. The film version, released in 1933, featured June Knight and Lillian Roth.

# GAY DIVORCE

**Music & lyrics:** Cole Porter
**Book:** Dwight Taylor
**Producers:** Dwight Deere Wiman & Tom Weatherly
**Director:** Howard Lindsay
**Choreographers:** Carl Randall, Barbara Newberry
**Cast:** Fred Astaire, Claire Luce, Luella Gear, Betty Starbuck, Erik Rhodes, Eric Blore, G. P. Huntley Jr.
**Songs:** "After You, Who?"; "Night and Day"; "How's Your Romance?"; "I've Got You on My Mind"; "Mister and Missus Fitch"
**New York run:** Ethel Barrymore Theatre, November 29, 1932; 248 p.

The first musical to play the Ethel Barrymore Theatre (on 47th Street west of Broadway), *Gay Divorce* was the only stage production in which Fred Astaire performed without sister Adele. In the story, adapted from an unproduced play, Astaire was seen as Guy Holden, a British novelist, who goes to a seaside resort to woo would-be divorcée Mimi Pratt (Claire Luce), primarily by convincing her — through song and dance — that night and day she is the one. Complications arise when Guy is mistaken for a professional corespondent (Erik Rhodes) who has been hired to ease Mimi's divorce. Though Astaire proved that he could carry both a weak plot and a new dancing partner, *Gay Divorce* (without the definite article, please) marked his final appearance on Broadway. The 1934 film version, retitled *The Gay Divorcee,* co-starred Fred with Ginger Rogers.

# AS THOUSANDS CHEER

**Music & lyrics:** Irving Berlin
**Sketches:** Moss Hart
**Producer:** Sam H. Harris
**Director:** Hassard Short
**Choreographer:** Charles Weidman
**Cast:** Marilyn Miller, Clifton Webb, Helen Broderick, Ethel Waters, Hal Forde, Jerome Cowan, Harry Stockwell, José Limon, Letitia Ide, Thomas Hamilton, Leslie Adams
**Songs:** "How's Chances?"; "Heat Wave"; "Lonely Heart"; "Easter Parade"; "Supper Time"; "Harlem on My Mind"; "Not for All the Rice in China"
**New York run:** Music Box, September 30, 1933; 400 p.

Though it was a revue, the Irving Berlin-Moss Hart *As Thousands Cheer* was considered a successor to the Berlin-Hart book musical, *Face the Music,* since it also dealt satirically with topics of current interest. In fact, it was so concerned with topicality that the entire show was structured in the form of a newspaper, with various stories and features — each one preceded by a blowup of a headline — depicted in songs, dances and sketches. In addition to general news, there were sections devoted to comics, rotogravure (an opportunity to show the Easter Parade of half a century earlier), society, theatre, the weather report ("Heat Wave"), and advice to the lovelorn ("Lonely Heart"). As might be expected in a lighthearted entertainment, serious topics were avoided except for Ethel Waters' purposely jarring "Supper Time," introduced by the headline "UNKNOWN NEGRO LYNCHED BY FRENZIED MOB." Newsworthy individuals impersonated in the noteworthy show were Barbara Hutton and Joan Crawford (by Marilyn Miller in her 12th and final Broadway appearance); Douglas Fairbanks Jr., John D. Rockefeller, and Mahatma Gandhi (by Clifton Webb); Louise Hoover, Aimee Semple MacPherson, Queen Mary, and the Statue of Liberty (by Helen Broderick); and Josephine Baker (by Miss Waters).

**As Thousands Cheer.** King George V (Leslie Adams) and Queen Mary (Helen Broderick) are upset to read of the latest romantic escapade involving the Prince of Wales (Thomas Hamilton). (Vandamm)

# ROBERTA

**Music:** Jerome Kern
**Lyrics & book:** Otto Harbach
**Producer:** Max Gordon
**Director:** (Hassard Short uncredited)
**Choreographer:** José Limon (John Lonergan uncredited)
**Cast:** Lyda Roberti, Bob Hope, Fay Templeton, Tamara, George Murphy, Sydney Greenstreet, Ray Middleton, Fred MacMurray
**Songs:** "Let's Begin"; "You're Devastating"; "Yesterdays"; "The Touch of Your Hand"; "I'll Be Hard to Handle" (lyric: Bernard Dougall); "Smoke Gets in Your Eyes"; "Something Had to Happen"
**New York run:** New Amsterdam Theatre, November 18, 1933; 295 p.

Based on Alice Duer Miller's popular novel, *Gowns by Roberta* (the original title was still used during the tryout), the production was expected to follow *The Cat and the Fiddle* and *Music in the Air* as another of Jerome Kern's well-integrated modern operettas set in present-day Europe. The work, however, turned out to be more of a formula musical comedy dependent upon sumptuously mounted production numbers (one was a fashion show), some comic interpolations, and a superior collection of songs — including "Smoke Gets in Your Eyes" and "Yesterdays" — that bore little relevance to the plot. Said plot had to do with a former All-American fullback, John Kent (Ray Middleton), who inherits a Paris dress salon owned by his Aunt Minnie (Fay Templeton). John also ends with Minnie's assistant, Russian Princess Stephanie (Tamara), as both business and marital partner. Bob Hope, in his first major Broadway role, played John's bandleader chum, Huckleberry Haines. Though *Roberta* was initially directed by Kern himself, the composer was replaced by the more experienced Hassard Short who refused program credit. In 1935, the first of two screen versions co-starred Irene Dunne, Fred Astaire, and Ginger Rogers. Columbia SC/ TW.

**Roberta.** Bob Hope catches Lyda Roberti and Ray Middleton in an embarrassing situation. (Vandamm)

**Ziegfeld Follies.** Willie Howard and Fanny Brice in the sketch based on *Sailor, Beware!*

# ZIEGFELD FOLLIES
**Music:** Vernon Duke, etc.
**Lyrics:** E. Y. Harburg, etc.
**Sketches:** Miscellaneous writers
**Producer:** Billie Burke Ziegfeld (Messrs. Shubert uncredited)
**Directors:** Bobby Connolly, Edward Clark Lilley, John Murray Anderson
**Choreographers:** Bobby Connolly, Robert Alton
**Cast:**   Fanny Brice, Willie & Eugene Howard, Everett Marshall, Jane Froman, Vilma & Buddy Ebsen, Patricia Bowman, Cherry & June Preisser, Eve Arden, Robert Cummings, Ina Ray Hutton
**Songs:** "I Like the Likes of You"; "Suddenly"; "What Is There to Say?"; "The Last Round-Up" (Billy Hill); "Wagon Wheels" (Peter DeRose-Hill)
**New York run:** Winter Garden, January 4, 1934; 182 p.

In the mid-Thirties the Shubert brothers offered five revues at the Winter Garden that won general approval for their high level of comedy, inventive staging, attractive decor, and musical quality. The first of these, the 1934 *Ziegfeld Follies*, had begun its tryout tour so unpromisingly, however, that director John Murray Anderson and choreographer Robert Alton were rushed in to replace Bobby Connolly. They just barely whipped things into shape in time for the Broadway opening. To add authenticity to the show, the nominal sponsor was Ziegfeld's widow, Billie Burke, and the leading comic attracton was *Follies* veteran Fanny Brice. Miss Brice did takeoffs on evangelist Aimee Semple MacPherson and strip-tease dancers, impersonated a bratty child known as Baby Snooks, and appeared with another great clown, Willie Howard, in a frantic burlesque of the play *Sailor, Beware!* The durable "I Like the Likes of You" was sung in the show by Robert Cummings and danced to by Vilma and Buddy Ebsen.

# NEW FACES

**Music, lyrics & sketches:** Miscellaneous writers
**Producer:** Charles Dillingham (Leonard Sillman uncredited)
**Director-choreographer:** Leonard Sillman
**Cast:** Leonard Sillman, Imogene Coca, Nancy Hamilton, Charles Walters, Henry Fonda, Teddy Lynch, James Shelton, Billie Heywood
**Songs:** "Lamplight" (James Shelton); "My Last Affair" (Haven Johnson); "The Gutter Song" (Shelton); "You're My Relaxation" (Charles Schwab-Robert Sour)
**New York run:** Fulton Theatre, March 15, 1934; 149 p.

Originally presented in Pasadena as *Low and Behold,* Leonard Sillman's *New Faces* had to give 137 auditions before the needed $15,000 was raised to open at the Fulton Theatre (then on 46th Street west of Broadway). Under the "supervision" of Elsie Janis, Sillman's dewy-eyed, intimate revue served much the same function as *The Garrick Gaieties* by providing a showcase for hitherto undiscovered talent — such as Henry Fonda, future film director Charles Walters, and chief comedienne Imogene Coca (though she had been around since 1925). Audiences particularly enjoyed Miss Coca's impish fan dance while bundled in an oversized polo coat, Nancy Hamilton's sketch in which "The Three Little Pigs" was presented in the manner of three recent dramas, and the song, "Lamplight," sung by its composer James Shelton. *New Faces* marked the 62nd and final Broadway musical credited to producer Charles Dillingham, who had merely lent the prestige of his name to the entertainment and who died five months after the opening. Sillman staged six subsequent editions of the tyro talent show, with the most successful offered in 1952 (see page 154.)

**New Faces.** Imogene Coca in her polo coat.

# LIFE BEGINS AT 8:40

**Music:** Harold Arlen
**Lyrics:** Ira Gershwin & E. Y. Harburg
**Sketches:** Miscellaneous writers
**Producers:** Messrs. Shubert
**Directors:** John Murray Anderson, Philip Loeb
**Choreographers:** Robert Alton, Charles Weidman
**Cast:**   Bert Lahr, Ray Bolger, Luella Gear, Frances Williams, Brian Donlevy, Dixie Dunbar, Earl Oxford
**Songs:** "You're a Builder-Upper"; "Fun to Be Fooled"; "What Can You Say in a Love Song?"; "Let's Take a Walk Around the Block"; "Things"
**New York run:** Winter Garden, August 27, 1934; 237 p.

The second of the Shubert-sponsored Winter Garden revues in the mid-Thirties, *Life Begins at 8:40* had something of the style of *The Band Wagon* and the topicality of *As Thousands Cheer*. With John Murray Anderson in overall charge, it was also the successor to the Anderson-directed *Ziegfeld Follies* that had opened the same year. (The show's title, which recalled Walter Pitkin's bestseller, *Life Begins at Forty*, referred to the time the curtain went up.) Again the accent was on comedy, with Bert Lahr winning praise for his newly acquired satirical skill, as revealed in his characterizations of a suicidally bent Frenchman, a stiff-upper-lip Englishman, and a pompous concert baritone sputtering about "the utter utter utter loveliness of things." Also well received were Ray Bolger's dance interpretation of the recent Max Baer-Primo Carnera championship fight and Luella Gear's takeoff on the peripatetic Eleanor Roosevelt breathlessly enumerating her day's activities.

# THE GREAT WALTZ

**Music:** Johann Strauss Jr.
**Lyrics:** Desmond Carter
**Book:** Moss Hart
**Producer:** Max Gordon
**Director:** Hassard Short
**Choreographer:** Albertina Rasch
**Cast:**   Marion Claire, Marie Burke, Guy Robertson, H. Reeves-Smith, Ernest Cossart, Alexandra Danilova
**Songs:** "You Are My Song"; "Love Will Find You"; "Like a Star in the Sky"; "With All My Heart"; "While You Love Me"; "Danube So Blue"
**New York run:** Center Theatre, September 22, 1934; 298 p.

One of the truly mammoth undertakings of the mid-Thirties, *The Great Waltz* opened at the 3,822-seat Center Theatre (then in Rockefeller Center one block south of the Radio City Music Hall) with 23 actors, 77 singers, 33 ballet dancers, 53 musicians, 90 backstage workers, and a wardrobe of over 500 costumes. The production cost, among the highest of any show to date, was $246,000. Based on an English version of a Viennese musical called *Waltzes from Vienna*, the operetta deals with the rivalry between Johann Strauss Sr. and Johann Strauss Jr., played by H. Reeves-Smith and Guy Robertson. After jealously thwarting his son's advancement, the old Waltz King — in the show's spectacular climax at Dommayer's Gardens — reluctantly abdicates his title when the younger man takes over the baton to conduct "The Blue Danube" (here titled "Danube So Blue"). Though critics were divided, *The Great Waltz* had a respectable run (at a $3.30 top), and reopened for an additional 49 performances in August 1935. AEI SC/ Capitol Los Angeles OC (1965)/ TW.

# ANYTHING GOES

**Music & lyrics:** Cole Porter
**Book:** Guy Bolton & P. G. Wodehouse, Howard Lindsay & Russel Crouse
**Producer:** Vinton Freedley
**Director:** Howard Lindsay
**Choreographer:** Robert Alton
**Cast:** William Gaxton, Ethel Merman, Victor Moore, Bettina Hall, Vera Dunn, Leslie Barrie, Vivian Vance, Helen Raymond, George E. Mack, Houston Richards
**Songs:** "I Get a Kick Out of You"; "There'll Always Be a Lady Fair"; "All Through the Night"; "You're the Top"; "Anything Goes"; "Blow, Gabriel, Blow"; "Be Like the Bluebird"; "The Gypsy in Me"
**New York run:** Alvin Theatre, November 21, 1934; 420 p.

Following the debacle of a musical comedy called *Pardon My English* early in 1933, producer Vinton Freedley had to flee the country to avoid creditors. To help clear his mind and regain his health, Freedley spent most of his time in a fishing boat off the Pearl Islands in the Gulf of Panama. While fishing he envisaged the perfect musical comedy with which he would launch his comeback: William Gaxton, Victor Moore, and Ethel Merman would play the leading roles, the score would be written by Cole Porter, and the libretto would be by the veteran team of Guy Bolton and P. G. Wodehouse who would tie everything together in a fun-filled story about a group of oddball characters on an ocean liner that is facing a possible shipwreck.

Once he returned to New York and paid off his debts, the producer rounded up his people for what was originally called *Bon Voyage*, then *Hard to Get*. With rehearsals about to begin, disaster struck when the *S.S. Morro Castle* went down in flames off the New Jersey coast with a loss of over 125 lives. Obviously, the script had to be changed. Since Bolton and Wodehouse were then in Europe, Freedley, in desperation, turned to his director, Howard Lindsay, who agreed to undertake the rewriting with a press agent and part-time librettist named Russel Crouse (thereby launching the celebrated team that would be responsible for a total of seven musical-comedy librettos and eight plays).

Though still taking place on shipboard, the new story eliminated the shipwreck but retained the leading characters of the original plot: nightclub singer Reno Sweeney (Merman), her chum Billy Crocker (Gaxton) who stows away to be near Hope Harcourt (Bettina Hall), the debutante he loves, and Moon-Face Mooney (Moore), Public Enemy No. 13, who masquerades as a clergyman to avoid the long arm of the FBI. It may have been created out of tragedy, but *Anything Goes* (the title was chosen to indicate the desperation with which the show was put together) turned out to be the fourth longest running musical of the Thirties as well as one of the decade's most durable attractions. Porter's score, considered his best to date, included three Merman trademarks — "I Get a Kick Out of You," "You're the Top" (a duet with Gaxton), and "Blow, Gabriel, Blow." During the Broadway run, Miss Merman was succeeded by Benay Venuta.

*Anything Goes* was revived Off Broadway in 1962 with Hal Linden, Eileen Rodgers, and Mickey Deems, and a number of Porter interpolations. It ran 239 performances. In 1987, it was given a new production at Lincoln Center's Vivian Beaumont Theatre, which had the longest run of all. during the engagement, Patti luPone was succeeded by Leslie Uggams, Howard McGillin by Gregg Edelman. (See page 277.) The 1936 film version offered Ethel Merman plus Bing Crosby and Charlie Ruggles; the 1956 film of the same name, also with Crosby, had nothing in common with the original except for five songs.
Smithsonian part OC; Epic OC (1962)/ TW.

**Anything Goes.** Ethel Merman leading the chorus in "Blow, Gabriel, Blow." (Vandamm)

# AT HOME ABROAD
**Music:** Arthur Schwartz
**Lyrics:** Howard Dietz
**Sketches:** Miscellaneous writers
**Producers:** Messrs. Shubert
**Directors:** Vincente Minnelli, Thomas Mitchell
**Choreographers:** Gene Snyder, Harry Losee
**Cast:** Beatrice Lillie, Ethel Waters, Herb Williams, Eleanor Powell, Paul Haakon, Reginald Gardiner, Eddie Foy Jr., Vera Allen, John Payne
**Songs:** "Hottentot Potentate"; "Paree"; "Thief in the Night"; "Love Is a Dancing Thing"; "Loadin' Time"; "What a Wonderful World"; "Get Yourself a Geisha"; "Got a Bran' New Suit"
**New York run:** Winter Garden, September 19, 1935; 198 p.

Structured in the form of an around-the-world cruise — though carefully avoiding such countries as Germany, Italy, and Russia — *At Home Abroad* provided theatregoers with the chance to be abroad at home as they savored the pleasures of a variety of comic and colorful locales. These included a London department store for Beatrice Lillie's classic tongue-twisting sketch about ordering two dozen double damask dinner napkins; an African jungle where Ethel Waters proclaims herself the "Hottentot Potentate"; the Moulin Rouge in Paris to offer Miss Lillie's paean to the wonders of the city; a Balkan country where Eleanor Powell taps out spy messages; a West Indies dockside for Miss Waters' throbbing description "Loadin' Time"; and a Japanese garden where Miss Lillie joins a bevy of Nipponese maidens in extolling the advantages of getting one's self a geisha. The third Shubert-sponsored Winter Garden revue of the mid-Thirties, *At Home Abroad* marked the first complete stage production directed by Vincente Minnelli. In 1948, Arthur Schwartz and Howard Dietz conducted a more limited revue tour, *Inside U.S.A.*, which also starred Beatrice Lillie. Smithsonian OC.

**Porgy and Bess.** Ruby Elzy and J. Rosamond Johnson in the saucer burial scene. Anne Brown and Todd Duncan are to their left. (Vandamm)

**Porgy and Bess.** The setting of Catfish Row, designed by Sergei Soudeikine. (Vandamm)

# PORGY AND BESS

**Music:** George Gershwin
**Lyrics:** DuBose Heyward, Ira Gershwin
**Book:** DuBose Heyward
**Producer:** Theatre Guild
**Director:** Rouben Mamoulian
**Cast:** Todd Duncan, Anne Brown, Warren Coleman, John W. Bubbles, Abbie Mitchell, Ruby Elzy, Georgette Harvey, Edward Matthews, Helen Dowdy, J. Rosamond Johnson
**Songs:** "Summertime" (Heyward); "A Woman Is a Sometime Thing" (Heyward); "My Man's Gone Now" (Heyward); "I Got Plenty o' Nuttin'" (Heyward, Gershwin); "Bess, You Is My Woman Now" (Heyward, Gershwin); "It Ain't Necessarily So" (Gershwin); "I Loves You, Porgy" (Heyward, Gershwin); "There's a Boat Dat's Leavin' Soon for New York" (Gershwin); "I'm on My Way" (Heyward)
**New York run:** Alvin Theatre, October 10, 1935; 124 p.

Universally accepted as the most popular opera written by an American composer, *Porgy and Bess* began life in 1925 as the novel *Porgy* by DuBose Heyward. Heyward's setting of Catfish Row in Charleston, South Carolina, and his dramatic story of the crippled beggar Porgy, the seductive Bess, the menacing Crown, and the slinky cocaine dealer Sportin' Life fired George Gershwin's imagination even before Heyward and his wife, Dorothy, adapted the book into a play two years later. After a number of delays, Gershwin began writing the opera late in 1933 with Heyward as librettist-lyricist and brother Ira Gershwin as co-lyricist. The composer's last Broadway score, the work was completed — including Gershwin's own orchestrations — in 20 months.

The initial production, with Todd Duncan and Anne Brown in the leads, was treated as such a major event that the larger dailies dispatched both their drama and music critics to cover the opening. It was not, however, a commercial success, though many of the solos and duets — "Summertime," "Bess, You Is My Woman Now," "I Got Plenty o' Nuttin'," "It Ain't Necessarily So" — soon caught on. Four revivals of *Porgy and Bess* have had extended Broadway runs. In 1942, again with Todd Duncan and Anne Brown but with Avon Long replacing John W. Bubbles as Sportin' Life, the musical ran successfully for 286 performances (at a $2.75 top ticket price) in a somewhat streamlined version with a smaller orchestra and no recitative. It was produced by Cheryl Crawford and directed by Robert Ross. The production then toured for 17 months, including a two-month return visit to New York. Ten years later, one of the most ambitious projects in theatre history was inaugurated with a four-year international tour directed by co-producer Robert Breen. Still more musical drama than opera, *Porgy and Bess* was performed in 23 cities in the United States and Canada, and — under the auspices of the State Department — in 28 countries throughout Europe (including well-publicized engagements in Leningrad and Moscow), the Middle East and Latin America. This company's 1953 stay in New York had the longest run the work has had to date. (See page 156.)

A mounting in 1976 by the Houston Grand Opera was staged at the Uris (now the Gershwin) Theatre on 51st Street west of Broadway. With an acclaimed performance by Clamma Dale as Bess and all the original musical portions restored, the production came closest to the composer's concept of the work as an opera. It was also the basis for the 1983 revival, the first adult, full-scale dramatic work ever staged at the 6,000-seat Radio City Music Hall. Two years later, on its 50th anniversary, *Porgy and Bess* entered the repertory of the Metropolitan Opera. In 1959, a screen adaptation was released with Sidney Poitier, Dorothy Dandridge, and Sammy Davis Jr.

MCA OC (1942); Columbia SC; RCA OC (1953); RCA OC (1976)/ Chilton (1973)/ TW.

# JUBILEE

**Music & lyrics:** Cole Porter
**Book:** Moss Hart
**Producers:** Sam H. Harris & Max Gordon
**Directors:** Hassard Short, Monty Woolley
**Choreographer:** Albertina Rasch
**Cast:** Mary Boland, June Knight, Melville Cooper, Charles Walters, Derek Williams, Mark Plant, Montgomery Clift, May Boley, Margaret Adams
**Songs:** "Why Shouldn't I?"; "Begin the Beguine"; "A Picture of Me Without You"; "Me and Marie"; "Just One of Those Things"
**New York run:** Imperial Theatre, October 12, 1935; 169 p.

Seeking suitable inspiration for an elegant song-and-dance entertainment, Cole Porter and Moss Hart took off on a four-and-a-half month, 34,000-mile cruise around the world. Their hegira resulted in an airy concoction sparked by the recent Silver Jubilee of Britain's King George V and Queen Mary. The tale concerns itself with what might happen if members of a mythical royal family — thanks to a supposed uprising — were given the chance to do what they wanted while gadding about town incognito. King Melville Cooper spends his time perfecting sleight-of-hand tricks, Queen Mary Boland is thrilled to meet Mowgli the movie ape man, Prince Charles Walters learns how to begin the beguine from dancer June Knight, and Princess Margaret Adams answers her own question in "Why Shouldn't I?" by having just one of those crazy flings with a Noel Coward-type playwright. Then it's back to the pomp and circumstance of the royal jubilee. Though beloved by her theatre-going subjects, Miss Boland had to return to Hollywood after only four months; her successor Laura Hope Crews couldn't keep the celebration going a month.

**Jubilee.** Mary Boland and Melville Cooper singing "Me and Marie." (Vandamm)

# JUMBO

**Music:** Richard Rodgers
**Lyrics:** Lorenz Hart
**Book:** Ben Hecht & Charles MacArthur
**Producer:** Billy Rose
**Directors:** John Murray Anderson, George Abbott
**Choreographer:** Allan K. Foster
**Cast:** Jimmy Durante, Paul Whiteman Orchestra, Donald Novis, Gloria Grafton, A. P. Kaye, A. Robins, Poodles Hanneford, Big Rosie, Tilda Getze
**Songs:** "Over and Over Again"; "The Circus Is on Parade"; "The Most Beautiful Girl in the World"; "My Romance"; "Little Girl Blue"
**New York run:** Hippodrome, November 16, 1935; 233 p.

The Hippodrome, once located on 43rd Street and 6th Avenue, was a huge barn of a theatre that had not been in use for five years when showman Billy Rose decided that it would be just the place to house the spectacular circus musical he named *Jumbo*. Designer Albert Johnson completely rebuilt the auditorium to make it resemble an actual circus, with a grandstand sloping up from a single circular revolving stage. The show marked the first of 34 musicals directed by George Abbott as well as the return to Broadway of Rodgers and Hart after almost three years in Hollywood. Plotted by Ben Hecht and Charles MacArthur to give plenty of opportunity for the specialty acts recruited from all over the world, the book had to do with a debt-ridden circus and what the well-meaning but inept publicity man Claudius B. Bowers (Jimmy Durante) does to help save the day. *Jumbo* cost an unprecedented $340,000 to open; it closed after rehearsing for six months and playing for five. The evening's highlight: the blue-tinted first-act finale, "Little Girl Blue," in which heroine Gloria Grafton (who had replaced Ella Logan before the premiere) dreams she is a child again being entertained by her favorite circus performers. Durante was also in the 1962 screen version, along with Doris Day and Martha Raye.

# ZIEGFELD FOLLIES

**Music:** Vernon Duke
**Lyrics:** Ira Gershwin
**Sketches:** David Freedman
**Producer:** Billie Burke Ziegfeld (Messrs. Shubert uncredited)
**Directors:** John Murray Anderson, Edward Clark Lilley
**Choreographers:** Robert Alton, George Balanchine
**Cast:** Fanny Brice, Bob Hope, Gertrude Niesen, Josephine Baker, Hugh O'Connell, Harriet Hoctor, Eve Arden, Judy Canova, Cherry & June Preisser, Nicholas Brothers, John Hoysradt, Stan Kavanaugh
**Songs:** "Island in the West Indies"; "Words Without Music"; "That Moment of Moments"; "I Can't Get Started"
**New York run:** Winter Garden, January 30, 1936; 115 p.

Fanny Brice returned for her second Shubert-sponsored *Ziegfeld Follies* (it was her 15th and final Broadway show), along with a number of holdovers from the 1934 edition. They were joined by ballet choreographer George Balanchine making his Broadway debut. The revue was deemed superior to its predecessor, with Miss Brice up to her old shtick kidding modern dancing and playing Baby Snooks, and Bob Hope getting the chance to butter up Eve Arden in the classic "I Can't Get Started." Another highlight was the first-act finale spoofing the latest Hollywood extravaganza, "The Broadway Gold Melody Diggers of 42nd Street." The *Follies* reopened in the fall for 112 additional performances with Jane Pickens, Gypsy Rose Lee, and Cass Daley joining the cast.

# ON YOUR TOES

**Music:** Richard Rodgers
**Lyrics:** Lorenz Hart
**Book:** Richard Rodgers, Lorenz Hart & George Abbott
**Producer:** Dwight Deere Wiman
**Director:** Worthington Miner (George Abbott uncredited)
**Choreographer:** George Balanchine
**Cast:** Ray Bolger, Luella Gear, Tamara Geva, Monty Woolley, Doris Carson, David Morris, Demetrios Vilan, George Church
**Songs:** "The Three B's"; "It's Got to Be Love"; "Too Good for the Average Man"; "There's a Small Hotel"; "The Heart Is Quicker Than the Eye"; "Quiet Night"; "Glad to Be Unhappy"; "On Your Toes"; "Slaughter on Tenth Avenue" (ballet)
**New York run:** Imperial Theatre, April 11, 1936; 315 p.

*On Your Toes* made a star of rubberlegged dancer Ray Bolger, and it also gave George Balanchine his first opportunity to create dances for a book musical. Most important, it signaled a major breakthrough in form by utilizing ballet as an integral part of the story. Junior Dolan (Bolger), an ex-vaudevillian now teaching music at Knickerbocker University, a WPA extension in New York, enlists the help of patroness Peggy Porterfield (Luella Gear) to persuade Sergei Alexandrovich (Monty Woolley), the director of the Russian Ballet, to stage a friend's jazzy "Slaughter on Tenth Avenue" ballet. While he may dream of sharing the pleasures of a small hotel with girlfriend Frankie Frayne (Doris Carson), Junior becomes involved with the company's prima ballerina, Vera Barnova (Tamara Geva), and even takes over the male lead in "Slaughter." This so enrages Vera's lover and regular dancing partner that he hires two thugs to kill Junior while he is performing on stage. To avoid being a target Junior keeps dancing even after the ballet is over, then — once the gunmen have been arrested — falls exhausted to the floor.

Richard Rodgers and Lorenz Hart had originally written the musical as a movie vehicle for Fred Astaire, but the dancer turned it down because he was afraid his public would not accept him without his trademark attire of top hat, white tie and tails. The team then rewrote the script as a stage musical and Lee Shubert took an option on it with Ray Bolger set for the male lead. When Shubert lost interest, the rights were picked up by Dwight Deere Wiman (it was the first of five Rodgers and Hart shows he would produce), with George Abbott joining the project as co-author and director. Production delays, however, prompted Abbott to withdraw as director, though he did return to restage the musical after its poorly-received Boston opening. Originally, Marilyn Miller and Gregory Ratoff were sought for the roles that went to Miss Geva and Mr. Woolley.

There have been two revivals of *On Your Toes* on Broadway. In 1954, Abbott and Balanchine put together a production starring Bobby Van, Vera Zorina (she had appeared in the role of the ballerina in London and in the movie version), and Elaine Stritch (who played Peggy and sang the interpolated "You Took Advantage of Me"). The general verdict was that the musical was hopelessly dated and it remained only two months. Twenty-nine years later, however, again staged by Abbott, it succeeded so well that it bested the original Broadway run. Natalia Makarova of the American Ballet Theatre made an impressive Main Stem debut in the show. She was replaced during the engagement by ballerinas Galina Panova and Valentina Kozlova, and Dina Merrill was replaced by Kitty Carlisle. (See page 264.) The 1939 movie, with Eddie Albert as Junior, used music only as background and for the ballets.

Columbia SC; MCA OC (1954); Polydor OC (1983)/ R&H.

**On Your Toes.** Luella Gear, Monty Woolley, Ray Bolger, and Demetrios Vilan. (White)

**On Your Toes.** Ray Bolger, George Church, and Tamara Geva in a dramatic moment from "Slaughter on Tenth Avenue." (White)

**Red, Hot and Blue!** Ethel Merman and Bob Hope. (Vandamm)

# RED, HOT AND BLUE!
**Music & lyrics:** Cole Porter
**Book:** Howard Lindsay & Russel Crouse
**Producer:** Vinton Freedley
**Director:** Howard Lindsay
**Choreographer:** George Hale
**Cast:** Jimmy Durante, Ethel Merman, Bob Hope, Polly Walters, Paul & Grace Hartman, Vivian Vance, Lew Parker
**Songs:** "Ours"; "Down in the Depths (on the Ninetieth Floor)"; "You've Got Something"; "It's De-Lovely"; "Ridin' High"; "Red, Hot and Blue"
**New York run:** Alvin Theatre, October 29, 1936; 183 p.

Anxious to repeat the success of *Anything Goes,* producer Vinton Freedley signed its three stars and its three writers for his next musical, *Red, Hot and Blue!* But after overhearing Freedley promise Ethel Merman that hers would be the most prominent role, William Gaxton and Victor Moore bowed out and were replaced by Bob Hope and Jimmy Durante. The show, which seemed to be aiming for *Of Thee I Sing*-type political satire, offered Miss Merman as Nails O'Reilly Duquesne, a manicurist-turned-wealthy widow, Hope as Bob Hale, her lawyer and love interest, and Durante as Policy Pinkle, the captain of the polo team at Larks Nest Prison. Pinkle is released to help win a Congressional committee's approval for Nails and Bob's national lottery in which the first prize goes to the ticket holder who finds a girl who had sat on a hot waffle iron when she was four. The Supreme Court, however, declares the lottery unconstitutional on the grounds that it might benefit the American people. Though no red hot smash, the musical served to introduce three certifiable Cole Porter standards: "It's De-Lovely," "Down in the Depths," and "Ridin' High." It is also remembered for the battle of the billing, which was resolved by crossing the names of Jimmy Durante and Ethel Merman above the show's title.
AEI OC.

Note that Vincente Minnelli's name is misspelled twice.

# THE SHOW IS ON
**Music & lyrics:** Miscellaneous writers
**Sketches:** David Freedman, Moss Hart
**Producers:** Messrs. Shubert
**Directors:** Vincente Minnelli, Edward Clark Lilley
**Choreographer:** Robert Alton, Harry Losee
**Cast:** Beatrice Lillie, Bert Lahr, Reginald Gardiner, Mitzi Mayfair, Paul Haakon, Gracie Barrie, Charles Walters, Vera Allen, Jack McCauley
**Songs:** "Now" (Vernon Duke-Ted Fetter); "Rhythm" (Richard Rodgers- Lorenz Hart); "Song of the Woodman" (Harold Arlen-E. Y. Harburg); "Long as You've Got Your Health" (Will Irwin-Harburg, Norman Zeno); "By Strauss" (George Gershwin-Ira Gershwin); "Little Old Lady" (Hoagy Carmichael-Stanley Adams)
**New York run:** Winter Garden, December 25, 1936; 237 p.

The fifth and final mid-Thirties revue presented by the Shuberts at the Winter Garden was one of the brightest, merriest, and most elegant of the decade's stage attractions. Featuring two superior clowns, Beatrice Lillie and Bert Lahr, *The Show Is On* was something of a successor to *At Home Abroad,* only this time the theme was around the world of show business. In songs, sketches, and production numbers, it looked in on a variety of phenomena and events — from excessively rhythmic pop singers to raffish burlesque shows, from John Gielgud's production of *Hamlet* (which is ruined by the outbursts of Miss Lillie's boorish socialite) to coquettish music-hall entertainers (Miss Lillie perched on a migratory half moon dispensing garters to favored gentlemen), and from he-man concert baritones (Lahr's classic "Song of the Woodman") to an old-fashioned tent show production of *Uncle Tom's Cabin. The Show Is On* returned briefly in the fall of 1937 with Rose King and Willie Howard.

# BABES IN ARMS

**Music:** Richard Rodgers
**Lyrics:** Lorenz Hart
**Book:** Richard Rodgers & Lorenz Hart
**Producer:** Dwight Deere Wiman
**Director:** Robert Sinclair
**Choreographer:** George Balanchine
**Cast:** Mitzi Green, Wynn Murray, Ray Heatherton, Duke McHale, Alfred Drake, Ray McDonald, Grace McDonald, Nicholas Brothers, Dan Dailey
**Songs:** "Where or When"; "Babes in Arms"; "I Wish I Were in Love Again"; "My Funny Valentine"; "Johnny One Note"; "Imagine"; "All at Once"; "The Lady Is a Tramp"; "You Are So Fair"
**New York run:** Shubert Theatre, April 14, 1937; 289 p.

With such songs as "I Wish I Were in Love Again," "Johnny One Note," "The Lady Is a Tramp," "My Funny Valentine," and "Where or When," *Babes in Arms* could claim more hits than any other Rodgers and Hart musical. In the high-spirited, youthful show, a group of teenagers, whose parents are out-of-work vaudevillians, stage a revue to keep from being sent to a work farm. Unfortunately, the show is a bomb. Later, when a transatlantic French flyer lands nearby, they are able to attract enough publicity to put on a successful show and build their own youth center. Because the sets were modest and the cast boasted no stellar names, producer Dwight Deere Wiman priced his tickets at a $3.85 top. Among the show's Broadway debuts were those of Alfred Drake (he sang the title song) and Dan Dailey. The 1939 movie version featured Judy Garland and Mickey Rooney.
Columbia SC/ R&H.

# I'D RATHER BE RIGHT

**Music:** Richard Rodgers
**Lyrics:** Lorenz Hart
**Book:** George S. Kaufman & Moss Hart
**Producer:** Sam H. Harris
**Director:** George S. Kaufman
**Choreographers:** Charles Weidman, Ned McGurn
**Cast:** George M. Cohan, Taylor Holmes, Joy Hodges, Austin Marshall, Marion Green, Mary Jane Walsh
**Songs:** "Have You Met Miss Jones?"; "Sweet Sixty-Five"; "We're Going to Balance the Budget"; "I'd Rather Be Right"; "Off the Record"
**New York run:** Alvin Theatre, November 2, 1937; 290 p.

*I'd Rather Be Right* was the most anxiously awaited theatrical event of the decade for two reasons: the central character was President Franklin D. Roosevelt and the part was being played by the legendary George M. Cohan, who was returning to the musical stage for the first time in ten years in the only song-and-dance show he ever appeared in that he did not write himself. The work, however, was considered not quite up to the satirical standards set by *Of Thee I Sing*, with which it was most frequently compared. The locale is New York's Central Park on the 4th of July. Peggy and Phil (Joy Hodges and Austin Marshall) hope to get married but Phil's boss won't give him a raise until Roosevelt balances the budget. Phil falls asleep and dreams that they meet FDR strolling through the park. After Phil explains the couple's dilemma, Roosevelt promises to help — which is only an excuse for some genial ribbing at the expense of Cabinet members, the Supreme Court, the PWA, fireside chats, Alf Landon, press conferences, and the President's decision to seek a third term.
Random House (1937)/ R&H.

**I'd Rather Be Right.** George M. Cohan as President Franklin D. Roosevelt giving a 4th of July speech. (Vandamm)

# PINS AND NEEDLES

**Music & lyrics:** Harold Rome
**Sketches:** Miscellaneous writers
**Producer:** ILGWU
**Director:** Charles Friedman
**Choreographer:** Gluck Sandor
**Cast:** ILGWU members
**Songs:** "Sing Me a Song With Social Significance"; "Sunday in the Park"; "Nobody Makes a Pass at Me"; "Chain Store Daisy"; "One Big Union for Two"; "Four Little Angels of Peace"; "Doin' the Reactionary"
**New York run:** Labor Stage, November 27, 1937; 1,108 p.

*Pins and Needles* was initially presented for a limited engagement at the tiny Labor Stage (formerly the Princess Theatre) by and for members of the International Ladies Garment Workers Union, but it soon attracted audiences in such droves that it kept on running until it overtook *Irene* as the long-run record holder for musicals. Though reflecting a basically liberal, pro-union slant, the attitude was generally good-humored as it took aim at warmongers, bigots, reactionaries, Nazis, Fascists, Communists, and the DAR — and it even managed a few digs at the labor movement itself. Retitled *New Pins and Needles* in 1939, the show moved to the Windsor Theatre, then on 48th Street east of 7th Avenue, at a top ticket price of $1.65. Among those associated with the revue, songwriter Harold Rome, making his professional debut, was the one most responsible for its special flavor and appeal. In September 1938, Rome joined George S. Kaufman and Moss Hart in creating *Sing Out the News,* a more polished variation on *Pins and Needles,* which proved less successful.
Columbia SC.

# HOORAY FOR WHAT!

**Music:** Harold Arlen
**Lyrics:** E. Y. Harburg
**Book:** Howard Lindsay & Russel Crouse
**Producers:** Messrs. Shubert
**Directors:** Vincente Minnelli, Howard Lindsay
**Choreographers:** Robert Alton, Agnes de Mille
**Cast:** Ed Wynn, Jack Whiting, Paul Haakon, June Clyde, Vivian Vance, Ruthanna Boris, Hugh Martin, Ralph Blane, Meg Mundy
**Songs:** "God's Country"; "I've Gone Romantic on You"; "Moanin' in the Mornin' "; "Down With Love"; "In the Shade of the New Apple Tree"
**New York run:** Winter Garden, December 1, 1937; 200 p.

Although it starred the clownish Ed Wynn, and even made room for his vaudeville specialties, *Hooray for What!* was primarily concerned with such weighty and timely matters as poison gas, munitions, diplomatic duplicity, espionage, and actual warfare. In the outlandish, satirical plot, Chuckles, a horticulturist, invents a gas to kill worms but then discovers that it can also kill humans. The invention sets off an arms race among the European powers who meet at a so-called Peace Conference in Geneva, where spies try to steal the formula from Chuckles' room at the Hotel de l'Espionage. When, using a mirror, a seductive spy copies the formula backwards, the gas turns out to be harmless and war is miraculously averted. *Hooray for What!* marked Agnes de Mille's first efforts as a Broadway choreographer, though most of her work was cut by the time the show reached New York.

# THE CRADLE WILL ROCK

**Music, lyrics & book:** Marc Blitzstein
**Producer:** Sam H. Grisman
**Director:** Orson Welles
**Cast:** Howard DaSilva, Will Geer, Hiram Sherman, Olive Stanton, John Hoysradt, Marc Blitzstein
**Songs:** "The Freedom of the Press"; "Honolulu"; "Art for Art's Sake"; "Nickel Under the Foot"; "The Cradle Will Rock"; "Joe Worker"
**New York run:** Windsor Theatre, January 3, 1938; 108 p.

One of the most controversial stage productions of the decade, Marc Blitzstein's *The Cradle Will Rock* was initially a project of the WPA's Federal Theatre, with John Houseman as producer and Orson Welles as director. A grim parable dealing with the struggle for union recognition in a steel town, the work was scheduled to open June 16, 1937, at the Maxine Elliott Theatre, with a ticket scale of 25¢, 40¢, and 55¢. Because of political pressure, the Federal Theatre cancelled the production at the last minute, but Welles was determined to put on the show anywhere and anyway he could. That same night, he managed to secure the Venice Theatre (once known as Jolson's 59th Street Theatre), where the actors — who were forbidden from appearing on any stage by their own union — performed from their seats in various parts of the theatre, while Blitzstein provided piano accompaniment. The musical gave 19 performances in this fashion.

When producer Sam Grisman offered *The Cradle Will Rock* at his Windsor Theatre, the cast did perform on stage, though there was no scenery and the music was still played by the composer at the piano. The story of this "Play in Music" is little more than an animated left-wing political cartoon. In Steeltown, USA, the noble union organizer Larry Foreman (Howard DaSilva) does battle against the powerful and corrupt Mr. Mister (Will Geer), who owns everything and everyone in town, and eventually leads the workers to victory. In addition to the labor-management struggle, Blitzstein also turned his attention to the issue of prostitution, contrasting the character of a wistful street walker with the venality of journalists, artists, educators, religious leaders, and doctors. *The Cradle Will Rock* had brief revivals in 1947 with Alfred Drake as Larry Foreman, in 1964 with Jerry Orbach, and in 1983 (in a John Houseman production) with Randle Mell. American Legacy OC; Composer OC (1964)/ Random House (1938)/ TW.

**The Cradle Will Rock.** Marc Blitzstein at the piano.

**I Married an Angel.** Vera Zorina and Dennis King.

# I MARRIED AN ANGEL
**Music:** Richard Rodgers
**Lyrics:** Lorenz Hart
**Book:** Richard Rodgers & Lorenz Hart
**Producer:** Dwight Deere Wiman
**Director:** Joshua Logan
**Choreographer:** George Balanchine
**Cast:** Dennis King, Vera Zorina, Vivienne Segal, Walter Slezak, Audrey Christie, Charles Walters
**Songs:** "Did You Ever Get Stung?"; "I Married an Angel"; "I'll Tell the Man in the Street"; "How to Win Friends and Influence People"; "Spring Is Here"; "A Twinkle in Your Eye"; "At the Roxy Music Hall"
**New York run:** Shubert Theatre, May 11, 1938; 338 p.

"Musical comedy has met its masters, and they have reared back and passed a 44th Street miracle," wrote Brooks Atkinson in the *Times* following the opening of *I Married an Angel.* That miracle had to do not only with the pleasures of the entertainment but also with the audience's total acceptance that the disillusioned hero's vow to marry only an angel actually comes true. The setting of this fantasy is Budapest where banker Willy Palaffi (Dennis King) finds that his celestial bride (Vera Zorina) causes all kinds of embarrassing problems with her heavenly honesty. Willy's sharp-tongued sister Peggy (Vivienne Segal) manages to save the marriage by dispensing such worldly advice to the angel as the proper use of a twinkle in her eye. The show's show stopper, unrelated to the proceedings or the locale, was the witty travesty of a typical Radio City Music Hall presentation. *I Married an Angel* was adapted by Rodgers and Hart from a Hungarian play on which they had previously based an unused movie script. The musical, the first of 14 staged by Joshua Logan, also marked the occasion of Zorina's Broadway debut. Jeanette MacDonald and Nelson Eddy were in the 1942 film.
AEI part OC/ R&H.

# HELLZAPOPPIN

**Music:** Sammy Fain, etc.
**Lyrics:** Charles Tobias, etc.
**Sketches:** Ole Olsen & Chic Johnson
**Producers:** Ole Olsen & Chic Johnson (Messrs. Shubert uncredited)
**Director:** Edward Duryea Dowling
**Cast:**  Ole Olsen & Chic Johnson, Barto & Mann, Radio Rogues, Hal Sherman, Ray Kinney
**Songs:** "Fuddle Dee Duddle"; "Abe Lincoln" (Earl Robinson-Alfred Hayes); "It's Time to Say Aloha"; "Boomps-a-Daisy" (Annette Mills)
**New York run:** 46th Street Theatre, September 22, 1938; 1,404 p.

It was more of a raucous vaudeville show than a revue, it featured no performers whose names could attract Broadway theatregoers, and it received generally unfavorable notices. Yet when this legendary freak success closed up shop it had bested the long-run record for musicals recently established by *Pins and Needles*. *Hellzapoppin* was basically the same rowdy act that Olsen and Johnson had been performing all over the country for 14 years. But customers were attracted to its lowbrow high jinks, especially such audience-participation gimmicks as dancing in the aisles, and such running gags as the one of the little man walking through the audience with a plant for Mrs. Jones that grows and grows and grows. Within two months after its opening the show was transferred to the Winter Garden where it remained for the rest of its engagement. Olsen and Johnson, along with Martha Raye, were in the 1941 screen version.

**Hellzapoppin.** Behind Ole Olsen and Chic Johnson are the Radio Rogues (Sidney Chatton, Jimmy Hollywood, Eddie Bartel). The girls are Sally Bond and Margie Young. (DeMirjian)

**Knickerbocker Holiday.** Walter Huston, Jeanne Madden, and ladies of New Amsterdam. (Lucas)

# KNICKERBOCKER HOLIDAY

**Music:** Kurt Weill
**Lyrics & book:** Maxwell Anderson
**Producer:** Playwrights' Company
**Director:** Joshua Logan
**Choreographers:** Carl Randall, Edwin Denby
**Cast:** Walter Huston, Ray Middleton, Jeanne Madden, Richard Kollmar, Robert Rounseville, Howard Freeman, Clarence Nordstrom
**Songs:** "There's Nowhere to Go but Up"; "It Never Was You"; "How Can You Tell an American?"; "September Song"; "The Scars"
**New York run:** Ethel Barrymore Theatre, October 19, 1938; 168 p.

A victim of Hitler's Germany, Kurt Weill settled in New York to become one of the Broadway theatre's most admired and influential composers. For *Knickerbocker Holiday,* the second of his eight American works, he was joined by playwright Maxwell Anderson to create what was probably the first musical to use an historical subject as the means through which views on contemporary matters could be expressed. Here the theme was totalitarianism versus democracy, as personified by Pieter Stuyvesant (Walter Huston), the autocratic governor of New Amsterdam in 1647, and Brom Broeck (Richard Kollmar), the freedom-loving "first American" who is opposed to any kind of government interference. The point became somewhat muddied when it appeared that Anderson's target was President Roosevelt rather than any of the peace-menacing dictators then in power. There was confusion of a more dramatic kind since Walter Huston, in his only Broadway musical, made Stuyvesant such a likable chap — especially when he sang of the anxieties of growing old in "September Song" — that audience sympathies tended to be with the wrong man. The 1944 screen version featured Nelson Eddy and Charles Coburn.
AEI OC/ Anderson House (1938)/ R&H.

**Leave It to Me!** Mary Martin.
(Vandamm)

# LEAVE IT TO ME!

**Music & lyrics:** Cole Porter
**Book:** Bella & Samuel Spewack
**Producer:** Vinton Freedley
**Director:** Samuel Spewack
**Choreographer:** Robert Alton
**Cast:**    William Gaxton, Victor Moore, Sophie Tucker, Tamara, Mary Martin,
Edward H. Robins, Alexander Asro, George Tobias, Gene Kelly
**Songs:** "Get Out of Town"; "From Now On"; "Most Gentlemen Don't Like
Love"; "My Heart Belongs to Daddy"; "I Want to Go Home"
**New York run:** Imperial Theatre, November 9, 1938; 291 p.

With a book distantly related to their own play, *Clear All Wires,* Bella and Samuel
Spewack came up with a spoof of Communism and U.S. diplomacy that offered
comedian Victor Moore one of his meatiest roles as mild-mannered Alonzo P.
"Stinky" Goodhue. Goodhue is unwillingly named Ambassador to the Soviet
Union because his ambitious wife (Sophie Tucker) has contributed generously to
President Roosevelt's re-election campaign. Aided by foreign correspondent
Buckley Joyce Thomas (William Gaxton), the Ambassador does everything he
can to be recalled, but each blunder only succeeds in making him a bigger hero.
Finally, he introduces a plan to ensure world peace — which, of course, no one
wants — and Stinky is soon happily on his way back to Kansas. Mary Martin
made a notable Broadway debut in *Leave It to Me!,* singing and coyly stripping
to "My Heart Belongs to Daddy" while being stranded on a Siberian railroad station with a male quartet that included Gene Kelly. Two months after the musical
closed it paid a two-week return visit to New York.
Chilton (1976)/ TW.

**The Boys from Syracuse.** Marcy Wescott, Wynn Murray, and Muriel Angelus singing "Sing for Your Supper." (Vandamm)

**The Boys from Syracuse.** Betty Bruce, Teddy Hart, and Eddie Albert. (Vandamm)

# THE BOYS FROM SYRACUSE

**Music:** Richard Rodgers
**Lyrics:** Lorenz Hart
**Book:** George Abbott
**Producer-director:** George Abbott
**Choreographer:** George Balanchine
**Cast:** Jimmy Savo, Teddy Hart, Eddie Albert, Wynn Murray, Ronald Graham, Muriel Angelus, Marcy Wescott, Betty Bruce, Burl Ives
**Songs:** "Falling in Love With Love"; "The Shortest Day of the Year"; "This Can't Be Love"; "He and She"; "You Have Cast Your Shadow on the Sea"; "Sing for Your Supper"; "What Can You Do With a Man?"
**New York run:** Alvin Theatre, November 23, 1938; 235 p.

The genesis of *The Boys from Syracuse* began when Rodgers and Hart, while working on another show, were discussing the fact that no one had yet written a Broadway musical based on a play by Shakespeare. Their obvious choice was *The Comedy of Errors* (whose plot Shakespeare had borrowed from Plautus' *Menaechmi*), partly because Hart's brother, Teddy Hart, was always being confused with another comic actor, Jimmy Savo. The action takes place in Ephesus in ancient Asia Minor, and the mildly ribald tale concerns the efforts of two boys from Syracuse, Antipholus and his servant Dromio (Eddie Albert and Jimmy Savo), to find their long-lost twins who — for reasons of plot confusion — are also named Antipholus and Dromio (Ronald Graham and Teddy Hart). Complications arise when the wives of the Ephesians, Adriana (Muriel Angelus) and her servant Luce (Wynn Murray), mistake the two strangers for their husbands, though the couples eventually get sorted out after Adriana's sister Luciana (Marcy Wescott) and the Syracuse Antipholus admit their love while protesting "This Can't Be Love." In 1963, an Off-Broadway revival had a longer run than the original. Allan Jones, Joe Penner, and Martha Raye were in the 1940 film.

In 1981, *Oh, Brother!,* a second musical adaptation of the same basic tale, had a brief stay on Broadway. Other musicals inspired by Shakespeare have been *Swingin' the Dream* (1939) and *Babes in the Wood* (1964), both from *A Midsummer Night's Dream; Kiss Me, Kate* (1948), from *The Taming of the Shrew; West Side Story* (1957) and *Sensations* (1970), both from *Romeo and Juliet; Love and Let Love* (1968), *Your Own Thing* (1968), and *Music Is* (1976), all from *Twelfth Night; Two Gentlemen of Verona* (1971); and *Rockabye Hamlet* (1976). Columbia SC; Capitol OC (1963)/ R&H.

**Too Many Girls.** Eddie Bracken and Hal LeRoy help and inebriated Desi Arnaz confront Marcy Wescott. (Vandamm)

# TOO MANY GIRLS

**Music:** Richard Rodgers
**Lyrics:** Lorenz Hart
**Book:** George Marion Jr.
**Producer-director:** George Abbott
**Choreographer:** Robert Alton
**Cast:** Marcy Wescott, Desi Arnaz, Hal LeRoy, Mary Jane Walsh, Diosa Costello, Richard Kollmar, Eddie Bracken, Leila Ernst, Van Johnson
**Songs:** "Love Never Went to College"; "Spic and Spanish"; "I Like to Recognize the Tune"; "I Didn't Know What Time It Was"; "She Could Shake the Maracas"; "Give It Back to the Indians"
**New York run:** Imperial Theatre, October 18, 1939; 249 p.

By 1939 — after such shows as *Leave It to Jane* and *Good News!* — a rah-rah college musical about football may not have been the most original idea along the Main Stem, but blessed with spirited songs by Rodgers and Hart, a youthful, talented cast, and fast-paced direction by George Abbott, *Too Many Girls* won high marks with both critics and public. Set in Pottawatomie College, Stop Gap, New Mexico (described as "one of those colleges that play football on Friday"), the musical featured an All-American backfield composed of Desi Arnaz, Hal LeRoy, Richard Kollmar (succeeded by Van Johnson for the tour), and Eddie Bracken, who also, unknown to her, act as bodyguards for wealthy coed Marcy Wescott. Soon boy students are pairing off with girl students, and Kollmar and Wescott get the chance to voice such sentiments as "Love Never Went to College" and "I Didn't Know What Time It Was." The 1940 movie version with Lucille Ball and Ann Miller also included members of the original cast.
Painted Smiles SC/ R&H.

# DUBARRY WAS A LADY

**Music & lyrics:** Cole Porter
**Book:** Herbert Fields & B. G. DeSylva
**Producer:** B. G. DeSylva
**Director:** Edgar MacGregor
**Choreographer:** Robert Alton
**Cast:**  Bert Lahr, Ethel Merman, Betty Grable, Benny Baker, Ronald Graham, Charles Walters, Kay Sutton
**Songs:** "When Love Beckoned (in Fifty-Second Street)"; "Well, Did You Evah?"; "But in the Morning, No"; "Do I Love You?"; "It Was Written in the Stars"; "Give Him the Oo-la-la"; "Katie Went to Haiti"; "Friendship"
**New York run:** 46th Street Theatre, December 6, 1939; 408 p.

Broadway's fifth longest-running musical of the Thirties, *DuBarry Was a Lady* was the first of three smash hits offered in succession by producer B.G. DeSylva. The show evolved through the merging of two ideas: Herbert Fields wanted to write a musical with Mae West as DuBarry and DeSylva wanted to write one about a washroom attendant in a swanky New York nightclub who is smitten by a Brenda Frazier-type debutante. Both concepts were combined by having the attendant, named Louis Blore, switch his affections to May Daly, the club's flashy singing star, and by having Louis — after taking a mickey finn — dream that he is King Louis XV and the singer his unaccommodating concubine. Ethel Merman and Bert Lahr, who stopped the show nightly with their raucous avowal of eternal friendship, were hailed as Broadway's royal couple, and Betty Grable won such favorable notice that she was soon whisked off to Hollywood stardom. During the Broadway run, Miss Merman was succeeded by Gypsy Rose Lee and Frances Williams. The show's movie version, in 1943, featured Lucille Ball, Gene Kelly, and Red Skelton.
TW.

**DuBarry Was a Lady.** Bert Lahr and Ethel Merman.

**Louisiana Purchase.** William Gaxton, Vera Zorina, Victor Moore, and Irene Bordoni at the Mardi Gras. (Lucas & Monroe)

# LOUISIANA PURCHASE

**Music & lyrics:** Irving Berlin
**Book:** Morrie Ryskind & B. G. DeSylva
**Producer:** B. G. DeSylva (Irving Berlin uncredited)
**Director:** Edgar MacGregor
**Choreographer:** George Balanchine
**Cast:** William Gaxton, Vera Zorina, Victor Moore, Irene Bordoni, Carol Bruce, Nick Long Jr., Hugh Martin, Ralph Blane, Edward H. Robins
**Songs:** "Louisiana Purchase"; "It's a Lovely Day Tomorrow"; "Outside of That I Love You"; "You're Lonely and I'm Lonely"; "Latins Know How"; "What Chance Have I?"; "The Lord Done Fixed Up My Soul"; "Fools Fall in Love"; "You Can't Brush Me Off"
**New York run:** Imperial Theatre, May 28, 1940; 444 p.

After playing a Vice President in *Of Thee I Sing* and *Let 'Em Eat Cake* and an Ambassador in *Leave It to Me!,* Victor Moore endeared himself to audiences again by impersonating a United States Senator in *Louisiana Purchase.* In the libretto, prompted by recent revelations of corruption involving the late political leader Huey Long, the seemingly innocent Senator Oliver P. Loganberry goes to New Orleans to investigate the shady operations of the Louisiana Purchasing Company. Jim Taylor (William Gaxton), the company's president, tries to block the probe by involving the incorruptible Senator first with Marina Van Linden (Vera Zorina), a Viennese refugee, then with Mme. Yvonne Bordelaise (Irene Bordoni), a local restaurateuse. Loganberry manages to get out of the trap by marrying Yvonne, but he is ultimately defeated when, being a politician, he is unwilling to cross the picket line in front of the building in which his hearings are to take place. The second of producer B. G. DeSylva's three hits in a row, *Louisiana Purchase* marked Irving Berlin's return to Broadway after an absence of almost seven years. Moore, Zorina, and Bordoni were joined by Bob Hope for the 1941 movie.

# CABIN IN THE SKY

**Music:** Vernon Duke
**Lyrics:** John Latouche
**Book:** Lynn Root
**Producers:** Albert Lewis & Vinton Freedley
**Directors:** George Balanchine, Albert Lewis
**Choreographer:** George Balanchine
**Cast:** Ethel Waters, Todd Duncan, Dooley Wilson, Katherine Dunham, Rex Ingram, J. Rosamond Johnson
**Songs:** "Taking a Chance on Love" (lyric with Ted Fetter); "Cabin in the Sky"; "Love Turned the Light Out"; "Honey in the Honeycomb"; "My Old Virginia Home (on the River Nile)"; "Do What You Wanna Do"
**New York run:** Martin Beck Theatre, October 25, 1940; 156 p.

The first major musical to play the Martin Beck Theatre (on 45th Street west of 8th Avenue), *Cabin in the Sky* was a parable of Southern Negro life with echoes of Ferenc Molnar's *Liliom* (which would be turned into the musical *Carousel*) and Marc Connelly's *The Green Pastures*. The fantasy deals with the struggle between the Lawd's General (Todd Duncan) and Lucifer Jr. (Rex Ingram) for the soul of shiftless Little Joe Jackson (Dooley Wilson), who has been fatally wounded in a street brawl. Because of the fervent prayers of Joe's devoted wife, Petunia (Ethel Waters), Joe is granted six months to make amends to allow him to get into Heaven. Lucifer Jr. offers temptation in the form of Georgia Brown (Katherine Dunham), but with Petunia's help Joe eventually manages to squeeze through the Pearly Gates. Miss Waters won resounding acclaim in this her only book musical, in which she sang the showstopper, "Taking a Chance on Love." In 1964, Rosetta LeNoire appeared in an adaptation which ran briefly Off Broadway. The 1943 film version gave Miss Waters the chance to repeat her role. Capitol OC (1964).

# PANAMA HATTIE

**Music & lyrics:** Cole Porter
**Book:** Herbert Fields & B. G. DeSylva
**Producer:** B. G. DeSylva
**Director:** Edgar MacGregor
**Choreographer:** Robert Alton
**Cast:** Ethel Merman, Arthur Treacher, James Dunn, Rags Ragland, Pat Harrington, Frank Hyers, Phyllis Brooks, Betty Hutton, Joan Carroll, June Allyson, Lucille Bremer, Vera Ellen, Betsy Blair
**Songs:** "My Mother Would Love You"; "I've Still Got My Health"; "Fresh as a Daisy"; "Let's Be Buddies"; "Make It Another Old-Fashioned, Please"; "I'm Throwing a Ball Tonight"
**New York run:** 46th Street Theatre, October 30, 1940; 501 p.

According to Ethel Merman, Hattie Maloney in *Panama Hattie* was an expansion of the Katie who went to Haiti in *DuBarry Was a Lady*. The show was the first in which Miss Merman received solo star billing and it had the longest run of the five musicals in which she was spotlighted singing the songs of Cole Porter. Ethel's Hattie is a brassy, gold-hearted nightclub owner in Panama City who becomes engaged to divorcé Nick Bullitt (James Dunn), a Philadelphia Main Liner. In order for the couple to marry, however, Hattie must first win the approval of Nick's snotty eight-year-old daughter (Joan Carroll), which she accomplishes through the conciliatory "Let's Be Buddies." *Panama Hattie* was the last of the three-in-a-row hits produced by B. G. DeSylva. In 1942, a movie version co-starred Ann Sothern and Red Skelton. TW.

# PAL JOEY

**Music:** Richard Rodgers
**Lyrics:** Lorenz Hart
**Book:** John O'Hara (George Abbott uncredited)
**Producer-director:** George Abbott
**Choreographer:** Robert Alton
**Cast:** Vivienne Segal, Gene Kelly, June Havoc, Jack Durant, Leila Ernst, Jean Casto, Van Johnson, Stanley Donen, Tilda Getze
**Songs:** "You Mustn't Kick It Around"; "I Could Write a Book"; "That Terrific Rainbow"; "Happy Hunting Horn"; "Bewitched"; "The Flower Garden of My Heart"; "Zip"; "Den of Iniquity"; "Take Him"
**New York run:** Ethel Barrymore Theatre, December 25, 1940; 374 p.

With its heel for a hero, its smoky nightclub ambiance, and its true-to-life, untrue-to-anyone characters, *Pal Joey* was a major breakthrough in bringing about a more adult form of musical theatre. The idea originated with author John O'Hara who suggested to Rodgers and Hart that they collaborate on a musical treatment of O'Hara's series of *New Yorker* short stories about Joey Evans, a small-time Chicago entertainer. In the libretto (written with an uncredited assist from producer-director George Abbott), Joey gets a job at Mike's Club where he is attracted to Linda English (Leila Ernst) but drops her in favor of the rich, bewitched dowager, Vera Simpson (Vivienne Segal). Vera builds a glittering nightclub, the Chez Joey, for her paramour, but she soon tires of him, and at the end — after an encounter with blackmailers Ludlow Lowell (Jack Durant) and Gladys Bumps (June Havoc) — Joey is off in search of other conquests. *Pal Joey* marked the only Broadway musical in which Gene Kelly played a major role.

Though it was well received, the musical had to wait until a 1952 revival to be fully appreciated. Miss Segal repeated her original role and Harold Lang played Joey. During the run Helen Gallagher was succeeded by Nancy Walker as Gladys. (See page 153). In 1976, *Pal Joey* returned to Broadway for two months with Joan Copeland and Christopher Chadman. The 1957 screen version featured Frank Sinatra, Rita Hayworth, and Kim Novak.
CSP part OC (1952); Capitol part OC (1952)/ Random House (1952)/ R&H.

**Pal Joey.** Gene Kelly, June Havoc, and Jack Durant. (Fred Fehl)

# LADY IN THE DARK

**Music:** Kurt Weill
**Lyrics:** Ira Gershwin
**Book:** Moss Hart
**Producer:** Sam H. Harris
**Directors:** Hassard Short, Moss Hart
**Choreographer:** Albertina Rasch
**Cast:**  Gertrude Lawrence, Victor Mature, Danny Kaye, Macdonald Carey, Bert Lytell, Evelyn Wyckoff, Margaret Dale, Ron Field
**Songs:** "One Life to Live"; "Girl of the Moment"; "This Is New"; "The Princess of Pure Delight"; "My Ship"; "Jenny"; "Tschaikowsky"
**New York run:** Alvin Theatre, January 23, 1941; 467 p.

Though he originally conceived it as a vehicle for Katharine Cornell, Moss Hart turned *Lady in the Dark* into a vehicle for Gertrude Lawrence by enlisting the services of Kurt Weill and Ira Gershwin and changing it from a play to a musical. The work is concerned with *Allure* magazine editor Liza Elliott, whose inability to make up her mind has led her to seek psychiatric help. This feeling of insecurity contributes to her doubts about marrying her lover, publisher Kendall Nesbitt (Bert Lytell), and makes her think she is falling in love with movie star Randy Curtis (Victor Mature). In the end, however, she realizes that the man who can cure her neuroses is really Charley Johnson (Macdonald Carey), the magazine's cynical advertising manager. How does she know? Charley can complete the song "My Ship," which Liza had learned as a child but is now unable to finish. ("Ah! Sweet Mystery of Life" had served a similar function in *Naughty Marietta*.) All other musical pieces in *Lady in the Dark* — including the tongue-twisting "Tschaikowsky" for Danny Kaye and the raucous showstopper "Jenny" for Miss Lawrence, both part of the colorful circus scene — are performed within the dreams that Liza reveals to her doctor.

*Lady in the Dark* closed for vacation in June 1941, then reopened in September with Lytell replaced by Paul McGrath, Mature by Willard Parker, Carey by Walter Coy, and Kaye by Eric Brotherson. Following a tour, the musical returned to Broadway in February 1943 and remained for 83 performances. Ginger Rogers and Ray Milland were in the 1944 movie version.

RCA OC; AEI OC; Columbia SC/ Random House (1941)/ R&H.

**Lady in the Dark.** Margaret Dale, Danny Kaye, and Gertrude Lawrence. (Vandamm)

# BEST FOOT FORWARD

**Music & lyrics:** Hugh Martin & Ralph Blane
**Book:** John Cecil Holm
**Producer:** George Abbott (Richard Rodgers uncredited)
**Director:** George Abbott
**Choreographer:** Gene Kelly
**Cast:** Rosemary Lane, Marty May, Gil Stratton Jr., Maureen Cannon, Nancy
Walker, June Allyson, Kenny Bowers, Victoria Schools, Tommy Dix,
Danny Daniels
**Songs:** "The Three B's"; "Buckle Down, Winsocki"; "Just a Little Joint With a
Jukebox"; "What Do You Think I Am?"; "Ev'ry Time"; "Shady Lady Bird"
**New York run:** Ethel Barrymore Theatre, October 1, 1941; 326 p.

Taking place at Winsocki, a Pennsylvania prep school, *Best Foot Forward* is all
about the complications that result from the arrival of Hollywood glamour girl
Gale Joy (Rosemary Lane) who, as a publicity stunt, has accepted the invitation
of Bud Hooper (Gil Stratton Jr.) to be his date at the annual prom. Not only does
this provoke hurt feelings on the part of Bud's steady girl, Helen Schlessinger
(Maureen Cannon), it also results in a near-riot when souvenir hungry prom-
trotters strip the movie star down to her essentials. (John Cecil Holm's libretto
was based on his own experience when, as a student at the Perkiomen School
near Philadelphia, he had invited movie star Betty Compson to be his prom date.
The story he wrote was his idea of what might have happened had she shown
up.) The rousing "Buckle Down, Winsocki" became the best-known song in the
show, which was the first to present Nancy Walker and June Allyson in major
roles. In 1963, an Off-Broadway revival performed a similar function for 17-year-
old Liza Minnelli and Christopher (then Ronald) Walken. The 1943 screen version
featured Lucille Ball, and Misses Walker and Allyson.
Cadence OC (1963)/ TW.

**Best Foot Forward.** June Allyson, Victoria Schools, and Nancy
Walker singing "The Three B's." (Vandamm)

**Let's Face It!** An awkward situation involving Houston Richards, Benny Baker, Mary Jane Walsh, Danny Kaye, and Jack Williams. (Vandamm)

# LET'S FACE IT!
**Music & lyrics:** Cole Porter
**Book:** Herbert & Dorothy Fields
**Producer:** Vinton Freedley
**Director:** Edgar MacGregor
**Choreographer:** Charles Walters
**Cast:** Danny Kaye, Eve Arden, Benny Baker, Mary Jane Walsh, Edith Meiser, Vivian Vance, Nanette Fabray, Mary Parker & Billy Daniel, Jack Williams, Houston Richards
**Songs:** "Farming"; "Ev'rything I Love"; "Ace in the Hole"; "Let's Not Talk About Love"; "A Little Rumba Numba"; "I Hate You, Darling"; "Melody in 4-F" (Sylvia Fine - Max Liebman)
**New York run:** Imperial Theatre, October 29, 1941; 547 p.

Producer Vinton Freedley got the idea for *Let's Face It!* while reading a newspaper account about a number of patriotic women who were so anxious to help the morale of World War II soldiers that they wrote to army camps requesting permission to entertain servicemen in their homes. Using a 1925 Broadway hit, *The Cradle Snatchers,* as foundation, the script by Herbert and Dorothy Fields was about three Southampton matrons who, having grown suspicious of their husbands' frequent hunting trips, have enlisted the service of three rookies from a nearby army camp for an evening of fun and games. The inevitable embarrassments occur when the husbands and their girl friends — as well as the soldiers' girl friends — show up at the party. Danny Kaye (in his first starring role) scored a hit particularly with special material coauthored by his wife, Sylvia Fine. Kaye was succeeded during the Broadway run by José Ferrer. Bob Hope and Betty Hutton were in the 1943 movie version.
Smithsonian OC.

115

**By Jupiter.** Ray Bolger and Bertha Belmore singing "Life With Father." (Vandamm)

# BY JUPITER

**Music:** Richard Rodgers
**Lyrics:** Lorenz Hart
**Book:** Richard Rodgers & Lorenz Hart
**Producers:** Dwight Deere Wiman & Richard Rodgers
**Director:** Joshua Logan
**Choreographer:** Robert Alton
**Cast:** Ray Bolger, Constance Moore, Benay Venuta, Ronald Graham, Bertha Belmore, Ralph Dumke, Vera Ellen, Margaret Bannerman
**Songs:** "Jupiter Forbid"; "Life With Father"; "Nobody's Heart"; "Ev'rything I've Got"; "Careless Rhapsody"; "Wait Till You See Her"
**New York run:** Shubert Theatre, June 3, 1942; 427 p.

Because of its ancient Greek characters and its Asia Minor setting, *By Jupiter* was something of a successor to the previous Rodgers and Hart hit, *The Boys from Syracuse.* The new work, which tried out in Boston under the title *All's Fair,* was based on the 1932 play, *The Warrior's Husband,* in which Katharine Hepburn had first attracted notice. The musical deals with the conflict between the Greeks and the legendary female warriors called Amazons, who live in a gynarchic land ruled by Queen Hippolyta (Benay Venuta). As one of his 12 labors, Hercules (Ralph Dumke) arrives with a Greek army led by Theseus (Ronald Graham) to steal the queen's magical girdle of Diana, the source of her strength. But when Hippolyta's sister Antiope (Constance Moore) takes one look at Theseus, she soon lays down her spear for love, a gesture her sister warriors only too willingly emulate. During the run, Miss Moore was succeeded by Nanette Fabray.

*By Jupiter*, which remained the longest on Broadway of any Rodgers and Hart musical during the team's partnership, was the last original show they wrote together. It could have stayed longer had not Ray Bolger (in his first starring role as Sapiens, the queen's husband) quit the cast to entertain American troops in the Far East. One curious aspect of the show's score is that "Wait Till You See Her," its best-known song, was dropped a month after the Broadway opening. In 1967, an Off-Broadway revival of *By Jupiter* ran for 118 performances. RCA OC (1967)/ R&H.

**This Is the Army.** Ezra Stone, Julie Oshins, and Philip Truex singing "The Army's Made a Man Out of Me." (Vandamm)

# THIS IS THE ARMY

**Music & lyrics:** Irving Berlin
**Sketches:** (uncredited)
**Producer:** Uncle Sam
**Directors:** Ezra Stone, Joshua Logan
**Choreographers:** Robert Sidney, Nelson Barclift
**Cast:** Ezra Stone, Burl Ives, Gary Merrill, Julie Oshins, Robert Sidney, Alan Manson, Earl Oxford, Nelson Barclift, Stuart Churchill, Philip Truex, Irving Berlin
**Songs:** "This Is the Army, Mr. Jones"; "The Army's Made a Man Out of Me"; "I Left My Heart at the Stage Door Canteen"; "Mandy"; "I'm Getting Tired So I Can Sleep"; "Oh, How I Hate to Get Up in the Morning"; "American Eagles"; "This Time"
**New York run:** Broadway Theatre, July 4, 1942; 113 p.

Having already written songs for the all-soldier show, *Yip Yip Yaphank,* during World War I, Irving Berlin followed up with songs for the all-soldier show, *This Is the Army,* during World War II. The revue, put together as a benefit for the Army Emergency Relief Fund, both kidded and extolled the military life in a song-and-dance mixture of horseplay, nostalgia, and patriotism. Though most of the show reflected a draftee's view of the Army, there was also room for tributes to the Navy and the Air Force. Highlights included the opening "Military Minstrel Show"; the scene at the Stage Door Canteen with soldiers impersonating celebrities who worked and performed there; Berlin himself leading his World War I buddies in singing, "Oh, How I Hate to Get Up in the Morning"; and the finale with the cast members in full battle dress booming their determination to make certain that this time would be the last. *This Is the Army* played a limited 12-week engagement in New York, was filmed in 1943 with Ronald Reagan, then toured overseas until October 1945. In 1946, the Broadway revue *Call Me Mister* dealt with the adjustment of World War II servicemen to civilian life. CSP OC.

**Oklahoma!** Joan Roberts singing "Many a New Day."

**Oklahoma!** Celeste Holm and Lee Dixon.

**Oklahoma!** Howard Da Silva and Alfred Drake singing "Pore Jud." (Vandamm)

# OKLAHOMA!

**Music:** Richard Rodgers
**Lyrics & book:** Oscar Hammerstein II
**Producer:** Theatre Guild
**Director:** Rouben Mamoulian
**Choreographer:** Agnes de Mille
**Cast:** Betty Garde, Alfred Drake, Joan Roberts, Joseph Buloff, Celeste Holm, Howard Da Silva, Lee Dixon, Joan McCracken, Bambi Linn, George S. Irving, George Church, Ralph Riggs, Marc Platt, Katharine Sergava
**Songs:** "Oh, What a Beautiful Mornin'"; "The Surrey With the Fringe on Top"; "Kansas City"; "I Cain't Say No"; "Many a New Day"; "People Will Say We're in Love"; "Pore Jud"; "Out of My Dreams"; "The Farmer and the Cowman"; "All er Nothin' "; "Oklahoma"
**New York run:** St. James Theatre, March 31, 1943; 2,212 p.

A recognized landmark in the evolution of the American musical theatre, *Oklahoma!* was the initial collaboration between Richard Rodgers and Oscar Hammerstein II (in all, they wrote nine Broadway shows together). Under the direction of Rouben Mamoulian and with choreography by Agnes de Mille (her first of 15 book musicals), the production not only fused story, songs, and dances, but introduced the dream ballet to reveal hidden fears and desires of the principal characters. In addition, the musical continued in the paths of *Show Boat* (written by Hammerstein) and *Porgy and Bess* (directed by Mamoulian) by further expanding Broadway's horizons in its depiction of the pioneering men and woman who had once tilled the land and tended the cattle of the American Southwest.

Based on Lynn Riggs' 1931 play *Green Grow the Lilacs, Oklahoma!* is set in Indian Territory soon after the turn of the century. The simple tale is mostly concerned with whether the decent Curly McLain (Alfred Drake) or the menacing Jud Fry (Howard Da Silva) will take Laurey Williams (Joan Roberts) to the box social. Though in a fit of pique, Laurey chooses Jud, she really loves Curly and they soon make plans to marry. At their wedding, there is a joyous celebration of Oklahoma's impending statehood, Jud is accidently killed in a fight with Curly, and the newlyweds prepare to ride off in their surrey with the fringe on top. A comic secondary plot has to do with a romantic triangle involving man-crazy Ado Annie Carnes (Celeste Holm), cowboy Will Parker (Lee Dixon), and peddler Ali Hakim (Joseph Buloff).

After trying out under the title *Away We Go!*, the show was renamed *Oklahoma!* for its Broadway engagement at the St. James Theatre (formerly Erlanger's). It remained there five years nine months, thereby setting a long-run record for musicals that it held until overtaken by *My Fair Lady* 15 years later. Among actors who replaced original-cast members were Howard Keel (Curly), Mary Hatcher (Laurey), and Shelley Winters (Ado Annie). A National Company toured for over a decade, including a return visit to New York that lasted 100 performances. The first road company was headed by Harry Stockwell (Curly), Evelyn Wyckoff (Laurey), Pamela Britton (Ado Annie), and David Burns (Ali Hakim). Those who subsequently toured included John Raitt (Curly), Florence Henderson (Laurey), and Barbara Cook (Ado Annie).

In 1969, the Music Theatre of Lincoln Center mounted a revival with Bruce Yarnell (Curly), Leigh Beery (Laurey), April Shawhan (Ado Annie), Margaret Hamilton (Aunt Eller), and Lee Roy Reams (Will). Ten years later, a new production directed by William Hammerstein (Oscar's son) returned to New York for eight months as part of a two-and-a-half year tour. (See page 255.) The 1955 movie version, the first film in Todd-AO, featured Gordon MacRae and Shirley Jones in the leading roles.

MCA OC; CSP part tour OC; RCA OC (1979)/ Random House (1943)/ R&H.

# THE MERRY WIDOW

**Music:** Franz Lehár
**Lyrics:** Adrian Ross, Robert Gilbert
**Book:** Sidney Sheldon & Ben Roberts
**Producer:** Yolanda Mero-Irion for the New Opera Co.
**Director:** Felix Brentano
**Choreographer:** George Balanchine
**Cast:** Jan Kiepura, Marta Eggerth, Melville Cooper, Ruth Matteson, Robert Rounseville, David Wayne, Ralph Dumke, Gene Barry, Lubov Roudenko, Milada Mladova
**Songs:** Same as original production
**New York run:** Majestic Theatre, August 4, 1943; 322 p.

(See page 15.)

# ONE TOUCH OF VENUS

**Music:** Kurt Weill
**Lyrics:** Ogden Nash
**Book:** S. J. Perelman & Ogden Nash
**Producer:** Cheryl Crawford
**Director:** Elia Kazan
**Choreographer:** Agnes de Mille
**Cast:** Mary Martin, Kenny Baker, John Boles, Paula Laurence, Teddy Hart, Ruth Bond, Sono Osato, Harry Clark, Allyn Ann McLerie, Helen Raymond, Lou Wills Jr., Pearl Lang
**Songs:** "One Touch of Venus"; "How Much I Love You"; "I'm a Stranger Here Myself"; "West Wind"; "Foolish Heart"; "The Trouble With Women"; "Speak Low"; "That's Him"; "Wooden Wedding"
**New York run:** Imperial Theatre, October 7, 1943; 567 p.

*One Touch of Venus* combined the music of composer Kurt Weill (it was his most lighthearted score) with the libretto of two celebrated humorists, poet Ogden Nash and short-story writer S.J. Perelman (it was their only Broadway book musical). In her first starring role, Mary Martin played a statue of Venus recently unveiled in a New York museum, the Whitelaw Savory Foundation of Modern Art, that comes to life after barber Rodney Hatch (Kenny Baker) places a ring on the statue's finger. There is much comic confusion when Savory (John Boles) falls in love with Venus and Venus falls in love with Rodney, but after dreaming of her humdrum life as a barber's wife in Ozone Heights, the goddess happily turns back to marble. Fortunately, Rodney meets a girl who looks just like the statue (Miss Martin, of course) who just loves living in Ozone Heights.

Though *One Touch of Venus* (whose hit song was the torchy "Speak Low") was a fantasy in the modern sophisticated vein of Rodgers and Hart's *I Married an Angel,* its origin was a short novel, *The Tinted Venus,* written in 1885 by the English author F. Anstey (né Thomas Anstey Guthrie) who had based his story on the Pygmalion myth. The musical's first draft, by Bella Spewack, suggested Marlene Dietrich for the role of Venus, but when the actress turned down the part the concept was changed from worldly exotic to youthfully innocent after Perelman and Nash replaced Spewack and Mary Martin replaced Dietrich. The movie version, released in 1948, starred Ava Gardner, Robert Walker, and Dick Haymes.
AEI OC/ Little, Brown (1943); Chilton (1973)/ TW.

**One Touch of Venus.** Barber Kenny Baker slipping the ring on statue Mary Martin's finger. (Vandamm)

# CARMEN JONES

**Music:** Georges Bizet
**Lyrics & book:** Oscar Hammerstein II
**Producer:** Billy Rose
**Directors:** Hassard Short, Charles Friedman
**Choreographer:** Eugene Loring
**Cast:** Muriel Smith (or Inez Matthews), Luther Saxon, Carlotta Franzell, Glenn Bryant, June Hawkins, Cosy Cole
**Songs:** "Dat's Love"; "You Talk Just Like My Maw"; "Dere's a Café on de Corner"; "Beat Out dat Rhythm on a Drum"; "Stan' Up and Fight"; "Whizzin' Away Along de Track"; "Dis Flower"; "My Joe"
**New York run:** Broadway Theatre, December 2, 1943; 502 p.

Adapting his libretto from Meilhac and Halevy's for the 1875 premiere production of *Carmen,* and adhering as closely as possible to the original form, Oscar Hammerstein II set his idiomatic lyrics to Georges Bizet's music and updated the story to World War II. Now Carmen is a worker in a parachute factory in the South (rather than a cigarette factory in Seville), Joe (Don José) is an army corporal who falls in love with the temptress, Cindy Lou (Micaela) is the country girl who loves Joe, and Husky Miller is the boxer (replacing Escamillo the bull fighter) who wins Carmen away from Joe. As did the original, the work ends in tragedy as Joe stabs Carmen to death outside a sports stadium while the crowd can be heard cheering Husky. In addition to the staging, Hassard Short was also responsible for the striking color schemes used throughout the production. *Carmen Jones* returned twice to New York during its year-and-a-half nationwide tour. The 1954 film adaptation featured Dorothy Dandridge, Harry Belafonte, and Diahann Carroll. MCA OC/ Knopf (1945)/ R&H.

# MEXICAN HAYRIDE

**Music & lyrics:** Cole Porter
**Book:** Herbert & Dorothy Fields
**Producer:** Michael Todd
**Directors:** Hassard Short, John Kennedy
**Choreographer:** Paul Haakon
**Cast:** Bobby Clark, June Havoc, George Givot, Wilbur Evans, Luba Malina, Corinna Mura, Paul Haakon, Edith Meiser, Bill Callahan, Candy Jones
**Songs:** "Sing to Me, Guitar"; "I Love You"; "There Must Be Someone for Me"; "Abracadabra"; "Carlotta"; "Girls"; "Count Your Blessings"
**New York run:** Winter Garden, January 28, 1944; 481 p.

One of Broadway's most lavish wartime attractions (it had a cast of 89), *Mexican Hayride* owed its success largely to its appealing Latin-flavored score by Cole Porter (including the hit ballad "I Love You"), its eye-dazzling decor, its rows of long-stemmed show girls, and — most of all — the buffooneries of prankish, leering Bobby Clark. Clark was seen as Joe Bascom, alias Humphrey Fish, a numbers racketeer on the lam in Mexico where, at a bull fight, he is mistakenly selected as the "Amigo Americano," or good-will ambassador. Alternately hailed by the populace and trailed by the police, Bascom bounds from Mexico City to Chepultepec, Xochimilco, and Taxco, assuming a number of disguises including that of a mariachi flute player and a tortilla-vending, cigar-chomping Indian squaw with a baby strapped to her back. Because of the sumptuousness of the production, the top ticket price was $5.50. Abbott and Costello (but no Porter songs) were in the 1948 Hollywood version. CSP OC.

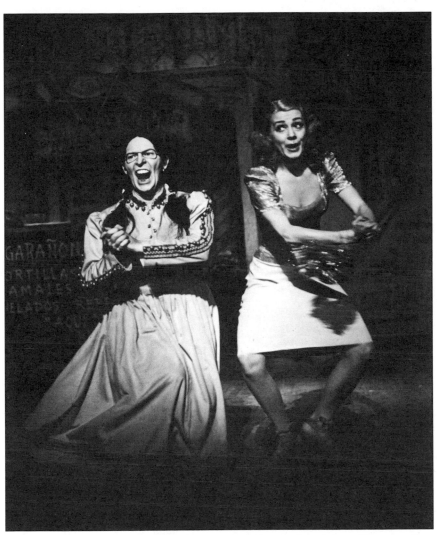

**Mexican Hayride.** Bobby Clark (in his squaw disguise) and June Havoc cutting up during the "Count Your Blessings" number.

# FOLLOW THE GIRLS

**Music:** Phil Charig
**Lyrics:** Dan Shaprio & Milton Pascal
**Book:** Guy Bolton, Eddie Davis & Fred Thompson
**Producers:** Dave Wolper & Albert Borde
**Directors:** Harry Delmar, Fred Thompson
**Choreographer:** Catherine Littlefield
**Cast:** Gertrude Niesen, Jackie Gleason, Buster West, Tim Herbert, Irina Baronova, Frank Parker, William Tabbert
**Songs:** "You're Perf"; "Twelve O'Clock and All Is Well"; "Follow the Girls"; "I Wanna Get Married"; "I'm Gonna Hang My Hat"
**New York run:** New Century Theatre, April 8, 1944; 882 p.

Though it was one of Broadway's most popular wartime attractions, *Follow the Girls* is all but forgotten today. The raucous and lively show did, however, make a star of Gertrude Niesen in her only book musical, and her rendition of "I Wanna Get Married" was an authentic musical-comedy showstopper. The disposable plot had something to do with a burlesque queen, Bubbles LaMarr, who becomes a favorite of sailors at the Spotlight Canteen in Great Neck, Long Island. The show, however, served to throw the spotlight not only on Miss Niesen as Bubbles, but also on the antics of Jackie Gleason as Goofy Gale and on the dancing of ballerina Irina Baronova. *Follow the Girls* was the first attraction to play the reopened and refurbished Jolson's 59th Street Theatre, renamed the New Century.

# SONG OF NORWAY

**Music & lyrics:** Robert Wright & George Forrest based on Edvard Grieg
**Book:** Milton Lazarus
**Producer:** Edwin Lester
**Directors:** Edwin Lester, Charles K. Freeman
**Choreographer:** George Balanchine
**Cast:** Irra Petina, Lawrence Brooks, Robert Shafer, Helena Bliss, Sig Arno, Alexandra Danilova, Maria Tallchief, Ruthanna Boris
**Songs:** "The Legend"; "Hill of Dreams"; "Freddy and His Fiddle"; "Now!"; "Strange Music"; "Midsummer's Eve"; "Three Loves"; "I Love You"; "Piano Concerto in A Minor" (instrumental)
**New York run:** Imperial Theatre, August 21, 1944; 860 p.

*Song of Norway* had its premiere a continent away from Broadway in July 1944, when it was presented by Edwin Lester's Los Angeles and San Francisco Civic Light Opera Association. Following in the tradition of *Blossom Time,* it offered a score based on themes by a classical composer combined with a biographical plot unencumbered by too much fidelity to historical accuracy. Here we have a romanticized tale of the early years of Edvard Grieg (Lawrence Brooks) who, with his friend, poet Rikard Nordraak (Robert Shafer), is anxious to bring new artistic glory to their beloved Norway. Though temporarily distracted from this noble aim by a dalliance in Rome with a flirtatious (and fictitious) Italian prima donna (Irra Petina), Grieg is so affected by the news of Nordraak's death that he returns home to his indulgent wife (Helena Bliss). Suitably inspired after singing a reprise of their love duet, "Strange Music," the composer creates the A-Minor Piano Concerto. *Song of Norway* which was presented by the New York City Opera in 1981, was filmed in 1970 with Tauralv Maurstad and Florence Henderson. For other musicals with scores based on classical themes, see *Blossom Time,* page 38.
MCA OC; Columbia OC (1958)/ TW.

# BLOOMER GIRL

**Music:** Harold Arlen
**Lyrics:** E. Y. Harburg
**Book:** Sig Herzig & Fred Saidy
**Producers:** John C. Wilson & Nat Goldstone
**Directors:** E. Y. Harburg, William Schorr
**Choreographer:** Agnes de Mille
**Cast:** Celeste Holm, David Brooks, Dooley Wilson, Joan McCracken, Richard Huey, Margaret Douglass, Mabel Taliaferro, Matt Briggs, Herbert Ross
**Songs:** "When the Boys Come Home"; "Evelina"; "It Was Good Enough for Grandma"; "The Eagle and Me"; "Right as the Rain"; "T'morra, T'morra"; "Sunday in Cicero Falls"; "I Got a Song"
**New York run:** Shubert Theatre, October 5, 1944; 654 p.

Continuing the Americana spirit of *Oklahoma!*, *Bloomer Girl* was not only concerned with the introduction of bloomers during the Civil War, it also covered various aspects of the women's reform movement and the struggle for civil rights. The action occurs in Cicero Falls, New York, in 1861, and covers the rebellion of Evelina Applegate (Celeste Holm) against her tyrannical father, a manufacturer of hoopskirts, who wants her to marry one of his salesmen. Evelina is so provoked that she joins her aunt, Amelia "Dolly" Bloomer (Margaret Douglass), in both her crusade for more practical clothing for women and in her abolitionist activities. Evelina's convictions, however, do not prevent her from singing the romantic duet, "Right as the Rain," with Jefferson Calhoun (David Brooks), a visiting Southern slaveholder, who is eventually won over to her cause. *Bloomer Girl* made a star of Celeste Holm (who was succeeded in her role by Nanette Fabray), and it was also noted for Agnes de Mille's "Civil War Ballet," depicting the anguish felt by women who must remain at home while their men are off fighting. The musical returned to New York for six weeks early in 1947.

Broadway has also seen the following Civil War musicals: *The Girl from Dixie* (1903), *Caroline* (1923), *My Maryland* (1927), *My Darlin' Aida* (1952), *Maggie Flynn* (1968), and *Shenandoah* (1975).
MCA OC/ TW.

**Bloomer Girl.** Joan McCracken showing off her bloomers to Celeste Holm and Margaret Douglass. (Vandamm)

# ON THE TOWN

**Music:** Leonard Bernstein
**Lyrics & book:** Betty Comden & Adolph Green
**Producers:** Oliver Smith & Paul Feigay
**Director:** George Abbott
**Choreographer:** Jerome Robbins
**Cast:** Sono Osato, Nancy Walker, Betty Comden, Adolph Green, John Battles, Cris Alexander, Alice Pearce, Allyn Ann McLerie
**Songs:** "New York, New York"; "Come Up to My Place"; "I Get Carried Away"; "Lonely Town"; "Lucky to Be Me"; "Ya Got Me"; "Some Other Time"
**New York run:** Adelphi Theatre, December 28, 1944; 463 p.

On the Town heralded the Broadway arrival of four major talents — composer Leonard Bernstein, writing partners Betty Comden and Adolph Green, and choreographer Jerome Robbins. Based on the Robbins-Bernstein ballet, Fancy Free, the musical expanded the work into a carefree tour of New York City, where three sailors — played by John Battles, Adolph Green, and Cris Alexander — become involved with three girls — Sono Osato, Betty Comden, and Nancy Walker — on a 24-hour shore leave. One of the sailors (Battles) becomes so smitten by the current winner of the subway's "Miss Turnstiles" competition (Miss Osato) that he and his buddies pursue her through the Museum of Natural History, Central Park, Times Square, and Coney Island. The Adelphi Theatre was once located on 54th Street east of 7th Avenue.

There have been two New York revivals of On the Town. Joe Layton staged an Off-Broadway version in 1959, with Harold Lang, Wisa D'Orso, and Pat Carroll, and Ron Field staged a Broadway version in 1971 with Ron Husmann, Donna McKechnie, Bernadette Peters, and Phyllis Newman. The movie adaptation, released in 1949, co-starred Gene Kelly, Vera-Ellen, Frank Sinatra, and Betty Garrett. MCA part OC; Columbia OC/ TW.

# UP IN CENTRAL PARK

**Music:** Sigmund Romberg
**Lyrics:** Dorothy Fields
**Book:** Herbert & Dorothy Fields
**Producer:** Michael Todd
**Director:** John Kennedy
**Choreographer:** Helen Tamiris
**Cast:** Wilbur Evans, Maureen Cannon, Betty Bruce, Noah Beery, Maurice Burke, Charles Irwin, Robert Rounseville
**Songs:** "Carousel in the Park"; "When You Walk in the Room"; "Close as Pages in a Book"; "The Big Back Yard"; "April Snow"
**New York run:** New Century Theatre, January 27, 1945; 504 p.

Celebrated for his lush scores for operettas in exotic locales (The Desert Song, The New Moon), Sigmund Romberg joined with lyricist Dorothy Fields to recapture the vintage Currier and Ives charms found up in New York's Central Park in the 1870s. The story, a combination of fact and fiction, deals with the efforts of John Matthews (Wilbur Evans), a New York Times reporter, to expose Tammany boss William Marcy Tweed (Noah Beery) and the other grafters who are lining their pockets with funds designated for the building of the park. Romance is supplied when John and Rosie Moore (Maureen Cannon), the daughter of a Tweed crony, vow love everlasting in their ardent duet, "Close as Pages in a Book." Deanna Durbin and Dick Haymes were in the 1948 movie version. MCA SC.

**Carousel.** The opening scene with John Raitt and Jan Clayton. (Vandamm)

# CAROUSEL

**Music:** Richard Rodgers
**Lyrics & book:** Oscar Hammerstein II
**Producer:** Theatre Guild
**Director:** Rouben Mamoulian
**Choreographer:** Ágnes de Mille
**Cast:** John Raitt, Jan Clayton, Murvyn Vye, Jean Darling, Christine Johnson, Eric Mattson, Bambi Linn, Peter Birch, Pearl Lang
**Songs:** "Carousel Waltz" (instrumental); "You're a Queer One, Julie Jordan"; "Mr. Snow"; "If I Loved You"; "Blow High, Blow Low"; "June Is Bustin' Out All Over"; "When the Children Are Asleep"; "Soliloquy"; "What's the Use of Wond'rin'?"; "You'll Never Walk Alone"; "The Highest Judge of All"
**New York run:** Majestic Theatre, April 19, 1945; 890 p.

With *Carousel*, Rodgers and Hammerstein solidified their position as the dominant creators of musical theatre in the Forties. Reunited for the production with their *Oklahoma!* colleagues, the partners transported Ferenc Molnar's 1921 fantasy *Liliom* from Budapest to a New England fishing village between 1873 and 1888. Billy Bigelow (John Raitt), a swaggering carnival barker, meets Julie Jordan (Jan Clayton), a local factory worker, and — in the soaring duet, "If I Loved You" — they are soon admitting their feelings for each other. After their marriage, Billy learns of his impending fatherhood — with his ambivalent emotions expressed in the "Soliloquy" — and, desperate for money, is killed in an attempted robbery. He is, however, allowed to return to earth to do one good deed. This is accomplished when, unseen by his daughter Louise (Bambi Linn), he shows up at her high school graduation to encourage the lonely girl to have confidence in herself by heeding the words to "You'll Never Walk Alone." For almost two years, *Carousel* at the Majestic Theatre (on 44th Street west of Broadway) played across the street from *Oklahoma!* at the St. James. During the Broadway run (the fifth longest of the decade), Raitt was replaced for a time by Howard Keel. The National Company traveled for one year nine months, ending its tour with a Broadway stand lasting 48 performances. Twenty years after the opening, John Raitt again played Billy Bigelow in a revival presented by the Music Theatre of Lincoln Center. The 1956 film version starred Gordon MacRae and Shirley Jones.
MCA OC; RCA OC (1965); MCA SC (1987)/ Random House (1945)/ R&H.

# THE RED MILL

**Music:** Victor Herbert
**Lyrics:** Henry Blossom, Forman Brown
**Book:** (uncredited)
**Producers:** Paula Stone & Hunt Stromberg Jr.
**Director:** Billy Gilbert
**Choreographer:** Aida Broadbent
**Cast:**  Eddie Foy Jr., Michael O'Shea, Odette Myrtil, Dorothy Stone, Charles Collins, Ann Andre, Lorna Byron
**Songs:** Same as original production
**New York run:** Ziegfeld Theatre, October 16, 1945; 531 p.

(See page 13.)

---

# SHOW BOAT

**Music:** Jerome Kern
**Lyrics & book:** Oscar Hammerstein II
**Producers:** Jerome Kern & Oscar Hammerstein II
**Directors:** Hassard Short, Oscar Hammerstein II
**Choreographer:** Helen Tamiris
**Cast:**  Jan Clayton, Ralph Dumke, Carol Bruce, Charles Fredericks, Buddy Ebsen, Colette Lyons, Kenneth Spencer, Pearl Primus, Talley Beatty
**Songs:** Same as original production plus "Nobody Else but Me"
**New York run:** Ziegfeld Theatre, January 5, 1946; 418 p.

(See page 60.)

**Show Boat.** Buddy Ebsen and Colette Lyons strutting through "Goodbye, My Lady Love." (Eileen Darby)

# ST. LOUIS WOMAN

**Music:** Harold Arlen
**Lyrics:** Johnny Mercer
**Book:** Arna Bontemps & Countee Cullen
**Producer:** Edward Gross
**Director:** Rouben Mamoulian
**Choreographer:** Charles Walters
**Cast:** Harold Nicholas, Fayard Nicholas, Pearl Bailey, Ruby Hill, Rex Ingram, June Hawkins, Juanita Hall, Lorenzo Fuller
**Songs:** "Cakewalk Your Lady"; "Come Rain or Come Shine"; "I Had Myself a True Love"; "Legalize My Name"; "Any Place I Hang My Hat Is Home"; "A Woman's Prerogative"; "Ridin' on the Moon"
**New York run:** Martin Beck Theatre, March 30, 1946; 113 p.

Though based on Arna Bontemps' novel, *God Sends Sunday, St. Louis Woman* seems also to have been a close relative of *Porgy and Bess.* Set in St. Louis in 1898, the musical tells of fickle Della Green (Ruby Hill in a part intended for Lena Horne), who is the woman of tough saloon owner Biglow Brown (Rex Ingram), but who falls for Li'l Augie (Harold Nicholas), a jockey with an incredible winning streak. Before Brown is killed by a discarded girlfriend, he puts a curse on Li'l Augie which ends both the winning streak and Della's affection. The two, however, are reunited for the final reprise of their ardent "Come Rain or Como Shine." In 1959, a revised version of *St. Louis Woman*, with other Harold Arlen songs added and now set in New Orleans, was performed in Amsterdam and Paris under the title *Free and Easy.*
Capitol OC/ N.A.L. (1973).

# CALL ME MISTER

**Music & lyrics:** Harold Rome
**Sketches:** Arnold Auerbach, Arnold B. Horwitt
**Producers:** Melvyn Douglas & Herman Levin
**Director:** Robert H. Gordon
**Choreographer:** John Wray
**Cast:** Betty Garrett, Jules Munshin, Bill Callahan, Lawrence Winters, Paula Bane, Maria Karnilova, George S. Irving
**Songs:** "Goin' Home Train"; "Along With Me"; "The Red Ball Express"; "Military Life"; "The Face on the Dime"; "South America, Take It Away"; "Call Me Mister"
**New York run:** National Theatre, April 18, 1946; 734 p.

With its theme dealing with servicemen readjusting to civilian life, *Call Me Mister* was something of a follow-up to *This Is the Army.* The show's cast consisted of ex-GIs and ex-USO entertainers, and it took a somewhat satirical, yet basically good-humored and optimistic attitude toward military life and demobilization. Its most popular number was "South America, Take It Away," performed by Betty Garrett as a rumba-hating canteen hostess. Its funniest sketch found the Air Corps getting its lumps as the flyers were shown enjoying the glamorous life while periodically offering toasts "To the Blue Lady of the Clouds." In a serious moment, the revue faced up to post-war racial discrimination when Lawrence Winters, as a former driver with the supplies-carrying "Red Ball Express," is unable to get a job as a truck driver. *Call Me Mister* played the National Theatre (now the Nederlander) on 41st Street west of 7th Avenue. The 1951 movie version (with plot) co-starred Betty Grable and Dan Dailey.
CSP OC.

# ANNIE GET YOUR GUN

**Music & lyrics:** Irving Berlin
**Book:** Herbert & Dorothy Fields
**Producers:** Richard Rodgers & Oscar Hammerstein II
**Director:** Joshua Logan
**Choreographer:** Helen Tamiris
**Cast:** Ethel Merman, Ray Middleton, Marty May, Kenny Bowers, Lea Penman, Betty Anne Nyman, William O'Neal, Lubov Roudenko, Daniel Nagrin, Harry Belaver, Ellen Hanley
**Songs:** "Doin' What Comes Natur'lly"; "The Girl That I Marry"; "You Can't Get a Man With a Gun"; "There's No Business Like Show Business"; "They Say It's Wonderful"; "Moonshine Lullaby"; "My Defenses Are Down"; "I'm an Indian Too"; "I Got Lost in His Arms"; "I Got the Sun in the Morning"; "Anything You Can Do"
**New York run:** Imperial Theatre, May 16, 1946; 1,147 p.

*Annie Get Your Gun* was the first of two shows Irving Berlin wrote for Ethel Merman (the other was *Call Me Madam*). The third longest running musical of the Forties, it was also the biggest Broadway hit of their respective careers. Originally, however, composer Jerome Kern was to have written the songs with lyricist Dorothy Fields (also the co-librettist), but Kern's death as he was about to begin the assignment brought Berlin into the project for both music and lyrics. The idea for the show, the only Rodgers and Hammerstein musical production without a Rodgers and Hammerstein score, is credited to Miss Fields who felt that Ethel Merman as Annie Oakley would be surefire casting.

Though unspecified, the period of the story is the mid-1880s. Annie Oakley, an illiterate hillbilly living near Cincinnati, demonstrates her remarkable marksmanship, and is persuaded — through the convincing claim "There's No Business Like Show Business" — to join Col. Buffalo Bill's travelling Wild West Show. Annie, who needs only one look to fall hopelessly in love with Frank Butler (Ray Middleton), the show's featured shooting ace, soon eclipses Butler as the main attraction, which doesn't help the cause of romance. She exhibits her skills at such locales as the Minneapolis Fair Grounds (where she hits the targets while riding on a motorcycle) and at Governor's Island, New York, where, in a shooting contest with Frank, she realizes that the only way to win the man is to let him win the match. The National Company's tour, which began in October 1947, lasted for one year seven months with Mary Martin heading the original touring cast. In 1966, Miss Merman recreated the role of Annie Oakley for a production sponsored by the Music Theatre of Lincoln Center. This revival, which also had Bruce Yarnell and Jerry Orbach in the cast, included a new Berlin song, "An Old-Fashioned Wedding." After a brief tour, the show played two months at the Broadway Theatre. Betty Hutton and Howard Keel were in the 1950 screen adaptation.

Following *Annie Get Your Gun,* other show business musical biographies have been written about Gypsy Rose Lee (Sandra Church in *Gypsy,* 1959); Edmund Kean (Alfred Drake in *Kean,* 1961); Sophie Tucker (Libi Staiger in *Sophie,* 1963); Laurette Taylor (Mary Martin in *Jennie,* 1963); Fanny Brice (Barbra Streisand in *Funny Girl,* 1964); George M. Cohan (Joel Grey in *George M!,* 1968); the Marx Brothers (Lewis J. Stadlen, Daniel Fortus, Irwin Pearl, and Alvin Kupperman in *Minnie's Boys,* 1970); Mack Sennett and Mabel Normand (Robert Preston and Bernadette Peters in *Mack & Mabel,* 1974); Phineas T. Barnum (Jim Dale in *Barnum,* 1980); Federico Fellini (Raul Julia in *Nine,* 1982); Tallulah Bankhead (Helen Gallagher in *Tallulah,* 1983); Marilyn Monroe (Alyson Reed in *Marilyn,* 1983); Ned Harrigan and Tony Hart (Harry Groener and Mark Hamill in *Harrigan 'n Hart,* 1985); and Ellie Greenfield (Dinah Manoff in *Leader of the Pack,* 1985).
MCA OC; RCA OC (1966)/ R&H.

Cover designed by Lucinda Ballard.

**Annie Get Your Gun.** "There's No Business Like Show Business" sing William O'Neal, Marty May, Ethel Merman, and Ray Middleton. (Vandamm)

131

# STREET SCENE

**Music:** Kurt Weill
**Lyrics:** Langston Hughes
**Book:** Elmer Rice
**Producers:** Dwight Deere Wiman & The Playwrights' Co.
**Director:** Charles Friedman
**Choreographer:** Anna Sokolow
**Cast:** Norman Cordon, Anne Jeffreys, Polyna Stoska, Brian Sullivan, Hope Emerson, Sheila Bond, Danny Daniels, Don Saxon, Juanita Hall
**Songs:** "Somehow I Never Could Believe"; "Ice Cream"; "Wrapped in a Ribbon and Tied in a Bow"; "Wouldn't You Like to Be on Broadway?"; "What Good Would the Moon Be?"; "Moon-Faced, Starry-Eyed"; "Remember That I Care"; "We'll Go Away Together"
**New York run:** Adelphi Theatre, January 9, 1947; 148 p.

Adapted by Elmer Rice from his 1929 play, *Street Scene* was the most operatic of all the Broadway productions with music by Kurt Weill. Something of a white Northern counterpart to *Porgy and Bess,* the work takes a melodramatic look at the inhabitants of a New York City tenement during an oppressively hot summer day. Among those inhabitants are the members of the Maurrant family — Anna (Polyna Stoska) whose loveless marriage (as revealed through the impassioned aria "Somehow I Never Could Believe") drives her to an affair that ends in tragedy; Anna's bullying, drunken husband Frank (Norman Cordon); and their frustrated daughter Rose (Anne Jeffreys) who cannot give herself either to the smooth-talking sharpie Harry Easter (Don Saxon) or to the earnest neighbor Sam Kaplan (Brian Sullivan). In 1959, *Street Scene* entered the repertory of the New York City Opera.
Columbia OC/ R&H.

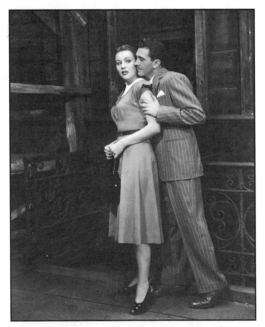

**Street Scene.** Anne Jeffreys and Don Saxon.
(Vandamm)

**Finian's Rainbow.** Albert Sharpe, David Wayne, and Anita Alvarez in a tense moment.

# FINIAN'S RAINBOW

**Music:** Burton Lane
**Lyrics:** E. Y. Harburg
**Book:** E. Y. Harburg & Fred Saidy
**Producers:** Lee Sabinson & William Katzell
**Director:** Bretaigne Windust
**Choreographer:** Michael Kidd
**Cast:** Ella Logan, Albert Sharpe, Donald Richards, David Wayne, Anita Alvarez, Robert Pitkin
**Songs:** "How Are Things in Glocca Morra?"; "If This Isn't Love"; "Look to the Rainbow"; "Old Devil Moon"; "Something Sort of Grandish"; "Necessity"; "When the Idle Poor Become the Idle Rich"; "When I'm Not Near the Girl I Love"; "That Great Come-and-Get-It Day"
**New York run:** 46th Street Theatre, January 10, 1947; 725 p.

E. Y. Harburg got the idea for *Finian's Rainbow* because he wanted to satirize an economic system that requires gold reserves to be buried at Fort Knox. He then began thinking of leprechauns and their legendary crock of gold that could grant three wishes. In the story that Harburg and Fred Saidy devised, Finian McLonergan (Albert Sharpe), an Irish immigrant, is in Rainbow Valley, Missitucky, to bury a crock of gold, which he is sure, will grow and make him rich. Also part of the fantasy are Og (David Wayne), the leprechaun whose crock has been stolen, Finian's daughter Sharon (Ella Logan), who dreams wistfully of Glocca Morra, Woody Mahoney (Donald Richards), a labor organizer who blames "That Old Devil Moon" for the way he feels about Sharon, and a bigoted Southern Senator, Billboard Rawkins (Robert Pitkin), who — as one of the three wishes — turns black. At the end, everyone comes to understand that riches are found not in gold but in people trusting one another. A 1960 revival had a brief Broadway run. The 1968 movie version starred Fred Astaire, Petula Clark, and Tommy Steele.
Columbia OC; RCA OC (1960)/ Berkley Books (1968)/ TW.

# SWEETHEARTS

**Music:** Victor Herbert
**Lyrics:** Robert B. Smith
**Book:** John Cecil Holm
**Producers:** Paula Stone & Michael Sloane
**Director:** John Kennedy
**Choreographers:** Catherine Littlefield, Theodore Adolphus
**Cast:**   Bobby Clark, Marjorie Gateson, Gloria Story, Mark Dawson, Robert Shackleton, June Knight, Cornell MacNeil
**Songs:** 6 cut from original production; "To the Land of My Own Romance" (lyric: Harry B. Smith) and "I Might Be Your Once-in-a-While" added.
**New York run:** Shubert Theatre, January 21, 1947; 288 p.

(See page 19.)

# BRIGADOON

**Music:** Frederick Loewe
**Lyrics & book:** Alan Jay Lerner
**Producer:** Cheryl Crawford
**Director:** Robert Lewis
**Choreographer:** Agnes de Mille
**Cast:**   David Brooks, Marion Bell, Pamela Britton, Lee Sullivan, George Keane, James Mitchell, William Hansen, Elliott Sullivan, Helen Gallagher, Hayes Gordon, Lidija Franklin
**Songs:** "Brigadoon"; "Down on MacConnachy Square"; "Waiting for My Dearie"; "I'll Go Home With Bonnie Jean"; "The Heather on the Hill"; "Come to Me, Bend to Me"; "Almost Like Being in Love"; "There but for You Go I"; "My Mother's Wedding Day"; "From This Day On"
**New York run:** Ziegfeld Theatre, March 13, 1947; 581 p.

By dealing with themes of substance, by their adherence to the concept of the integrated musical, and by their ability to make the past come vividly alive to modern audiences, Lerner and Loewe established their special niche in the musical theatre while still laying claim to being the stylistic heirs of Rodgers and Hammerstein. *Brigadoon,* their third Broadway musical and first hit, was motivated partly by Lerner's fondness for the works of James M. Barrie and partly by a German story, *Germelshausen,* by Friedrich Gerstäcker.

The fantasy is about two American tourists, Tommy Albright and Jeff Douglas (David Brooks and George Keane), who stumble upon a mist-clouded Scottish town that, they eventually discover, reawakens only one day every hundred years. Tommy, who enjoys wandering through the heather on the hill with a local lass, Fiona MacLaren (Marion Bell), returns to New York after learning of the curse that has caused the town's excessively somnolent condition. True love, however, pulls him back to the highlands. The tale was made believable not only through its evocative score but also through Agnes de Mille's ballets, especially the emotion-charged "Sword Dance" performed by James Mitchell during a wedding ceremony and the anguished "Funeral Dance" performed by Lidija Franklin.

A Broadway revival of *Brigadoon* in 1980 did not remain awake very long, but a 1986 production by the New York City Opera was well received. Hollywood's 1954 version co-starred Gene Kelly, Cyd Charisse, and Van Johnson. RCA OC/ Coward-McCann (1947); Chilton (1973)/ TW.

**Brigadoon.** George Keane, David Brooks, and William Hansen. (Vandamm)

# HIGH BUTTON SHOES

**Music:** Jule Styne
**Lyrics:** Sammy Cahn
**Book:** Stephen Longstreet (George Abbott, Phil Silvers uncredited)
**Producers:** Monte Proser & Joseph Kipness
**Director:** George Abbott
**Choreographer:** Jerome Robbins
**Cast:** Phil Silvers, Nanette Fabray, Jack McCauley, Mark Dawson, Joey Faye, Lois Lee, Sondra Lee, Helen Gallagher, Nathaniel Frey, Johnny Stewart, Paul Godkin
**Songs:** "Can't You Just See Yourself?"; "You're My Girl"; "Papa, Won't You Dance With Me?"; "On a Sunday by the Sea"; "I Still Get Jealous"
**New York run:** New Century Theatre, October 9, 1947; 727 p.

*High Button Shoes*, Jule Styne's initial Broadway assignment, offered Phil Silvers his first starring opportunity in the typical role of a brash, bumbling con artist. Though Stephen Longstreet was credited with adapting the story from his own semi-autobiographical novel, *The Sisters Liked Them Handsome,* the musical was completely rewritten by director George Abbott, with an assist from Silvers. In the plot, set in New Brunswick, New Jersey, in 1913, Harrison Floy (Silvers) hoodwinks the Longstreet family into letting him sell some of the valueless property they own. After running off with the profits to Atlantic City (where Jerome Robbins' classic "Keystone Kops" ballet is staged), Floy loses and recovers the money — then loses it forever by betting on the wrong college football team. The musical's showstopper was an old-fashioned song-and-dance polka, "Papa, Won't You Dance With Me?," performed by Nanette Fabray and Jack McCauley.
RCA OC/ TW.

# ALLEGRO

**Music:** Richard Rodgers
**Lyrics & book:** Oscar Hammerstein II
**Producer:** Theatre Guild
**Director:** Agnes de Mille (Oscar Hammerstein II uncredited)
**Choreographer:** Agnes de Mille
**Cast:** John Battles, Annamary Dickey, William Ching, John Conte, Muriel O'Malley, Lisa Kirk, Roberta Jonay
**Songs:** "A Fellow Needs a Girl"; "You Are Never Away"; "So Far"; "Money Isn't Ev'rything"; "The Gentleman Is a Dope"; "Allegro"
**New York run:** Majestic Theatre, October 10, 1947; 315 p.

The third Rodgers and Hammerstein Broadway musical, *Allegro* was their first with a story that had not been based on a previous source. It was a particularly ambitious undertaking, with a theme dealing with the corrupting effect of big institutions on the young and idealistic. The saga is told through the life of a doctor, Joseph Taylor Jr. (John Battles), from his birth in a small midwest American town to his 35th year. We follow Joe's progress as he grows up, goes to school, marries a local belle (Roberta Jonay), joins the staff of a large Chicago hospital that panders to wealthy hypochondriacs, discovers that his wife is unfaithful, and, in the end, returns to his home town with his adoring nurse (Lisa Kirk) to rededicate his life to healing the sick and helping the needy. The show's innovations included a Greek chorus to comment on the action both to the actors and the audience, and the use of multi-level performing areas with nonrepresentational sets.
RCA OC/ Random House (1947)/ R&H.

# MAKE MINE MANHATTAN

**Music:** Richard Lewine
**Lyrics & sketches:** Arnold B. Horwitt
**Producer:** Joseph Hyman
**Directors:** Hassard Short, Max Liebman
**Choreographer:** Lee Sherman
**Cast:** Sid Caesar, David Burns, Sheila Bond, Joshua Shelley, Kyle McDonnell, Danny Daniels, Nelle Fisher, Ray Harrison, Jack Kilty, Larry Carr
**Songs:** "Phil the Fiddler"; "Saturday Night in Central Park"; "I Fell in Love With You"; "My Brudder and Me"; "Gentleman Friend"
**New York run:** Broadhurst Theatre, January 15, 1948; 429 p.

Partly because of the increasing importance of books in book musicals and partly because of the increasing influence of television, 1948 was the last year in which traditional revues found large and receptive audiences. Adhering to its titular request, *Make Mine Manhattan* took a mostly satirical but always light-hearted look at the city's most prominent borough as it covered such matters as the forthcoming establishment of the United Nations' permanent home, the pretentions of Rodgers and Hammerstein's *Allegro*, the distinctive menu at the Schrafft's restaurant chain, the continuous cacophony of street noises, and — recognizing the existence of two other boroughs — the problems of a Bronx boy who must use an intricate series of subway trains to travel to see his girl at the far end of Brooklyn. Sid Caesar, who did imitations, including one of a penny gum machine, was succeeded for the tour by Bert Lahr.
Painted Smiles SC.

# INSIDE U.S.A.

**Music:** Arthur Schwartz
**Lyrics:** Howard Dietz
**Sketches:** Arnold Auerbach, Arnold B. Horwitt, Moss Hart
**Producer:** Arthur Schwartz
**Director:** Robert H. Gordon
**Choreographer:** Helen Tamiris
**Cast:** Beatrice Lillie, Jack Haley, John Tyers, Herb Shriner, Valerie Bettis, Lewis Nye, Carl Reiner, Thelma Carpenter, Estelle Loring, Eric Victor, Talley Beatty, Jack Cassidy
**Songs:** "Inside U.S.A."; "Blue Grass"; "Rhode Island Is Famous for You"; "Haunted Heart"; "At the Mardi Gras"; "My Gal Is Mine Once More"; "First Prize at the Fair"
**New York run:** New Century Theatre, April 30, 1948; 399 p.

Expanding the geographical area of the recently opened *Make Mine Manhattan*, and contracting it from their 1935 revue *At Home Abroad*, Arthur Schwartz and Howard Dietz put together an All-American revue, *Inside U.S.A.*, which borrowed nothing more than the title from John Gunther's sociological survey. With Beatrice Lillie and Jack Haley as comical cicerones, the itinerary included visits to Pittsburgh (where a choral society takes on industrial pollution), the Kentucky Derby (for a lament of one whose lover has been lost betting the ponies), a San Francisco waterfront (the scene of the ballad "Haunted Heart"), the Wisconsin State Fair, the New Orleans Mardi Gras (Bea Lillie is queen), a Wyoming rodeo, and Alberquerque (where two Indians, Miss Lillie and Haley, resolutely refuse to take the country back). *Inside U.S.A.* was the last of seven revues written by Schwartz and Dietz.

# LOVE LIFE

**Music:** Kurt Weill
**Lyrics & book:** Alan Jay Lerner
**Producer:** Cheryl Crawford
**Director:** Elia Kazan
**Choreographer:** Michael Kidd
**Cast:** Nanette Fabray, Ray Middleton, Johnny Stewart, Cheryl Archer, Jay Marshall
**Songs:** "Here I'll Stay"; "Progress"; "I Remember It Well"; "Green-Up Time"; "Economics"; "Mr. Right"
**New York run:** 46th Street Theatre, October 7, 1948; 252 p.

The only collaboration between Kurt Weill and Alan Jay Lerner, *Love Life* was a highly unconventional work. Billed as "A Vaudeville," it related the story of a non-aging couple (Nanette Fabray and Ray Middleton) and their two children from 1791 to the present, with the theme being the gradual changes in the relationship between people as life in America becomes more complex. The musical pieces were incorporated into the show mostly as commentaries on the characters and situations, in much the same way that Weill had used songs in his early German works. As for the musical's structure, there was no linear plot — with beginning, middle and end — but rather a series of separate but connecting scenes interspersed with vaudeville acts through which the authors conveyed their views. Not quite the format for a long-running smash, perhaps, but the show's innovations did turn up in later productions such as *Company* and *A Chorus Line* (nonlinear stories), *Hallelujah, Baby!* (characters did not age over a long period of time), and *Chicago* (conceived as "A Musical Vaudeville").

# WHERE'S CHARLEY?

**Music & lyrics:** Frank Loesser
**Book:** George Abbott
**Producers:** Cy Feuer & Ernest Martin
**Director:** George Abbott
**Choreographer:** George Balanchine
**Cast:** Ray Bolger, Allyn Ann McLerie, Byron Palmer, Doretta Morrow, Horace Cooper, Jane Lawrence, Paul England, Cornell MacNeil
**Songs:** "The New Ashmoleon Marching Society and Students' Conservatory Band"; "My Darling, My Darling"; "Make a Miracle"; "Lovelier Than Ever"; "Once in Love With Amy"; "At the Red Rose Cotillion"
**New York run:** St. James Theatre, October 11, 1948; 792 p.

*Where's Charley?* was based on Brandon Thomas's durable 1892 London farce, *Charley's Aunt*. The first Broadway book musical with a score by Frank Loesser (he wrote five shows in all), the musical is concerned with the madcap doings that result when Oxford undergraduates Charley Wykeham (Ray Bolger) and Jack Chesney (Byron Palmer) entertain their proper lady friends, Amy Spettigue (Allyn Ann McLerie) and Kitty Verdun (Doretta Morrow), in their rooms. To do so, Charley must also play chaperon by disguising himself as his own rich aunt "from Brazil where the nuts come from." Transvestite misunderstanding results in complications when the "aunt" must flee the amorous advances of the girls' money-hungry guardian, and when the real aunt makes an unexpected appearance. The show gave Ray Bolger his biggest hit, plus the nightly opportunity to lead the audience in joining him in singing "Once in Love With Amy." Bolger brought the touring company back to Broadway in 1951 for 48 performances, and repeated his part in the 1952 movie version.
M-E London OC (1958)/ MTI.

# AS THE GIRLS GO

**Music:** Jimmy McHugh
**Lyrics:** Harold Adamson
**Book:** William Roos
**Producer:** Michael Todd
**Director:** Howard Bay
**Choreographer:** Hermes Pan
**Cast:** Bobby Clark, Irene Rich, Bill Callahan, Kathryn Lee, Betty Jane Watson, Hobart Cavanaugh, Betty Lou Barto, Dick Dana, Gregg Sherwood, Jo Sullivan, Buddy Schwab
**Songs:** "As the Girls Go"; "You Say the Nicest Things, Baby"; "There's No Getting Away from You"; "Lucky in the Rain"; "Father's Day"
**New York run:** Winter Garden, November 13, 1948; 420 p.

A throwback to the days when a great personality could carry a musical to success without any help from the book, *As the Girls Go* was a gaudy, rowdy, fast-paced song-and-dance show totally dependent on the antics of one of the theatre's outstanding clowns, Bobby Clark, here making his final Broadway appearance. Clark played Waldo Wellington, the husband of the first woman President of the United States (Irene Rich), and initially the production was planned as a political satire in the tradition of *Of Thee I Sing.* After a disastrous tryout in Boston, however, the plot was largely discarded as Clark leered, pranced, chased Amazonian show girls, blew soap bubbles out of a trumpet, masqueraded as a female barber, and, without looking, tossed his hat clear across the stage and onto a hatrack. During the run, Fran Warren replaced Betty Jane Watson in the romantic lead. *As the Girls Go* was the first Broadway attraction to charge $7.20 for orchestra seats.

# LEND AN EAR

**Music, lyrics & sketches:** Charles Gaynor
**Producers:** William Katzell, Franklin Gilbert, William Eythe
**Directors:** Gower Champion, Hal Gerson
**Choreographer:** Gower Champion
**Cast:** William Eythe, Carol Channing, Yvonne Adair, Gene Nelson, Jennie Lou Law, Gloria Hamilton, Bob Scheerer
**Songs:** "Give Your Heart a Chance to Sing"; "Doin' the Old Yahoo Step"; "Molly O'Reilly"; "Who Hit Me?"
**New York run:** National Theatre, December 16, 1948; 460 p.

Billed as "An Intimate Musical Revue" (there were 21 in the cast), *Lend an Ear* was the first of 14 musicals to be directed and choreographed by Gower Champion. It also revealed the triple talents of writer Charles Gaynor, and it marked the Broadway debut of a squeaky-voiced, saucer-eyed blonde named Carol Channing. Initially presented seven years earlier in Pittsburgh, the youthful show came to New York after a successful engagement in Los Angeles. Among its satirical topics: psychoanalysts; the influence of gossip columnists; a tourist-eye view of Santo Domingo; a third-rate opera company that must speak its lines because it cannot afford orchestral accompaniment; queens of the silent screen; and "The Gladiola Girl," an encapsulated typical musical comedy of the mid-Twenties about flappers and lounge lizards on a Long Island estate where everyone dances "The Old Yahoo Step."
Samuel French (1971)*/ SF.

**Kiss Me, Kate.** Alfred Drake taming his shrew Patricia Morison. (Eileen Darby)

# KISS ME, KATE

**Music & lyrics:** Cole Porter
**Book:** Samuel & Bella Spewack
**Producers:** Saint Subber & Lemuel Ayers
**Director:** John C. Wilson
**Choreographer:** Hanya Holm
**Cast:** Alfred Drake, Patricia Morison, Harold Lang, Lisa Kirk, Harry Clark, Jack Diamond, Annabelle Hill, Lorenzo Fuller, Marc Breaux
**Songs:** "Another Op'nin', Another Show"'; "Why Can't You Behave?"'; "Wunderbar"; "So in Love"; "We Open in Venice"; "Tom, Dick or Harry"; "I've Come to Wive It Wealthily in Padua"; "I Hate Men"; "Were Thine That Special Face"; "Too Darn Hot"; "Where Is the Life That Late I Led?"; "Always True to You in My Fashion"; "Bianca"; "Brush Up Your Shakespeare"; "I Am Ashamed That Women Are So Simple" (lyric: Shakespeare)
**New York run:** New Century Theatre, December 30, 1948; 1,070 p.

After having collaborated ten years earlier on *Leave It to Me!*, Cole Porter and the husband-wife team of Samuel and Bella Spewack were reunited for *Kiss Me, Kate,* the composer's biggest hit and the fourth longest running musical of the Forties. The idea for the show began germinating in 1935 when producer Saint Subber, then a stagehand for the Theatre Guild's production of *The Taming of the Shrew*, became aware that its stars, Alfred Lunt and Lynn Fontanne, quarrelled in private almost as much as did the charaters they were portraying in the play. *Kiss Me, Kate* takes place backstage and onstage at Ford's Theatre in Baltimore, from five p.m. to midnight during one day of a tryout of a musical version of *The Taming of the Shrew*. In the plot, egotistical actor-producer Fred Graham (Alfred Drake) and his temperamental co-star and ex-wife, Lili Vanessi (Patricia Morison) fight and make up and eventually demonstrate their enduring affection for each other — just like Shakespeare's Petruchio and Kate. A subplot involves actress Lois Lane (Lisa Kirk) whose romance with actor Bill Calhoun (Harold Lang) is complicated by Bill's weakness for gambling.

Because of the musical's construction, it is possible to follow the story of *The Taming of the Shrew* even though the play-within-the-play is offered only in excerpts. For his lyrics in the musical numbers sung during *The Shrew's* performance, Porter made use of such Shakespearean lines as "I come to wive it wealthily in Padua," "Were thine that special face," "Where is the life that late I led?," and Kate's finale speech beginning "I am ashamed that women are so simple." The more modern sentiments — "Why Can't You Behave?," "So in Love," "Too Darn Hot," and "Always True to You in My Fashion" — were restricted to the theatre's backstage area.

*Kiss Me, Kate* (the title is from Petruchio's last command in *The Taming of the Shrew)* marked Alfred Drake's first starring part on Broadway and the only major musical in which Patricia Morison originated a leading role. (She won it after it had been rejected by Jarmila Novotna, Mary Martin, Lily Pons, and Jeanette MacDonald.) During the run, Drake was succeeded by Keith Andes and Ted Scott, Miss Morison by Anne Jeffreys, Lisa Kirk by Betty Ann Grove, and Harold Lang by Danny Daniels. The National Company, which toured for one year 11 months, started out with a cast headed by Andes, Jeffreys, Julie Wilson, and Marc Platt, with the first three eventually succeeded by Bob Wright, Frances McCann, and Betty George. In 1953, the Hollywood version put Howard Keel, Kathryn Grayson, Ann Miller, and Tommy Rall in the leads. For other musicals based on Shakespeare, see *The Boys from Syracuse,* page 107.
Columbia OC; Capitol OC/ Knopf (1953); Chilton (1973)/ TW.

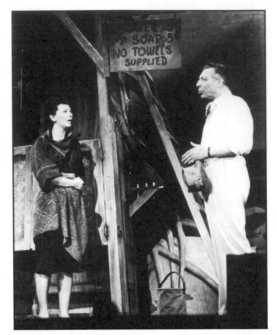

**South Pacific.** Mary Martin and Ezio Pinza.

**South Pacific.** William Tabbert singing "Younger Than Spring-time" to Betta St. John.

# SOUTH PACIFIC

**Music:** Richard Rodgers
**Lyrics:** Oscar Hammerstein II
**Book:** Oscar Hammerstein II & Joshua Logan
**Producers:** Richard Rodgers & Oscar Hammerstein II, Leland Hayward & Joshua Logan
**Director:** Joshua Logan
**Cast:** Mary Martin, Ezio Pinza, Myron McCormick, Juanita Hall, William Tabbert, Betta St. John, Martin Wolfson, Harvey Stephens, Richard Eastham, Henry Slate, Fred Sadoff, Archie Savage
**Songs:** "A Cockeyed Optimist"; "Some Enchanted Evening"; "Bloody Mary"; "There Is Nothin' Like a Dame"; "Bali Ha'i"; "I'm Gonna Wash That Man Right Outa My Hair"; "A Wonderful Guy"; "Younger Than Springtime"; "Happy Talk"; "Honey Bun"; "You've Got to Be Carefully Taught"; "This Nearly Was Mine"
**New York run:** Majestic Theatre, April 7, 1949; 1,925 p.

The catalyst for the musical was director Joshua Logan who, early in 1948, strongly urged Rodgers and Hammerstein to adapt a short story in James Michener's wartime collection *Tales of the South Pacific* as their next Broadway production. "Fo' Dolla," the story Logan recommended, was about Lt. Joe Cable's tender and tragic romance with a Polynesian girl, but it struck the partners as too close to *Madama Butterfly* to sustain interest throughout an entire evening. Their solution was to make this a secondary plot while using another Michener tale, "Our Heroine," as the main story. That one had to do with the unlikely attraction between Nellie Forbush, a naive Navy nurse from Little Rock, and Emile de Becque, a worldly French planter living on a Pacific island, who fall in love on an enchanted evening. Both stories were combined by having Cable and de Becque go on a dangerous mission together behind Japanese lines, from which only de Becque returns. One of the musical's major themes — expressed through the song "You've Got to Be Carefully Taught" — is the folly of the racial prejudice, an issue that comes up when Emile tells Nellie that he had lived with a native woman who bore him two children.

*South Pacific* was the first of two musicals (the other was *The Sound of Music*) in which Mary Martin, who played Nellie, was seen as a Rodgers and Hammerstein heroine, and it marked the Broadway debut of Metropolitan Opera basso Ezio Pinza, who played de Becque. It was the second longest running musical of the decade as well as the second musical to be awarded the Pulitzer Prize for drama. Among actors who appeared in the production during its Broadway tenure were Martha Wright and Cloris Leachman (both played Nellie), Ray Middleton (de Becque), Shirley Jones (one of the nurses), Gene Saks (Professor), and Jack Weston (Stewpot).

The touring company, which was seen in 118 cities over a period of five years, had a cast originally headed by Janet Blair (Nellie), Richard Eastham (de Becque), Diosa Costello (Bloody Mary), Ray Walston (Luther), Julia Migenes (de Becque's daughter), and Alan Baxter (Comdr. Harbison). Cast replacements on the road included Connie Russell (Nellie), Irene Bordoni (Bloody Mary), and David Burns and Benny Baker (Luther). In 1967, *South Pacific* was revived by the Music Theatre of Lincoln Center with Florence Henderson and Giorgio Tozzi in the leads; 20 years later it was staged by the New York City Opera. The 1958 screen version co-starred Mitzi Gaynor and Rossano Brazzi (with Tozzi's voice). Columbia OC; Columbia OC (1967); CBS SC (1986)/ Random House (1949)/ R&H.

# MISS LIBERTY

**Music & lyrics:** Irving Berlin
**Book:** Robert E. Sherwood
**Producers:** Irving Berlin, Robert E. Sherwood & Moss Hart
**Director:** Moss Hart
**Choreographer:** Jerome Robbins
**Cast:** Eddie Albert, Allyn Ann McLerie, Mary McCarty, Charles Dingle, Philip Bourneuf, Ethel Griffies, Herbert Berghof, Tommy Rall, Janice Rule, Maria Karnilova, Dody Goodman
**Songs:** "Little Fish in a Big Pond"; "Let's Take an Old-Fashioned Walk"; "Homework"; "Paris Wakes Up and Smiles"; "Only for Americans"; "Just One Way to Say I Love You"; "You Can Have Him"; "Give Me Your Tired, Your Poor" (poem: Emma Lazarus)
**New York run:** Imperial Theatre, July 15, 1949; 308 p.

*Miss Liberty* boasted impressive credentials: songs by Irving Berlin, book by Robert E. Sherwood (his only musical), and direction by Moss Hart. If the results fell somewhat short of expectations, the show was still very much in the Americana mold of *Oklahoma!* and *Bloomer Girl* that offered a comforting view of the past to make audiences feel confident about the future. Here the story — set in New York and Paris in 1885 — deals with the rivalry between two newspapers, the *Herald* and the *World*, and the search for the model who posed for the Statue of Liberty. When the wrong model is brought to New York amid much hoopla, there is the inevitable consternation when the error is discovered. A happy ending is devised, however, just in time for the statue's dedication when all join in singing "Give Me Your Tired, Your Poor."
Columbia OC/ Samuel French (1986)*/ SF.

# LOST IN THE STARS

**Music:** Kurt Weill
**Lyrics & book:** Maxwell Anderson
**Producer:** Playwrights' Company
**Director:** Rouben Mamoulian
**Cast:** Todd Duncan, Leslie Banks, Warren Coleman, Inez Matthews, Julian Mayfield, Frank Roane, Sheila Guyse, Herbert Coleman
**Songs:** "The Hills of Ixipo"; "Thousands of Miles"; "Train to Johannesburg"; "The Little Grey House"; "Trouble Man"; "Lost in the Stars"; "Stay Well"; "Cry, the Beloved Country"; "Big Mole"; "A Bird of Passage"
**New York run:** Music Box, October 30, 1949; 273 p.

Regarding the musical adaptation of Alan Paton's novel of South Africa, *Cry, the Beloved Country,* Kurt Weill once explained, "We wanted to treat the race problem as part of the human problem. The tragedy through which we are living is the tragedy of all men, white or black, rich or poor, young or old." After Absalom Kumalo (Julian Mayfield), the son of black minister Stephen Kumalo (Todd Duncan), accidentally kills a white man in an attempted robbery in Johannesburg, he is courageous enough to admit his guilt and face hanging, even though his companions, protesting their innocence, go free. As Absalom is about to die, Stephen is visited by the father of the slain man. Though James Jarvis (Leslie Banks) is a firm believer in apartheid, he admires the minister for his courage and honesty, and the play ends with each man saying, "I have a friend." *Lost in the Stars* was Kurt Weill's last Broadway production. In 1958, the work became part of the repertory of the New York City Opera, and in 1972 it was presented on Broadway with Brock Peters as Stephen Kumalo. Peters and Melba Moore were in the 1974 film version.
MCA OC/ Chilton (1976)/ R&H.

**Miss Liberty.** Allyn Ann McLerie, Eddie Albert, Mary McCarty, Charles Dingle, Maria Karnilova, and Tommy Rall lead the cast in singing "Give Me Your Tired, Your Poor."

**Lost in the Stars.** Warren Coleman, Todd Duncan, and Herbert Coleman. (Karger-Pix)

# GENTLEMEN PREFER BLONDES

**Music:** Jule Styne
**Lyrics:** Leo Robin
**Book:** Joseph Stein & Anita Loos
**Producers:** Herman Levin & Oliver Smith
**Director:** John C. Wilson
**Choreographer:** Agnes de Mille
**Cast:** Carol Channing, Yvonne Adair, Jack McCauley, Eric Brotherson, Alice Pearce, Rex Evans, Anita Alvarez, George S. Irving, Mort Marshall, Howard Morris, Charles "Honi" Coles, Cholly Atkins
**Songs:** "Bye, Bye, Baby"; "A Little Girl from Little Rock"; "Just a Kiss Apart"; "It's Delightful Down in Chile"; "Diamonds Are a Girl's Best Friend"
**New York run:** Ziegfeld Theatre, December 8, 1949; 740 p.

Based on Anita Loos' popular 1926 novel and play of the same name, *Gentlemen Prefer Blondes* took a satirical look at the wild and wacky Twenties, though there was no attempt at parodying the songs and styles as in the manner of Sandy Wilson's *The Boy Friend.* Carol Channing, in her first major role, scored such a success as the gold-digging little girl from Little Rock that she was elevated to stardom during the show's run. The scenes occur mostly aboard the *Ile de France,* which is taking Lorelei Lee and her chum Dorothy Shaw (Yvonne Adair) to Paris, courtesy of Lorelei's generous friend, button tycoon Gus Esmond (Jack McCauley). En route, the girls meet a number of accommodating gentlemen, including Sir Francis Beekman (Rex Evans) who loses a diamond tiara to Lorelei (who thereby wins a best friend) and Henry Spofford (Eric Brotherson), a Philadelphia Main Liner who loses his heart to Dorothy. The 1953 movie version offered Marilyn Monroe and Jane Russell, plus a hybrid score.

In 1973, a new stage version, called *Lorelei,* retained ten songs from the original score and added five new ones by Jule Styne, Betty Comden and Adolph Green. Carol Channing again headed the cast which included Tamara Long (Dorothy), Peter Palmer (Gus), Lee Roy Reams (Henry), and Jack Fletcher (Sir Francis). The book, now credited to Kenny Solms and Gail Parent, retained the same basic story, except for a modern-day prologue and epilogue that found Lorelei reminiscing about the past. After touring 11 months, *Lorelei* opened on Broadway in January 1974, and gave 320 performances.
Columbia OC; MGM OC (1973, 1974).

**Gentlemen Prefer Blondes.** Carol Channing singing "Diamonds Are a Girl's Best Friend." (Fred Fehl)

**Call Me Madam.** Ethel Merman as Sally Adams. (Vandamm)

# CALL ME MADAM
**Music & lyrics:** Irving Berlin
**Book:** Howard Lindsay & Russel Crouse
**Producer:** Leland Hayward
**Director:** George Abbott
**Choreographer:** Jerome Robbins
**Cast:** Ethel Merman, Paul Lukas, Russell Nype, Galina Talva, Pat Harrington, Alan Hewitt, Tommy Rall, Nathaniel Frey
**Songs:** "The Hostess With the Mostes' on the Ball"; "Can You Use Any Money Today?"; "Marrying for Love"; "It's a Lovely Day Today"; "They Like Ike"; "The Best Thing for You"; "You're Just in Love"
**New York run:** Imperial Theatre, October 12, 1950; 644 p.

Once President Harry S. Truman named Washington party-giver Perle Mesta Ambassador to Luxembourg, the foundation was laid for a musical-comedy satire that would kid politics, foreign affairs, and the familiar sight of the comically gauche American abroad. Once Ethel Merman and Irving Berlin joined Howard Lindsay and Russel Crouse in the enterprise, the foundation was laid for a solid Broadway hit. The story, according to the program, takes place "in two mythical countries, one is Lichtenburg, the other the United States of America." When Sally Adams, the hostess with the mostes' on the ball, becomes Ambassador to the tiny duchy, she surprises and charms the local gentry, especially Foreign Minister Cosmo Constantine (Paul Lukas), with her no-nonsense, undiplomatic manner. In a subplot, Sally's young aide Kenneth Gibson (Russell Nype) finds himself falling for Lichtenburg's Princess Marie (Galina Talva), a condition that prompts the ambassador to itemize the symptoms in the classic contrapuntal duet, "You're Just in Love." In a running gag, Sally periodically chats with President Truman on the telephone, thereby justifying the nightly gimmick of Truman look-alike Irving Fisher taking a bow during the curtain calls. The film version, also starring Ethel Merman, was released in 1953. Three years later, Miss Merman appeared in *Happy Hunting,* another Lindsay-Crouse stage musical contrasting American brashness with European courtliness that was also sparked by a topical event, the wedding of Grace Kelly and Prince Rainier of Monaco. RCA OC (minus Merman); MCA OC (only Merman)/ Irving Berlin Ltd., London (1956)*/ MTI.

# GUYS AND DOLLS

**Music & lyrics:** Frank Loesser
**Book:** Abe Burrows
**Producers:** Cy Feuer & Ernest Martin
**Director:** George S. Kaufman
**Choreographer:** Michael Kidd
**Cast:** Robert Alda, Vivian Blaine, Sam Levene, Isabel Bigley, Pat Rooney Sr., B. S. Pully, Stubby Kaye, Tom Pedi, Johnny Silver, Peter Gennaro, Onna White, Buddy Schwab
**Songs :** "Fugue for Tinhorns"; "Follow the Fold"; "The Oldest Established"; "I'll Know"; "A Bushel and a Peck"; "Adelaide's Lament"; "Guys and Dolls"; "If I Were a Bell"; "My Time of Day"; "I've Never Been in Love Before"; "Take Back Your Mink"; "More I Cannot Wish You"; "Luck Be a Lady"; "Sue Me"; "Sit Down, You're Rockin' the Boat"; "Marry the Man Today"
**New York run:** 46th Street Theatre, November 24, 1950; 1,200 p.

Though it turned out to be one of Broadway's most hilarious musical comedies — as well as an acknowledged classic in the field — *Guys and Dolls* was originally planned as a serious romantic story. Much impressed by the success of *South Pacific*, producers Cy Feuer and Ernest Martin felt that if such a compelling musical play could be written about the unlikely romance between naive Nellie Forbush and sophisticated Emile de Becque, an equally affecting story could be created out of the unlikely romance between a pure-at-heart Salvation Army-type reformer and a slick Broadway gambler, the two leading characters in Damon Runyon's short story "The Idyll of Miss Sarah Brown." For the score, the producers enlisted Frank Loesser (with whom they had been associated on *Where's Charley?*), then tried some 11 librettists though none came up with an acceptable script. The last of these writers, Jo Swerling, had a contract giving him primary credit as author no matter how many subsequent changes might be made, which is the reason his name always appears on programs as co-librettist. After so many script rejections, Feuer and Martin changed their minds and now decided that *Guys and Dolls* could only work if it were played for laughs. This led them to Abe Burrows, a radio and television comedy writer without theatrical experience, who wrote an entirely new book that he fitted to Loesser's already existing score.

In this so-called "Musical Fable of Broadway," the high-minded lowlifes and spunky do-gooders of Damon Runyon's world come colorfully alive in such characters as Sky Masterson (Robert Alda), the bet-on-anything gambler; Nathan Detroit (Sam Levene), the perpetually harried organizer of the oldest established permanent floating crap game in New York, who bets Sky that he can't make the next girl he sees fall in love with him; Miss Sarah Brown (Isabel Bigley) of the Save-a-Soul Mission on Times Square, who *is* the next girl Sky sees and who does succumb; and Miss Adelaide (Vivian Blaine), the main attraction at the Hot Box nightclub, whose psychosomatic perpetual cold stems from her being engaged to Nathan for 14 years. One of the show's memorable scenes occurs in the mission where Nicely-Nicely Johnson (Stubby Kaye) confesses his sins in the rousing "Sit Down, You're Rockin' the Boat." *Guys and Dolls* was the fifth longest-running Broadway musical of the Fifties. Its touring company traveled for two years four months with a cast originally headed by Allan Jones (Sky), Pamela Britton (Adelaide), Julie Oshins (Nathan), and Jan Clayton (Sarah).

A Broadway revival of *Guys and Dolls* with an all-black cast was mounted in 1976. In it were James Randolph (Sky), Norma Donaldson (Adelaide), Robert Guillaume (Nathan), Ernestine Jackson (Sarah), and Ken Page (Nicely-Nicely). The run lasted 239 performances. The film version, released in 1955, starred Marlon Brando, Vivian Blaine, Frank Sinatra, and Jean Simmons.
MCA OC; Motown OC (1976)/ Doubleday Anchor (1956)/ MTI.

**Guys and Dolls.** Sam Levene and Vivian Blaine singing "Sue Me." (Eileen Darby)

**Guys and Dolls.** Robert Alda throws the dice as Stubby Kaye, B. S. Pully, Johnny Silver, and Sam Levene watch. (Eileen Darby)

**The King and I.** Anna and son (Gertrude Lawrence and Sandy Kennedy) arrive in Bangkok. (Vandamm)

**The King and I.** ''Shall We Dance?'' Anna (Gertrude Lawrence) asks the King (Yul Brynner). (Vandamm)

# THE KING AND I

**Music:** Richard Rodgers
**Lyrics & book:** Oscar Hammerstein II
**Producers:** Richard Rodgers & Oscar Hammerstein II
**Director:** John van Druten
**Choreographer:** Jerome Robbins
**Cast:** Gertrude Lawrence, Yul Brynner, Dorothy Sarnoff, Doretta Morrow, Larry Douglas, Johnny Stewart, Sandy Kennedy, Lee Becker Theodore, Gemze de Lappe, Yuriko, Baayork Lee
**Songs:** "I Whistle a Happy Tune"; "My Lord and Master"; "Hello, Young Lovers"; "March of the Siamese Children" (instrumental); "A Puzzlement"; "Getting to Know You"; "We Kiss in a Shadow"; "Shall I Tell You What I Think of You?"; "Something Wonderful"; "I Have Dreamed"; "Shall We Dance?"
**New York run:** St. James Theatre, March 29, 1951; 1,246 p.

Upon reading Margaret Landon's novel, *Anna and the King of Siam,* and seeing the film version, Gertrude Lawrence became convinced that this would be the ideal vehicle for her return to the musical stage. She first sounded out Cole Porter about the project, then turned to Rodgers and Hammerstein who, though aware of her vocal limitations, readily agreed to write and produce it. Based on the diaries of an adventurous Englishwoman, Anna Leonowens, the story of *The King and I* (a title Miss Lawrence never liked) is set in Bangkok in the early 1860s. Anna, the new governess and teacher to King Mongkut's many children, has frequent clashes with the autocratic, semi-barbaric ruler, but eventually — and discretely — comes to love him. She exerts great influence in helping to democratize the country, and after the King's death remains as adviser to his successor, Crown Prince Chulalongkorn (Johnny Stewart). A tragic secondary plot concerns the furtive romance between Tuptim (Doretta Morrow), one of Mongkut's wives, and her lover Lun Tha (Larry Douglas). Of dramatic importance in the plot was Jerome Robbins' narrative ballet, "The Small House of Uncle Thomas," based on *Uncle Tom's Cabin.*

Cast as the King was Yul Brynner, a virtually unknown actor who won the role after attempts had been made to interest Rex Harrison, Noël Coward, and Alfred Drake (Drake did replace Brynner briefly during the run). Following Miss Lawrence's death in September 1952, Anna was played successively by Constance Carpenter, Annamary Dickey, and Patricia Morison. *The King and I's* Broadway run was the fourth longest of the decade, and the musical toured for over a year and a half with Miss Morison and Brynner.

Though in 1964 Darren McGavin played the Siamese monarch opposite Risë Stevens' Anna in the premiere production of the Music Theatre of Lincoln Center, and others have played it throughout the country, the role of King Mongkut became the virtual personal property of Yul Brynner. By the sheer force of his personality and without any change in the script, he managed to switch the dramatic spotlight from Anna to the King. In 1956, Brynner co-starred in the film version with Deborah Kerr. Twenty years later, now solo starred, he began touring in a new stage production (with Constance Towers as Anna) that played New York in 1977 (see page 248), and London 1979. Brynner resumed touring in 1981 and returned to New York in December 1984, with Mary Beth Peil as Anna. By the end of this engagement, King Yul had had a reign lasting 4,625 performances.

MCA OC; RCA OC (1964); RCA OC (1977)/ Random House (1951)/ R&H.

# A TREE GROWS IN BROOKLYN

**Music:** Arthur Schwartz
**Lyrics:** Dorothy Fields
**Book:** George Abbott & Betty Smith
**Producers:** George Abbott & Robert Fryer
**Director:** George Abbott
**Choreographer:** Herbert Ross
**Cast:** Shirley Booth, Johnny Johnston, Marcia Van Dyke, Nomi Mitty, Nathaniel Frey, Harland Dixon, Lou Wills Jr.
**Songs:** "Make the Man Love Me"; "I'm Like a New Broom"; "Look Who's Dancing"; "Love Is the Reason"; "I'll Buy You a Star"; "He Had Refinement"; "Growing Pains"
**New York run:** Alvin Theatre, April 19, 1951; 270 p.

Far removed from the sophisticated revues and book musicals Arthur Schwartz and Dorothy Fields were usually associated with was this sentimental, nostalgic view of a Brooklyn working-class family at the turn of the century. Betty Smith, who had originally written her autobiographical novel as a play, shared adaptation credit with director-producer George Abbott for a work that was initially supposed to have a score by Irving Berlin. The story relates the saga of the Nolan clan: the charming but weak Johnny (Johnny Johnston), who finds relief in the bottle; his hard-working, devoted wife Katie (Marcia Van Dyke); their daughter Francie (Nomi Mitty), who idolizes her father; and Katie's sister, the amiable, available Cissy (Shirley Booth), whose affairs with a string of unwed husbands help lighten the basically tragic story. Miss Booth, who scored an impressive hit, was seen two years later in *By the Beautiful Sea,* another Arthur Schwartz-Dorothy Fields musical that was also set in turn-of-the-century Brooklyn. Columbia OC/ Harper (1951).

# PAINT YOUR WAGON

**Music:** Frederick Loewe
**Lyrics & book:** Alan Jay Lerner
**Producer:** Cheryl Crawford
**Director:** Daniel Mann
**Choreographer:** Agnes de Mille
**Cast:** James Barton, Olga San Juan, Tony Bavaar, James Mitchell, Kay Medford, Gemze de Lappe, Marijane Maricle
**Songs:** "I Talk to the Trees"; "What's Goin' on Here?"; "They Call the Wind Maria"; "I Still See Elisa"; "Another Autumn"; "Wand'rin' Star"
**New York run:** Shubert Theatre, November 12, 1951; 289 p.

Filling their musical play with authentic incidents and backgrounds, Lerner and Loewe struck it rich both musically and dramatically with a work that captured the flavor of the roistering, robust California gold fields of 1853. James Barton, returning to the musical stage for the first time in 20 years, took the part of Ben Rumson, a grizzled prospector whose daughter Jennifer (Olga San Juan) discovers gold near their camp. Word of the strike quickly spreads and before long there are over 4,000 inhabitants of the new town of Rumson. Jennifer, who has fallen in love with Julio (Tony Bavaar), a Mexican prospector, goes East to school but returns to Julio when the gold strike peters out. Rumson is now virtually a ghost town, and Ben is left with nothing but his hopes and dreams. During the Broadway run, Barton was succeeded by Burl Ives and Eddie Dowling. The 1969 film version, with Clint Eastwood, Lee Marvin and Jean Seberg told a different story.
RCA OC/ Coward-McCann (1952)/ TW.

# PAL JOEY

**Music:** Richard Rodgers
**Lyrics:** Lorenz Hart
**Book:** John O'Hara (George Abbott uncredited)
**Producers:** Jule Styne & Leonard Key
**Directors:** Robert Alton, David Alexander
**Choreographer:** Robert Alton
**Cast:** Vivienne Segal, Harold Lang, Helen Gallagher, Lionel Stander, Patricia Northrop, Elaine Stritch, Helen Wood, Barbara Nichols, Jack Waldron, Robert Fortier
**Songs:** Same as original production
**New York run:** Broadhurst Theatre, January 3, 1952; 540 p.

(See page 112.)

**Pal Joey.** Harold Lang (as Joey) is distracted by Patricia Northrop much to the irritation of patroness Vivienne Segal. (Eileen Darby)

# NEW FACES OF 1952
**Music, lyrics & sketches:** Miscellaneous writers
**Producer:** Leonard Sillman
**Directors:** John Murray Anderson, John Beal
**Choreographer:** Richard Barstow
**Cast:** Ronny Graham, Eartha Kitt, Robert Clary, June Carroll, Virginia de Luce, Alice Ghostley, Carol Lawrence, Paul Lynde
**Songs:** "Lucky Pierre" (Ronny Graham); "Guess Who I Saw Today" (Murray Grand-Elisse Boyd); "Love Is a Simple Thing" (Arthur Siegel-June Carroll); "Boston Beguine" (Sheldon Harnick); "Lizzie Bordon" (Michael Brown); "I'm in Love with Miss Logan" (Graham); "Penny Candy" (Siegel-Carroll); "Monotonous" (Siegel-Carroll)
**New York run:** Royale Theatre, May 16, 1952; 365 p.

Of the seven *New Faces* revues assembled by Leonard Sillman, the 1952 edition was the most admired, both for the talent of the performers and the cleverness of the writing. Among the numbers were "Boston Beguine," Alice Ghostley's revelation of improper behavior in a proper surrounding; "Lizzie Borden," a sprightly hoedown celebrating an unsightly deed; "Guess Who I Saw Today," a rueful ballad of infidelity sung by June Carroll; "Monotonous," in which Eartha Kitt purred about her boring life; Ronny Graham's sendup of Truman Capote called "Oedipus Goes South"; Mel Brooks' burlesque of *Death of a Salesman*, in which a pickpocket feels betrayed by a son who shuns the family business; and Paul Lynde's speech, while swathed in bandages, about his misadventures on an African safari. The Royale Theatre is on 45th Street west of Broadway. In 1954, the film version was released with the original performers. RCA OC.

# WISH YOU WERE HERE
**Music & lyrics:** Harold Rome
**Book:** Arthur Kober & Joshua Logan
**Producers:** Leland Hayward & Joshua Logan
**Director:** Joshua Logan
**Choreographer:** Joshua Logan (Jerome Robbins uncredited)
**Cast:** Sheila Bond, Jack Cassidy, Patricia Marand, Sidney Armus, Paul Valentine, Harry Clark, Florence Henderson, Tom Tryon, Larry Blyden, Phyllis Newman, Reid Shelton
**Songs:** "Social Director"; "Goodbye Love"; "Could Be"; "Tripping the Light Fantastic"; "Where Did the Night Go?"; "Summer Afternoon"; "Don José of Far Rockaway"; "Wish You Were Here"; "Flattery"
**New York run:** Imperial Theatre, June 25, 1952; 598 p.

It was known as the musical with the swimming pool, but *Wish You Were Here* had other things going for it, including a cast of ingratiating actors, a warm and witty score by Harold Rome, and a director, Joshua Logan, who wouldn't stop making improvements even after the Broadway opening (among them were new dances choreographed by Jerome Robbins). The musical, which Arthur Kober and Logan adapted from Kober's 1937 play, *Having Wonderful Time,* is set in Camp Karefree, an adult summer camp "where friendships are formed to last a whole lifetime through," and is concerned with middle-class New Yorkers trying to make the most of a two-week vacation in the Catskills. Mainly it's about Teddy Stern (Patricia Marand), a secretary from Brooklyn, who finds true love — after a series of misunderstandings — with Chick Miller (Jack Cassidy), a law student working as a waiter by day and a dancing partner by night. RCA OC/ MTI.

# WONDERFUL TOWN

**Music:** Leonard Bernstein
**Lyrics:** Betty Comden & Adolph Green
**Book:** Joseph Fields & Jerome Chodorov
**Producer:** Robert Fryer
**Director:** George Abbott (Jerome Robbins uncredited)
**Choreographer:** Donald Saddler
**Cast:** Rosalind Russell, George Gaynes, Edie Adams, Henry Lascoe, Dort Clark, Dody Goodman, Nathaniel Frey, Joe Layton
**Songs:** "Christopher Street", "Ohio"; "One Hundred Easy Ways"; "What a Waste"; "A Little Bit in Love"; "A Quiet Girl"; "Conga!"; "Swing!"; "It's Love"; "Wrong Note Rag"
**New York run:** Winter Garden, February 25, 1953; 559 p.

Because it again showed New York as just about the liveliest, friendliest place on earth, and because it again had a score by Leonard Bernstein, Betty Comden and Adolph Green and direction by George Abbott, *Wonderful Town* is generally accepted as the successor to *On The Town*. The songwriters, in fact, became involved in the project only five weeks before rehearsals when they took over the assignment from Leroy Anderson and Arnold Horwitt, who had bowed out over a disagreement with librettists Joseph Fields (brother of Herbert and Dorothy) and Jerome Chodorov. The musical was based on Ruth McKinney's *New Yorker* short stories — which Fields and Chodorov had already turned into the 1940 Broadway hit *My Sister Eileen* — and concerns the adventures of Miss McKinney and her sister in Greenwich Village after arriving from Ohio seeking careers. Ruth has problems getting her stories accepted by *The Manhatter* magazine and Eileen (Edie Adams) has problems warding off admirers. On a freelance newspaper assignment, Ruth gets to interview seven over-amorous, Conga-dancing Brazilian naval cadets, who cause a near-riot. Though this lands Ruth in jail, she also manages to land a handsome magazine editor (George Gaynes). Rosalind Russell, as Ruth, scored resoundingly in her only major musical-comedy role, and was succeeded during the run by Carol Channing.
MCA OC/ Random House (1953); Chilton (1976)/ TW.

**Wonderful Town.** Edie Adams and Rosalind Russell singing "Ohio." (Vandamm)

# PORGY AND BESS

**Music:** George Gershwin
**Lyrics:** DuBose Heyward, Ira Gershwin
**Book:** DuBose Heyward
**Producers:** Blevins Davis & Robert Breen
**Director:** Robert Breen
**Cast:**   LeVern Hutcherson (or Leslie Scott, Irving Barnes), Leontyne Price (or Urylee Leonardos), Cab Calloway, John McCurry, Helen Colbert, Helen Thigpen, Georgia Burke, Helen Dowdy
**Songs:** Same as original production
**New York run:** Ziegfeld Theatre, March 10, 1953; 305 p.

(See page 91.)

# CAN-CAN

**Music & lyrics:** Cole Porter
**Book:** Abe Burrows
**Producers:** Cy Feuer & Ernest Martin
**Director:** Abe Burrows
**Choreographer:** Michael Kidd
**Cast:**   Lilo, Peter Cookson, Hans Conried, Gwen Verdon, Erik Rhodes, Dania Krupska, Phil Leeds, DeeDee Wood
**Songs:** "Never Give Anything Away"; "C'est Magnifique"; "Come Along With Me"; "Live and Let Live"; "I Am in Love"; "Montmart' "; "Allez-vous-en"; "Never Never Be an Artist"; "It's All Right With Me"; "I Love Paris"; "Can-Can"
**New York run:** Shubert Theatre, May 7, 1953; 892 p.

To make sure that his script for *Can-Can* would be historically authentic, Abe Burrows traveled to Paris where he researched the records of the courts, the police, and the Chamber of Deputies. To his surprise, Burrows discovered that there were then a number of blue-nose organizations devoted to the suppression of such immoral exhibitions as the high-kicking, derriere-baring dance. This gave him the outline for his plot. Set in 1893, it tells of La Mome Pistache who is so distressed about the investigation of her Bal du Paradis — where the chief attraction is the Can-Can — that she tries to vamp the highly moral investigating judge, Aristide Forestier. Eventually, the two fall in love and when the case comes to trial, Forestier himself takes over the defense and wins acquittal. Though originally intended for Carol Channing, the role of Pistache went to the French actress Lilo (who introduced "I Love Paris"), but most of the kudos were for Gwen Verdon (who stopped the show with an Apache dance and the sexy "Garden of Eden" ballet) in her first major Broadway role.

In 1981, *Can-Can* again kicked up its heels — albeit briefly — in a revival starring Zizi Jeanmaire and Ron Husmann that was directed by Burrows. The altered Hollywood version, released in 1960, featured Frank Sinatra, Shirley MacLaine, and Maurice Chevalier.
Capitol OC/ TW.

**Me and Juliet.** Isabel Bigley singing "I'm Your Girl" to Bill Hayes. (Eileen Darby)

# ME AND JULIET
**Music:** Richard Rodgers
**Lyrics & book:** Oscar Hammerstein II
**Producers:** Richard Rodgers & Oscar Hammerstein II
**Director:** George Abbott
**Choreographer:** Robert Alton
**Cast:** Isabel Bigley, Bill Hayes, Joan McCracken, Ray Walston, Mark Dawson, George S. Irving, Barbara Carroll, Shirley MacLaine
**Songs:** "A Very Special Day"; "Marriage-Type Love"; "Keep It Gay"; "The Big Black Giant"; "No Other Love"; "It's Me"; "I'm Your Girl"
**New York run:** Majestic Theatre, May 28, 1953; 358 p.

Writing in the lighter form of musical comedy rather than in their more accustomed "serious" form of musical play, Rodgers and Hammerstein created *Me and Juliet* as their Valentine to show business. The action — in *Kiss Me, Kate* fashion — takes place both backstage and onstage of a theatre during the performance of a play. Here the tale concerns a romance between a singer in the chorus (Isabel Bigley) and the assistant stage manager (Bill Hayes) whose newfound bliss is temporarily threatened by the jealous, heavy-drinking electrician (Mark Dawson). The melody of the show's best-known song, "No Other Love," had been previously used as background for the "Beneath the Southern Cross" episode in the NBC-TV series, *Victory at Sea. Me and Juliet* was the 29th and penultimate Broadway musical choreographed by Robert Alton. RCA OC/ Random House (1953)/ R&H.

# KISMET

**Music & lyrics:** Robert Wright & George Forrest based on Alexander Borodin
**Book:** Charles Lederer & Luther Davis
**Producers:** Charles Lederer, Edwin Lester
**Director:** Albert Marre
**Choreographer:** Jack Cole
**Cast:** Alfred Drake, Doretta Morrow, Joan Diener, Henry Calvin, Richard Kiley, Steve Reeves, Beatrice Kraft
**Songs:** "Sands of Time"; "Rhymes Have I"; "Not Since Nineveh"; "Baubles, Bangles and Beads"; "Stranger in Paradise"; "Night of My Nights"; "And This Is My Beloved"; "The Olive Tree"
**New York run:** Ziegfeld Theatre, December 3, 1953; 583 p.

The story of *Kismet* was adapted from a 1911 play by Edward Knoblock that was closely identified with Otis Skinner. The music of *Kismet* was adapted from themes Alexander Borodin composed for such works as the "Polovtsian Dances" ("Stranger in Paradise") and the D-Major String Quartet ("And This Is My Beloved," "Baubles, Bangles and Beads"). In this "Musical Arabian Night," the action occurs within a 24-hour period from dawn to dawn in ancient Baghdad, where a roguish public poet (Alfred Drake) assumes the identity of Hajj the beggar and has a series of unlikely adventures. By the time they have ended, he has drowned the wicked Wazir (Henry Calvin), has seen his daughter Marsinah (Doretta Morrow) wedded to the handsome Caliph (Richard Kiley), has been appointed Emir of Baghdad, and has gone off into the desert with the Wazir's luscious wife Lalume (Joan Diener). Before coming to New York, *Kismet* had first been presented in the summer of 1953 by Edwin Lester's Los Angeles and San Francisco Civic Light Opera Association. The film version, with Howard Keel and Ann Blyth, was released in 1955.

In 1965 the musical was revived by the Music Theatre of Lincoln Center with Alfred Drake again giving a bravura performance, and in 1985 it was added to the repertory of the New York City Opera. An all-black variation, *Timbuktu,* arrived on Broadway in 1978 and remained for 221 performances. It kept the music but switched the locale to the ancient African kingdom of Mali, and its cast was headed by Eartha Kitt, Ira Hawkins, Melba Moore, and Gilbert Price. For other musicals with scores based on classical themes, see *Blossom Time* page 38.
Columbia OC; RCA OC (1965)/ Random House (1954)/ MTI.

**The Threepenny Opera.** Lotte Lenya as Jenny.

# THE THREEPENNY OPERA

**Music:** Kurt Weill
**Lyrics & book:** Marc Blitzstein
**Producers:** Carmen Capalbo & Stanley Chase
**Director:** Carmen Capalbo
**Cast:** Lotte Lenya, Scott Merrill, Leon Lishner, Jo Sullivan, Charlotte Rae, Beatrice Arthur, Gerald Price, John Astin, Joseph Beruh, Gerrianne Raphael
**Songs:** "The Ballad of Mack the Knife"; "Army Song"; "Love Song"; "Pirate Jenny"; "Tango-Ballad"; "Ballad of the Easy Life"; "Barbara Song"; "Useless Song"; "Solomon Song"
**New York run:** Theatre de Lys, March 10, 1954; 95 p. Reopened: September 20, 1955; 2,611 p.

The reason for the two engagements noted above is that the initial showing of Marc Blitzstein's English-language version of the Kurt Weill-Bertold Brecht *Die Dreigroschenoper* at the Theatre de Lys (now the Lucille Lortel) had to be terminated because of a prior booking. Led by critic Brooks Atkinson, public demand brought it back 15 months after the closing, with cast replacements including Frederic Downs for Leon Lishner, Jane Connell for Charlotte Rae, Tige Andrews for Gerald Price, Eddie Lawrence for Joseph Beruh, and Chris Chase for Gerrianne Raphael. At this writing, the return engagement is the second longest running production ever mounted Off Broadway. In its original form, the work was presented in Berlin in 1928 on the 200th anniverasy of *The Beggar's Opera* — credited as the first ballad opera, or musical comedy — on which it was based. The play's bitter, raffish view of contemporary morality, combined with its jingly, beer-hall tunes, quickly made it a favorite throughout Europe, and in 1933 the first American adaptation had a brief run on Broadway.

Set in Victorian London, *The Threepenny Opera* spins the tale of Macheath (Scott Merrill), an outlaw known as Mack the Knife. Mack marries Polly Peachum (Jo Sullivan), the daughter of the leader of Soho's underworld, but he is betrayed by his in-laws and is sent to Newgate Prison. After being freed by Lucy Brown (Beatrice Arthur), the police chief's daughter, Mack is again betrayed — this time by Jenny the whore (Lotte Lenya, Weill's widow, who had originated the role in Berlin). Sentenced to be hanged, Mack receives a last-minute reprieve from the queen, thus providing the play with a mock-heroic ending. Among the more than 200 actors who played the 22 parts during the show's run were Carole Cook, Valerie Bettis, and Dolly Haas (Jenny); James Mitchell and Jerry Orbach (Mack); Pert Kelton and Nancy Andrews (Mrs. Peachum); Georgia Brown (Lucy); Edward Asner (Peachum); and Estelle Parsons (Mrs. Coaxer). The 1964 film version featured Hildegarde Neff and Kurt Jurgens.

In 1976, Joseph Papp's New York Shakespeare Festival at Lincoln Center offered an even more abrasive version of *The Threepenny Opera* in an adaptation by Ralph Manheim and John Willett. With a cast headed by Raul Julia (Mack) and Ellen Greene (Jenny), the show also played Broadway for a total run of 307 performances.

*The Beggar's Opera,* the 18th Century English musical that had inspired the German version, was first presented in America in 1750. Its most recent production was in 1972 when the Chelsea Theatre of Brooklyn staged a revival that was also shown at an Off Broadway theatre in Manhattan. It ran 253 performances. Another variation, *Beggar's Holiday,* updating the scene to modern America, opened on Broadway in 1946. The music was by Duke Ellington, the lyrics and libretto by John Latouche, and the cast included Alfred Drake, Zero Mostel, and Bernice Parks.

Polydor OC; Columbia OC (1976)/ R&H.

**The Golden Apple.** Salesman Jonathan Lucas displays his wares for Kaye Ballard, Priscilla Gillette, and Stephen Douglass. (Vandamm)

# THE GOLDEN APPLE

**Music:** Jerome Moross
**Lyrics & book:** John Latouche
**Producers:** T. Edward Hambleton & Norris Houghton
**Director:** Norman Lloyd
**Choreographer:** Hanya Holm
**Cast:**     Priscilla Gillette, Stephen Douglass, Kaye Ballard, Jack Whiting, Bibi Osterwald, Jonathan Lucas, Portia Nelson, Jerry Stiller, Dean Michener, Shannon Bolin
**Songs:** "My Love Is on the Way"; "It's the Going Home Together"; "Helen Is Always Willing"; "Lazy Afternoon"; "Windflowers"
**New York run:** Phoenix Theatre, March 11, 1954; 173 p.

Using Homer's *Odyssey* and *Iliad* as models, Jerome Moross and John Latouche updated the epics to the period between 1900 and 1910 and relocated the action in the state of Washington. With spoken dialogue cut to a minimum, the story is told through a steady stream of musical numbers (including the popular hit, "Lazy Afternoon") and relates the consternation caused in the town of Angel's Roost (near Mt. Olympus) when a salesman named Paris (Jonathan Lucas) flies in in a balloon and abducts old Menelaus' always-willing wife, Helen (Kaye Ballard). The stalwart Ulysses (Stephen Douglass), who has just returned from the Spanish-American War, feels so duty-bound to retrieve the errant Helen that he leaves his wife Penelope (Priscilla Gillette) to go in search of the pair. Ulysses stays away ten years, during which time he resists various temptations, whips Paris in a bareknuckles fight, and is finally reunited with his incredibly patient spouse. Following its well-received opening at the downtown Phoenix Theatre, *The Golden Apple* moved uptown to the Alvin where it had a disappointingly short run.
Elektra OC/ Random House (1954)/ TW.

# THE PAJAMA GAME

**Music & lyrics:** Richard Adler & Jerry Ross
**Book:** George Abbott & Richard Bissell
**Producers:** Frederick Brisson, Robert Griffith & Harold Prince
**Directors:** George Abbott & Jerome Robbins
**Choreographer:** Bob Fosse
**Cast:** John Raitt, Janis Paige, Eddie Foy Jr., Carol Haney, Reta Shaw, Ralph Dunn, Stanley Prager, Peter Gennaro, Shirley MacLaine
**Songs:** "I'm Not at All in Love"; "I'll Never Be Jealous Again"; "Hey, There"; "Once a Year Day"; "Small Talk"; "There Once Was a Man"; "Steam Heat"; "Hernando's Hideaway"
**New York run:** St. James Theatre, May 13, 1954; 1,063 p.

When Frank Loesser was approached to write the score for the musical adaptation of Richard Bissell's novel, *7½ Cents,* he had to turn it down, but he did recommend a young team, Richard Adler and Jerry Ross, who had never before written songs for a book musical. Their work — including such hits as "Hey, There" and "Hernando's Hideaway" — was impressive and so was the show, which Bissell, another Broadway newcomer, adapted in collaboration with veteran director George Abbott. (Other neophytes involved were co-director Jerome Robbins, choreographer Bob Fosse, and the trio of producers.)

The *Pajama Game* is concerned with the activities at the Sleep-Tite Pajama Factory in Cedar Rapids, Iowa, where Sid Sorokin (John Raitt), the new plant superintendent, has taken a shine to Babe Williams (Janis Paige), a union activist. Their romance suffers a setback when the workers go on strike for a seven-and-a-half cents hourly raise, but eventually management and labor are again singing in tune. During the run, chorus dancer Shirley MacLaine attracted notice when she substituted for Carol Haney in the "Steam Heat" number and was soon off to Hollywood. The musical toured for two years with Larry Douglas and Fran Warren. In 1973, the show was revived briefly on Broadway with a cast headed by Hal Linden, Barbara McNair, and Cab Calloway. John Raitt and Eddie Foy, Jr. repeated their original roles in the 1957 movie, which also starred Doris Day.

In 1958, Richard Bissell's novel, *Say, Darling,* which the author had based on his experience with *The Pajama Game,* was itself turned into a musical by Bissell, his wife Marian, and Abe Burrows. Burrows also directed, and Jule Styne, Betty Comden and Adolph Green supplied nine songs. The show ran 10 months. Columbia OC/ Random House (1954)/ MTI.

**The Pajama Game.** The picnic scene with Shirley MacLaine, John Raitt, and Janis Paige. (Talbot)

# THE BOY FRIEND

**Music, lyrics & book:** Sandy Wilson
**Producers:** Cy Feuer & Ernest Martin
**Director:** Vida Hope (Cy Feuer uncredited)
**Choreographer:** John Heawood
**Cast:**   Julie Andrews, John Hewer, Eric Berry, Ruth Altman, Bob Scheerer, Ann
Wakefield, Millicent Martin, Dilys Lay, Stella Claire, Buddy Schwab
**Songs:** "The Boy Friend"; "Won't You Charleston With Me?"; "I Could Be Happy
With You"; "Sur La Plage"; "A Room in Bloomsbury"; "The Riviera";
"It's Never Too Late to Fall in Love"; "Poor Little Pierrette"
**New York run:** Royale Theatre, September 30 ,1954; 485 p.

Though he was the first British writer of musicals since Noël Coward to win success in New York, composer-lyricist-librettist Sandy Wilson has, to date, seen
only one of his works performed on Broadway. *The Boy Friend,* which had
opened in London (where it would achieve a run of 2,048 performances), was in
the tradition of Charles Gaynor's "Gladiola Girl" in *Lend an Ear* in that it offered
an affectionate sendup of musical comedies of the Twenties, with the songs not
only recalling the styles of that era but also establishing their own musical individuality. The tale is set in 1926 on the Riviera where Polly Browne, an English heiress attending Mme. Dubonnet's finishing school, meets Tony who, though of
noble lineage, is posing as a delivery boy. They fall in love to such sweet sentiments as "I Could Be Happy With You" ("If you could be happy with me"), and
though they have the expected misunderstanding, are happily reunited when,
costumed as Pierrette and Pierrot, they both show up at the Carnival Ball. The
musical also served to introduce Broadway to the charms of Julie Andrews who
played Polly.

*The Boy Friend* enjoyed an even longer run in a 1958 Off Broadway production that lasted 763 performances. Ellen McCown played Polly, Gerrianne Raphael her friend Maisie, and Bill Mullikin was Tony. The musical was again revived,
this time on Broadway, in 1970, with Judy Carne (Polly), Sandy Duncan (Maisie),
and Ronald Young (Tony). This version remained for four months. The cast of the
1972 film treatment included Twiggy and Tommy Tune.
RCA OC; MCA OC (1970)/ Dutton (1955)/ MTI.

**The Boy Friend.** Julie Andrews with
Millicent Martin, Dilys Lay, Ann Wakefield,
and Stella Claire. (Eileen Darby)

**Peter Pan.** "I'm Flying" sings Mary Martin as Peter Pan. (John Engstead)

# PETER PAN
**Music:** Mark Charlap*; Jule Styne**
**Lyrics:** Carolyn Leigh*; Betty Comden & Adolph Green**
**Play:** James M. Barrie
**Producers:** Richard Halliday, Edwin Lester
**Director-choreographer:** Jerome Robbins
**Cast:** Mary Martin, Cyril Ritchard, Kathy Nolan, Margalo Gillmore, Joe E. Marks, Sondra Lee, Joseph Stafford, Robert Harrington
**Songs:** "Tender Shepherd"*; "I've Got to Crow"*; "Neverland"**; "I'm Flying"*; "Wendy"**; "I Won't Grow Up"*; "Mysterious Lady"**; "Captain Hook's Waltz"**
**New York run:** Winter Garden, October 20, 1954; 152 p.

When Jerome Robbins decided that the time was ripe to stage a new version of *Peter Pan,* with Mary Martin as the boy who wouldn't grow up and Cyril Ritchard as Captain Hook, he initially planned to use only a few incidental songs by new-comers Mark Charlap and Carolyn Leigh. After the play began evolving into a full-fledged musical, however, he went to the more experienced team of Jule Styne, Betty Comden and Adolph Green for the additional numbers. Following its unveiling as part of Edwin Lester's Los Angeles and San Francisco Civic Light Opera series, the show came to New York offering such pleasures as Miss Martin singing and flying at the same time and Ritchard playing the villainous Hook as a giggling, mincing Restoration dandy.

Peter Pan was first presented in New York in 1905 with Maude Adams as Peter, a role she virtually made her own for eight years. It was revived in 1924 with Marilyn Miller singing two songs by Jerome Kern, and in 1950 with Jean Arthur, Boris Karloff plus five songs by Leonard Bernstein. That version lasted nine months. A 1979 revival, starring Sandy Duncan in a production based on the 1954 musical, turned out to be the longest running — or flying — *Peter Pan* ever performed in New York. (See page 254.)
RCA OC/ SF.

**Fanny.** Ezio Pinza and Walter Slezak.
(Zinn Arthur)

# FANNY

**Music & lyrics:** Harold Rome
**Book:** S. N. Behrman & Joshua Logan
**Producers:** David Merrick & Joshua Logan
**Director:** Joshua Logan
**Choreographer:** Helen Tamiris
**Cast:** Ezio Pinza, Walter Slezak, Florence Henderson, William Tabbert, Nejla Ates, Gerald Price, Alan Carney
**Songs:** "Restless Heart"; "Never Too Late for Love"; "Why Be Afraid to Dance?"; "Welcome Home"; "I Like You"; "Fanny"; "To My Wife"; "Love Is a Very Light Thing"; "Be Kind to Your Parents"
**New York run:** Majestic Theatre, November 4, 1954; 888 p.

*Fanny* takes us to the colorful, bustling port of Marseilles "not so long ago" for a musical version of Marcel Pagnol's French film trilogy, *Marius, Fanny,* and *César.* Compressed into one story, the heavily plotted tale — with its intensely emotional score — concerns Marius (William Tabbert), who yearns to go to sea; his father, César (Ezio Pinza), the local café owner; Panisse (Walter Slezak), a well-to-do middle-aged sail maker; and Fanny Cabanis (Florence Henderson), the girl beloved by both Marius and Panisse. Though Fanny conceives a child with Marius just before he ships off, Panisse marries her and brings up the boy as his own. When Marius returns demanding both Fanny and their son, César convinces him that Panisse has the more rightful claim. Years later, however, the dying Panisse dictates a letter to Marius offering him Fanny's hand in marriage.

Although Rodgers and Hammerstein had been sought to write it, *Fanny* became a collaboration between Harold Rome and Joshua Logan, who had worked together on *Wish You Were Here,* plus playwright S.N. Behrman. It also marked the first of 27 Broadway musicals produced by David Merrick. During the Broadway run, Pinza was succeeded by another former Metropolitan Opera star, Lawrence Tibbett, and Slezak by Billy Gilbert. No songs were retained for the 1960 movie version with Leslie Caron, Maurice Chevalier, and Charles Boyer.
RCA OC/ Random House (1955)/ TW.

**House of Flowers.** Pearl Bailey as Mme. Fleur. (Zinn Arthur)

# HOUSE OF FLOWERS
**Music:** Harold Arlen
**Lyrics:** Truman Capote & Harold Arlen
**Book:** Truman Capote
**Producer:** Saint Subber
**Director:** Peter Brook
**Choreographer:** Herbert Ross
**Cast:** Pearl Bailey, Diahann Carroll, Juanita Hall, Ray Walston, Dino DiLuca, Geoffrey Holder, Rawn Spearman, Frederick O'Neal, Carmen De Lavallade, Alvin Ailey, Arthur Mitchell
**Songs:** "A Sleepin' Bee"; "Smellin' of Vanilla"; "House of Flowers"; "Two Ladies in de Shade of de Banana Tree"; "I'm Gonna Leave Off Wearin' My Shoes"; "I Never Has Seen Snow"
**New York run:** Alvin Theatre, December 30, 1954; 165 p.

The genesis of *House of Flowers* occurred in 1948 when Truman Capote was visiting Port-au-Prince, Haiti, where he enjoyed frequenting the lively local bordellos. He first wrote a short story about one such establishment, then turned it into the libretto for a Broadway musical. Producer Saint Subber brought in Harold Arlen who also shared lyric-writing chores with Capote. In the plot, Madame Fleur (Pearl Bailey) is the protective, domineering horticulturist of the House of Flowers, which is in competition with a similar enterprise run by Madame Tango (Juanita Hall). Fleur is delighted to discover a new floral attraction named Ottilie (Diahann Carroll), but the innocent girl gives up all possibilities of professional advancement in favor of keeping herself for the equally innocent Royal (Rawn Spearman). *House of Flowers,* the first musical directed by Peter Brook, is particularly remembered for its colorful Oliver Messel sets and its atmospheric Harold Arlen music. In 1968, a somewhat revised version was offered Off Broadway with Josephine Premice as Madame Fleur.
Columbia OC; UA OC (1968)/ Random House (1968).

# PLAIN AND FANCY

**Music:** Albert Hague
**Lyrics:** Arnold B. Horwitt
**Book:** Joseph Stein & Will Glickman
**Producers:** Richard Kollmar & James Gardiner
**Director:** Morton Da Costa
**Choreographer:** Helen Tamiris
**Cast:** Richard Derr, Barbara Cook, David Daniels, Shirl Conway, Stefan Schnabel, Gloria Marlowe, Nancy Andrews
**Songs:** "It Wonders Me"; "Plenty of Pennsylvania"; "Young and Foolish"; "This Is All Very New to Me"; "Follow Your Heart"; "I'll Show Him"
**New York run:** Mark Hellinger Theatre, January 27, 1955; 461 p.

Like *Brigadoon, Plain and Fancy* used the visit of two sophisticated New Yorkers to a strange rural community so that audiences might become acquainted with its special customs and traditions. Here visitors Don King and Ruth Winters (Richard Derr and Shirl Conway) have come to Bird-in-Hand, Pennsylvania, to sell a farm Don owns to Amish farmer Jacob Yoder (Stefan Schnabel), a member of a fundamentalist religious sect that gets along without telephones, automobiles, indoor plumbing, or even buttons. Yoder has arranged an unwanted marriage for his daughter, Katie (Gloria Marlowe), though her young and foolish heart still belongs to her childhood sweetheart Peter Reber (David Daniels). When Yoder's barn is struck by lightning and burns down, Peter is blamed for putting a hex on it and he is shunned by members of the community. By rescuing his brother from a carnival brawl, however, he proves himself worthy of their — and Katie's — esteem. The Mark Hellinger Theatre, originally a movie house named the Hollywood, stands at 51st Street and Broadway.
Capitol OC/ Random House (1955)/ SF.

# SILK STOCKINGS

**Music & lyrics:** Cole Porter
**Book:** George S. Kaufman, Leueen McGrath & Abe Burrows
**Producers:** Cy Feuer & Ernest Martin
**Director:** Cy Feuer
**Choreographer:** Eugene Loring
**Cast:** Hildegarde Neff, Don Ameche, Gretchen Wyler, George Tobias, Leon Belasco, Henry Lascoe, David Opatoshu, Julie Newmar, Onna White
**Songs:** "Paris Loves Lovers"; "It's a Chemical Reaction, That's All"; "All of You"; "Too Bad"; "Satin and Silk"; "Without Love"; "Silk Stockings"; "The Red Blues"
**New York run:** Imperial Theatre, February 24, 1955; 478 p.

Cole Porter's last Broadway musical — and his sixth with a French setting — was based on the popular 1939 film, *Ninotchka,* in which Greta Garbo was seen as a dour Russian official who succumbs to the charms of both Paris and a French count played by Melvyn Douglas. In the musical, Ninotchka (Hildegarde Neff) is again doubly seduced, though this time the man is the fast-talking American talent agent Steve Canfield (Don Ameche), involved in convincing a Soviet composer to write the score for a gaudy movie version of *War and Peace.* During the Philadelphia tryout, prospects for the show looked so bleak that co-producer Cy Feuer took over as director from George S. Kaufman, and Abe Burrows was summoned to take over as librettist from Kaufman and Leueen McGrath (then Mrs. Kaufman). The movie version was released in 1957 with Fred Astaire and Cyd Charisse in the leads.
RCA OC/ TW.

# DAMN YANKEES

**Music & lyrics:** Richard Adler & Jerry Ross
**Book:** George Abbott & Douglass Wallop (Richard Bissell uncredited)
**Producers:** Frederick Brisson, Robert Griffith & Harold Prince
**Director:** George Abbott
**Choreographer:** Bob Fosse
**Cast:** Gwen Verdon, Stephen Douglass, Ray Walston, Russ Brown, Shannon Bolin, Rae Allen, Jean Stapleton, Nathaniel Frey, Robert Shafer
**Songs:** "Heart"; "Shoeless Joe from Hannibal, Mo."; "A Little Brains — a Little Talent"; "Whatever Lola Wants"; "Near to You"; "Two Lost Souls"
**New York run:** 46th Street Theatre, May 5, 1955; 1,019 p.

*Damn Yankees* was something of a stylistic follow-up to *The Pajama Game* since it was put together by the same songwriters, librettist-director, choreographer, producers, music director (Harold Hastings), and orchestrator (Don Walker). With the author as collaborator, they adapted the work from Douglass Wallop's novel, *The Year the Yankees Lost the Pennant,* and managed to turn it into such a clean hit that it broke the longheld jinx against shows dealing with baseball. In this variation on the *Faust* legend (which had been used in musical theatre as far back as *The Black Crook* in 1866), a middle-aged Washington Senators fan (Robert Shafer) is so devoted that he sells his soul to the devil (Ray Walston as "Mr. Applegate") just for a chance to play on his favorite team. Suddenly transformed into a young man, now named Joe Hardy (Stephen Douglass), the fan not only joins the team but becomes its ace pitcher and hitter. Fortunately for him, there is a contractural escape clause, and Applegate — even aided by the seductive Lola (Gwen Verdon) who usually gets what she wants — cannot prevent Joe from returning home to his wife at the end of a year. (Miss Verdon, who also appeared in the 1958 screen version, was elevated to stardom during the show's run.) The touring company, led by Sherry O'Neil and Bobby Clark (in his last stage role as Applegate), traveled for one year four months.
RCA OC/ Random House (1956)/ MTI.

**Damn Yankees.** Gwen Verdon and Ray Walston. (Talbot)

167

# MY FAIR LADY

**Music:** Frederick Loewe
**Lyrics & book:** Alan Jay Lerner
**Producer:** Herman Levin
**Director:** Moss Hart
**Choreographer:** Hanya Holm
**Cast:** Rex Harrison, Julie Andrews, Stanley Holloway, Cathleen Nesbitt, Robert Coote, John Michael King, Christopher Hewett, Reid Shelton
**Songs:** "Why Can't the English?"; "Wouldn't It Be Loverly?"; "With a Little Bit of Luck"; "I'm an Ordinary Man"; "The Rain in Spain"; "I Could Have Danced All Night"; "On the Street Where You Live"; "Show Me"; "Get Me to the Church on Time"; "A Hymn to Him"; "Without You"; "I've Grown Accustomed to Her Face"
**New York run:** Mark Hellinger Theatre, March 15, 1956; 2,717 p.

The most influential musical of the Fifties and one of the most distinguished productions of all time came about as a result of the efforts of Hungarian film producer Gabriel Pascal, who devoted the last two years of his life to a quest for writers to adapt George Bernard Shaw's 1914 play *Pygmalion* into a stage musical. After being rejected by the likes of Rodgers and Hammerstein and Noël Coward, Pascal won the committment of Alan Jay Lerner and Frederick Loewe once they decided to use most of Shaw's original dialogue and to expand the action to include scenes at Tottenham Court Road, the Ascot races, and the Embassy Ball. They were also scrupulous to maintain the Shavian flavor in the songs, most apparent in such pieces as "Why Can't the English?," "Show Me," "Get Me to the Church on Time," and "Without You."

Shaw's concern with class distinction and his belief that barriers would fall if all Englishmen would learn to speak their language properly was conveyed through a story about Eliza Doolittle, a scruffy cockney flower seller in Covent Garden, who takes lessons from phonetician Henry Higgins to help her qualify for a job in a florist shop. Eliza succeeds so well that she outgrows her social station and, in a development added by librettist Lerner, even gets the misogynous speech professor to fall in love with her — or at least grow accustomed to her face. Rex Harrison (who played Higgins), Julie Andrews (who won the part of Eliza after Mary Martin had turned it down), and Stanley Holloway (as Eliza's roistering father, Alfred P. Doolittle) all became forever identified with their roles in *My Fair Lady* which, for over nine years, was the longest running musical in Broadway history. The touring company, originally headed by Brian Aherne and Anne Rogers, traveled for six years nine months.

Two major revivals were staged in New York. In 1976, the musical ran for 377 performances with Ian Richardson, Christine Andreas, and George Rose. In 1981, it lasted 119 with Rex Harrison, Nancy Ringham, and Milo O'Shea. Harrison and Holloway repeated their roles in the 1964 movie version, also starring Audrey Hepburn.

A previous musical based on a Shaw play was the 1909 *Chocolate Soldier* (from *Arms and the Man*); a subsequent musical was the 1968 *Her First Roman* (from *Caesar and Cleopatra*). The notable success of *My Fair Lady* prompted a number of adaptations — offered on Broadway and off — of classics of British literature: Jane Austen's *Pride and Prejudice* (*First Impressions*, 1959); William Wycherley's *The Country Wife* (*She Shall Have Music*, 1959); Oscar Wilde's *The Importance of Being Earnest* (*Ernest in Love*, 1960); Sheridan's *The Rivals* (*All in Love*, 1961); Goldsmith's *She Stoops to Conquer* (*O, Marry Me!*, 1961); Dickens' *Oliver Twist* (*Oliver!*, 1963); H.G. Wells' *Kipps* (*Half a Sixpence*, 1965); Dickens' *Pickwick Papers* (*Pickwick*, 1965); and Arnold Bennett's *Buried Alive* (*Darling of the Day*, 1968).

Columbia OC; Columbia OC (1976); London SC (1987)/ Coward-McCann (1956)/ TW.

**My Fair Lady.** Stanley Holloway, with cronies Gordon Dilworth and Rod McLennon, singing "With A Little Bit of Luck." (Friedman-Abeles)

**My Fair Lady.** Robert Coote, Julie Andrews, and Rex Harrison in "The Rain in Spain" number. (Friedman-Abeles)

# THE MOST HAPPY FELLA

**Music, lyrics & book:** Frank Loesser
**Producers:** Kermit Bloomgarden & Lynn Loesser
**Director:** Joseph Anthony
**Choreographer:** Dania Krupska
**Cast:** Robert Weede, Jo Sullivan, Art Lund, Susan Johnson, Shorty Long, Mona Paulee
**Songs:** "Somebody Somewhere"; "The Most Happy Fella"; "Standing on the Corner"; "Joey, Joey, Joey"; "Rosabella"; "Abbondanza"; "Sposalizio"; "Happy to Make Your Acquaintance"; "Big 'D' "; "My Heart Is So Full of You"; "Warm All Over"
**New York run:** Imperial Theatre, May 3, 1956; 676 p.

Serving as his own librettist, composer-lyricist Frank Loesser adapted Sidney Howard's 1924 play, *They Knew What They Wanted,* into a cohesive, ambitious work, with more than 30 separate musical numbers including arias, duets, trios, quartets, and choral pieces, plus recitatives. Robust, emotional expressions ("Joey, Joey, Joey," "My Heart Is So Full of You") were interspersed with more traditional Broadway specialties ("Big 'D'," "Standing on the Corner"), though in the manner of an opera the program credits did not list individual selections.

Set in California's Napa Valley, *The Most Happy Fella* is about Tony Esposito (Robert Weede), an aging Italian vineyard owner, who proposed by mail to Rosabella (Jo Sullivan), a San Francisco waitress, and she accepts, partly because Tony has sent her a photograph of Joe (Art Lund), his handsome ranch foreman. Rosabella is so upset at finding Tony physically unattractive that on her wedding night she gives herself to Joe. Tony is distraught over his wife's pregnancy, but there is a reconciliation, and the vintner (somewhat similar to the situation in *Fanny* ) offers to raise the child as his own. In 1979, *The Most Happy Fella* was revived on Broadway with Giorgio Tozzi as Tony.
Columbia OC/ MTI.

**The Most Happy Fella.** Robert Weede and neighbors singing the title song. (Arthur Cantor)

# LI'L ABNER

**Music:** Gene de Paul
**Lyrics:** Johnny Mercer
**Book:** Norman Panama & Melvin Frank
**Producers:** Norman Panama, Melvin Frank & Michael Kidd
**Director-choreographer:** Michael Kidd
**Cast:** Edie Adams, Peter Palmer, Howard St. John, Stubby Kaye, Charlotte Rae, Tina Louise, Joe E. Marks, Julie Newmar, Grover Dale
**Songs:** "If I Had My Druthers"; "Jubilation T. Cornpone"; "Namely You"; "The Country's in the Very Best of Hands"; "Oh, Happy Day"
**New York run:** St. James Theatre, November 15, 1956; 693 p.

Following the lead of *Finian's Rainbow, Li'l Abner* was a musical fantasy set in a rural Southern community that aimed satirical darts at existing social conditions. Here the main targets are the government's propensity for bull-dozing areas for atom-bomb tests, right-wing militarists, inefficient politicians, and conformity. Based on the comic strip by Al Capp (who, ironically, would later adopt some of the views the show derided), *Li'l Abner* takes place in Dogpatch, U.S.A., where mini-skirted Daisy Mae (Edie Adams) is forever trying to get dimwitted Abner Yokum (Peter Palmer) to marry her, where Marryin' Sam (Stubby Kaye) exuberantly leads the townspeople in singing the praises of the South's most incompetent general, Jubilation T. Cornpone, and where the annual big event (as well as the musical's big production number) is the frenetic man-chasing race on Sadie Hawkins' Day. The 1959 movie again featured Peter Palmer as Abner.

Comic strips also supplied the bases for such other Broadway musicals as *Buster Brown* (1905), *Little Nemo* (1908), *Bringing Up Father* (1925), *It's a Bird It's a Plane It's Superman* (1966), *You're a Good Man, Charlie Brown* (1967), *Annie* (1977), *Snoopy* (1982), and *Doonesbury* (1983). Columbia OC/ TW.

# BELLS ARE RINGING

**Music:** Jule Styne
**Lyrics & book:** Betty Comden & Adolph Green
**Producer:** Theatre Guild
**Director:** Jerome Robbins
**Choreographers:** Jerome Robbins, Bob Fosse
**Cast:** Judy Holliday, Sydney Chaplin, Jean Stapleton, Eddie Lawrence, Dort Clark, George S. Irving, Peter Gennaro, Bernie West
**Songs:** "It's a Perfect Relationship"; "Hello, Hello There!"; "Is It a Crime?"; "I Met a Girl"; "Long Before I Knew You"; "Just in Time"; "Drop That Name"; "The Party's Over"; "I'm Going Back"
**New York run:** Shubert Theatre, November 29, 1956; 924 p.

Ever since appearing with Judy Holliday in a nightclub revue, Betty Comden and Adolph Green had wanted to write a musical for her. The story they eventually hit upon was one in which Miss Holliday played Ella Peterson, a chatty telephone operator at the Susanswerphone service (run by Jean Stapleton) who gets so involved with one client, playwright Jeff Moss (Sydney Chaplin), that — without revealing her identity — she arranges to meet him and help him overcome his writer's block. They also sing and dance in the subway, entertain fellow New Yorkers in Central Park, and fall in love. With Miss Holliday's winning performance and a score containing three enduring songs ("Long Before I Knew You," "Just in Time," and "The Party's Over"), *Bells Are Ringing* had the longest run of the eight musicals written together by Styne, Comden and Green. Miss Holliday repeated her role in the 1960 movie version, which also starred Dean Martin. Columbia OC/ Random House (1957)/ TW.

**Candide.** Max Adrian, Louis Edmonds, Barbara Cook, and Robert Rounseville. (Friedman-Abeles)

# CANDIDE

**Music:** Leonard Bernstein
**Lyrics:** Richard Wilbur, etc.
**Book:** Lillian Hellman
**Producer:** Ethel Linder Reiner
**Director:** Tyrone Guthrie
**Cast:** Max Adrian, Robert Rounseville, Barbara Cook, Irra Petina, William Olvis, Louis Edmonds, Conrad Bain
**Songs:** "The Best of All Possible Worlds"; "Oh, Happy We"; "It Must Be So"; "Glitter and Be Gay"; "I Am Easily Assimilated" (lyric: Bernstein); "Eldorado" (lyric: Hellman); "Bon Voyage"; "What's the Use?"; "Make Our Garden Grow"
**New York run:** Martin Beck Theatre, December 1, 1956; 73 p.

Based on Voltaire's classic satire on mindless optimism, *Candide* covers the travels and travails of the eponymous hero (Robert Rounseville) who journeys from his home in Westphalia searching for his beloved Cunegonde (Barbara Cook) in Lisbon (during the Spanish Inquisition), Paris, Buenos Aires, Venice, and back to Westphalia. Throughout the tale the gullible young man remains firm in his belief — as espoused by his philosophy professor, Dr. Pangloss (Max Adrian) — that "this is the best of all possible worlds." In the end, at last reunited with Cunegonde, Candide (like the hero of the later musical, *Pippin*) comes to realize that perfection can never be attained and that one must accept life's realities and try to do one's best. Despite the musical's highly praised score (Leonard Bernstein's original lyricist, John Latouche, had died early in the preparation) and attractive production, the show's initial run lasted less than three months.

In 1973, a revised version was staged by the Chelsea Theatre Center of Brooklyn. Hugh Wheeler contributed a new libretto, Stephen Sondheim some new lyrics, and Harold Prince a total-theatre concept. Following its limited run, the musical was successfully remounted at the Broadway Theatre. The auditorium was completely remodeled, with musicians playing from various parts of the house, and the audience seated on stools surrounded by ten different acting areas linked by ramps, bridges, platforms, and trap doors. (See page 239.) In 1982, *Candide* was added to the repertory of the New York City Opera.
Columbia OC; Columbia OC (1973); New World OC (1982)/ Random House (1957)/ MTI.

# NEW GIRL IN TOWN

**Music & lyrics:** Bob Merrill
**Book:** George Abbott
**Producers:** Frederick Brisson, Robert Griffith & Harold Prince
**Director:** George Abbott
**Choreographer:** Bob Fosse
**Cast:**   Gwen Verdon, Thelma Ritter, George Wallace, Cameron Prud'homme, Mark Dawson
**Songs:** "Sunshine Girl"; "Flings"; "It's Good to Be Alive"; "Look at 'Er"; "At the Check Apron Ball"; "If That Was Love"
**New York run:** 46th Street Theatre, May 14, 1957; 431 p.

Composer-lyricist Bob Merrill had first conceived of the idea of a musical version of Eugene O'Neill's 1921 play *Anna Christie* as a movie under the title of *A Saint She Ain't.* When that was abandoned he found director George Abbott highly receptive to its possibilities as a stage musical, particularly as a vehicle for Gwen Verdon. In the story, set near New York's waterfront at the turn of the century, barge captain Chris Christopherson (Cameron Prud'homme) is excited at the news that his daughter Anna will be returning from St. Paul. When she does appear, she is quickly sized up by Chris' slattern friend Marthy (Thelma Ritter) as a street walker. After Anna joins her father on his barge, she meets sailor Matt Burke (George Wallace), and they fall in love. When she tells her story to the two men they get smashed, but fortunately there is a reconciliation. In 1959, Merrill wrote the songs for *Take Me Along,* based on another O'Neill play *Ah, Wilderness!*
RCA OC/ Random House (1958)/ MTI.

**New Girl in Town.** Harvey Hohnecker, Gwen Verdon, and Harvey Jung dancing "At the Check Apron Ball." (Friedman-Abeles)

Carol Lawrence and Larry Kert.

**West Side Story.** The Jets performing the "Gee, Officer Krupke" number. (Eileen Darby)

# WEST SIDE STORY

**Music:** Leonard Bernstein
**Lyrics:** Stephen Sondheim
**Conception:** Jerome Robbins
**Book:** Arthur Laurents
**Producers:** Robert Griffith & Harold Prince
**Director:** Jerome Robbins
**Choreographers:** Jerome Robbins & Peter Gennaro
**Cast:** Carol Lawrence, Larry Kert, Chita Rivera, Art Smith, Mickey Calin, Ken LeRoy, Lee Becker Theodore, David Winter, Tony Mordente, Eddie Roll, Martin Charnin
**Songs:** "Something's Coming"; "Maria"; "Tonight"; "America"; "Cool"; "One Hand, One Heart"; "I Feel Pretty"; "Somewhere"; "Gee, Officer Krupke"; "A Boy Like That"; "I Have a Love"
**New York run:** Winter Garden, September 26, 1957; 732 p.

In 1949, Jerome Robbins brought together composer Leonard Bernstein and playwright Arthur Laurents (his first experience as a librettist) to work on a modern musical version of *Romeo and Juliet*. Called *East Side Story*, it was about a Jewish boy's star-crossed romance with an Italian Catholic girl set against the clashing street gangs on New York's lower East Side. Heavy schedules, however, forced the trio to suspend the project for six years and by the time they got together again the conflict seemed dated. Far more timely, they now felt, would be the love story of a native-born boy of Polish descent and a newly arrived Puerto Rican girl set against the clashing street gangs on the city's West Side. At this time Bernstein decided against writing his own lyrics and he turned the task over to Stephen Sondheim, a 27-year-old Broadway neophyte.

In *West Side Story,* Tony (Larry Kert), once the leader of the Jets street gang, now tries to keep his distance from his former group and the rival Puerto Rican Sharks. He becomes particularly committed to peaceful coexistence once he meets a girl named Maria (Carol Lawrence) at a high school dance, and — with Maria's fire escape as a balcony — they express their mutual devotion to the soaring sentiments of "Tonight." But after Tony kills Maria's brother Bernardo (Ken LeRoy) while trying to break up a rumble, warfare erupts anew, and even Maria's best friend, Anita (Chita Rivera), urges her to stay away from Tony. In the end, Tony is killed by one of the Sharks and Maria is left grieving over his body.

With its galvanic choreography, compelling music and lyrics, and unflinching look at contemporary street life, *West Side Story* was a jolting work, not alone for its theme but for its advanced use of dance within the framework of a musical play. After cutting short its initial Broadway run to go on tour, the company returned to New York ten weeks later for an additional 249 performances.

Since then there have been two major revivals. In 1968, the Music Theatre of Lincoln Center sponsored a production that ran for 89 performances. Tony was played by Kurt Peterson, Maria by Victoria Mallory, and Anita by Barbara Luna. In 1980, the musical was mounted at the Minskoff Theatre under Robbins' direction, and had a 333-performance run. The cast was headed by Ken Marshall, Jossie de Guzman, and Debbie Allen. The film version, with Richard Beymer, Natalie Wood, George Chakiris, and Rita Moreno, was released in 1961. For other Broadway musicals based on Shakespeare, see *The Boys from Syracuse,* page 107.

Columbia OC; DGG SC (1985)/ Random House (1958); Chilton (1973)/ MTI.

# JAMAICA

**Music:** Harold Arlen
**Lyrics:** E.Y. Harburg
**Book:** E.Y. Harburg & Fred Saidy (Joseph Stein uncredited)
**Producer:** David Merrick
**Driector:** Robert Lewis
**Choreographer:** Jack Cole
**Cast:** Lena Horne, Ricardo Montalban, Josephine Premice, Adelaide Hall, Ossie Davis, Erik Rhodes, Joe Adams, Alvin Ailey, Billy Wilson
**Songs:** "Pretty to Walk With"; "Push the Button"; "Little Biscuit"; "Cocoanut Sweet"; "Pity the Sunset"; "Take It Slow, Joe"; "Ain't It the Truth?"; "I Don't Think I'll End It All Today"
**New York run:** Imperial Theatre, October 31, 1957; 558 p.

Aided by evocative music, provocative lyrics, lush decor, and the sparkling presence of Lena Horne, *Jamaica* overcame a weak book to become one of the hits of the season. Something of a Caribbean companion to Harold Arlen's most recent musical *House of Flowers,* the new work dealt with a fisherman named Koli (Ricardo Montalban), who enjoys the simple life on mythical Pigeon Island near Jamaica, and Savannah (Miss Horne), his inamorata who yearns for the glittering, mechanized life on another mythical island called Manhattan. After being tempted by a slick pearl dealer, Savannah — to no one's surprise — is content to remain with Koli in their tropical paradise. Originally, Harry Belafonte was to have been starred in the show but illness forced his replacement by the equally stellar Lena Horne, thereby altering the story's emphasis.
RCA OC/ TW.

**Jamaica.** Ricardo Montalban and Lena Horne.
(Friedman-Abeles)

# THE MUSIC MAN

**Music, lyrics & book:** Meredith Willson
**Producer:** Kermit Bloomgarden
**Director:** Morton Da Costa
**Choreographer:** Onna White
**Cast:** Robert Preston, Barbara Cook, David Burns, Pert Kelton, Iggie Wolfington, The Buffalo Bills, Eddie Hodges, Helen Raymond
**Songs:** "Rock Island"; "Trouble"; "Goodnight My Someone"; "Seventy-Six Trombones"; "Sincere"; "The Sadder-but-Wiser Girl"; "Marian the Librarian"; "My White Knight"; "Wells Fargo Wagon"; "Shipoopi"; "Lida Rose"; "Gary, Indiana"; "Till There Was You"
**New York run:** Majestic Theatre, December 19, 1957; 1,375 p.

It took eight years to write — including over 30 drafts and 40 songs — but by the time it was produced on Broadway, *The Music Man* had clearly established newcomer Meredith Willson among the most impressive talents of the musical theatre. The idea for the show had first been suggested by Willson's friend, Frank Loesser, who enjoyed listening to the composer's tales of growing up in a small Iowa town. Though the plot was credited in part to Frank Lacey, the musical emerged as a very personal expression through which Willson captured all the innocent charm of a bygone America. The story begins on the Fourth of July, 1912, in River City, Iowa. Enter "Professor" Harold Hill, who has arrived to hornswoggle the citizens into believing he can teach the local youngsters how to play in a marching band that would rival the once-mammoth parade featuring "Seventy-Six Trombones." But instead of skipping town before the instruments arrive, Hill is persuaded to remain by the town's librarian, Marian Paroo (Barbara Cook). The musical ends with the children being hailed by their parents, even though they can barely produce any recognizable sound from their instruments.

The role of Professor Harold Hill was rejected by a number of actors, including Danny Kaye, Dan Dailey, Phil Harris, and Gene Kelly, before it went to Robert Preston who gave a memorably dynamic performance in his first appearance on the musical stage. Preston also repeated the part in the 1962 movie version. During the show's Broadway run, the third longest of the decade's musicals, Preston was succeeded by Eddie Albert and Bert Parks. For the road tour, which lasted three years seven months, Forrest Tucker played the professor and Joan Weldon was Marian. *The Music Man* returned briefly to New York in 1980, with a cast headed by Dick Van Dyke and Meg Bussert. Capitol OC/ Putnam (1958)/ MTI.

**The Music Man.** Barbara Cook and Robert Preston singing "Till There Was You." (Friedman-Abeles)

**Flower Drum Song.** Miyoshi Umeki singing "A Hundred Million Miracles," accompanied by Juanita Hall and Keye Luke. (Friedman-Abeles)

# FLOWER DRUM SONG

**Music:** Richard Rodgers
**Lyrics:** Oscar Hammerstein II
**Book:** Oscar Hammerstein II & Joseph Fields
**Producers:** Richard Rodgers, Oscar Hammerstein II & Joseph Fields
**Director:** Gene Kelly
**Choreographer:** Carol Haney
**Cast:** Miyoshi Umeki, Larry Blyden, Pat Suzuki, Juanita Hall, Ed Kenney, Keye Luke, Arabella Hong, Jack Soo, Anita Ellis
**Songs:** "You Are Beautiful"; "A Hundred Million Miracles"; "I Enjoy Being a Girl"; "I Am Going to Like It Here"; "Don't Marry Me"; "Grant Avenue"; "Love, Look Away"; "Sunday"
**New York run:** St. James Theatre, December 1, 1958; 600 p.

Upon reading Chin Y. Lee's novel, *The Flower Drum Song,* librettist Joseph Fields bought the dramatic rights and then took the idea to Rodgers and Hammerstein. The resulting production — the only Broadway musical ever directed by Gene Kelly — dealt in a lighthearted way with the conflict between San Francisco's traditionalist older Chinese-Americans and their Americanized children who are anxious to break away. Mei Li (Miyoshi Umeki), a timid "picture bride" from China, has arrived to fulfill her contract to marry Sammy Fong (Larry Blyden), a local nightclub owner, but Sammy prefers Linda Low (Pat Suzuki), who quite obviously enjoys being a girl. The problem is resolved when Sammy's friend Wang Ta (Ed Kenney) conveniently falls in love with Mei Li. Miyoshi Umeki appeared in the 1961 film version, along with Nancy Kwan and James Shigeta. Columbia OC/ Farrar, Straus (1959)/ R&H.

# REDHEAD

**Music:** Albert Hague
**Lyrics:** Dorothy Fields
**Book:** Herbert & Dorothy Fields, Sidney Sheldon, David Shaw
**Producers:** Robert Fryer & Lawrence Carr
**Director-choreographer:** Bob Fosse
**Cast:** Gwen Verdon, Richard Kiley, Leonard Stone, Doris Rich, Cynthia Latham
**Songs:** "The Right Finger of My Left Hand"; "Just for Once"; "Merely Marvel-ous"; "The Uncle Sam Rag"; "Erbie Fitch's Twitch"; "My Girl Is Just Enough Woman for Me"; "Look Who's In Love"
**New York run:** 46th Street Theatre, February 5, 1959; 452 p.

One of the theatre's rare musical whodunits, *Redhead* had been in the works — it was first called *The Works* — ever since 1950 when Herbert and Dorothy Fields began writing it with Beatrice Lillie in mind for the starring role. Six years later, with Sidney Sheldon joining them, they rewrote it for Gewn Verdon, but there were further complications caused by Miss Verdon's contract with Robert Fryer and Lawrence Carr to star in a musical being written by David Shaw. The problem was solved when the producers decided to switch their activities to *Redhead* and Shaw was added to the roster of writers. The show, which was the first to charge $9.20 for orchestra seats, also marked Bob Fosse's initial effort as a director as well as choreographer. The story takes place in London in the early 1900s. At the Simpson Sisters' Waxworks, where all the wax images are made by Essie Whimple, a model of a recently murdered young woman offends her brother, Tom Baxter (Richard Kiley). Essie and Tom join forces to solve the murder which, after Essie gets the chance to perform "Erbie Fitch's Twitch" at the Odeon Music Hall, they do.
RCA OC/ MTI.

**Redhead.** Richard Kiley and Gwen Verdon in a tense situation. (Friedman-Abeles)

# DESTRY RIDES AGAIN

**Music & lyrics:** Harold Rome
**Book:** Leonard Gershe
**Producer:** David Merrick
**Director-choreographer:** Michael Kidd
**Cast:**  Andy Griffith, Dolores Gray, Scott Brady, Jack Prince, Swen Swenson, Marc Breaux, George Reeder
**Songs:** "Ballad of the Gun"; "I Know Your Kind"; "Anyone Would Love You"; "Once Knew a Fella"; "That Ring on the Finger"; "I Say Hello"
**New York run:** Imperial Theatre, April 23, 1959; 473 p.

Hollywood's classic Western had been filmed three times before David Merrick decided to turn the durable sagebrush saga into a Broadway musical. A whoopin', shootin', hollerin' show, it starred Andy Griffith (in his only musical) as Thomas Jefferson Destry Jr., the violence-hating sheriff, and Dolores Gray as the peppery saloon entertainer known as Frenchy. The story, set in the brawling frontier town of Bottleneck just before the turn of the century, involves the traditional confrontation between good guys and bad guys in scenes set in such equally traditional locales as the Last Chance Saloon and Rose Lovejoy's establishment in Paradise Alley. Contrary to the movie industry's morals code that never permitted a happy ending for a woman of easy virtue, Frenchy is not killed protecting Destry but ends up in his arms. The show's choreographic highlight: the crackling, whipcracking dance performed by outlaws Swen Swenson, Marc Breaux, and George Reeder.
MCA OC/ TW.

**Destry Rides Again.** An embarrassing moment when Destry accidentally tears off part of Frenchy's dress. Andy Griffith, Scott Brady, and Dolores Gray. (Friedman-Abeles)

**Once Upon a Mattress.** Carol Burnett explaining
that she's really so "Shy." (Friedman-Abeles)

# ONCE UPON A MATTRESS

**Music:** Mary Rodgers
**Lyrics:** Marshall Barer
**Book:** Jay Thompson, Dean Fuller & Marshall Barer
**Producers:** T. Edward Hambleton, Norris Houghton, William & Jean Eckart
**Director:** George Abbott
**Choreographer:** Joe Layton
**Cast:** Joseph Bova, Carol Burnett, Allen Case, Jack Gilford, Anne Jones, Matt Mattox, Harry Snow, Jane White
**Songs:** "Many Moons Ago"; "In a Little While"; "Shy"; "Sensitivity"; "Happily Ever After"; "Very Soft Shoes"
**New York run:** Phoenix Theater, May 11, 1959; 460 p.

*Once Upon a Mattress* was first created as a one-act musical by Mary Rodgers (daughter of Richard Rodgers) and Marshall Barer at an adult summer camp. With Jay Thompson and Dean Fuller, they expanded the work, based on the fairy tale *The Princess and the Pea,* into a full evening's entertainment. Carol Burnett made a notable stage debut in the show as Princess Winnifred who arrives dripping wet in the throne room of an ancient kingdom because, as she explains, "I swam the moat." She is there as a contender for the hand of Prince Dauntless the Drab (Joseph Bova), whose domineering mother, Queen Agravain (Jane White), has decreed that he will wed only a true princess of royal blood. Winnifred passes the test being unable to sleep on a pile of mattresses with a pea on the bottom — though, as the finale reveals — her sleeplessness was really caused by a helpful Minstrel (Harry Snow) who had filled her bed with all sorts of uncomfortable objects. After opening at the downtown Phoenix Theatre, *Once Upon A Mattress* then played the Alvin, the Winter Garden, the Cort, and the St. James. MCA OC/ R&H.

# GYPSY

**Music:** Jule Styne
**Lyrics:** Stephen Sondheim
**Book:** Arthur Laurents
**Producers:** David Merrick & Leland Hayward
**Director-choreographer:** Jerome Robbins
**Cast:** Ethel Merman, Jack Klugman, Sandra Church, Lane Bradbury, Maria Karnilova, Paul Wallace, Jacqueline Mayro, Karen Moore, Joe Silver
**Songs:** "Let Me Entertain You"; "Some People"; "Small World"; "Little Lamb"; "You'll Never Get Away from Me"; "If Momma Was Married"; "All I Need Is the Girl"; "Everything's Coming Up Roses"; "Together"; "You Gotta Have a Gimmick"; "Rose's Turn"
**New York run:** Broadway Theatre, May 21, 1959; 702 p.

With Ethel Merman giving the performance of her life as Gypsy Rose Lee's ruthless mother and with an exceptionally strong score and story, *Gypsy* was one of the musical theatre's most distinguished achievements. The germination of the show began with producer David Merrick, who needed to read but one chapter of Miss Lee's autobiography to convince him of its stage potential. Stephen Sondheim, joining *West Side Story* colleagues Arthur Laurents and Jerome Robbins, was originally to have supplied the music as well as the lyrics, but Miss Merman wanted a more experienced composer and Jule Styne was brought in. The Styne-Sondheim team created such overwhelming expressions of raw ambition as "Some People" and "Everything's Coming Up Roses" that they soon took their place among Miss Merman's most closely identified songs.

In the story, Mama Rose is determined to escape from a life of playing bingo and paying rent by pushing the vaudeville career of her younger daughter June (Lane Bradbury); after June elopes with a hoofer, she focuses all her attention on her older, less talented daughter, Louise (Sandra Church). Eventually, Louise becomes burlesque stripper Gypsy Rose Lee, and Rose suffers a breakdown — expressed through the shattering "Rose's Turn" — when she realizes that she is no longer needed in her daughter's career. Mama Rose was the last stage role Ethel Merman created and the first in which she toured. In 1974, a new production of *Gypsy* opened in New York after playing in London. Angela Lansbury starred, Arthur Laurents directed, and it ran 120 performances. The film version, in 1962, put Rosalind Russell, Natalie Wood, and Karl Malden in the leads. For other show-business musical biographies, see *Annie Get Your Gun,* page 130.
Columbia OC; RCA OC (1974)/ Random House (1960); Chilton (1973)/ TW.

**Gypsy.** Sandra Church, Ethel Merman, and Jack Klugman. (Friedman-Abeles)

**Gypsy.** Ethel Merman doing her climactic "Rose's Turn." (Friedman-Abeles)

# TAKE ME ALONG
**Music & lyrics:** Bob Merrill
**Book:** Joseph Stein & Robert Russell
**Producer:** David Merrick
**Director:** Peter Glenville
**Choreographer:** Onna White
**Cast:** Jackie Gleason, Walter Pidgeon, Eileen Herlie, Robert Morse, Una Merkel, Peter Conlow, Susan Luckey, Valerie Harper
**Songs:** "I Would Die"; "Sid Ol' Kid"; "Staying Young"; "I Get Embarrassed"; "We're Home"; "Take Me Along"; "Promise Me a Rose"; "Nine O'Clock"; "But Yours"
**New York run:** Shubert Theatre, October 22, 1959; 448 p.

Having written a score for a musical version of Eugene O'Neill's somber *Anna Christie,* Bob Merrill followed it up with a score for a musical version of O'Neill's 1933 sentimental comedy, *Ah, Wilderness!* Though casting the exuberant Jackie Gleason as the bibulous Sid Davis tended to divert the focus from the main story, *Take Me Along* was a faithful rendering of the playwright's view of an adolescent's growing pains.

The action takes place in the cozy environs of Centerville, Connecticut, during July 1910. Young Richard Miller (Robert Morse), the son of newspaper publisher Nat Miller (Walter Pidgeon), ardently woos Muriel Macomber (Susan Luckey) by quoting literary morsels that her father finds so objectionable he withdraws his advertisements from Nat's paper. With Muriel forbidden to see him, Richard goes on a binge; once they are reconciled he gets ready to go to Yale. A secondary plot concerns Sid's repeated efforts to quit drinking, get a steady job, and marry Nat's spinster sister Lily (Eileen Herlie). During the Broadway run, Pidgeon was succeeded by Sidney Blackmer and Gleason by William Bendix. The musical's Broadway revival in 1985 gave only one performance.
RCA OC/ TW.

# THE SOUND OF MUSIC

**Music:** Richard Rodgers
**Lyrics:** Oscar Hammerstein II
**Book:** Howard Lindsay & Russel Crouse
**Producers:** Leland Hayward, Richard Halliday, Richard Rodgers & Oscar Hammerstein II
**Director:** Vincent J. Donehue
**Choreographer:** Joe Layton
**Cast:** Mary Martin, Theodore Bikel, Patricia Neway, Kurt Kasznar, Marion Marlowe, Lauri Peters, Brian Davies, John Randolph, Nan McFarland, Joey Heatherton
**Songs:** "The Sound of Music"; "Maria"; "My Favorite Things"; "Do-Re-Mi"; "Sixteen Going on Seventeen"; "The Lonely Goatherd"; "How Can Love Survive?"; "So Long, Farewell"; "Climb Ev'ry Mountain"; "An Ordinary Couple"; "Edelweiss"
**New York run:** Lunt-Fontanne Theatre, November 16, 1959; 1,443 p.

The second longest running Broadway musical of the Fifties, *The Sound of Music* also marked the 35th and final work of Oscar Hammerstein II, who died nine months after the opening (his last lyric was for "Edelweiss"). Primarily at the urging of director Vincent J. Donehue, the story was adapted as a star vehicle for Mary Martin from Maria Von Trapp's autobiography *The Trapp Family Singers* and also the German film version. Miss Martin's husband, Richard Halliday, and Leland Hayward became partners in sponsoring the project and Howard Lindsay and Russel Crouse were engaged to write the book. Initially, they planned to use only authentic music sung by the Trapps in their concerts plus an additional song to be supplied by Rodgers and Hammerstein. When the songwriters balked at this arrangement, they were asked to contribute the entire score and they also joined Halliday and Hayward as producers.

The musical, set in 1938, takes place in Salzburg in the Austrian Tyrol. Maria Rainer, a free-spirited postulant at Nonnberg Abbey, has been giving her superiors concern because of her fondness for taking off to the mountains listening to the sound of music. At the request of the Mother Abbess (Patricia Neway), — and as something of a variation on *The King and I* — Maria is hired as governess to the seven children of the wealthy, autocratic Capt. Georg Von Trapp (Theodore Bikel). Maria soon wins the affection of her charges — in part by teaching them such songs as "Do-Re-Mi," "The Lonely Goatherd," and "So Long, Farewell." Though Von Trapp is engaged to the socially prominent Elsa Schraeder (Marion Marlowe), he and Maria fall in love and marry. Their happiness, however, is almost immediately shattered by the German invasion of Austria. The Von Trapp family, which has become celebrated for its amateur concerts, gives a final performance before heeding the message of "Climb Ev'ry Mountain" and fleeing over the Alps to the safety of Switzerland. A subplot in *The Sound of Music* concerns the teenage romance between Von Trapp's daughter Liesl (Lauri Peters) and Rolf Gruber, an incipient Nazi (Brian Davies).

During the Broadway run (the Lunt-Fontanne Theatre, where the show opened, was once the Globe), Miss Martin was succeeded by Martha Wright, Jeannie Carson, and Nancy Dussault. In 1961, Jon Voight took over the part of Rolf. Florence Henderson and John Myhers originally headed the touring company which traveled two years nine months. The popular movie version, which came out in 1965, co-starred Julie Andrews and Christopher Plummer. Columbia OC/ Random House (1960)/ R&H.

**The Sound of Music.** Theodore Bikel, Marion Marlowe, and Kurt Kasznar. (Friedman-Abeles)

**The Sound of Music.** Brian Davies and Lauri Peters. (Toni Frissell)

**The Sound of Music.** Mary Martin and Theodore Bikel lead the Trapp Family in "Edelweiss." (Friedman-Abeles)

# LITTLE MARY SUNSHINE

**Music, lyrics & book:** Rick Besoyan
**Producers:** Howard Barker, Cynthia Baer, Robert Chambers
**Directors:** Ray Harrison, Rick Besoyan
**Choreographer:** Ray Harrison
**Cast:** Eileen Brennan, William Graham, John McMartin, Elmarie Wendel
**Songs:** "Look for a Sky of Blue"; "Tell a Handsome Stranger"; "Once in a Blue Moon"; "Colorado Love Call"; "Every Little Nothing"; "Do You Ever Dream of Vienna?"; "Naughty, Naughty Nancy"
**New York run:** Orpheum Theatre, November 18, 1959; 1,143 p.

*Little Mary Sunshine* was a witty, melodious takeoff on the *Rose-Marie* school of robust heroics and excessively ardent love songs. Its engagement at the Orpheum Theatre on lower 2nd Avenue is currently the seventh longest of any Off-Broadway musical. Set in the Colorado Rockies early in the century, the tale is primarily concerned with Mary Potts (Eileen Brennan), proprietress of the Colorado Inn, and valorous Capt. "Big Jim" Warrington of the Forest Rangers (William Graham), who gets to rescue his beloved just in time for their echoing "Colorado Love Call" duet. The production marked the impressive New York theatre debuts of both Eileen Brennan and composer-lyricist-librettist Rick Besoyan. Besoyan (who died in 1970 at the age of 45) followed up in 1963 with *The Student Gypsy,* a less successful spoof of European mythical-kingdom operettas, which also featured Miss Brennan. The earliest operetta burlesque on Broadway was Rodgers and Hart's "Rose of Arizona" in the 1926 *Garrick Gaieties.*
Capitol OC/Samuel French, London(1960)*/ SF

# FIORELLO!

**Music:** Jerry Bock
**Lyrics:** Sheldon Harnick
**Book:** Jerome Weidman & George Abbott
**Producers:** Robert Griffith & Harold Prince
**Director:** George Abbott
**Choreographer:** Peter Gennaro
**Cast:** Tom Bosley, Patricia Wilson, Ellen Hanley, Howard Da Silva, Mark Dawson, Nathaniel Frey, Pat Stanley, Eileen Rodgers, Ron Husmann
**Songs:** "Politics and Poker"; "The Name's LaGuardia"; "I Love a Cop"; "Till Tomorrow"; "When Did I Fall in Love?"; "Little Tin Box"
**New York run:** Broadhurst Theatre, November 23, 1959; 795 p.

New York's favorite mayor, Fiorello LaGuardia, was a peppery, pugnacious reformer whose exuberant personality readily lent itself to depiction on the musical stage. With Tom Bosley making an auspicious Broadway bow in the title role, *Fiorello!* encompassed the ten-year period in LaGuardia's life before he became mayor. Beginning with his surprise election to Congress prior to World War I, it includes such events as his enlistment in the Air Force, his first race for mayor against the unbeatable James J. Walker (who was himself the subject of a 1969 musical *Jimmy,* with Frank Gorshin in the title part), the death of LaGuardia's first wife, the revelation of Walker's cronies with their hands caught in little tin boxes, and the preparations for the victorious LaGuardia campaign of 1933 which he won as a Fusion candidate. *Fiorello!* had the distinction of being the third musical to be awarded the Pulitzer Prize for drama. A year after the show's opening, its composer, lyricist, librettists, director, producers, music director (Harold Hastings), and orchestrator (Irwin Kostal) were reunited for *Tenderloin,* which was about another New York reformer just before the turn of the century.
Capitol OC/ Random House (1960); Chilton (1976)/ TW.

**Fiorello!** Tom Bosley, Patricia Wilson, Nathaniel Frey, and Ellen Hanley singing "Till Tomorrow." (Eileen Darby)

# GREENWILLOW
**Music & lyrics:** Frank Loesser
**Book:** Lesser Samuels & Frank Loesser
**Producer:** Robert Willey
**Director:** George Roy Hill
**Choreographer:** Joe Layton
**Cast:** Anthony Perkins, Cecil Kelloway, Pert Kelton, Ellen McCown, William Chapman, Grover Dale
**Songs:** "A Day Borrowed from Heaven"; "The Music of Home"; "Gideon Briggs, I Love You"; "Summertime Love"; "Walking Away Whistling"; "Never Will I Marry"; "Faraway Boy"
**New York run:** Alvin Theatre, March 8, 1960; 95 p.

B.J. Chute's novel was turned into a homespun fantasy that had to do with quaint superstitions and folklore of a mythical village located on the Meander River — or somewhere down the road from Brigadoon and Glocca Morra. The whimsical tale takes up the conflict of young Gideon Briggs (Anthony Perkins) who would like nothing better than to remain at home and marry his summertime love, Dorrie (Ellen McCown), but who fears that the curse of his family's "call to wander soli-tary" will someday make him run off to sail distant seas. Though tarrying on Broadway only three months, *Greenwillow* has long been admired for the airy, otherworldly charms of Frank Loesser's atypical score. The production also marked Anthony Perkins' first — and so far only — Broadway musical. Columbia OC.

187

# BYE BYE BIRDIE

**Music:** Charles Strouse
**Lyrics:** Lee Adams
**Book:** Michael Stewart
**Producer:** Edward Padula
**Director-choreographer:** Gower Champion
**Cast:** Chita Rivera, Dick Van Dyke, Kay Medford, Paul Lynde, Dick Gautier, Michael J. Pollard, Susan Watson, Charles Nelson Reilly
**Songs:** "An English Teacher"; "The Telephone Hour"; "How Lovely to Be a Woman"; "Put on a Happy Face"; "One Boy"; "One Last Kiss"; "A Lot of Livin' to Do"; "Kids"; "Baby, Talk to Me"; "Rosie"
**New York run:** Martin Beck Theatre, April 14, 1960; 607 p.

*Bye Bye Birdie* provided the launching pad for the Broadway careers of songwriters Charles Strouse and Lee Adams, librettist Michael Stewart, and director-choreographer Gower Champion (his first of nine book musicals). It was also the earliest musical about the rock and roll phenomenon and the effect of its idols on impressionable teenagers. The attitude, however, was generally sympathetic toward adolescent emotions, offering something of a fresh-air antidote to the picture of modern youth conveyed by *West Side Story.* The singing idol in this case is Conrad Birdie (suggesting Elvis Presley), and the young people he is shown affecting are the clean-cut kids of Sweet Apple, Ohio. Birdie is managed by Albert Peterson (Dick Van Dyke) who, with his secretary Rose Grant (Chita Rivera), contrives a publicity stunt involving Kim McAfee (Susan Watson) kissing Birdie on Ed Sullivan's television show just before he is drafted into the Army. Complications involve Kim's jealous boyfriend (Michael J. Pollard) and her exasperated father (Paul Lynde), as well as Albert's querulous mother (Kay Medford) and his relationship with Rose, who wants him to get out of the music business and become an English teacher. During the run, Dick Van Dyke was succeeded by Gene Rayburn, Chita Rivera by Gretchen Wyler. Van Dyke repeated his role in the 1963 film version (also starring Ann-Margret), and Miss Rivera repeated her role in the short-lived 1981 sequel, *Bring Back Birdie* (also with Donald O'Connor). Columbia OC/ DBS Publications (1962)/ TW.

**The Fantasticks.** Jerry Orbach, Rita Gardner, and Kenneth Nelson. (Friedman-Abeles))

# THE FANTASTICKS

**Music:** Harvey Schmidt
**Lyrics & book:** Tom Jones
**Producer:** Lore Noto
**Director:** Word Baker
**Cast:** Jerry Orbach, Rita Gardner, Kenneth Nelson, William Larson, Hugh Thomas, Tom Jones, George Curley, Richard Stauffer
**Songs:** "Try to Remember"; "Much More"; "It Depends on What You Pay"; "Soon It's Gonna Rain"; "I Can See It"; "Plant a Radish"; "Round and Round"; "They Were You"
**New York run:** Sullivan Street Playhouse, May 3, 1960; (still running 11/1/89)

The statistics alone are, well, fantastic. No other New York stage production has ever played so many performances (over 12,280 as of November 1, 1989) and there is still no end in sight. Moreover, by the time of the show's 27th year at the 150-seat Greenwich Village theatre, there had been over 10,000 productions throughout the World, of which some 500 were performed in more than 66 foreign countries. There have also been 15 national touring companies. As for profits, the original backers have so far received a return of over 9,620% on their initial investment of $16,500. Curiously, the original critical reception was not encouraging and producer Lore Noto seriously considered closing the show after its first week. But an Off Broadway award, the popularity of the song "Try to Remember," and, most important, word of mouth, all helped turn the musical's fortunes around.

The whimsical fantasy is concerned with the theme of seasonal rebirth — or the paradox of "why Spring is born out of Winter's laboring pains." The tale, freely adapted from Edmond Rostand's 1894 play, *Les Romanesques,* is told with a cast of eight and performed on a platform with a minimum of props. The neighboring fathers (Hugh Thomas and William Larsen) of Luisa and Matt (Rita Gardner and Kenneth Nelson), though good friends, feel they must appear as enemies to make sure that their progenies fall in love. Having thought up this bit of logic they next find a way to reverse themselves by hiring El Gallo (Jerry Orbach), aided by The Old Actor (Tom Jones) and The Indian (George Curley), to perform a mock rape by moonlight so that Matt might prove his valor, thus paving the way for a reconciliation. But daylight reveals the parental deception, the lovers quarrel, and the young man goes off to see the world. After a number of degrading experiences, he returns home to Luisa's waiting arms firm in the knowledge that "without a hurt the heart is hollow."

To date, the New York company has had over 34 El Gallos (including Bert Convy, David Cryer, and Keith Charles), over 32 Luisas (including Eileen Fulton, Betsy Joslyn, Kathryn Morath, and Judy Blazer), and over 26 Matts (including Craig Carnelia and Bruce Cryer). F. Murray Abraham played The Old Actor in 1967, and producer Lore Noto played the Boy's Father from 1970 to 1986.

Harvey Schmidt and Tom Jones had originally written the musical under the title *Joy Comes to Dead Horse,* in which the characters were Mexican and Anglo families living on adjoining ranches in the American Southwest. Dissatisfied with the overblown concept, they cut the story down to one act, reduced the number of characters, and retitled the show *The Fantasticks*. It was staged in this fashion at Barnard College in the summer of 1959. Lore Noto saw it there, and at his urging Schmidt and Jones rewrote it once again, this time as an intimate two-act musical.

Polydor OC/ Drama Book Shop (1964)/ MTI.

# IRMA LA DOUCE

**Music:** Marguerite Monnot
**Lyrics & book:** Julian More, David Heneker & Monty Norman
**Producer:** David Merrick
**Director:** Peter Brook
**Choreographer:** Onna White
**Cast:** Elizabeth Seal, Keith Michell, Clive Revill, George S. Irving, Stuart Damon, Fred Gwynne, Elliott Gould
**Songs:** "The Bridge of Caulaincourt"; "Our Language of Love"; "Dis-Donc"; "Irma la Douce"; "There Is Only One Paris for That"
**New York run:** Plymouth Theatre, September 29, 1960; 524 p.

Broadway's first hit with music by a French composer, *Irma la Douce* originated in Paris in 1956 with book and lyrics by Alexandre Breffort and ran for four years. The English-language adaptation opened two years later in London and gave 1,512 performances. With Elizabeth Seal, Keith Michell, and Clive Revill recreating their roles in New York — Miss Seal was the only female member of the cast — the production at the Plymouth Theatre (on 45th Street west of Broadway) was a virtual carbon of the West End original. In the story, Irma is a pure-at-heart Parisian prostitute and Nestor (Mr. Michell) is a poor student who is anxious to have Irma all for his own. The student gets the idea to disguise himself as an aged benefactor named Oscar who supposedly has enough money to be the lady's only patron. Nestor, however, grows jealous of Irma's affection for Oscar and "kills" him. He is sent to Devil's Island, but manages to escape, prove his innocence, and return to his beloved. All the songs — including the chief ballad, "Our Language of Love" — were cut from the 1963 film version starring Shirley MacLaine and Jack Lemmon.
Columbia OC/ TW.

**Irma la Douce.** The main performers in the scene are Keith Michell, Elizabeth Seal, and Clive Revill. (Friedman-Abeles)

# THE UNSINKABLE MOLLY BROWN

**Music & lyrics:** Meredith Willson
**Book:** Richard Morris
**Producers:** Theatre Guild & Dore Schary
**Director:** Dore Schary
**Choreographer:** Peter Gennaro
**Cast:** Tammy Grimes, Harve Presnell, Cameron Prud'homme, Mony Dalmes, Edith Meiser, Mitchell Gregg, Christopher Hewett
**Songs:** "I Ain't Down Yet"; "Belly Up to the Bar, Boys"; "Colorado, My Home"; "I'll Never Say No to You"; "My Own Brass Bed"; "Are You Sure?"; "Dolce Far Niente"
**New York run:** Winter Garden, November 3, 1960; 532 p.

Providing Tammy Grimes with her most rewarding role in a musical, *The Unsinkable Molly Brown* retold the saga of a near-legendary figure of the Colorado silver mines who rose from a poverty-stricken background in Hannibal, Missouri, through her spunky determination to be "up where the people are," and by having the good fortune to marry a lucky prospector, "Leadville Johnny" Brown (Harve Presnell). After failing to crash Denver society, Molly drags Johnny off to Europe where despite her gaucheries, or because of them, she becomes a social leader in Monte Carlo. Molly almost loses Johnny, but following her heroism displayed during the sinking of the *Titanic,* she wins back her husband and wins over the elite of Denver. The score Meredith Willson turned out was much in the same Americana vein as *The Music Man,* complete with breezy marches, rugged male choruses, back country dance numbers, and revivalistic exhortations. The movie version came out in 1964 with Debbie Reynolds as Molly and Presnell again as Johnny.
Capitol OC/ Putnam (1961)/ MTI.

**The Unsinkable Molly Brown.** Tammy Grimes and Harve Presnell. (Friedman-Abeles)

**Camelot.** Julie Andrews and Richard Burton.
(Friedman-Abeles)

**Camelot.** Julie Andrews leading the courtiers in "The Lusty Month of
May." (Friedman-Abeles)

# CAMELOT

**Music:** Frederick Loewe
**Lyrics & book:** Alan Jay Lerner
**Producers:** Alan Jay Lerner, Frederick Loewe & Moss Hart
**Director:** Moss Hart (Alan Jay Lerner uncredited)
**Choreographer:** Hanya Holm
**Cast:** Richard Burton, Julie Andrews, Roddy McDowall, Robert Coote, Robert Goulet, M'el Dowd, John Cullum, Bruce Yarnell, David Hurst, Michael Kermoyan
**Songs:** "I Wonder What the King Is Doing Tonight"; "The Simple Joys of Maiden-hood"; "Camelot"; "Follow Me"; "C'est Moi"; "The Lusty Month of May"; "Then You May Take Me to the Fair"; "How to Handle a Woman"; "Before I Gaze at You Again"; "If Ever I Would Leave You"; "What Do the Simple Folk Do?"; "Fie on Goodness!"; "I Loved You Once in Silence"; "Guenevere"
**New York run:** Majestic Theatre, December 3, 1960; 873 p.

Lerner and Loewe's first Broadway undertaking following their spectacular success, *My Fair Lady,* was based on T.H. White's retelling of the Arthurian legend, *The Once and Future King.* Originally titled *Jenny Kissed Me, Camelot* reunited the composer and lyricist with director Moss Hart (who joined Lerner and Loewe as co-producer), fair lady Julie Andrews, Col. Blimpish actor Robert Coote, choreographer Hanya Holm, scene designer Oliver Smith, music director Franz Allers, and orchestrators Robert Russell Bennett and Philip J. Lang. During the tryout, Moss Hart (who died a year later) was hospitalized with a heart attack and Lerner temporarily took over as director. The show had the biggest advance sale in Broadway history up to that time.

The opulently mounted production was a somewhat somber affair that dealt with the chivalrous Knights of the Round Table and the tragic romantic triangle involving noble King Arthur (Richard Burton), his errant Queen Guenevere (Julie Andrews), and Arthur's trusted Sir Lancelot du Lac (Robert Goulet). At the end, with his kingdom in ruins and his wife with another man, the King can still urge a young boy to tell everyone the story "that once there was a fleeting wisp of glory call Camelot." The touring company, which traveled for a year and a half, had a cast headed by William Squire (Arthur), Kathryn Grayson (Guenevere), Robert Peterson (Lancelot), Jan Moody (Morgan Le Fay), and Arthur Treacher (King Pellinore).

In 1980, Richard Burton recreated his original role in a touring revival that played a limited New York engagement in July. Christine Ebersole played Guenevere and Richard Muenz was Lancelot. Because of ill health, Burton was succeeded on the road by Richard Harris who also came back briefly to New York — in November 1981 — with Meg Bussert now playing the queen. In all, this company toured for almost three years. Harris had previously played King Arthur in the 1967 film version, which also starred Vanessa Redgrave (Guenevere) and Franco Nero (Lancelot).

A previous — and far more lighthearted — view of King Arthur's court was found in Rodgers and Hart's 1927 hit, *A Connecticut Yankee.*
Columbia OC/ Random House (1961); Chilton (1976)/ TW.

# DO RE MI

**Music:** Jule Styne
**Lyrics:** Betty Comden & Adolph Green
**Book:** Garson Kanin
**Producer:** David Merrick
**Director:** Garson Kanin
**Choreographers:** Marc Breaux & DeeDee Wood
**Cast:** Phil Silvers, Nancy Walker, John Reardon, David Burns, George Mathews, George Givot, Nancy Dussault
**Songs:** "It's Legitimate"; "I Know About Love"; "Cry Like the Wind"; "Fireworks"; "What's New at the Zoo?"; "The Late Late Show"; "Adventure"; "Make Someone Happy"
**New York run:** St. James Theatre, December 26, 1960; 400 p.

A raucous satire on the music business — with special emphasis on the jukebox industry — *Do Re Mi* was full of characters reminiscent of the raffish denizens of *Guys and Dolls.* It was particularly blessed by offering two outstanding clowns in Phil Silvers as the pushiest of patsies and Nancy Walker as his long-suffering spouse. The story, which Garson Kanin adapted from his own novel, concerns Hubie Cram, a would-be bigshot, who induces three retired slot-machine mobsters (David Burns, George Mathews, and George Givot) to muscle in on the jukebox racket. Though this does not make him the fawned-upon tycoon he has always dreamed of becoming, Hubie does succeed in turning a waitress (Nancy Dussault) into a singing star. He also shows his musical knowledge by instructing a group of studio musicians on how each one is to play his instrument. His modest comment: "You hang around, you learn."
RCA OC/ TW.

**Do Re Mi.** "It's Legitimate" sing Phil Silvers, George Mathews, George Givot, and David Burns. (Friedman-Abeles)

# CARNIVAL

**Music & lyrics:** Bob Merrill
**Book:** Michael Stewart
**Producer:** David Merrick
**Director-choreographer:** Gower Champion
**Cast:** Anna Maria Alberghetti, James Mitchell, Kaye Ballard, Pierre Olaf, Jerry Orbach, Henry Lascoe, Anita Gillette
**Songs:** "Direct from Vienna"; "Mira"; "Yes, My Heart"; "Love Makes the World Go Round"; "Beautiful Candy"; "Grand Imperial Cirque de Paris"; "Always Always You"; "She's My Love"
**New York run:** Imperial Theatre, April 13, 1961; 719 p.

Though the 1953 movie *Lili* had but one song, it did have two extended dance sequences which qualified it as the first screen musical to be adapted as a stage musical. Since the single song was "Hi Lili, Hi Lo," it presented a challenge for Bob Merrill to come up with a "theme" for *Carnival* with the same flavor but sufficiently distinctive on its own. He met the challenge with "Love Makes the World Go Round," whose melody from a wheezing concertina opens the show on a bare, pre-dawn setting as the weary members of a seedy French carnival set up the tents. With this strikingly effective opening (there is no overture), director Gower Champion reaffirmed his reputation for imaginative stagecraft, which was later bolstered by a joyously self-deluding dance number as the company proudly imagines itself as the "Grand Imperial Cirque de Paris." In the story, Anna Maria Alberghetti appeared as the waif who comes from the town of Mira to join the carnival where she falls for the egotistical magician Marco the Magnificent (James Mitchell), befriends the show's puppets, and ends in the arms of the disillusioned crippled puppeteer (Jerry Orbach). During the Broadway run, Miss Alberghetti was succeeded by Susan Watson and sister Carla Alberghetti. Polydor OC/ DBS Publications (1968)/ TW.

# MILK AND HONEY

**Music & lyrics:** Jerry Herman
**Book:** Don Appell
**Producer:** Gerald Oestreicher
**Director:** Albert Marre
**Choreographer:** Donald Saddler
**Cast:** Robert Weede, Mimi Benzell, Molly Picon, Tommy Rall, Lanna Saunders, Juki Arkin
**Songs:** "Shalom"; "Milk and Honey"; "There's No Reason in the World"; "That Was Yesterday"; "Let's Not Waste A Moment"; "Like A Young Man"; "As Simple As That"
**New York run:** Martin Beck Theatre, October 10, 1961, 543 p.

For his initial Broadway assignment, composer-lyricist Jerry Herman joined playwright Don Appell to create the first musical with an Israeli setting. After spending some weeks in Israel, the writers agreed on a story concerning American tourists so that the score would not have to be written entirely in a minor key. *Milk and Honey* (originally titled *Shalom*) was primarily about a romance that blooms in a desert *moshav* between a middle-aged man separated from his wife (Robert Weede) and an almost middle-aged widow (Mimi Benzell). Though Phil would like Ruth to remain with him, she is unhappy about an extended non-matrimonial relationship, and — when last seen — Phil is on his way to make one final appeal for a divorce. Comic relief was provided by Molly Picon (a star of the Yiddish theatre in her only Broadway musical) as a husband-hunting widow. RCA OC/ TW.

**How to Succeed in Business Without Really Trying.** Robert Morse and Bonnie Scott. (Friedman-Abeles)

# HOW TO SUCCEED IN BUSINESS WITHOUT REALLY TRYING

**Music & lyrics:** Frank Loesser
**Book:** Abe Burrows
**Producers:** Cy Feuer & Ernest Martin
**Director:** Abe Burrows
**Choreographers:** Bob Fosse, Hugh Lambert
**Cast:** Robert Morse, Rudy Vallee, Bonnie Scott, Virginia Martin, Charles Nelson Reilly, Ruth Kobart, Sammy Smith, Donna McKechnie
**Songs:** "Coffee Break"; "The Company Way"; "A Secretary Is Not a Toy"; "Grand Old Ivy"; "Paris Original"; "Rosemary"; "I Believe in You"; "Brotherhood of Man"
**New York run:** 46th Street Theatre, October 14, 1961; 1,417 p.

The program credit for *How to Succeed in Business Without Really Trying* indicates that the musical was based on Shepherd Mead's tongue-in-cheek manual, but since the book had no plot Abe Burrows' script was actually based on an unproduced play by Jack Weinstock and Willie Gilbert (whose program credit, also incorrect, indicates that they were co-librettists). That play had been sent to producers Cy Feuer and Ernest Martin who then enlisted Burrows and Frank Loesser, their *Guys and Dolls* team, to turn it into a musical comedy. Bob Fosse was brought in during rehearsals to take charge of the musical staging.

In the sassy sendup of the Horatio Alger myth, our disarmingly boyish hero J. Pierpont Finch (Robert Morse) owes his advancement — from window washer to Chairman of the Board of the World Wide Wicket Company — not to hard work but to his ability to make others work hard for him. As it traces Finch's step-by-step back-stabbing way up the corporate ladder, the show skewers such aspects of Big Business as nepotism, old-school ties, the coffee break, the office party, the sycophantic yes-men, the executive washroom (where Finch serenades his image in the mirror with the worshipful "I Believe in You"), and the boardroom presentation. The musical became the fourth to win the Pulitzer Prize for drama. Robert Morse and Rudy Vallee, who played J.B. Biggley, the stuffy president of the company, were also in the 1967 movie.
RCA OC/ Frank Music, London (1963)*/ MTI.

# NO STRINGS

**Music & lyrics:** Richard Rodgers
**Book:** Samuel Taylor
**Producer:** Richard Rodgers
**Director-choreographer:** Joe Layton
**Cast:**  Richard Kiley, Diahann Carroll, Polly Rowles, Noelle Adam, Bernice Massi, Don Chastain, Alvin Epstein, Mitchell Gregg
**Songs:** "The Sweetest Sounds"; "Loads of Love"; "La La La"; "Nobody Told Me"; "Look No Further"; "Maine"; "No Strings"
**New York run:** 54th Street Theatre, March 15, 1962; 580 p.

One appearance on the Jack Paar television show was all it took for Diahann Carroll to convince Richard Rodgers that she should be starred on Broadway in a Richard Rodgers musical. *No Strings,* the musical that resulted, was Rodgers' first production after the death of his partner, Oscar Hammerstein II, and the only one for which the composer also supplied his own lyrics. The work proved to be highly innovative in a number of ways: it placed the orchestra backstage, it put musicians onstage to accompany singers, it had the principals and chorus move scenery and props in full view of the audience, and — conforming to the show's title — it removed the string section from the orchestra. In addition, it was concerned with an interracial love affair, though the matter of race was never discussed. The leading characters were Barbara Woodruff (Miss Carroll), a high fashion model living in Paris, and David Jordan (Richard Kiley), a former Pulitzer Prize-winning novelist now a sponging "Europe bum." After meeting they enjoy hearing the sweetest sounds in such romantic surroundings as Monte Carlo, Honfleur, Deauville, and St. Tropez. The story ends, with no strings attached, as the writer returns home alone to Maine to try to resume his career. During the run, Kiley and Miss Carroll were succeeded by Howard Keel and Barbara McNair, who then toured. The 54th Street Theatre, formerly the Adelphi, was renamed the George Abbott before it was demolished.
Capitol OC/ Random House (1962)/ R&H.

**No Strings.** Diahann Carroll and Richard Kiley.
(Friedman-Abeles)

# A FUNNY THING HAPPENED ON THE WAY TO THE FORUM

**Music & lyrics:** Stephen Sondheim
**Book:** Burt Shevelove & Larry Gelbart
**Producer:** Harold Prince
**Director:** George Abbott (Jerome Robbins uncredited)
**Choreographer:** Jack Cole
**Cast:** Zero Mostel, John Carradine, Raymond Walburn, Jack Gilford, David Burns, Ruth Kobart, Brian Davies, Preshy Marker, Ronald Holgate, Eddie Phillips
**Songs:** "Comedy Tonight"; "Love I Hear"; "Free"; "Lovely"; "Pretty Little Picture"; "Everybody Ought to Have a Maid"; "I'm Calm"; "Impossible"; "Bring Me My Bride"; "That'll Show Him"
**New York run:** Alvin Theatre, May 8, 1962; 964 p.

Having already written a musical at Yale inspired by the farcical plays of Titus Maccius Plautus (254 BC-184 BC), Burt Shevelove got together with Larry Gelbart and Stephen Sondheim to give Broadway a taste of what once convulsed Roman audiences. To come up with a suitable script — which would also adhere to the classic unities of time, place and action — the writers researched all 21 of the playwright's surviving comedies, then put together an original story incorporating such typical, laugh-catching Plautus characters as the conniving slave, the callow hero (named Hero), the doddering old man, the seductive courtesan, the lustful husband and his shrewish wife, and the macho warrior. One situation in the musical — regarding the doddering old man who is kept from entering his house because he thinks it is haunted — was discovered in a play with the curiously prophetic title of *Mostellaria*.

Originally intended as a vehicle for Phil Silvers, then for Milton Berle, *A Funny Thing Happened on the Way to the Forum* opened with Zero Mostel as Pseudolus, a slave who is forced to go through a series of outlandish adventures before being allowed his freedom. Though Broadway audiences immediately took to George Abbott's frantically paced show, the outlook had not looked promising during the pre-New York tryout and director Jerome Robbins was called in. His most important change: beginning the musical with the song "Comedy Tonight," which set just the right mood for the madcap doings that followed. In addition to being Harold Prince's first solo producing effort, the show was the first Broadway offering with music as well as lyrics by Stephen Sondheim. During the run, Mostel was succeeded by Dick Shawn, David Burns by Frank McHugh (as Senex, a lascivious slave owner), Jack Gilford by Lee Goodman (as Hysterium, a nervous slave) and John Carradine by Erik Rhodes (as Marcus Lycus, a dealer in courtesans). The touring cast included Jerry Lester (Pseudolus), Paul Hartman (Senex), Arnold Stang (Hysterium), Erik Rhodes (Marcus Lycus), Edward Everett Horton (Erronius, the doddering old man), and Donna McKechnie (Philia, a slave).

In 1972, Phil Silvers got his chance to play Pseudolus in a well-received revival whose run was cut short by the star's illness. Larry Blyden, who was also co-producer, appeared as Hysterium, and others in the cast were Mort Marshall (Senex), Carl Ballantine (Lycus), and Reginald Owen (Erronius). Burt Shevelove was the director. Both Mostel (as Pseudolus) and Silvers (as Lycus) were in the 1966 screen version along with Jack Gilford.
Capitol OC/ Dodd, Mead (1963)/ MTI.

**A Funny Thing Happened on the Way to the Forum.** John Carradine and Zero Mostel. (Friedman-Abeles)

## STOP THE WORLD — I WANT TO GET OFF

**Music, lyrics & book:** Leslie Bricusse & Anthony Newley
**Producer:** David Merrick
**Director:** Anthony Newley
**Choreographers:** Virginia Mason, John Broome
**Cast:** Anthony Newley, Anna Quayle, Jennifer Baker, Susan Baker
**Songs:** "Typically English"; "Gonna Build a Mountain"; "Once in a Lifetime"; "Someone Nice Like You"; "What Kind Of Fool Am I?"
**New York run:** Shubert Theatre, October 3, 1962; 555 p.

A hit in London a year before it was presented in New York, *Stop the World — I Want to Get Off* unveiled the multiple talents of the British team of Leslie Bricusse and Anthony Newley. Newley starred in the musical, in which he played Littlechap, and the allegorical tale had much to say about man's drive for fame and power and the disillusionment that sets in once these goals are attained. (Rodgers and Hammerstein had previously dealt with the same general theme in *Allegro*.) In a setting designed by Sean Kenny to resemble a circus tent, Littlechap — wearing white-face clown makeup — rises in the world of business and politics after marrying the boss's daughter (Anna Quayle). Not above a little philandering with Russian, German, and American girls (all played by Miss Quayle), Littlechap ends his days ruminating — in "What Kind of Fool Am I?" — about his misspent life. Newley was succeeded during the run by Joel Grey, and his part in the 1966 movie was played by Tony Tanner. A revised adaptation came back to Broadway in 1978 with Sammy Davis Jr. Davis also did a film version of this verison under the modest rubric *Sammy Stops the World.* Polydor OC/ TW.

# LITTLE ME

**Music:** Cy Coleman
**Lyrics:** Carolyn Leigh
**Book:** Neil Simon
**Producers:** Cy Feuer & Ernest Martin
**Directors:** Cy Feuer & Bob Fosse
**Choreographer:** Bob Fosse
**Cast:** Sid Caesar, Virginia Martin, Nancy Andrews, Mort Marshall, Joey Faye, Swen Swenson, Peter Turgeon, Mickey Deems, Gretchen Cryer
**Songs:** "The Other Side of the Tracks"; "I Love You"; "Be a Performer"; "Boom-Boom"; "I've Got Your Number"; "Real Live Girl"; "Poor Little Hollywood Star"; "Here's to Us"
**New York run:** Lunt-Fontanne Theatre, November 17, 1962; 257 p.

Although Neil Simon's wickedly funny, outlandishly plotted libretto for *Little Me* was based on Patrick Dennis' novel about the rise of a voluptuous beauty from Drifters' Row, Venezuela, Illinois, to a Southampton estate, it was written primarily to show off the protean comic gifts of Sid Caesar playing all seven of the men who figured prominently in our heroine's life. Chief among the Caesar characterizations was Noble Eggleston, the over-achieving snob who loves poor Belle Schlumpfert as much as he is able ("considering you're riffraff and I am well-to-do"), studies medicine and law at Harvard and Yale, becomes a flying ace in World War I, wins election as governor of both North and South Dakota, and, eventually, is the man with whom Belle literally walks into the sunset. The actor was also seen as Amos Pinchley, an 88-year-old miserly banker; Val du Val, a flashy French entertainer; Fred Poitrine, the hick soldier who marries Belle and quickly expires; Otto Schnitzler, a dictatorial Hollywood director; Prince Cherney, the lachrymose impoverished ruler of the duchy of Rosenzweig; and Noble Jr., an over-achieving chip who studies both at Juilliard and Georgia Tech to become a musical engineer. Highlights of the score were the wistful "Real Live Girl," sung by World War I doughboys, and the sassy, seductive "I've Got Your Number," sung and danced by Swen Swenson, as Belle's faithful admirer.

In 1982, a revised version of *Little Me* — with James Coco, Victor Garber and Mary Gordon Murray — had a disappointingly short run on Broadway. RCA OC/ Random House (1977)/ TW.

**Little Me.** Sid Caesar (as Amos Pinchley) and Virginia Martin. (Friedman-Abeles)

# OLIVER!

**Music, lyrics & book:** Lionel Bart
**Producers:** David Merrick & Donald Albery
**Director:** Peter Cole
**Cast:** Clive Revill, Georgia Brown, Bruce Prochnik, Willoughby Goddard, Hope Jackman, Danny Sewell, David Jones, Geoffrey Lumb
**Songs:** "Food Glorious Food"; "Where Is Love?"; "Consider Yourself"; "You've Got to Pick a Pocket or Two"; "It's a Fine Life"; "Oom-Pah-Pah"; "I'd Do Anything"; "As Long as He Needs Me"; "Who Will Buy?"; "Reviewing the Situation"
**New York run:** Imperial Theatre, January 6, 1963; 774 p.

Lionel Bart's *Oliver!,* which opened in London in 1960, held the West End long-run record for a musical until overtaken by *Jesus Christ Superstar,* and its Broadway facsimilie—also directed by Peter Cole and designed by Sean Kenny—was the longest running musical import until overtaken by *Evita.* Adapted from Charles Dickens' *Oliver Twist,* the stage version offered a somewhat jollied up view of the ordeal of an orphan (played by Bruce Prochnik) who dares to ask for more food at the workhouse, is sent out into the cruel world, falls in with a band of juvenile pickpockets under the benign controlof Fagin (Clive Revill), and is eventually rescued from a life of fraternal crime by kindly, wealthy Mr. Brownlow (Geoffrey Lumb), who turns out to be Oliver's grandfather. Kenny's ingenious, atmospheric settings were much admired as were the tuneful, rousing score. The work, however, did not last long in a 1984 revival with Ron Moody (the London and 1968 film version Fagin) and Patti LuPone.

Five other Dickens novels were seen on Broadway in musical adaptations: *Barnaby Rudge* (*Dolly Varden,* 1902); *The Posthumous Papers of the Pickwick Club* (*Mr. Pickwick,* 1903; *Pickwick,* 1965); *A Christmas Carol* (*Comin' Uptown,* 1979); *David Copperfield* (*Copperfield,* 1981); *The Mystery of Edwin Drood* 1985). For other musicals based on British literary classics, see *My Fair Lady,* page 168.
RCA OC/TW.

**Oliver!** Georgia Brown, David Jones, Bruce Prochnik, and Clive Revill in the "I'd Do Anything" number. (Friedman-Abeles)

**She Loves Me.** Daniel Massey and Barbara Cook. (Eileen Darby)

# SHE LOVES ME

**Music:** Jerry Bock
**Lyrics:** Sheldon Harnick
**Book:** Joe Masteroff
**Producer-director:** Harold Prince
**Choreographer:** Carol Haney
**Cast:** Barbara Cook, Daniel Massey, Barbara Baxley, Jack Cassidy, Ludwig Donath, Nathaniel Frey, Ralph Williams
**Songs:** "Days Gone By"; "Tonight at Eight"; "Will He Like Me?"; "Dear Friend"; "Ice Cream"; "She Loves Me"; "A Trip to the Library"; "Grand Knowing You"; "Twelve Days to Christmas"
**New York run:** Eugene O'Neill Theatre, April 23, 1963; 301 p.

With its beguiling European setting, attractive characters, tender love story, and, most important, closely integrated, melody drenched score, *She Loves Me* recalled the atmosphere and charm of the Kern-Harbach *The Cat and the Fiddle* and the Kern-Hammerstein *Music in the Air.* The new musical, the first to be directed as well as produced by Harold Prince, was based on a Hungarian play, *Parfumerie,* by Miklos Laszlo, that had already been used as the basis for two films, *The Shop Around the Corner* and *In the Good Old Summertime.* Set in the 1930s in "A City in Europe" — which could only be Budapest — the tale is concerned with the people who work in Maraczek's Parfumerie, principally the constantly squabbling sales clerk Amalia Balash (Barbara Cook) and the manager Georg Nowack (Daniel Massey). It is soon revealed that they are anonymous pen pals who agree to meet one night at the Café Imperiale, though neither knows the other's identity. Georg realizes who Amalia is when he sees her waiting for him in the restaurant, but he doesn't let on and the unhappy Amalia pours out her heart in a longing plea to her unknown "Dear Friend." After she calls in sick, their relationship blossoms into love when Georg brings her ice cream; eventually, he is emboldened to reveal his identity by quoting from one of Amalia's letters.

*She Loves Me,* which would have starred Julie Andrews had she not been tied up with a film, was one of the few musicals to play the Eugene O'Neill Theatre on 49th Street west of Broadway.
Polydor OC/ Dodd, Mead (1963)/ TW.

# 110 IN THE SHADE

**Music:** Harvey Schmidt
**Lyrics:** Tom Jones
**Book:** N. Richard Nash
**Producer:** David Merrick
**Director:** Joseph Anthony
**Choreographer:** Agnes de Mille
**Cast:** Robert Horton, Inga Swenson, Stephen Douglass, Will Geer, Steve Roland, Anthony Teague, Lesley Ann Warren, Gretchen Cryer
**Songs:** "Love, Don't Turn Away"; "Rain Song"; "You're Not Foolin' Me"; "Old Maid"; "Everything Beautiful Happens at Night"; "Melisande"; "Simple Little Things"; "Little Red Hat"; "Is It Really Me?"
**New York run:** Broadhurst Theatre, October 24, 1963; 330 p.

Harvey Schmidt and Tom Jones followed their runaway Off-Broadway hit, *The Fantasticks,* with an equally wistful and appealing score for *110 in the Shade,* which N. Richard Nash adapted from his own 1954 play, *The Rainmaker.* The action of the story takes place in a drought-stricken Western town on a hot summer day from dawn to midnight. The sudden appearance of a brash rainmaker, Bill Starbuck (Robert Horton in a part first announced for Hal Holbrook), lifts the spirits of all but plain Lizzie Curry (Inga Swenson) who calls him a fake. Lizzie, whose life is as parched as the weather, is attracted to the flamboyant con man and they make love while the town is enjoying its annual picnic. Starbuck wants Lizzie to run away with him, but since her dreams are really only of simple little things, she is happy to remain with the more dependable suitor, Sheriff File (Stephen Douglass). Then darned if a miracle doesn't happen and the rains come. RCA OC/ TW.

**110 in the Shade.** Robert Horton and Inga Swenson. (Friedman-Abeles)

# HELLO, DOLLY!

**Music & lyrics:** Jerry Herman
**Book:** Michael Stewart
**Producer:** David Merrick
**Director-choreographer:** Gower Champion
**Cast:** Carol Channing, David Burns, Eileen Brennan, Sondra Lee, Charles Nelson Reilly, Jerry Dodge, Gordon Connell, Igors Gavon, Alice Playten, David Hartman
**Songs:** "It Takes a Woman"; "Put on Your Sunday Clothes"; "Ribbons Down My Back"; "Dancing"; "Before the Parade Passes By"; "Hello, Dolly!"; "It Only Takes a Moment"; "So Long, Dearie"
**New York run:** St. James Theatre, January 16, 1964; 2,844 p.

For over ten months — until it was overtaken by *Fiddler on the Roof* — *Hello, Dolly!* held the record as Broadway's longest running musical. Its tryout tour, however, was hardly a harbinger of even a moderate success. New writers had to be called in, three songs were dropped and three added (including the first-act finale, "Before the Parade Passes By"), and Jerry Dodge replaced one of the two leading juveniles. But director Gower Champion made it all work and the musical won a rousing Broadway reception.

The turn-of-the-century tale centers around Dolly Gallagher Levi, a New York matchmaker engaged to help a pompous Yonkers merchant, Horace Vandergelder (David Burns), in his pursuit of a mate. But the matchmaker sets her cap for Vandergelder herself, and eventually he acknowledges that it fits. Along the way, the exuberant Dolly helps two of Vandergelder's clerks, Barnaby Tucker and Cornelius Hackl (Jerry Dodge and Charles Nelson Reilly) enjoy a night at the Harmonia Gardens restaurant with dressmaker Irene Malloy and her assistant Minnie Fay (Eileen Brennan and Sondra Lee). After her grand entrance into the restaurant, Dolly sets off a rousing, high-kicking reception by the waiters welcoming her back to a once favored haunt.

*Hello, Dolly!* had an unusually lengthy history. Its first version, in 1835, was a London play, *A Day Well Spent,* by John Oxenford. Seven years later, *Einen Jux Will er Sich Machen (He Wants to Have a Lark),* a Viennese variation by Johann Nestroy, was produced. In 1938, Thornton Wilder turned the Nestroy play into *The Merchant of Yonkers,* and 17 years after that he rewrote it as *The Matchmaker.* Both Wilder plays had Broadway runs. Another forerunner of *Hello, Dolly!* was the 1891 musical, *A Trip to Chinatown.*

Once Ethel Merman had turned down the chance to be the first song-and-dance Dolly, Carol Channing seized the opportunity to make it one of her two most closely identified roles. During the Broadway run she was succeeded by Ginger Rogers, Martha Raye, Betty Grable, Bibi Osterwald, Pearl Bailey (who starred in an all-black company and was frequently spelled by Thelma Carpenter), Phyllis Diller, and — at last — Ethel Merman. David Burns was replaced by Max Showalter, and Cab Calloway had the Vandergelder part opposite Miss Bailey. During Miss Merman's tenure, Russell Nype played Cornelius. The show returned to New York in 1974 with Miss Bailey and Billy Daniels leading an all-black cast, and in 1978 it came back with Miss Channing and Eddie Bracken as part of a year-and-a-half tour. In 1965, Mary Martin and Loring Smith headed the first touring company, which played the Far East (primarily for U.S. troops) and London. A second company toured two years nine months originally with Miss Channing (succeeded by Eve Arden and Dorothy Lamour) and Horace MacMahon. A third company, starring Miss Grable (then Miss Rogers and Miss Lamour) traveled for two years four months. The show's film version, released in 1969, co-starred Barbra Streisand and Walter Matthau.

RCA OC (Channing); RCA OC (Bailey); RCA OC (Martin)/ DBS (1966)/ TW.

Carol Channing

Ginger Rogers

Martha Raye

Betty Grable

Pearl Bailey

# WHAT MAKES SAMMY RUN?

**Music & lyrics:** Ervin Drake
**Book:** Budd & Stuart Schulberg
**Producer:** Joseph Cates
**Director:** Abe Burrows
**Choreographer:** Matt Mattox
**Cast:** Steve Lawrence, Sally Ann Howes, Robert Alda, Bernice Massi, Barry Newman, Walter Klavun
**Songs:** "A Tender Spot"; "My Home Town"; "A Room Without Windows"; "Something to Live For"; "The Friendliest Thing"
**New York run:** 54th Street Theatre, February 27, 1964; 540 p.

Unscrupulous Sammy Glick was first immortalized in Budd Schulberg's novel about the double dealing world of Hollywood. In the musical version, adapted by Schulberg and his brother Stuart, he was something of a relative to *How to Succeed's* J. Pierpont Finch, as the story covers Sammy's rise from his days as a newspaper copy boy, through his job as a script writer at World Wide Pictures and his affair with fellow-writer Kit Sargent (Sally Ann Howes), to his elevation as studio chief and his marriage to his boss's nymphomaniac daughter (Bernice Massi). At the play's end, left without friends and with an unfaithful wife, Sammy is still running. Playing the role of Sammy was nightclub and recording star Steve Lawrence, who helped turn a vision of romantic isolation, "A Room Without Windows," into a popular song hit.
Columbia OC/ Random House (1965)/ TW.

**Funny Girl.** Barbra Streisand singing "I'm the Greatest Star" as Danny Meehan watches. (Henry Grossman)

# FUNNY GIRL

**Music:** Jule Styne
**Lyrics:** Bob Merrill
**Book:** Isobel Lennart
**Producer:** Ray Stark
**Directors:** Jerome Robbins, Garson Kanin
**Choreographer:** Carol Haney
**Cast:** Barbra Streisand, Sydney Chaplin, Kay Medford, Danny Meehan, Jean Stapleton, Roger DeKoven, Joseph Macaulay, Lainie Kazan, Buzz Miller, George Reeder, Larry Fuller
**Songs:** "I'm the Greatest Star"; "Cornet Man"; I Want to Be Seen With You Tonight"; "People"; "You Are Woman"; "Don't Rain on My Parade"; "Sadie, Sadie"; "Who Are You Now?"; "The Music That Makes Me Dance"
**New York run:** Winter Garden, March 26, 1964; 1,348 p.

The funny girl of the title refers to Fanny Brice, and the story, told mostly in flashback, covers the major events in the life of the celebrated comedienne — her discovery by impresario Florenz Ziegfeld, her triumphs in the *Ziegfeld Follies,* her infatuation with and stormy marriage to smooth-talking con man Nick Arnstein, and the breakup of that marriage after Nick has served time for masterminding the theft of Wall Street securities. Film producer Ray Stark, Miss Brice's son-in-law, had long wanted to make a movie based on the Fanny Brice story, but he became convinced that it should first be done on the stage. Mary Martin, Anne Bancroft, and Carol Burnett had all turned down the leading part before it was won by Barbra Streisand, whose only other Broadway experience had been in a supporting role in *I Can Get It for You Wholesale.* Miss Streisand succeeded so well — her recording of "People" was a hit before *Funny Girl* opened — that she became even more renowned than the woman she portrayed.

At first there was hope that the *Gypsy* team of Jule Styne and Stephen Sondheim would be reunited to write the score, but Sondheim wasn't interested and Styne contacted Bob Merrill. Some of their songs, however, virtually replaced those used in comparable situations in *Gypsy* — "I'm the Greatest Star" for "Some People," "Don't Rain on My Parade" for "Everything's Coming Up Roses," and "The Music That Makes Me Dance" (which suggested Fanny Brice's closely identified theme song, "My Man") for "Rose's Turn." When Jerome Robbins, the original director, walked out in a dispute with the author, he was succeeded by Bob Fosse, who didn't stay long, then by Garson Kanin, who quit after Robbins was lured back.

The musical was variously announced under such titles as *A Very Special Person, My Man,* and *The Luckiest People* before David Merrick (who was to have been the show's co-producer) suggested *Funny Girl.* Numerous script alterations — including 40 rewrites of the final scene alone — and five opening-night postponements were required before the show was considered ready for its official premiere. During the Broadway run, Miss Streisand was followed by Mimi Hines, and Sydney Chaplin, who played Nick Arnstein, by Johnny Desmond. The road company, which toured for 13 months was headed by Marilyn Michaels (Fanny), Anthony George (Nick), and Lillian Roth (Fanny's mother). Miss Streisand also starred in the 1968 film version and its 1975 sequel, *Funny Lady.* For other show-business musical biographies, see *Annie Get Your Gun,* page 130.
Capitol OC/ Random House (1964)/ TW.

# HIGH SPIRITS

**Music, lyrics & book:** Hugh Martin & Timothy Gray
**Producers:** Lester Osterman, Robert Fletcher & Richard Horner
**Director:** Noël Coward (Gower Champion uncredited)
**Choreographer:** Danny Daniels
**Cast:**  Beatrice Lillie, Tammy Grimes, Edward Woodward, Louise Troy
**Songs:** "Was She Prettier Than I?"; "The Bicycle Song"; "Forever and a Day";
   "I Know Your Heart"; "Faster Than Sound"; "If I Gave You"; "Home
   Sweet Heaven"; "Something Is Coming to Tea"
**New York run:** Alvin Theatre, April 7, 1964; 375 p.

Hugh Martin and Timothy Gray had wanted to adapt Noël Coward's 1941 play
*Blithe Spirit* as early as 1953, but permission was not granted until seven years
later. In their musical version — initially titled *Faster Than Sound* — Beatrice
Lillie (in her 13th and final Broadway appearance) portrayed the antic spiritualist
Mme. Arcati who disrupts the second marriage of writer Charles Condomine
(Edward Woodward) by bringing the shade of his first wife, Elvira (Tammy
Grimes), back from the dead. In an attempt to take her former husband with her
to the spirit world, Elvira accidentally causes the death of Ruth (Louise Troy), the
second wife, who takes revenge by playing some ghostly tricks of her own. As
director, Noël Coward made sure that *High Spirits* was in the proper blithe spirit
of his play, but friction during the Philadelphia tryout between him and Miss Lillie
prompted Mr. Coward's replacement by Gower Champion.
ABC Paramount OC/ TW.

**Fiddler on the Roof.** Tevye (Zero Mostel) is none too happy that daughter
Tzeitel (Joanna Merlin) is marrying a poor tailor (Austin Pendleton).
(Friedman-Abeles)

# FIDDLER ON THE ROOF

**Music;** Jerry Bock
**Lyrics:** Sheldon Harnick
**Book:** Joseph Stein
**Producer:** Harold Prince
**Director-choreographer:** Jerome Robbins
**Cast:** Zero Mostel, Maria Karnilova, Beatrice Arthur, Joanna Merlin, Austin Pendleton, Bert Convy, Julia Migenes, Michael Granger, Tanya Everett, Leonard Frey, Maurice Edwards
**Songs:** "Tradition"; "Matchmaker, Matchmaker"; "If I Were a Rich Man"; "Sabbath Prayer"; "To Life"; "Miracle of Miracles"; "Sunrise, Sunset"; "Now I Have Everything"; "Do You Love Me?"; "Far from the Home I Love"; "Anatevka"
**New York run:** Imperial Theatre, September 22, 1964; 3,242 p.

One of Broadway's classic musicals, *Fiddler on the Roof* defied the accepted rules of commercial success by dealing with persecution, poverty, and the problems of holding on to traditions in the midst of a hostile world. But despite a story and setting that many thought had limited appeal, the theme struck such a universal response that the fiddler was perched precariously on his roof for seven years nine months, thus becoming the longest running production — musical or nonmusical — in Broadway history. (The record, however, was broken by *Grease* in December 1979.)

The plot is set in the Jewish village of Anatevka, Russia, in 1905, and deals mainly with the efforts of Tevye (Zero Mostel), a dairyman, his wife Golde (Maria Karnilova), and their five daughters to cope with their harsh existence. Tzeitel (Joanna Merlin), the oldest daughter, marries a poor tailor (Austin Pendleton), after Tevye had promised her to a well-to-do middle-aged butcher (Michael Granger). Hodel (Julia Migenes), the second daughter, marries a revolutionary (Bert Convy) and follows him to Siberia. Chava (Tanya Everett), the third daughter, marries out of her religion. When, at the end, the Czar's Cossacks destroy Anatevka, Tevye, still holding on to his faith and his traditions, bravely prepares to take what's left of his family to America. Though Zero Mostel became closely identified with the role of Tevye he proved not to be indispensable, since the musical had no trouble continuing with his successors Luther Adler, Herschel Bernardi, Harry Goz, Jerry Jarrett, Paul Lipson, and Jan Peerce. Six actresses replaced Maria Karnilova as Golde, including Martha Schlamme, Dolores Wilson, and Peg Murray. During the Broadway engagement, Pia Zadora took over as Bielke, the youngest daughter, and Bette Midler was seen for a time as Tzeitel. In 1976, *Fiddler on the Roof* came back to New York with Mostel and Thelma Lee in the leading roles; in 1981, it returned — at Lincoln Center's New York State Theatre — with Herschel Bernardi and Maria Karnilova. The national tour, originally featuring Luther Adler and Dolores Wilson, was on the road for two years three months. Topol, who played Tevye in London, was seen in the 1971 screen version which also featured Norma Crane and Molly Picon.

The idea for *Fiddler on the Roof* was planted when Jerry Bock, Sheldon Harnick, and Joseph Stein decided to make a musical out of Sholom Aleichem's short story, "Tevye and His Daughters." They took the first draft to producer Harold Prince who advised them that no other director but Jerome Robbins could possibly give the material the universal quality that it required. The first choice for Tevye was Danny Kaye; among others considered at various times were Howard Da Silva, Tom Bosley, and Danny Thomas.

RCA OC/ Crown (1964); Chilton (1973)/ MTI.

# GOLDEN BOY

**Music:** Charles Strouse
**Lyrics:** Lee Adams
**Book:** Clifford Odets, William Gibson
**Producer:** Hillard Elkins
**Director:** Arthur Penn
**Choreographer:** Donald McKayle
**Cast:** Sammy Davis Jr., Billy Daniels, Paula Wayne, Kenneth Tobey, Ted Beniades, Louis Gossett, Jaime Rogers, Lola Falana
**Songs:** "Night Song"; "Don't Forget 127th Street"; "Lorna's Here"; "This Is the Life"; "While the City Sleeps"; "I Want to Be With You"
**New York run:** Majestic Theatre, October 20, 1964; 569 p.

For his first offering as a Broadway producer, Hillard Elkins hit upon the idea that by changing the leading character in Clifford Odets' 1937 drama *Golden Boy* from an Italian-American boxer named Joe Bonaparte to a Negro American boxer named Joe Wellington, the result would be a musical play of substance and significance. Odets himself agreed to write the libretto but his death during the show's early stages created major problems that remained unsolved until playwright William Gibson took over the adaptation and Arthur Penn replaced the original director during the tryout. With Sammy Davis Jr. giving a sensitive performance as the young man who breaks out of his Harlem surroundings by becoming a professional fighter, and with such effectively choreographed scenes as the opening gym workout and the climactic prizefight, *Golden Boy* won a favorable Broadway decision and remained almost a year and a half.
Capitol OC/ Atheneum (1965)/ SF.

# DO I HEAR A WALTZ?

**Music:** Richard Rodgers
**Lyrics:** Stephen Sondheim
**Book:** Arthur Laurents
**Producer:** Richard Rodgers
**Director:** John Dexter
**Choreographer:** Herbert Ross
**Cast:** Elizabeth Allen, Sergio Franchi, Carol Bruce, Madeline Sherwood, Julienne Marie, Stuart Damon, Fleury D'Antonakis, Jack Manning
**Songs:** "Someone Woke Up"; "This Week Americans"; "What Do We Do? We Fly!"; "Someone Like You"; "Here We Are Again"; "Take the Moment"; "Moon in My Window"; "We're Gonna Be All Right"; "Do I Hear a Waltz?"; "Stay"; "Thank You So Much"
**New York run:** 46th Street Theatre, March 18, 1965; 220 p.

Since Stephen Sondheim was something of a protégé of Oscar Hammerstein II, it was almost inevitable that Richard Rodgers would team up with him after Hammerstein's death. Their single joint effort resulted in *Do I Hear a Waltz?*, which Arthur Laurents adapted from his own play, *The Time of the Cuckoo,* first produced in 1952. Taking place in Venice, the tale concerns Leona Samish (Elizabeth Allen), who has an intense but foredoomed affair with Renato Di Rossi (Sergio Franchi), a married shopkeeper. Though initially, there was to have been no dancing in the musical, the authors felt during the Boston tryout that the rueful story needed more movement and choreographer Herbert Ross was called in. His contribution was most apparent in the scene in which Leona — who has always been sure she will know true love if she hears an imaginary waltz — hears it, sings about it, and dances to it.
Columbia OC/ Random House (1966)/ R&H.

# HALF A SIXPENCE

**Music & lyrics:** David Heneker
**Book:** Beverly Cross
**Producers:** Allen-Hodgdon, Stevens Productions, Harold Fielding
**Director:** Gene Saks
**Choreographer:** Onna White
**Cast:** Tommy Steele, Ann Shoemaker, James Grout, Carrie Nye, Polly James, Grover Dale, Will Mackenzie, John Cleese
**Songs:** "Half a Sixpence"; "Money to Burn"; "She's Too Far Above Me"; "If the Rain's Got to Fall"; "Long Ago"; "Flash Bang Wallop"
**New York run:** Broadhurst Theatre, April 25, 1965; 512 p.

H.G. Wells' novel, *Kipps,* supplied the basis for this period musical in which Tommy Steele (for whom it was written) starred in London in 1963, in New York in 1965, and on film in 1967. *Half a Sixpence* is about Arthur Kipps, an orphan who becomes a draper's apprentice in Folkestone, England, at the turn of the century. Arthur inherits a fortune, becomes engaged to highborn Helen Walsingham (Carrie Nye), breaks off the engagement to marry Ann Pornick (Polly James), a working class girl, loses his money to Helen's brother (John Cleese) in a phony business scheme, and ends up contentedly as the owner of a book shop. There were some changes in the score for the New York engagement, which was enlivened by Onna White's rousing dances, especially the high-kicking, banjo-plucking "Money to Burn." During the run, Steele was succeeded by Tony Tanner, Joel Grey, and Dick Kalman. For other Broadway musicals based on British literary classics, see *My Fair Lady,* page 168.
RCA OC/ Dramatic Publ. Co. (1967)*/ DPC.

**Half a Sixpence.** Tommy Steele playing the banjo for his pub cronies in the "Money to Burn" number. (Friedman-Abeles)

**The Roar of the Greasepaint — The Smell of the Crowd.** Cyril Ritchard and Anthony Newley. (Henry Grossman)

# THE ROAR OF THE GREASEPAINT — THE SMELL OF THE CROWD

**Music, lyrics & book:** Leslie Bricusse & Anthony Newley
**Producer:** David Merrick
**Director:** Anthony Newley
**Choreographer:** Gillian Lynne
**Cast:** Anthony Newley, Cyril Ritchard, Sally Smith, Gilbert Price, Joyce Jillson
**Songs:** "A Wonderful Day Like Today"; "Where Would You Be Without Me?"; "My First Love Song"; "Look at That Face"; "The Joker"; "Who Can I Turn To?"; "Feeling Good"; "Nothing Can Stop Me Now!"; "My Way"; "Sweet Beginning"
**New York run:** Shubert Theatre, May 16, 1965; 232 p.

*The Roar of the Greasepaint — The Smell of the Crowd* was another allegorical musical in the same style as the previous Anthony Newley-Leslie Bricusse *Stop the World — I Want to Get Off.* Again Newley starred and directed, Sean Kenny designed the symbolic set (this one resembling a huge gaming table), and David Merrick was the producer. Here the writers are concerned with the weighty theme of Playing the Game, which covers such universal topics as religion (the supplicating ballad, "Who Can I Turn To?," is addressed to God), hunger, work, love, success, death, and rebellion. Leading the cast were Cyril Ritchard as Sir, representing ruling class authority, and Anthony Newley as Cocky, representing the masses who submissively play the game according to the existing rules — no matter how unfair they are. In the end, emboldened by a character called The Negro (Gilbert Price), Cocky challenges Sir's dominance, and they both realize that power must be shared between them. Though the musical folded in England without opening in London, Merrick secured the American rights and sent the production on a 13½-week tryout tour, thus allowing the infectious music-hall type songs to win favor before the show reached Broadway.
RCA OC/ TW.

# ON A CLEAR DAY YOU CAN SEE FOREVER

**Music:** Burton Lane
**Lyrics & book:** Alan Jay Lerner
**Producer:** Alan Jay Lerner
**Director:** Robert Lewis
**Choreographer:** Herbert Ross
**Cast:** Barbara Harris, John Cullum, Titos Vandis, William Daniels, Clifford David, Rae Allen
**Songs:** "Hurry! It's Lovely Up Here"; "On a Clear Day"; "On the S.S. Bernard Cohn"; "She Wasn't You"; "Melinda"; "What Did I Have That I Don't Have?"; "Wait Till We're Sixty-Five"; "Come Back to Me"
**New York run:** Mark Hellinger Theatre, October 17, 1965; 280 p.

Alan Jay Lerner's fascination with the phenomenon of extrasensory perception (ESP) led to his teaming with composer Richard Rodgers in 1962 to write a musical called *I Picked a Daisy*. When that partnership failed to work out, Lerner turned to Burton Lane, and the show was retitled *On a Clear Day You Can See Forever*. Though Barbara Harris was the only actress ever considered for the female lead, at least six actors were announced for the male lead until it went to Louis Jordan — and *he* was replaced by John Cullum during the Boston tryout. The musical (the first with a top ticket price of $11.90) is concerned with Daisy Gamble who can predict the future and, when hypnotized by Dr. Mark Bruckner, can also recall her life as Melinda Wells in 18th Century London. When Mark's infatuation with Melinda makes her something of a rival to the real-life alter ego, Daisy runs away. In the end, however, his stirring plea "Come Back to Me" is so persuasive that the couple is reunited. The 1970 film version starred Barbra Streisand and Yves Montand.
RCA OC/ Random House (1966)/ TW.

**On a Clear Day You Can See Forever.** John Cullum and Barbara Harris. (Bert Andrews)

**Man of La Mancha.** Richard Kiley as Don Quixote. (Bob Golby)

# MAN OF LA MANCHA

**Music:** Mitch Leigh
**Lyrics:** Joe Darion
**Book:** Dale Wasserman
**Producers:** Albert Selden & Hal James
**Director:** Albert Marre
**Choreographer:** Jack Cole
**Cast:**  Richard Kiley, Joan Diener, Irving Jacobson, Ray Middleton, Robert Rounseville, Jon Cypher, Gerrianne Raphael
**Songs:** "Man of La Mancha"; "Dulcinea"; "I Really Like Him"; "Little Bird, Little Bird"; "To Each His Dulcinea"; "The Impossible Dream"; "Knight of the Woeful Countenance"
**New York run:** ANTA Washington Square Theater, November 22, 1965; 2,328 p.

When, in *Man of La Mancha,* the dauntless, demented Don Quixote proclaims his quest to dream the impossible dream, the words not only expressed the theme of the musical but they could also have applied to the production itself. Though it won acclaim off Broadway (the theatre in which it opened, on West 4th Street, is no longer standing) and on Broadway (when it was transferred to the Martin Beck in March 1968), the idea of a windmill-tilting old gaffer as hero of a musical hardly seemed a formula for a successful run. Nor was there any encouraging track record for the show's composer, lyricist, or librettist. In fact, after the musical first tried out at the Goodspeed Opera House in Connecticut, it was considered so special that it was deliberately unveiled in New York far from the theatre district. Yet after its run of five years seven months, *Man of La Mancha* went into the record books as the third longest running musical of the Sixties.

The idea of transforming Dale Wasserman's television play, *I, Don Quixote,* into a musical first occurred to director Albert Marre. Originally, the score was to have been a collaboration between composer Mitch Leigh and co-lyricists W.H. Auden and Chester Kallman, and Michael Redgrave was announced for the role of the Don. The plot of *Man of La Mancha* unfolds as a story that novelist Miguel de Cervantes y Saavedra, imprisoned for debts during the Spanish Inquisition, tells to his fellow prisoners. In addition to Don Quixote, the major characters are the Don's faithful servant Sancho (Irving Jacobson) and the serving wench Aldonza (Joan Diener), whom the Don worships as the virginal Dulcinea and for whom he does battle to be worthy of knighthood. Though she scorns him for his foolishness, Aldonza is eventually won over — as the Don lays dying — to believing in his dream.

Richard Kiley gave his most celebrated performance as the Man of La Mancha, a role he relinquished during the run to José Ferrer, John Cullum, David Atkinson, Hal Holbrook, Bob Wright, Claudio Brook (from Mexico), Keith Michell (from England), Somegoro Ichikawa (from Japan), Charles West (from Australia), and Gideon Singer (from Israel). James Coco took over the small part of the Barber in 1966, and Joey Faye replaced Irving Jacobson as Sancho in 1968. The National Company toured for three years six months, with José Ferrer playing the original lead. In 1972, Kiley, Diener, and Jacobson were reunited when *Man of La Mancha* gave 140 performances at Lincoln Center's Vivian Beaumont Theatre. Kiley also played the Don in New York in 1977, heading a cast that included Emily Yancy and Tony Martinez, and remained for 124 performances. The 1972 screen version starred Peter O'Toole, Sophia Loren, and James Coco (as Sancho). Historic note: In 1889, Reginald De Koven and Harry B. Smith collaborated on an operetta based on the same story. Called *Don Quixote,* it was tried out in Chicago but never reached New York.

MCA OC/ Random House (1966); Chilton (1976)/ TW.

**Sweet Charity.** Gwen Verdon singing "If My Friends Could See Me Now." (Friedman-Abeles)

# SWEET CHARITY

**Music:** Cy Coleman
**Lyrics:** Dorothy Fields
**Book:** Neil Simon
**Producers:** Robert Fryer, Lawrence Carr, Sylvia & Joseph Harris
**Director-choreographer:** Bob Fosse
**Cast:** Gwen Verdon, John McMartin, Helen Gallagher, Thelma Oliver, James Luisi, Ruth Buzzi, Barbara Sharma
**Songs:** "Big Spender"; "If My Friends Could See Me Now"; "There's Gotta Be Something Better Than This"; "The Rhythm of Life"; "Baby Dream Your Dreams"; "Sweet Charity"; "Where Am I Going?"; "I'm a Brass Band"
**New York run:** Palace Theatre, January 29, 1966; 608 p.

Charity Hope Valentine — with her heart not only on her sleeve but tattooed on her arm — is a New York taxi dancer who knows there's gotta be something better to do than work at the Fan-Dango Ballroom. She gets innocently involved with an Italian movie star (James Luisi), then seriously involved with straight-laced Oscar Lindquist (John McMartin) after they meet in a stuck elevator at the 92nd Street "Y." Though Oscar eventually asks Charity to be his wife, the revelation of her employment makes the union impossible, and when last seen Charity is still a girl who lives "hopefully ever after."

The play's heroine was brought touchingly to life by Gwen Verdon after Bob Fosse, her husband at the time, decided to adapt as well as direct a musical treatment of Federico Fellini's film *Nights of Cabiria.* Originally intended as the first half of a double bill of one-act musicals, *Sweet Charity* was fleshed out to two acts when Neil Simon took over the writing. The musical was also the first legitimate show to play the Palace, the legendary vaudeville mecca on Broadway at 47th Street. A revival was mounted in 1986 (see page 272), with Debbie Allen (succeeded by Ann Reinking) as Charity, and a 1969 screen version starred Shirley MacLaine. The 1973 musical *Seesaw,* also with songs by Coleman and Fields and a book (though uncredited) by Neil Simon, was another New York tale of an ill-matched too-trusting kook and a too-square guy.

Columbia OC; EMI OC (1986)/ Random House (1966)/ TW.

# MAME

**Music & lyrics:** Jerry Herman
**Book:** Jerome Lawrence & Robert E. Lee
**Producers:** Robert Fryer, Lawrence Carr, Sylvia & Joseph Harris
**Director:** Gene Saks
**Choreographer:** Onna White
**Cast:**   Angela Lansbury, Beatrice Arthur, Jane Connell, Willard Waterman, Frankie Michaels, Charles Braswell, Jerry Lanning
**Songs:** "It's Today"; "Open a New Window"; "My Best Girl"; "We Need a Little Christmas"; "Mame"; "Bosom Buddies"; "That's How Young I Feel"; "If He Walked Into My Life"
**New York run:** Winter Garden, May 24, 1966; 1,508 p.

Once Mary Martin had turned down the title role in *Mame*, some 40 other actresses had to be eliminated before the part went to Angela Lansbury — who quickly established herself as one of the reigning queens of Broadway. Her vehicle, the fifth longest running musical of the Sixties, was an adaptation of Patrick Dennis' novel, *Auntie Mame*, which had also been the basis of the 1954 play. The show's musical-comedy lineage, however, could be traced to *Hello, Dolly!*, since it again spotlighted an antic, middle-aged matchmaking widow, and it again had a bubbling score by Jerry Herman including another strutting title song.

Set mostly in and around Mame's home at 3 Beekman Place, New York, the tale covers the period from 1928 to 1946. Firmly dedicated to the credo that "Life is a banquet and most poor sons-of-bitches are starving to death," Mame Dennis brings up her orphaned nephew Patrick (Frankie Michaels) in an aggressively permissive atmosphere as she urges him to live life to the fullest by opening a new window every day. After being wiped out by the stock market crash, Mame lands a part in — and manages to ruin — a musical comedy starring her bosom buddy Vera Charles (Beatrice Arthur), then recoups her fortunes by marrying Southern aristocrat Beauregard Jackson Pickett Burnside (Charles Braswell). Even Beau's death climbing an Alp cannot deter the indomitable Mame, whose final triumph is steering Patrick out of the clutches of a birdbrained snob and into the arms of a more appropriate mate. During the Broadway run, Miss Lansbury was followed by Celeste Holm, Janis Paige, Jane Morgan, and Ann Miller. Heading the four road companies were, respectively, Miss Holm, Miss Lansbury, Susan Hayward, and Janet Blair. Miss Lansbury also starred in a 1983 Broadway revival which had a brief run. The 1974 Hollywood version found Miss Arthur repeating her original role in a cast headed by Lucille Ball and Robert Preston. Columbia OC/ Random House (1967)/ TW.

**Mame.** Bosom buddies Angela Lansbury and Beatrice Arthur. (Friedman-Abeles)

# THE APPLE TREE

**Music:** Jerry Bock
**Lyrics:** Sheldon Harnick
**Book:** Jerry Bock & Sheldon Harnick, with Jerome Coopersmith
**Producer:** Stuart Ostrow
**Director:** Mike Nichols
**Choreographers:** Herbert Ross, Lee Theodore
**Cast:** Barbara Harris, Larry Blyden, Alan Alda, Carmen Alvarez, Robert Klein
**Songs:** "Here in Eden"; "Eve"; "Beautiful, Beautiful World"; "Go to Sleep, Whatever You Are"; "It's a Fish"; "What Makes Me Love Him"; "Oh, to Be a Movie Star"; "Gorgeous"
**New York run:** Shubert Theatre, October 18, 1966; 463 p.

While they were initially to have been linked by the unifying theme of man, woman, and the devil, the three one-act musicals that comprised *The Apple Tree* had nothing in common except for some subtle interrelated musical themes and a whimsical reference to the color brown. In Broadway's first — and so far only — musical triple bill, Act I was based on Mark Twain's "The Diary of Adam and Eve" and dealt with the dawn of humanity and innocence; Act II was based on Frank R. Stockton's short story "The Lady or the Tiger?," in which a warrior's fate, unresolved in the plot, was determined by the choice of door he enters; and Act III was based on Jules Feiffer's fantasy, "Passionella," about a poor chimney sweep who yearned to become — and did become — a mooooooooooovie star. Though originally to have been directed by Gower Champion, *The Apple Tree* marked Mike Nichols' first association with a musical. Historic note: A full-length musical version of "The Lady or the Tiger?" was presented on Broadway in 1888 with DeWolf Hopper in the lead.
Columbia OC/ Random House (1967)/ MTI.

**Cabaret.** Lotte Lenya and Jack Gilford singing "It Couldn't Please Me More." (Friedman-Abeles)

**Cabaret.** "Willkommen, bienvenue, welcome," sings Joel Grey. (Friedman-Abeles)

# CABARET

**Music:** John Kander
**Lyrics:** Fred Ebb
**Book:** Joe Masteroff
**Producer-director:** Harold Prince
**Choreographer:** Ron Field
**Cast:** Jill Haworth, Jack Gilford, Bert Convy, Lotte Lenya, Joel Grey, Peg Murray, Edward Winter
**Songs:** "Willkommen"; "Don't Tell Mama"; "Perfectly Marvelous"; "Two Ladies"; "It Couldn't Please Me More"; "Tomorrow Belongs to Me"; "The Money Song"; "Married"; "If You Could See Her"; "Cabaret"
**New York run:** Broadhurst Theatre, November 20, 1966; 1,165 p.

Claiming derivation from both Christopher Isherwood's *Berlin Stories* and John van Druten's 1951 dramatization, *I Am a Camera, Cabaret* turned a sleazy Berlin nightclub into a metaphor for the decadent world of pre-Hitler Germany, with the floorshow numbers used as commentaries on situations in the plot. At the Kit Kat Klub, where the epicene Master of Ceremonies (Joel Grey) bids one and all "Willkommen, bienvenue, welcome," the star attraction is the hedonistic British expatriate Sally Bowles (Jill Haworth), who also beckons customers with her own siren song to "Come to the cabaret, old chum." The main stories revolve around Sally's brief liaison with Clifford Bradshaw (Bert Convy), an American writer, and the more tragic romance between Fraulein Schneider (Lotte Lenya), a pragmatic landlady, and her Jewish suitor Herr Schultz (Jack Gilford). Helping to recreate the mood of a world in decay was the fluid direction of Harold Prince (it was his idea to add the Master of Ceremonies as a unifying symbol), a John Kander-Fred Ebb score that purposely evoked Kurt Weill, and the settings of Boris Aronson that recalled the paintings of George Grosz.

During the Broadway run, Miss Haworth was succeeded by Anita Gillette, Melissa Hart, and Tandy Cronyn. For the tour, which lasted one year seven months, the leads were taken by Miss Hart, Leo Fuchs (Schultz), Gene Rupert (Clifford), Signe Hasso (Fraulein), and Robert Salvio (MC). The 1972 film version retained Joel Grey (who also starred in the 1987 Broadway revival), but added Liza Minnelli, Michael York, Marisa Berenson, and a new story line.
Columbia OC/ Random House (1967); Chilton (1976)/ TW.

**I Do! I Do!** Robert Preston and Mary Martin.
(Friedman-Abeles)

# I DO! I DO!

**Music:** Harvey Schmidt
**Lyrics & book:** Tom Jones
**Producer:** David Merrick
**Director:** Gower Champion
**Cast:** Mary Martin, Robert Preston
**Songs:** "I Love My Wife"; "My Cup Runneth Over"; "Love Isn't Everything";
"Nobody's Perfect"; "The Honeymoon Is Over"; "Where Are the
Snows?"; "When the Kids Get Married"; "Someone Needs Me"; "Roll
Up the Ribbons"
**New York run:** 46th Street Theatre, December 5, 1966; 560 p.

*I Do! I Do!* may have been the first Broadway musical ever to have a cast consisting entirely of two people, but since those people were Mary Martin and Robert Preston, no one could possibly have felt the need for anyone else on stage. In all other ways, however, the musical —which was adapted from Jan de Hartog's 1951 play, *The Fourposter* — was an ambitious undertaking, covering 50 years in the life of a married couple, Agnes and Michael, from their wedding day to the day they move out of their house. In between, they bring up a family, quarrel, threaten to break up, have a reconciliation, plan for a life without children in the house, and reveal in song exactly what they mean to each other. Apart from its stars, who were followed on Broadway by Carol Lawrence and Gordon MacRae, the production was especially noted for Gower Champion's inventive direction. A later musical with only two characters — but each with three alter egos — was the 1979 hit, *They're Playing Our Song.*
RCA OC/ MTI.

# YOU'RE A GOOD MAN, CHARLIE BROWN

**Music, lyrics & book:** Clark Gesner
**Producers:** Arthur Whitelaw & Gene Persson
**Director:** Joseph Hardy
**Choreographer:** Patricia Birch
**Cast:** Bill Hinnant, Reva Rose, Karen Johnson, Bob Balaban, Skip Hinnant, Gary Burghoff
**Songs:** "You're a Good Man, Charlie Brown"; "My Blanket and Me"; "The Kite"; "Book Report"; "T.E.A.M. (The Baseball Game)"; "Little Known Facts"; "Suppertime"; "Happiness"
**New York run:** Theatre 80 St. Marks, March 7, 1967; 1,597 p.

With Charles Schultz's appealing comic strip "Peanuts" as general inspiration, Clark Gesner created a musical out of events in "a day made up of little moments picked from all the days of Charlie Brown, from Valentine's Day to the baseball season, from wild optimism to utter despair, all mixed with the lives of his friends (both human and non-human) and strung together on the string of a single day, from bright uncertain morning to hopeful starlit evening." The human characters, none supposedly older than six, include crabby, authoritarian Lucy (Reva Rose), music-loving Schroeder (Skip Hinnant), sweet and innocent Patty (Karen Johnson), blanket-hugging Linus (Bob Balaban), and perplexed, uncertain and eternally put-upon Charlie Brown himself (Gary Burghoff). The non-human character, of course, is Charlie Brown's highly imaginative pet dog Snoopy (Bill Hinnant), who likes to pretend that he's a World War I flying ace forever in search of the infamous Red Baron.

Gesner at first had no plans for his "Peanuts" songs other than as a recording, and initially MGM issued the album as part of its kiddie line. Producer Arthur Whitelaw, however, persuaded the writer to put together a theatrical concept, and he presented it at a tiny East Village theatre where it remained four years. Between 1967 and 1971, six road companies were performing throughout the United States. A second musical based on the "Peanuts" characters was *Snoopy*, written by Larry Grossman and Hal Hackaday. It opened Off Broadway in 1982 and ran for 152 performances. For other musicals taken from American comic strips, see *Li'l Abner*, page 171.
Polydor OC/ Random House (1967)/ TW.

**You're a Good Man, Charlie Brown.** Karen Johnson, Bob Balaban, Skip Hinnant, Reva Rose, Bill Hinnant, and Gary Burghoff. (Lawrence Belling)

# YOUR OWN THING

**Music & lyrics:** Hal Hester & Danny Apolinar
**Book:** Donald Driver
**Producers:** Zev Bufman & Dorothy Love
**Director:** Donald Driver
**Cast:** Leland Palmer, Marian Mercer, Rusty Thacker, Tom Ligon, Danny Apolinar, Michael Valenti, John Kuhner
**Songs:** "The Flowers"; "I'm Me!"; "Come Away Death" (lyric: Shakespeare); "I'm on My Way to the Top"; "The Now Generation"; "The Middle Years"
**New York run:** Orpheum Theatre, January 13, 1968; 933 p.

An Off-Broadway musical of the Now, Me-Too and Let-It-All-Hang-Out Generation, *Your Own Thing* retold in contemporary style (accompanied by film and slide projections) the story of Shakespeare's *Twelfth Night* as it might apply to a twin brother and sister singing team (Tom Ligon and Leland Palmer) who are shipwrecked on Manhattan Island. Once the siblings split up, much confusion is caused when sister Viola disguises herself in male attire to join The Four Apocalypse, a rock group at a discotheque owned by Olivia (Marian Mercer). Thinking Viola a man, Olivia is attracted to her, but matters eventually get sorted out — Olivia happily settles for twin brother Sebastian and Viola wins Orson (Rusty Thacker), the group's manager. Coincidentally, shortly before *Your Own Thing* opened, another musical based on *Twelfth Night,* called *Love and Let Love,* began a brief Off-Broadway run. After it closed, Marcia Rodd, who played Olivia, took over the same part in *Your Own Thing.* Additional cast replacements were Raul Julia (Orson) and Sandy Duncan (Viola). For other musicals based on Shakespeare, see *The Boys from Syracuse,* page 107.
RCA OC/ Dell (1970)/ TW.

# THE HAPPY TIME

**Music:** John Kander
**Lyrics:** Fred Ebb
**Book:** N. Richard Nash
**Producer:** David Merrick
**Director-choreographer:** Gower Champion
**Cast:** Robert Goulet, David Wayne, Mike Rupert, Julie Gregg, George S. Irving, Charles Durning
**Songs:** "The Happy Time"; "Tomorrow Morning"; "Please Stay"; "I Don't Remember You"; "The Life of the Party"; "Seeing Things"; "A Certain Girl"
**New York run:** Broadway Theatre, January 18, 1968; 286 p.

A gentle, nostalgic look at a French-Canadian family, *The Happy Time* was adapted from the novel by Robert Fontaine and the play by Samuel Taylor. The story is primarily concerned with the coming of age of Bibi Bonnard (Mike Rupert) and his desire to see the world with his Uncle Jacques (Robert Goulet), a footloose magazine photographer who has returned to his family for a brief visit. But Bibi's plans to run off with Jacques are opposed by the usually permissive Grandpère Bonnard (David Wayne) who manages — with Jacques' help — to convince Bibi to remain at home. The use of blow-up photographs to establish the mood for the various scenes was one of director Gower Champion's most effective touches. *The Happy Time* bore a certain resemblance to *110 in the Shade,* a previous musical by N. Richard Nash that had also been presented by David Merrick. That one also offered a smooth-talking visitor to a small town who excites the people's imagination, and leaves them with renewed appreciation of their own values.
RCA OC/ Dramatic Publ. Co. (1969)*/ DPC.

# GEORGE M!

**Music & lyrics:** George M. Cohan
**Book:** Michael Stewart, John & Fran Pascal
**Producers:** David Black, Konrad Matthaei, Lorin Price
**Director-choreographer:** Joe Layton
**Cast:** Joel Grey, Betty Ann Grove, Jerry Dodge, Jill O'Hara, Bernadette Peters, Jamie Donnelly, Jacqueline Alloway, Loni Ackerman
**Songs:** "Musical Comedy Man"; "All Aboard for Broadway"; "My Town"; "Billie"; "Ring to the Name of Rose"; "Give My Regards to Broadway"; "Forty-Five Minutes from Broadway"; "So Long, Mary"; "Mary's a Grand Old Name"; "Yankee Doodle Dandy"; "Nellie Kelly, I Love You"; "Harrigan"; "Over There"; "You're a Grand Old Flag"
**New York run:** Palace Theatre, April 10, 1968; 427 p.

In this biographical musical celebrating the achievements of composer-lyricist-librettist-playwright-director-producer-actor-singer-dancer George M. Cohan, the story takes us from his birth in Providence, Rhode Island, in 1878, through his successes and failures and ends with his final Broadway triumph in 1937 playing President Roosevelt in *I'd Rather Be Right,* the only musical in which he appeared that he did not write himself. With Joel Grey as the pushy, not entirely sympathetic flag-waving hero, the show devoted its first-act finale to the reconstruction of the scene — familiar to anyone who has seen James Cagney in the movie *Yankee Doodle Dandy* — in which Cohan introduced "Give My Regards to Broadway" on the Southampton pier in *Little Johnny Jones.* For other show-business biographies see *Annie Get Your Gun,* page 130.
Columbia OC/ TW.

**George M!** Joel Grey strutting through "Give My Regards to Broadway." (Friedman-Abeles)

# HAIR

**Music:** Galt MacDermot
**Lyrics & book:** Gerome Ragni & James Rado
**Producer:** Michael Butler
**Director:** Tom O'Horgan
**Choreographer:** Julie Arenal
**Cast:** Steve Curry, Ronald Dyson, Sally Eaton, Leata Galloway, Paul Jabara, Diane Keaton, Lynn Kellogg, Melba Moore, Shelley Plimpton, James Rado, Gerome Ragni, Lamont Washington
**Songs:** "Aquarius"; "Manchester England"; "Ain't Got No"; "I Got Life"; "Hair"; "Frank Mills"; "Hare Krishna"; "Where Do I Go?"; "Easy to Be Hard"; "Good Morning Starshine"; "Let the Sunshine In"
**New York run:** Biltmore Theatre, April 29, 1968; 1,750 p.

As much a product of its time as *Pins and Needles* and *This Is the Army* were of theirs, *Hair* grew out of the emotional turmoil of the Vietnam War years with its concomitant anti-establishment movement that produced a generation of drug-influenced, sex-obsessed social dropouts. With barely a discernable story line, this loosely structured musical celebrated the untethered lifestyle of hippies and flower children who welcomed the dawning of the Age of Aquarius by opposing the draft, the work ethic, and accepted standards of behavior and dress.

The "American Tribal Love-Rock Musical" (as it was billed) was first presented on October 29, 1967 under the direction of Gerald Freedman at Joseph Papp's New York Shakespeare Festival Public Theatre near Astor Place. At a $2.50 ticket price, it remained for about a month and a half, then moved to a Broadway nightclub called Cheetah. At that point, Michael Butler, a fledgling producer, took over the show for a Broadway run at the Biltmore Theatre (on 47th Street west of Broadway). Butler had it restaged by Tom O'Horgan, rechoreographed, redesigned, recostumed, relighted, and reorchestrated, and there were cast changes such as Lynn Kellogg for Jill O'Hara, Melba Moore for Jonelle Allen, and coauthor James Rado for Walker Daniels in the role of a draftee who spends his last civilian hours with a tribe of hippies. During its run — the fourth longest of a musical during the Sixties — *Hair* achieved something of a Broadway breakthrough by ending the first act in semi-darkness with the entire cast totally starkers. At one time, seven road companies were touring the United States. In 1977, Butler revived the musical but this time it ran only a month. The 1979 film version had a cast headed by John Savage, Treat Williams, and Beverly D'Angelo.

RCA OC (1967); RCA OC (1968)/ Pocket Books (1969); Stein & Day (1979)/ TW.

**Hair.** James Rado and Gerome Ragni. (Dagmar)

**Zorba.** Maria Karnilova and Herschel Bernardi in the "Y'assou" number. (Friedman-Abeles)

# ZORBA

**Music:** John Kander
**Lyrics:** Fred Ebb
**Book:** Joseph Stein
**Producer-director:** Harold Prince
**Choreographer:** Ron Field
**Cast:** Herschel Bernardi, Maria Karnilova, John Cunningham, Carmen Alvarez, Lorraine Serabian, James Luisi
**Songs:** "Life Is"; "The First Time"; "The Top of the Hill"; "No Boom Boom"; "The Butterfly"; "Only Love"; "Y'assou"; "Happy Birthday"; "I Am Free"
**New York run:** Imperial Theatre, November 17, 1968; 305 p.

Although it reunited the *Cabaret* team of composer John Kander, lyricist Fred Ebb, and producer-director Harold Prince, *Zorba* was more of an Aegean counterpart to *Fiddler on the Roof,* with its larger-than-life aging hero and its stageful of earthy, ethnic types. It also had the same producer, librettist, set designer (Boris Aronson), and costume designer (Patricia Zipprodt), and its leading roles were played by two *Fiddler* alumni, Herschel Bernardi and Maria Karnilova. The story, however, was far grimmer, and the people of Crete a colder, more menacing lot than the colorful villagers of Anatevka. The tale involves the ebulient Zorba (Bernardi) with a studious young man named Nikos (John Cunningham) who has inherited an abandoned mine on the island of Crete. This sets off a series of tragic events, including the suicide of a Cretan youth out of unrequited love for a young Widow (Carmen Alvarez), the vengeful murder of the Widow by the youth's family, the discovery that the mine is inoperable, and the death of Hortense (Maria Karnilova), a coquettish French cocotte in love with Zorba. Nothing, however, can dampen Zorba's lust for life and his determination to live it to the fullest.

The production, the first to charge $15 for Saturday night orchestra seats, was based on Nikos Kazantzakis's novel *Zorba the Greek,* which became a 1964 movie with Anthony Quinn and Lila Kedrova, directed by Michael Cacoyannis. Cacoyannis also directed Quinn and Kedrova in a new production of the musical in 1983. It began its cross-country tour early in the year, had a longer Broadway run than the original, then toured again through July 1986. (See page 268.) Capitol OC; RCA OC (1983)/ Random House (1969)/ SF.

# PROMISES, PROMISES

**Music:** Burt Bacharach
**Lyrics:** Hal David
**Book:** Neil Simon
**Producer:** David Merrick
**Director:** Robert Moore
**Choreographer:** Michael Bennett
**Cast:** Jerry Orbach, Jill O'Hara, Edward Winter, Norman Shelly, A. Larry Haines, Marian Mercer, Ken Howard, Donna McKechnie
**Songs:** "You'll Think of Someone"; "She Likes Basketball"; "Knowing When to Leave"; "Wanting Things"; "Whoever You Are"; "A Young Pretty Girl Like You"; "I'll Never Fall in Love Again"; "Promises, Promises"
**New York run:** Shubert Theatre, December 1, 1968; 1,281 p.

Two of the most successful pop song writers of the mid-Sixties, Burt Bacharach and Hal David, made a worthy — and so far only — contribution to the Broadway theatre with their score for *Promises, Promises*. Adapted from the 1960 movie, *The Apartment*, the musical followed such other recent offerings as *How to Succeed in Business Without Really Trying, I Can Get It for You Wholesale,* and *What Makes Sammy Run?* by revealing yet another method of getting ahead in the business world. Chuck Baxter (Jerry Orbach), the faceless hero of *Promises, Promises,* does it simply by lending his apartment to various executives of Consolidated Life for their extramarital dalliances. Among them is J.D. Sheldrake (Edward Winter) whose paramour, Fran Kubelik (Jill O'Hara), just happens to be the girl beloved by Chuck. Fran eventually reciprocates his feeling when he rescues her from a suicide attempt after J.D. decides to go back to his wife.

During the Broadway run, Orbach was succeeded by Tony Roberts, Miss O'Hara by Jenny O'Hara (her sister) and Lorna Luft. Roberts and Melissa Hart headed the road company which toured for 14 months.
United Artists OC/ Random House (1969)/ TW.

# DAMES AT SEA

**Music:** Jim Wise
**Lyrics & book:** George Haimsohn & Robin Miller
**Producers:** Jordan Hott & Jack Millstein
**Director-choreographer:** Neal Kenyon
**Cast:** Bernadette Peters, David Christmas, Steve Elmore, Tamara Long
**Songs:** "It's You"; "That Mister Man of Mine"; "Choo-Choo Honeymoon"; "The Sailor of My Dreams"; "Good Times Are Here to Stay"; "Dames at Sea"; "Raining in My Heart"; "Singapore Sue"; "Star Tar"
**New York run:** Bouwerie Lane Theatre, December 20, 1968; 575 p.

*Dames at Sea,* an affectionate spoof of early Hollywood musicals, was inspired in part by the same 1933 backstage movie on which the more elaborate *42nd Street* was later based. In this imaginative six-character show, Ruby (Bernadette Peters), a sweet young thing fresh from Centerville, Utah, lands a job in the chorus of a Broadway-bound musical, *Dames at Sea,* meets sailor-songwriter Dick (David Christmas), and... well, you know what happens. One switch, though, is that because the musical in preparation loses its theatre and must be performed on the deck of a battleship, Ruby gets her big break when the star (Tamara Long) can't go on because she's seasick. During the run, Miss Peters was succeeded by Pia Zadora, Bonnie Franklin, Barbara Sharma, and Loni Ackerman. The musical, which returned for an additional 170 performances at the Plaza 9 Music Hall in the Plaza Hotel, was revived Off Broadway in 1985.
Columbia OC/ Samuel French (1969)*/ SF.

# 1776

**Music & lyrics:** Sherman Edwards
**Book:** Peter Stone
**Producer:** Stuart Ostrow
**Director:** Peter Hunt
**Choreographer:** Onna White
**Cast:** William Daniels, Howard Da Silva, Paul Hecht, Clifford David, Ken Howard, Virginia Vestoff, Ronald Holgate, Betty Buckley
**Songs:** "Sit Down, John"; "The Lees of Old Virginia"; "But Mr. Adams"; "He Plays the Violin"; "Cool, Cool, Considerate Men"; "Momma Look Sharp"; "The Egg"; "Molasses to Rum"; "Is Anybody There?"
**New York run:** 46th Street Theatre, March 16, 1969; 1,217 p.

After researching the project for seven years, Sherman Edwards took two-and-a-half years to write the songs and the libretto for a musical history lesson about the signing of the Declaration of Independence. During preparations, however, the more experienced librettist Peter Stone was brought in. Sticking to the actual events with as much fidelity as possible, Edwards and Stone concentrated their musical on the debates, intrigues, and compromises involving the delegates to the second Continental Congress that met for three stifling summer months in Philadelphia to produce the historic document. Major figures in the production were such advocates of independence as John Adams of Massachusetts (William Daniels), Benjamin Franklin of Pennsylvania (Howard Da Silva), Thomas Jefferson (Ken Howard) and Richard Henry Lee (Ronald Holgate) both of Virginia, and such opponents as John Dickinson of Pennsylvania (Paul Hecht) and Edward Rutledge of South Carolina (Clifford David). Although the writers based their work on historical fact, they did take such liberties as having the debate on the wording of the Declaration occur before, not after, the actual vote for independence. Also altered was the signing of the document, which actually took many months to complete but which — for dramatic effectiveness — was made to take place on the 4th of July, the day the Declaration was proclaimed.

*1776* was the only musical by Sherman Edwards, who died in 1981. During the Broadway engagement, Daniels was succeeded by John Cunningham, Da Silva by Jay Garner, and David by John Cullum. The touring company, which traveled for two years two months, included Patrick Bedford (Adams), Rex Everhart (Franklin), George Hearn (Dickinson), and Jon Cypher (Jefferson). Daniels, Da Silva, Howard, and Holgate were also in the 1972 screen version. For other musicals about the American Revolution, see *Dearest Enemy*, page 48.
Columbia OC/ Viking (1969); Chilton (1973)/ MTI.

**1776.** William Daniels, Howard Da Silva, Betty Buckley, and Ken Howard. (Martha Swope)

# PURLIE

**Music:** Gary Geld
**Lyrics:** Peter Udell
**Book:** Ossie Davis, Philip Rose, Peter Udell
**Producer-director:** Philip Rose
**Choreographer:** Louis Johnson
**Cast:** Cleavon Little, Melba Moore, John Heffernan, Sherman Hemsley, Novella Nelson, George Faison
**Songs:** "Walk Him Up the Stairs"; "New Fangled Preacher Man"; "Purlie"; "Skinnin' a Cat"; "I Got Love"; "First Thing Monday Mornin' "
**New York run:** Broadway Theatre, March 15, 1970: 688 p.

With little ballyhoo, *Purlie* opened on Broadway to generally favorable notices and enthusiastic audiences, and became the sleeper hit of the season. The musical was adapted from the 1961 play *Purlie Victorious,* a folkish satire on racial stereotypes written by co-librettist Ossie Davis, and is concerned with the efforts of a self-styled new-fangled preacher man (Cleavon Little) to buy the Big Bethel Church in a rural Georgia town. This puts Purlie in confrontation with the bigoted plantation owner, Cap'n Cotchipee (John Heffernan), who also wants the church. Eventually, of course, the Cap'n is outsmarted and Purlie emerges victorious with both his church and his new wife Lutiebelle (Melba Moore). Robert Guillaume, who succeeded Cleavon Little during the Broadway run, toured in the musical which returned briefly to New York at the end of 1972.
Ampex OC/ Samuel French (1971)*/ SF.

# APPLAUSE

**Music:** Charles Strouse
**Lyrics:** Lee Adams
**Book:** Betty Comden & Adolph Green
**Producers:** Joseph Kipness & Lawrence Kasha
**Director-choreographer:** Ron Field
**Cast:** Lauren Bacall, Len Cariou, Robert Mandan, Ann Williams, Brandon Maggart, Penny Fuller, Lee Roy Reams, Bonnie Franklin
**Songs:** "Think How It's Gonna Be"; "But Alive"; "Who's That Girl?"; "Applause"; "Fasten Your Seat Belts"; "Welcome to the Theatre"; "One of a Kind"; "Something Greater"
**New York run:** Palace Theatre, March 30, 1970; 896 p.

It took only one Broadway musical for Lauren Bacall to join the roster of powerhouse female stars who have won distinction in the theatre. And she did it by appearing as another powerhouse female star, Margo Channing, in a musical version of the 1950 movie, *All About Eve.* The genesis of *Applause* took place in 1966 when Charles Strouse and Lee Adams were signed to create the score. Miss Bacall agreed to be in the show two years later, but it was not until early 1969 that the original librettist was replaced by Betty Comden and Adolph Green. The ambitions, tensions, insecurities, loyalties, and disloyalties of the theatre were exposed in a somewhat farfetched tale in which theatre doyenne Margo Channing befriends an adoring fan, Eve Harrington (Penny Fuller), who promptly schemes to take over her part, her man, and anything else needed to help Eve's career. Though Margo is not a musical-comedy star, thereby eliminating show-within-a-show numbers, Ron Field found opportunities for dance routines in such hangouts as a Greenwich Village gay bar and Joe Allen's restaurant. During the Broadway run, the leading role was assumed by Anne Baxter (Eve in the movie) and Arlene Dahl.
MCA OC/ Random House (1971); Chilton (1976)/ TW.

# COMPANY

**Music & lyrics:** Stephen Sondheim
**Book:** George Furth
**Producer-director:** Harold Prince
**Choreographer:** Michael Bennett
**Cast:** Dean Jones, Elaine Stritch, Barbara Barrie, John Cunningham, Charles Kimbrough, Donna McKechnie, Charles Braswell, Susan Browning, Steve Elmore, Beth Howland, Pamela Myers, Merle Louise
**Songs:** "Company"; "The Little Things You Do Together"; "Sorry-Grateful"; "You Could Drive a Person Crazy"; "Someone Is Waiting"; "Another Hundred People"; "Getting Married Today"; "What Would We Do Without You?"; "Barcelona"; "The Ladies who Lunch"; "Being Alive"
**New York run:** Alvin Theatre, April 26, 1970: 706 p.

*Company* was the first of six Broadway musicals created by the most influential and daring team of the Seventies, composer-lyricist Stephen Sondheim and director Harold Prince. In putting this work together they avoided the conventional dramatic structure of the linear story by using five separate stories dealing with marriage that were held together by a single character who influences and is influenced by his "good and crazy" married friends. Moreover, it was a bold example of the concept musical — in which the style of telling is as important as what is being told — with songs used as commentaries on the situations and characters, and the actors performing in a cage-like skeletal setting (by Boris Aronson) that made use of stairways, an elevator, and projections.

Initially, *Company* was a collection of 11 one-act plays by George Furth. Prince, however, saw it as a musical reflecting how life in a big city influences various couples, and Furth then revised three of the plays and added two others. The character of the bachelor Robert was brought in to connect the episodes, with the occasion of his 35th birthday party used as a framework. While the couples are less than idyllically happy — they fight, make plans to divorce, smoke pot, drink too much — the general philosophy, summed up in Robert's closing solo "Being Alive," is that it's better to be married than single.

Because of illness, Dean Jones, the original Robert, was replaced by Larry Kert within a month after the Broadway opening. During the run, Elaine Stritch, as a middle-aged guzzler who has the sardonic show-stopper "The Ladies who Lunch," was succeeded by Jane Russell and Vivian Blaine. The show's year-long tour had a cast headed by George Chakiris and Miss Stritch.
Columbia OC/ Random House (1970); Chilton (1973)/ MTI.

**Company.** Susan Browning, Donna McKechnie, and Pamela Myers. (Martha Swope)

**The Rothschilds.** Hal Linden as Mayer Rothschild. (Martha Swope)

# THE ROTHSCHILDS

**Music:** Jerry Bock
**Lyrics:** Sheldon Harnick
**Book:** Sherman Yellen
**Producers:** Lester Osterman & Hillard Elkins
**Director-choreographer:** Michael Kidd
**Cast:** Hal Linden, Paul Hecht, Leila Martin, Keene Curtis, Jill Clayburgh, Chris Sarandon
**Songs:** "One Room"; "He Tossed a Coin"; "Sons"; "Rothschild and Sons"; "I'm in Love! I'm in Love!"; "In My Own Lifetime"
**New York run:** Lunt-Fontanne Theatre, October 19, 1970; 507 p.

Adapted from Frederic Morton's best-selling account of the rise of the international banking family, *The Rothschilds* had several points of similarity with *Fiddler on the Roof.* Its songs were written by the same team, Jerry Bock and Sheldon Harnick (it was their seventh and last work together), the subject matter also concerned the struggle of European Jews to live in an oppressive world, and it even substituted a family of five sons for a family of five daughters. But unlike their poor Anatevka relatives, the Rothschilds did manage to escape the bonds of the Frankfort ghetto and, led by Mayer Rothschild (Hal Linden), work their way up to a position of wealth and affluence all over Europe. Actually, Bock and Harnick had been offered the story while they were still working on *Fiddler,* and it wasn't until some time later, when the musical had a new libretto by Sherman Yellen, that they felt it was sufficiently strong enough to withstand inevitable comparisons.
Columbia OC/ SF.

# NO, NO, NANETTE

**Music:** Vincent Youmans
**Lyrics:** Irving Caesar
**Book:** Burt Shevelove
**Producer:** Pyxidium Ltd. (Cyma Rubin)
**Director:** Burt Shevelove
**Choreographer:** Donald Saddler
**Cast:** Ruby Keeler, Jack Gilford, Bobby Van, Helen Gallagher, Patsy Kelly, Susan Watson, Roger Rathburn, Loni Ackerman
**Songs:** Same as original production, plus "I've Confessed to the Breeze" (lyric: Otto Harbach); "Take a Little One-Step" (lyric: Zelda Sears)
**New York run:** 46th Street Theatre, January 19, 1971; 861 p.

(See page 47.)

**No, No, Nanette.** Helen Gallagher and Bobby Van dancing to "You Can Dance With Any Girl at All." (Friedman-Abeles)

**Follies.** Alexis Smith singing "Could I Leave You?" (Martha Swope)

# FOLLIES

**Music & lyrics:** Stephen Sondheim
**Book:** James Goldman
**Producer:** Harold Prince
**Directors:** Harold Prince & Michael Bennett
**Choreographer:** Michael Bennett
**Cast:** Alexis Smith, Gene Nelson, Dorothy Collins, John McMartin, Yvonne DeCarlo, Fifi D'Orsay, Mary McCarty, Ethel Shutta, Arnold Moss, Ethel Barrymore Colt, Michael Bartlett, Sheila Smith, Justine Johnston, Virginia Sandifer, Kurt Peterson, Victoria Mallory, Marti Rolph
**Songs:** "Waiting for the Girls Upstairs"; "Ah, Paris!"; "Broadway Baby"; "The Road You Didn't Take"; "In Buddy's Eyes"; "Who's That Woman?"; "I'm Still Here"; "Too Many Mornings"; "The Right Girl"; "Could I Leave You?"; "Losing My Mind"; "The Story of Lucy and Jessie"
**New York run:** Winter Garden, April 4, 1971; 522 p.

Taking place at a reunion of performers who had appeared in various editions of the *Weismann Follies* (a fictitious counterpart of the Ziegfeld revue), the musical dealt with the reality of life as contrasted with the unreality of the theatre, a theme it explored principally through the lives of two couples, the upper-class, unhappy Phyllis and Ben Stone (Alexis Smith and John McMartin) and the middle-class, unhappy Sally and Buddy Plummer (Dorothy Collins and Gene Nelson). The second of the Stephen Sondheim-Harold Prince musicals, *Follies* also depicted these couples as they were in their youth, a flashback device that prompted the composer to come up with songs purposely reminiscent of the styles of some of the theatre's great songwriters of the past. In 1985, a highly acclaimed all-star concert version was staged at Avery Fisher Hall. The musical bore a certain kinship with *Company,* which also was about jaded, ambivalent characters, took a disenchanted view of marriage, and used the structural device of a party to bring a group of people together.
Capitol OC; RCA OC (1985)/Random House (1971)/ MTI.

# GODSPELL

**Music & lyrics:** Stephen Schwartz
**Book:** John-Michael Tebelak
**Producers:** Edgar Lansbury, Stuart Duncan, Joseph Beruh
**Director:** John-Michael Tebelak
**Cast:** Lamar Alford, David Haskell, Johanne Jonas, Robin Lamont, Sonia Manzano, Jeffrey Mylett, Stephen Nathan
**Songs:** "Prepare Ye the Way of the Lord"; "Save the People"; "Day by Day"; "All for the Best"; "All Good Gifts"; "Light of the World"; "Turn Back, O Man"; "We Beseech Thee"; "On the Willows"
**New York run:** Cherry Lane Theatre, May 17, 1971; 2,651 p.

The Seventies brought the Bible to the New York musical stage. Genesis supplied the source of both *Two by Two* (Noah and the Ark) in 1970 and *Joseph and the Amazing Technicolor Dreamcoat* in 1976 (performed at the Brooklyn Academy of Music); the Gospel According to St. Matthew was the origin of *Godspell* in 1971, *Jesus Christ Superstar* also in 1971, and *Your Arms Too Short to Box With God* in 1976. *Godspell* was a whimsical retelling of the last seven days of Christ, with Jesus in clownlike makeup sporting a superman "S" on his shirt; his disciples dressed like flower children; and the parables enacted in a frolicsome, contemporary manner. The work was first shown in nonmusical form as a workshop production at Café La Mama. When it was decided to turn *Godspell* into a musical, songs were then added by Stephen Schwartz. The show was presented in a Greenwich Village theatre for three months, then moved to the Promenade (on Broadway and 76th Street) for a total run of 2,124 performances, making it currently the fourth longest running Off-Broadway musical. The show's official "on" Broadway opening took place June 22, 1976, at the Broadhurst, where it ran for 527 performances. At one time there were seven road companies touring the United States. *Godspell* was revived in 1988 and gave 248 Off-Broadway performances. The film version, released in 1973, featured Victor Garber and David Haskell.
Arista OC/ TM.

# JESUS CHRIST SUPERSTAR

**Music:** Andrew Lloyd Webber
**Lyrics:** Tim Rice
**Conception:** Tom O'Horgan
**Producer:** Robert Stigwood
**Director:** Tom O'Horgan
**Cast:** Jeff Fenholt, Yvonne Elliman, Ben Vereen, Barry Dennen, Anita Morris
**Songs:** "Heaven on Their Minds"; "What's the Buzz?"; "Everything's Alright"; "I Don't Know How to Love Him"; "King Herod's Song"; "Could We Start Again, Please?"; "Superstar"
**New York run:** Mark Hellinger Theatre, October 12, 1971; 720 p.

Even though conceived as a theatre work, *Jesus Christ Superstar* appeared as a record before being presented on the stage because composer Andrew Lloyd Webber and lyricist Tim Rice were unable to find a producer willing to take a chance on so daring a production. Once it became a Gold Record album, however, the path was smoothed for its Broadway premiere. The self-described "rock opera" retold the last seven days of Christ in such a flamboyant, campy, and mind-blowing fashion that despite a mixed press and the opposition from various religious groups the show became a media hype and a boxoffice hit. The movie version was released in 1973 with Ted Neeley and Carl Anderson.
MCA OC/ Stein & Day (1979)/ MTI.

# TWO GENTLEMEN OF VERONA
**Music:** Galt MacDermot
**Lyrics:** John Guare
**Book:** John Guare & Mel Shapiro
**Producer:** Joseph Papp for the New York Shakespeare Festival
**Director:** Mel Shapiro
**Choreographer:** Jean Erdman
**Cast:** Jonelle Allen, Diana Davila, Clifton Davis, Raul Julia, Norman Matlock, Alix Elias, John Bottoms, Stockard Channing
**Songs:** "Follow the Rainbow"; "Bring All the Boys Back Home"; "Night Letter"; "Who Is Silvia?" (lyric: Shakespeare); "Calla Lily Lady"
**New York run:** St. James Theatre, December 1, 1971; 627 p.

*Two Gentlemen of Verona* was originally scheduled to be presented without songs as part of the New York Shakespeare Festival's series of free productions in Central Park. At the recommendation of director Mel Shapiro, a rock score was added to help give the modern adaptation of the play the proper contemporary flavor. The show proved so popular in its open-air presentation in the Summer of 1971 that it was transferred to Broadway, where its blend of anachronistic colloquialisms, ethnic references, and the Bard's own words (the song "Who Is Silvia?" uses the original text) won a receptive audience. The story spins the tale of two Veronese friends, the noble Valentine (Clifton Davis) and the ignoble Proteus (Raul Julia), whose adventures in Milan are complicated by Julia (Diana Davila), who loves Proteus, and Silvia (Jonelle Allen), who Loves Valentine. For other musicals based on Shakespeare, see *The Boys from Syracuse,* page 107. ABC OC/ Holt, Rinehart (1971); Stein & Day (1979)/ TW.

# GREASE
**Music, lyrics & book:** Jim Jacobs & Warren Casey
**Producers:** Kenneth Waissman & Maxine Fox
**Director:** Tom Moore
**Choreographer:** Patricia Birch
**Cast:** Adrienne Barbeau, Barry Bostwick, Carole Demas, Timothy Meyers
**Songs:** "Summer Nights"; "Freddy, My Love"; "Greased Lightnin' "; "Mooning"; "Look at Me, I'm Sandra Dee"; "We Go Together"; "It's Raining on Prom Night"; "Beauty School Dropout"; "Alone at a Drive-In Movie"; "There Are Worse Things I Could Do"
**New York run:** Eden Theatre, February 14, 1972; 3,388 p.

A surprise runaway hit, *Grease* opened at the Off-Broadway Eden Theatre (formerly the Phoenix), then moved on Broadway to the Broadhurst and then the Royale. And there it remained until April 13, 1980, for a record run that was not overtaken until *A Chorus Line* danced past the mark. The show, which began life as a five-hour amateur production in a Chicago trolley barn, took a satirically on-target view of the dress, manners, morals, and music of teenagers at the beginning of the rock and roll era. Set in the fictitious Rydell High School in Chicago, it is chiefly concerned with the attraction between greaser Danny Zuko (Barry Bostwick) and prim and proper Sandy Dumbrowski (Carole Demas), who eventually learns that there is little virtue in virtue. Mocking individuality and championing conformity, the musical hit a responsive chord in youthful audiences that could identify with teenagers having little on their minds except hanging out and making out. On Broadway, Danny was played by nine actors including Treat Williams. John Travolta, who was Danny in the 1978 movie opposite Olivia Newton-John, played Doody in the first of three touring companies. Polydor OC/ Pocket Books (1972); Stein & Day (1979)/ SF.

# SUGAR

**Music:** Jule Styne
**Lyrics:** Bob Merrill
**Book:** Peter Stone
**Producer:** David Merrick
**Director-choreographer:** Gower Champion
**Cast:** Robert Morse, Tony Roberts, Cyril Ritchard, Elaine Joyce, Sheila Smith, Steve Condos, Pamela Blair
**Songs:** "Sun on My Face"; "Sugar"; "What Do You Give to a Man Who's Had Everything?"; "When You Meet a Man in Chicago"
**New York run:** Majestic Theatre, April 9, 1972; 505 p.

Given the creative talents involved and the fact that it was based on the popular 1959 movie *Some Like It Hot, Sugar* might have been expected to be a more distinguised offering than it was. But there was so much dissention during the show's preparations (at one point the composer, lyricist and librettist were all threatened with replacement) that it was something of a miracle that the musical did turn out to be both entertaining and profitable. In the farcical story, set in 1931, Robert Morse and Tony Roberts played two dance-band musicians who witness the St. Valentine's Day gangland massacre in Chicago. They manage to escape from Spats Palazzo's thugs by disguising themselves as members of an all-girl orchestra, Sweet Sue and Her Society Syncopaters, which takes them to Miami for a series of romantic complications resulting when boys are mistaken for girls. Elaine Joyce appeared as Sugar Kane, the part immortalized on the screen by Marilyn Monroe.
United Artists OC/ TW.

# DON'T BOTHER ME, I CAN'T COPE

**Music & lyrics:** Micki Grant
**Conception:** Vinnette Carroll
**Producers:** Edward Padula & Arch Lustberg
**Director:** Vinnette Carroll
**Choreographer:** George Faison
**Cast:** Alex Bradford, Hope Clarke, Micki Grant, Bobby Hill, Arnold Wilkerson
**Songs:** "Don't Bother Me, I Can't Cope"; "Fighting for Pharaoh"; "Good Vibrations"; "It Takes a Whole Lot of Human Feeling"; "Thank Heaven for You"
**New York run:** Playhouse Theatre, April 19, 1972; 1,065 p.

A generally good-humored look at the social problems faced by black people today, *Don't Bother Me, I Can't Cope* was essentially a procession of musical numbers, both sung and danced, based on gospel, rock, calypso, and folk music. The show originated as a workshop project of Vinnette Carroll's Urban Arts Corps Theatre, after which it made appearances in Washington, Philadelphia, and Detroit before opening in New York at the Playhouse Theatre (on 48th Street east of 7th Avenue). Though stressing black pride and dignity, this "Musical Entertainment" still found room for some tongue-in-cheek self kidding which helped give it a broad enough appeal to keep it running on Broadway for two and one-half years.
Polydor OC/ Samuel French (1972)*/ SF.

**Pippin.** Ben Vereen, flanked by Ann Reinking and Candy Brown, in the "Magic to Do" number. (Martha Swope)

# PIPPIN

**Music & lyrics:** Stephen Schwartz
**Book:** Roger O. Hirson (Bob Fosse uncredited)
**Producer:** Stuart Ostrow
**Director-choreographer:** Bob Fosse
**Cast:** Eric Berry, Jill Clayburgh, Leland Palmer, Irene Ryan, Ben Vereen, John Rubinstein, Ann Reinking
**Songs:** "Magic to Do"; "Corner of the Sky"; "Simple Joys"; "No Time at All"; "Morning Glow"; "On the Right Track"; "Kind of Woman"; "Extraordinary"; "Love Song"
**New York run:** Imperial Theatre, October 23, 1972; 1,944 p.

Stephen Schwartz collaborated on the original version of *Pippin* — called *Pippin Pippin* — when he was still a student at Carnegie Tech, but it was not until the success of *Godspell* that a producer was willing to take a chance on him or his work. As insurance, however, Stuart Ostrow brought in playwright Roger O. Hirson to rewrite the book and, most signifcantly, Bob Fosse to serve as director-choreographer. Fosse, also the uncredited co-librettist, put his conceptual stamp on the musical by expanding it into a razzle-dazzle magic show within the framework of a *commedia dell'arte* performance. Helping to give the production a unifying concept was another Fosse touch, the half-God half-Devil Leading Player (Ben Vereen), a character developed from the Master of Ceremonies in *Cabaret.*

In the tale, Pippin (John Rubinstein), the son of Charlemagne (Eric Berry), is a Candide-like figure seeking glory first in war, then as a lover, and finally as a leader of social causes. After failing at all three, he is happy to compromise by settling down to middle-class domesticity with a widow named Catherine (Jill Clayburgh). During the Broadway run — the fourth longest of the decade — Betty Buckley succeeded Miss Clayburgh, and Dorothy Stickney took over as the fifth actress to play Berthe, Pippin's grandmother, whose showstopper was the vaudeville sing-along, "No Time at All." Two road companies toured in *Pippin,* the second of which traveled a full year.
Motown OC/ Drama Book Specialists (1975)/ MTI.

# A LITTLE NIGHT MUSIC

**Music & lyrics:** Stephen Sondheim
**Book:** Hugh Wheeler
**Producer-director:** Harold Prince
**Choreographer:** Patricia Birch
**Cast:** Glynis Johns, Len Cariou, Hermione Gingold, Victoria Mallory, Laurence Guittard, Patricia Elliott, Mark Lambert, D. Jamin-Bartlett, George Lee Andrews
**Songs:** "Night Waltz"; "The Glamorous Life"; "Remember?"; "You Must Meet My Wife"; "Liaisons"; "In Praise of Women"; "Every Day a Little Death"; "A Weekend in the Country"; "It Would Have Been Wonderful"; "Send in the Clowns"; "The Miller's Son"
**New York run:** Shubert Theatre, February 25, 1973; 600 p.

Not Mozart's K. 525 but Ingmar Bergman's 1955 film *Sommarnattens Leende (Smiles of a Summer Night)* was the inspiration for *A Little Night Music,* which offered a wry, witty view of a group of men and women from the standpoints of age and social position. The work claimed two musical innovations: the entire Stephen Sondheim score was composed in 3/4 time (or multiples thereof) and it had an overture sung by a quintet (whose members reappeared throughout the evening in the manner of a Greek chorus). It also contained, in "Send in the Clowns," the best known song the composer has written to date.

Taking place in Sweden at the turn of the century, the story deals with the complicated romantic world of a middle-aged lawyer, Fredrik Egerman (Len Cariou); his virginal child-bride Anne (Victoria Mallory); his son Henrik (Mark Lambert), who is in love with Anne; his former mistress, the actress Desirée Armfeldt (Glynis Johns); Desirée's current lover, the vain, aristocratic Count Carl-Magnus Malcolm (Laurence Guittard); and the count's suicidal wife, Charlotte (Patricia Elliott). The proper partners are paired off at a weekend at the country house of Desirée's mother (Hermoine Gingold), a former concubine of assorted members of the nobility. The musical toured for a year with Jean Simmons, Margaret Hamilton, and George Lee Andrews. A film version, in 1978, co-starred Elizabeth Taylor, Len Cariou, Diana Rigg, and Hermione Gingold.
Columbia OC/ Dodd, Mead (1973); Chilton (1976)/ MTI.

**A Little Night Music.** Len Cariou and Glynis Johns. (Martha Swope)

**Irene.** Debbie Reynolds and Patsy Kelly singing "Mother, Angel, Darling." (Friedman-Abeles)

# IRENE

**Music:** Harry Tierney, etc.
**Lyrics:** Joseph McCarthy, etc.
**Book:** Joseph Stein, Hugh Wheeler, Harry Rigby
**Producers:** Harry Rigby, Albert Selden, Jerome Minskoff
**Director:** Gower Champion
**Choreographer:** Peter Gennaro
**Cast:** Debbie Reynolds, Patsy Kelly, George S. Irving, Monte Markham, Ruth Warrick, Janie Sell, Carmen Alvarez
**Songs:** "Alice Blue Gown"; "They Go Wild, Simply Wild Over Me" (music: Fred Fisher); "Mother, Angel, Darling" (Charles Gaynor); "The Last Part of Ev'ry Party"; "Irene"; "You Made Me Love You" (music: James Monaco); "I'm Always Chasing Rainbows"(music: Harry Carroll) (added)
**New York run:** Minskoff Theatre, March 13, 1973; 604 p.

(See page 32.)

# RAISIN

**Music:** Judd Woldin
**Lyrics:** Robert Brittan
**Book:** Robert Nemiroff & Charlotte Zaltzberg (Joseph Stein uncredited)
**Producer:** Robert Nemiroff
**Director-choreographer:** Donald McKayle
**Cast:** Virginia Capers, Joe Morton, Ernestine Jackson, Ralph Carter, Debbie Allen, Robert Jackson, Ted Ross
**Songs:** "Whose Little Angry Man"; "A Whole Lotta Sunlight"; "Sweet Time"; "You Done Right"; "He Come Down This Morning"; "Sidewalk Tree"; "Not Anymore"; "Measure the Valleys"
**New York run:** 46th Street Theatre, October 18, 1973; 847 p.

Faithfully adapted from Lorraine Hansberry's 1959 play, *A Raisin in the Sun, Raisin* offered a warm, touching picture of a black family living in Chicago's Southside ghetto in the 1950s. Matriarch Lena Younger (Virginia Capers) wants to use her late husband's insurance money to buy a house in the white neighborhood of Clybourne Park, while her son, Walter Lee (Joe Morton), wants to use it to buy a liquor store. Lena gives Walter Lee part of the money for the store, but one of his partners absconds with it, and Walter Lee is faced with the temptation of buckling under and selling the house back to the Clybourne Park Association. At the end, with pride intact, the Youngers prepare to move into their new home. Miss Capers, who won high praise for her performance, headed the touring company for a year and a half. The play's title was taken from a poem by Langston Hughes — "What happens to a dream deferred?/ Does it dry up/ Like a raisin in the sun?"
Columbia OC/ Samuel French (1978)*/ SF.

# CANDIDE

**Music:** Leonard Bernstein
**Lyrics:** Richard Wilbur, etc.
**Book:** Hugh Wheeler
**Producer:** Chelsea Theatre Center of Brooklyn
**Director:** Harold Prince
**Choreographer:** Patricia Birch
**Cast:** Lewis J. Stadlen, Mark Baker, Maureen Brennan, Sam Freed, June Gable, Deborah St. Darr
**Songs:** "Life Is Happiness Indeed" (lyric: Stephen Sondheim); "The Best of All Possible Worlds"; "Oh, Happy We"; "It Must Be So"; "Glitter and Be Gay"; "Auto Da Fé" ("What a Day") (lyric: Sondheim); "This World" (lyric: Sondheim); "I Am Easily Assimilated" (lyric: Bernstein); "Bon Voyage"; "Make Our Garden Grow"
**New York run:** Broadway Theatre, March 10, 1974; 740 p.

(See page 172.)

# THE MAGIC SHOW

**Music & lyrics:** Stephen Schwartz
**Book:** Bob Randall
**Producers:** Edgar Lansbury, Joseph Beruh, Ivan Reitman
**Director-choreographer:** Grover Dale
**Cast:** Doug Henning, Dale Soules, David Ogden Stiers, Anita Morris
**Songs:** "Up to His Old Tricks"; "Lion Tamer"; "Style"; "The Goldfarb Variations"; "West End Avenue"
**New York run:** Cort Theatre, May 28, 1974; 1,920 p.

The fact that the program credit, "MAGIC BY DOUG HENNING," was on the same line and in the same size letters as that of the songwriter and the librettist indicates the importance of Henning's contribution. For *The Magic Show* was little more than a sleight-of-hand show accompanied by a slight-of-substance plot — something about an ambitious young magician at a seedy Passaic, New Jersey, nightclub who triumphs over a jealous old-timer — plus a collection of ten songs. While Henning won praise as an illusionist, his bag of tricks was not his exclusive property since Joe Adalbo took over the part during half the show's run at the Cort Theatre (on 48th Street east of 7th Avenue). The fifth longest running Broadway musical of the 1970s, *The Magic Show* was Stephen Schwartz's third in a row — the others were *Godspell* and *Pippin* — to play over 1,900 performances.
Bell OC.

**The Magic Show.** Doug Henning manages to separate Anita Morris. (Kenn Duncan)

**The Wiz.** Andre De Shields and Tiger Haynes. (Martha Swope)

# THE WIZ

**Music & Lyrics:** Charlie Smalls
**Book:** William F. Brown
**Producer:** Ken Harper
**Director:** Geoffrey Holder (Gilbert Moses uncredited)
**Choreographer:** George Faison
**Cast:** Tiger Haynes, Ted Ross, Hinton Battle, Stephanie Mills, Clarice Taylor, Mabel King, Andre De Shields, Tasha Thomas, DeeDee Bridgewater
**Songs:** "He's the Wizard"; "Ease on Down the Road"; "Slide Some Oil to Me"; "Be a Lion"; "Don't Nobody Bring Me No Bad News"; "If You Believe"
**New York run:** Majestic Theatre, January 5, 1975; 1,672 p.

Though following such illustrious *Wizard of Oz* predecessors as the stage version of 1903 and the screen version of 1939, *The Wiz* was an original concept with an all-black cast, a new rock score, and dialogue that made the fairytale relevant to modern audiences. It still, however, told the same basic story about Dorothy (Stephanie Mills), the little girl from Kansas who is blown by a tornado into Munchkinland in the Land of Oz, meets the Scarecrow (Hinton Battle), the Tinman (Tiger Haynes), and the Lion (Ted Ross) on the Yellow Brick Road, defeats the evil witch (Mabel King), and has an audience with the supposedly all-powerful Wizard (Andre De Shields). Though the Wiz is a phony, he does convince Dorothy that she can do anything she wants if she just believes in herself.

The idea for *The Wiz* originated with producer Ken Harper who had to surmount myriad problems in guiding the show to Broadway. After almost shutting down the musical in Baltimore, he replaced director Gilbert Moses with Geoffrey Holder (also the costume designer) in Detroit, and posted the closing notice on opening night in New York. But a concerted publicity and advertising campaign —plus favorable audience reaction — helped produce a real miracle, and *The Wiz* went on to a four-year run. It also spawned two touring companies that traveled for three years. The 1978 movie version featured Diana Ross, Michael Jackson, Nipsey Russell, Ted Ross, Lena Horne, and Richard Pryor.
Atlantic OC/ Stein & Day (1979)/ SF.

# SHENANDOAH

**Music:** Gary Geld
**Lyrics:** Peter Udell
**Book:** James Lee Barrett, with Philip Rose, Peter Udell
**Producers:** Philip Rose, Gloria & Louis Sher
**Director:** Philip Rose
**Choreographer:** Robert Tucker
**Cast:**  John Cullum, Donna Theodore, Penelope Milford, Joel Higgins, Ted Agress, Gordon Halliday, Chip Ford
**Songs:** "I've Heard It All Before"; "Next to Lovin' I Like Fightin' "; "The Pickers Are Comin' "; "Meditation"; "We Make a Beautiful Pair"; "Violets and Silverbells"; "Freedom"; "The Only Home I Know"
**New York run:** Alvin Theatre, January 7, 1975; 1,050 p.

Of all the movies that have been turned into Broadway musicals, the 1965 release, *Shenandoah,* would seem to have been the most unsuitable. A strongly anti-war polemic, the story is set in the Shenandoah Valley of Virginia during the Civil War. Charlie Anderson (John Cullum), the widowed patriarch of a family of farmers, is determined that the only cause in which any of his six sons will take up arms is in defense of their land. When his youngest son is kidnapped by Northern soldiers, however, Charlie and most of his family go off to find him. While they are away, the eldest son, his wife and baby are all killed, and there is further suffering before what is left of the Anderson family have an emotional reunion in church. First tried out at the Goodspeed Opera House in Connecticut, *Shenandoah* had an appealing Rodgers and Hammerstein flavor and it enjoyed an unexpected long run. It was revived briefly in 1989 with John Cullum. For other musicals about the Civil War, see *Bloomer Girl,* page 125.
RCA OC/ Samuel French (1975)*/ SF.

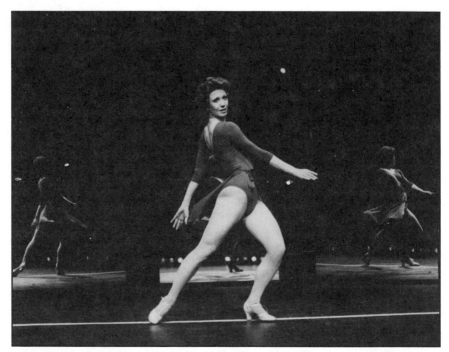

**A Chorus Line.** Donna McKechnie performing "The Music and the Mirror." (© Martha Swope)

# A CHORUS LINE

**Music:** Marvin Hamlisch
**Lyrics:** Edward Kleban
**Conception:** Michael Bennett
**Book:** James Kirkwood & Nicholas Dante
**Producer:** Joseph Papp for the New York Shakespeare Festival
**Director:** Michael Bennett
**Choreographers:** Michael Bennett & Bob Avian
**Cast:** Kelly Bishop, Pamela Blair, Wayne Cilento, Kay Cole, Patricia Garland, Baayork Lee, Priscilla Lopez, Robert LuPone, Donna McKechnie, Michel Stuart, Thommie Walsh, Sammy Williams
**Songs:** "I Hope I Get It"; "At the Ballet"; "Nothing"; "The Music and the Mirror"; "One"; "What I Did for Love"
**New York run:** Public Theatre, April 15, 1975; (still running 11/1/89)

Although it dealt with the hopes, fears, frustrations, and insecurities of a specific group of dancers auditioning for a chorus line, the musical skillfully conveyed the universal experience of anyone who has ever stood in line in an effort to present his or her qualifications for a job. Since that means just about all of us, *A Chorus Line* has managed to create such a strong empathetical bond with its audiences that it has become far and away the longest running production — musical or dramatic — ever staged on Broadway.

Director-choreographer Michael Bennett — who also receives program credit for having "conceived" the show — had long wanted to stage a work that would be a celebration of chorus dancers, known as "gypsies," who contribute so much and receive so little glory. Early in 1974, Bennett rented a studio where he invited 24 dancers to talk about themselves and their careers. Out of these rap sessions came some 30 hours of taped revelations, which gave the director the idea of creating his musical in the form of an audition. After he and Nicholas Dante, one of his dancers, had edited the tapes, producer Joseph Papp offered to sponsor the project as a workshop production at his New York Shakespeare Festival Public Theatre. Marvin Hamlisch and Edward Kleban were engaged to write the score, and playwright James Kirkwood was brought in to work with Dante on the book. The show opened at the Newman Theatre (part of the Public Theatre's complex) in mid April 1975, at a $10 top ticket price. Word of mouth made it a hit even before the critics were invited to view it on May 21, and it remained at the downtown playhouse for 101 performances. On July 25, 1975, *A Chorus Line* moved to the Shubert Theatre, went on to win the Pulitzer Prize for drama, and — at this writing — it is still running on Broadway.

Avoiding a linear plot structure, the musical is basically a series of vignettes as 18 applicants vie for places in an eight-member chorus line. Goaded by a largely unseen — and rather sadistic — director named Zach (Robert LuPone), each applicant in turn reveals truths that, supposedly, will help the director make his final choices. Among those auditioning are Cassie (Donna McKechnie), a former featured dancer now down on her luck who was once romantically involved with Zach; the street-smart but vulnerable Sheila (Kelly Bishop) who recalls how she had been attracted to dancing because "everything was beautiful at the ballet"; the still-hopeful Diana (Priscilla Lopez), who had once failed a method acting class; the voluptuous Val (Pamela Blair) who uses silicone to enlarge her talent; and the pathetic Paul (Sammy Williams) who relates his humiliating experience as a drag queen.

There have been two touring companies of *A Chorus Line,* the first traveling for seven years, the second for five years eight months. The film version was released in 1985.
Columbia OC.

**Chicago.** Lawyer Jerry Orbach coaches murderess Gwen Verdon how to appear demure in the courtroom. (Martha Swope)

# CHICAGO

**Music:** John Kander
**Lyrics:** Fred Ebb
**Book:** Fred Ebb & Bob Fosse
**Producers:** Robert Fryer & James Cresson
**Director-choreographer:** Bob Fosse
**Cast:** Gwen Verdon, Chita Rivera, Jerry Orbach, Barney Martin, Mary McCarty, M. O'Haughey, Graciela Daniele
**Songs:** "All That Jazz"; "All I Care About"; "Roxie"; "My Own Best Friend"; "Mr. Cellophane"; "Razzle Dazzle"; "Class"; "Nowadays"
**New York run:** 46th Street Theatre, June 3, 1975; 898 p.

Bob Fosse first planned a musical production of Maurine Dallas Watkins' 1926 play as early as the mid-Fifties, with Gwen Verdon as the star and Robert Fryer as the producer. It took some 13 years, however, for him to clear the rights to the story of Roxie Hart, a married chorus girl who kills her faithless lover, avoids prison through the histrionic efforts of razzle-dazzle lawyer Billy Flynn (Jerry Orbach), and ends up as a vaudeville headliner with another "scintillating sinner," Velma Kelly (Chita Rivera). Though the show was a scathing indictment of American huckstering, vulgarity, and decadence, its atmosphere strongly recalled the Berlin of *Cabaret,* which also had songs by John Kander and Fred Ebb and whose film version was directed by Bob Fosse.

In Fosse's conceptual treatment, which had much in common with his *commedia dell'arte* approach in *Pippin, Chicago* was created as "A Musical Vaudeville" with a Master of Ceremonies introducing each number as if it were a variety act. (A previous effort to combine vaudeville within a musical play was the Kurt Weill-Alan Jay Lerner *Love Life.*) Soon after *Chicago's* Broadway opening, Miss Verdon was temporarily replaced by Liza Minnelli because of illness; during the run she was succeeded by Ann Reinking.
Arista OC/ Samuel French (1976)*/ SF.

# PACIFIC OVERTURES

**Music & lyrics:** Stephen Sondheim
**Book:** John Weidman
**Producer-director:** Harold Prince
**Choreographer:** Patricia Birch
**Cast:** Mako, Soon-Teck Oh, Yuki Shimoda, Sab Shimono, Isao Sato
**Songs:** "There Is No Other Way"; "Four Black Dragons"; "Chrysanthemum Tea"; "Welcome to Kanagawa"; "Someone in a Tree"; "Please Hello"; "A Bowler Hat"; "Pretty Lady"; "Next"
**New York run:** Winter Garden, January 11, 1976; 193 p.

Few Broadway musicals have ever dared so much on so many levels as *Pacific Overtures*. In recounting the history of the emergence of Japan from a serenely isolated country to its present position in the forefront of international commerce, the musical covers a 120-year period, beginning with Comm. Matthew Perry's threateningly persuasive visit to the Floating Kingdom in 1853, and taking us through changes in social order, customs and dress that were the price Japan paid for its present-day affluence. To present such an ambitiously didactic work, the musical's creators chose to relate the saga not only from the Japanese point of view but also through an approximation of the ancient form of Japanese theatre known as Kabuki. Moreover, Stephen Sondheim's score, while accessible to Occidental ears, was a far more faithful recreation of Oriental music and poetic expression than had ever before been attempted on Broadway. Also adding to the show's dramatic impact were director Harold Prince's lavish conceptual approach and the stunning visual effects created by designer Boris Aronson. In 1984, a revival of *Pacific Overtures* was offered in a scaled-down, Off-Broadway production.
RCA OC/ Dodd, Mead (1977)/ MTI.

# I LOVE MY WIFE

**Music:** Cy Coleman
**Lyrics & book:** Michael Stewart
**Producers:** Terry Allen Kramer & Harry Rigby
**Director:** Gene Saks
**Choreographer:** Onna White
**Cast:** Ilene Graff, Lenny Baker, Joanna Gleason, James Naughton
**Songs:** "Love Revolution"; "Someone Wonderful I Missed"; "Sexually Free"; "Hey There, Good Times"; "Lovers on Christmas Eve"; "Everybody Today Is Turning On"; "I Love My Wife"
**New York run:** Ethel Barrymore Theatre, April 17, 1977; 872 p.

The sexual revolution of the 1960s hit Broadway a bit late with a musical about mate-swapping in the sinful citadel of Trenton, New Jersey. At the urging of the husbands, two happily married, well-adjusted couples agree to catch up with the amoral freedom they've been hearing and reading about by having themselves a *ménage à quatre*. Of course, since they are such basically decent, clean-living people, they abandon the idea at the last minute because — as the men agree in song — "I love my wife." The idea for the musical began when Michael Stewart saw a French farce in which songs were introduced by lip-synching actors without any attempt to fit them into the story line. *I Love My Wife* followed this general concept by using the musical numbers — sung by both the four actors and an instrumental quartet that turns up throughout the show — to make observations on the morals and mores of the time. During the run, Tom and Dick Smothers were among those who succeeded Lenny Baker and James Naughton.
Atlantic OC/ Samuel French (1980)*/ SF.

**Annie.** Annie (Andrea McArdle), Daddy Warbucks (Reid Shelton), and Sandy. (Martha Swope)

**Annie.** Orphans Diana Barrows, Robyn Finn, Donna Graham, Danielle Brisebois, Shelley Bruce, and Janine Ruane singing "You're Never Fully Dressed Without a Smile." (Martha Swope)

# ANNIE

**Music:** Charles Strouse
**Lyrics:** Martin Charnin
**Book:** Thomas Meehan
**Producer:** Mike Nichols
**Director:** Martin Charnin
**Choreographer:** Peter Gennaro
**Cast:** Andrea McArdle, Reid Shelton, Dorothy Loudon, Sandy Faison, Robert Fitch, Barbara Erwin, Raymond Thorne, Laurie Beechman, Danielle Brisebois, Shelley Bruce
**Songs:** "Maybe"; "It's the Hard-Knock Life"; "Tomorrow"; "Little Girls"; "I Think I'm Gonna Like It Here"; "N.Y.C."; "Easy Street"; "You're Never Fully Dressed Without a Smile"; "Something Was Missing"; "I Don't Need Anything but You"; "Annie"; "A New Deal for Christmas"
**New York run:** Alvin Theatre, April 21, 1977; 2,377 p.

The idea of turning Harold Gray's "Little Orphan Annie" comic strip into a musical was the inspiration of lyricist-director Martin Charnin, who then contacted playwright Thomas Meehan and composer Charles Strouse to join him in the project. Though their initial reaction was an unqualified "Ughhh," Meehan and Strouse were soon won over by Charnin's approach, which was to use only the three continuing characters in the strip — Annie, Daddy Warbucks, and Annie's mutt Sandy — and fit them into an original story. Because Meehan saw Annie as "a metaphorical figure standing for innate decency, courage and optimism in the face of hard times, pessimism and despair," he decided to set his fable in New York City in the midst of the Depression. Annie (Andrea McArdle), an 11-year-old foundling at the Municipal Orphanage, yearns for her parents to rescue her from the clutches of mean-spirited, bibulous Agatha Hannigan (Dorothy Loudon), the orphanage's matron. Presently, a miraculous parent-figure does show up in the person of billionaire Oliver Warbucks (Reid Shelton) whose secretary, Grace Farrell (Sandy Faison), has invited Annie to spend Christmas with him. Warbucks, in fact, becomes so fond of the child that he plans to adopt her, a situation that is temporarily blocked by the machinations of Miss Hannigan. But the industrialist enlists the aid of his friend President Roosevelt (Raymond Thorne), and everyone — at least everyone who believes that tomorrow is only a day away — looks forward to having a New Deal for Christmas. (It should be noted that Lionel Bart's musical *Oliver!* is also about a young orphan who escapes a life of deprivation by being adopted by a wealthy gentleman.)

When tried out at the Goodspeed Opera House in Connecticut (where Miss McArdle replaced another girl shortly before the opening and Miss Loudon was not yet in the cast), *Annie* won the approval of Mike Nichols who offered to produce it on Broadway. The show was quickly adopted by theatregoers who made it the third longest running musical of the 1970s. During the run, Warbucks was also played by Keene Curtis, John Schuck, Harve Presnell, and Rhodes Reason; Annie by Shelley Bruce, Sarah Jessica Parker, Allison Smith, and Alyson Kirk; and Miss Hannigan by Alice Ghostley, Dolores Wilson, Betty Hutton, Marcia Lewis, Ruth Kobart, and June Havoc. There were four road companies of *Annie,* with the first traveling three and a half years. In 1982, the movie version was released with Albert Finney, Aileen Quinn, Ann Reinking, and Carol Burnett.

For other musicals taken from comic strips, see *Li'l Abner,* page 171. Columbia OC/ MTI.

# THE KING AND I

**Music:** Richard Rodgers
**Lyrics & book:** Oscar Hammerstein II
**Producers:** Lee Guber & Shelly Gross
**Director:** Yuriko
**Choreographer:** Jerome Robbins recreated by Yuriko
**Cast:**   Yul Brynner, Constance Towers, Michael Kermoyan, Hye-Young Choi,
          Martin Vidnovic, June Angela, Susan Kikuchi, John Michael King, Gene
          Profanato, Marianne Tatum
**Songs:** Same as original production
**New York run:** Uris Theatre, May 2, 1977; 696 p.

See page 151.

**The King and I.** King Yul Brynner giving a royal command to governess Constance Towers. (Ernst Haas)

**On the Twentieth Century.**
Kevin Kline, John Cullum, and
Judy Kaye. (Martha Swope)

# ON THE TWENTIETH CENTURY

**Music:** Cy Coleman
**Lyrics & book:** Betty Comden & Adolph Green
**Producers:** Robert Fryer, Mary Lea Johnson, James Cresson, etc.
**Director:** Harold Prince
**Choreographer:** Larry Fuller
**Cast:** John Cullum, Madeline Kahn, Imogene Coca, George Coe, Dean
Dittman, Kevin Kline, Judy Kaye, George Lee Andrews
**Songs:** "On the Twentieth Century"; "I Rise Again"; "Veronique"; "Never";
"Our Private World"; "Repent"; "We've Got It All"
**New York run:** St. James Theatre, February 19, 1978; 449 p.

Ben Hecht and Charles MacArthur's 1932 show-business farce, *Twentieth Century* (which they had based on a play by Bruce Millholland) was turned into a musical that was not so much backstage as on track, since most of the action takes place aboard the Twentieth Century Limited (in a stunning art-deco set by Robin Wagner) as it speeds from Chicago to New York. Producer-director Oscar Jaffee (John Cullum), the flamboyant High Priest of Broadway now in desperate straights, makes a last-ditch effort to rise again by signing tempestuous movie star Lily Garland (Madeline Kahn), to act in his next epic, *The Passion of Mary Magdalene.* Oscar, who had once been Lily's mentor and lover — and had changed her name from Mildred Plotka — must now also contend with Lily's latest love, actor Bruce Granit (Kevin Kline), and a rival producer, Max Jacobs (George Lee Andrews). But we know that the two are meant for each other when Lily, tricked into signing Oscar's contract, affixes the name Peter Rabbit.

Though the character of Oscar Jaffee had been originally modeled after David Belasco and Jed Harris, Cullum played him as John Barrymore, with the love-hate relationship of Oscar and Lily also recalling Fred and Lili in *Kiss Me, Kate.* Two months after the opening, Miss Kahn was replaced by Judy Kaye. Columbia OC/ Drama Book Specialists (1981)/ SF.

# DANCIN'

**Music & lyrics:** Miscellaneous writers
**Producers:** Jules Fisher, Shubert Organization, Columbia Pictures
**Director-choreographer:** Bob Fosse
**Cast:** Sandahl Bergman, Rene Ceballos, Christopher Chadman, Wayne Cilento, Vicki Frederick, Edward Love, Ann Reinking, Charles Ward
**Songs:** 23 musical pieces from Bach to Jerry Jeff Walker
**New York run:** Broadhurst Theatre, March 27, 1978; 1,774 p.

An extension of Bob Fosse's previous work in *Pippin* and *Chicago* — plus Michael Bennett's in *A Chorus Line* — *Dancin'* represented the final triumph of the Broadway choreographer by doing away with practically everything else but. In essence, it was Fosse's attempt to create a popular-dance version of a ballet program performed on Broadway for a commercial run, and it succeeded so well in attracting an audience — especially foreign visitors who might have difficulty in following a book musical — that it remained in New York for four years three months, and toured for over a year. The precision, grace and sheer vitality of the dancers (particularly Ann Reinking) merited high praise in such numbers as the easy-going, high-strutting "I Wanna Be a Dancin' Man," performed by the entire company; the dithyrambic recreation of Benny Goodman's "Sing, Sing, Sing"; and the finale, "America," a collage of ten routines by turn comic, ironic, and rousing.

# THE BEST LITTLE WHOREHOUSE IN TEXAS

**Music & lyrics:** Carol Hall
**Book:** Larry L. King & Peter Masterson
**Producer:** Universal Pictures (Stevie Phillips)
**Directors:** Peter Masterson & Tommy Tune
**Choreographer:** Tommy Tune
**Cast:** Carlin Glynn, Henderson Forsythe, Delores Hall, Pamela Blair, Jay Garner, Clint Allmon
**Songs:** "A Li'l Ole Bitty Pissant Country Place"; "Girl, You're a Woman"; "Twenty-Four Hours of Lovin' "; "Texas Has a Whorehouse in It"; "Bus from Amarillo"; "Good Old Girl"; "Hard Candy Christmas"
**New York run:** Entermedia Theatre, April 17, 1978; 1,703 p.

The legendary Texas brothel known as the Chicken Ranch (so-called because in the Depression customers were allowed to pay with poultry) was in existence from the 1840s to 1973, when it was shut down through the efforts of a crusading, oilier-than-thou Houston radio commentator and his vigilante Watch Dogs. The story of the brothel and its last days became the subject of a raunchy, romping musical that was tried out at the Actor's Studio, opened at the Off-Broadway Entermedia Theatre (formerly the Eden), where it played 64 performances, then moved to the 46th Street Theatre on June 19. The show was put together entirely by four transplanted Texans who wanted to collaborate on a musical about the Lone Star State that would be, in the words of songwriter Carol Hall, "funny and nostalgic and tender." Carlin Glynn played Miss Mona Stangley, the whorehouse proprietor, and Henderson Forsythe the blunt-talking local sheriff, Ed Earl Dodd, who had once been Mona's lover. Alexis Smith was seen as Miss Mona in the second of three road companies that toured for three and a half years. The film version, released in 1982, co-starred Dolly Parton and Burt Reynolds. MCA OC/ Samuel French (1983)*/ SF.

# AIN'T MISBEHAVIN'

**Music:** Fats Waller
**Lyrics:** Miscellaneous writers
**Conception:** Murray Horwitz & Richard Maltby Jr.
**Producers:** Emanuel Azenberg, Dasha Epstein, Shubert Organization, Jane Gaynor, Ron Dante
**Director:** Richard Maltby Jr.
**Choreographer:** Arthur Faria
**Cast:** Nell Carter, Andre De Shields, Armelia McQueen, Ken Page, Charlaine Woodard
**Songs:** 30 written or recorded by Fats Waller
**New York run:** Longacre Theatre, May 9, 1978; 1,604 p.

While it was not the first entertainment presented on or off Broadway to feature the songs of a particular composer or lyricist, *Ain't Misbehavin'*, "The New Fats Waller Musical Show," was such a popular attraction that it opened the way for two subsequent "catalogue" musicals, *Eubie!,* spotlighting the work of Eubie Blake, and *Sophisticated Ladies,* which did the same for Duke Ellington. *Ain't Misbehavin'* began as a limited-run cabaret entertainment at the Manhattan Theatre Club on February 8, 1978. Its enthusiastic reception prompted its transfer to Broadway at the Longacre Theatre, where Charlaine Woodard replaced Irene Cara. Among the numbers performed were 18 written by Waller either as songs or instrumental pieces (some with new lyrics by Richard Maltby Jr. and Murray Horwitz) and 12 others that Waller recorded. Through costuming, decor, and arrangements, the show evoked the flavor of a Harlem nightclub in theThirties, with the playful spirit of Waller himself coming through in the performances and the staging. During the Broadway run, Miss Woodard was succeeded by Debbie Allen. The musical's touring company traveled for two years seven months. In 1988 the show had a brief Broadway revival.
RCA OC/ MTI.

**Ain't Misbehavin'.** Armelia McQueen, Ken Page, Charlaine Woodard, Andre De Shields, and Nell Carter. (Martha Swope)

# I'M GETTING MY ACT TOGETHER AND TAKING IT ON THE ROAD

**Music:** Nancy Ford
**Lyrics & book:** Gretchen Cryer
**Producer:** Joseph Papp for the New York Shakespeare Festival
**Director:** Word Baker
**Cast:** Gretchen Cryer, Joel Fabiani, Betty Aberlin, Don Scardino
**Songs:** "Natural High"; "Miss America"; "Dear Tom"; "Old Friend"; "Strong Woman Number"; "Happy Birthday"
**New York run:** Public Theatre, June 14, 1978; 1,165 p.

In all their works to date, composer Nancy Ford and lyricist-librettist Gretchen Cryer have been preeminently identified as feminist writers. *I'm Getting My Act Together and Taking It on the Road,* by far their most personal expression, even had the central role, that of a divorced 39-year-old pop singer attempting a come-back, played by Miss Cryer herself. The story finds her auditioning a new act for her dubious manager (Joel Fabiani), in which she presents herself as honestly as she can, without makeup or fancy gowns or any kind of audience-pandering. Through her songs, the singer gradually becomes the embodiment of the out-spoken, totally liberated woman who knows exactly who she is and where she is going. After six months at the New York Shakespeare Festival Public Theatre, the musical was transferred to the Circle in the Square in Greenwich Village. Dur-ing the run, Miss Cryer was succeeded by Virginia Vestoff, Betty Aberlin, Carol Hall, Betty Buckley, Anne Kaye, Nancy Ford, and Phyllis Newman.
CSP OC/ Samuel French (1980)*/ SF.

# THEY'RE PLAYING OUR SONG

**Music:** Marvin Hamlisch
**Lyrics:** Carole Bayer Sager
**Book:** Neil Simon
**Producer:** Emanuel Azenberg
**Director:** Robert Moore
**Choreographer:** Patricia Birch
**Cast:** Lucie Arnaz, Robert Klein
**Songs:** "Fallin' "; "If He Really Knew Me"; "They're Playing Our Song"; "Just for Tonight"; "When You're in My Arms"; "Right"
**New York run:** Imperial Theatre, February 11, 1979; 1,082 p.

*They're Playing Our Song* was based in part on composer Marvin Hamlisch's own frequently stormy affair with his then lyricist-in-residence, Carole Bayer Sager. In this musical *drame à clef,* Vernon Gersch, a wise-cracking, neurotic songwriter who likes to spend his time telling his troubles to a tape recorder, and Sonia Walsk, a wise-cracking, neurotic lyric writer whose wardrobe is made up of used theatre costumes, try to have both a professional and a personal rela-tionship despite constant interruptions caused by telephone calls from Sonia's former lover for whom she still feels great affection. To tell their story, the au-thors hit upon the notion — as in *I Do! I Do!* — of using only two characters, though in this case each one has three singing alter egos. Four actors succeeded Robert Klein during the Broadway run (including Tony Roberts and Victor Garber), and five succeeded Lucie Arnaz (including Stockard Channing and Anita Gillette). The show's first road company (with Garber and Ellen Greene) toured for two years; the second (with John Hammil and Lorna Luft) for one year three months.
Casablanca OC/ Random House (1980)/ SF.

**Sweeney Todd.** Angela Lansbury and Len Cariou.
(Martha Swope)

# SWEENEY TODD
**Music & lyrics:** Stephen Sondheim
**Book:** Hugh Wheeler
**Producers:** Richard Barr, Charles Woodward, Robert Fryer, etc.
**Director:** Harold Prince
**Choreographer:** Larry Fuller
**Cast:** Angela Lansbury, Len Cariou, Victor Garber, Ken Jennings, Merle Louise, Edmund Lyndeck, Sarah Rice
**Songs:** "The Ballad of Sweeney Todd"; "The Worst Pies in London"; "Johanna"; "Pretty Women"; "Epiphany"; "A Little Priest"; "By the Sea"; "Not While I'm Around"
**New York run:** Uris Theatre, March 1, 1979; 557 p.

Easily the most grisly musical ever presented for a commercial Broadway run, the near-operatic *Sweeney Todd* was a bold, even audience-intimidating attack on the cannibalizing effects of the Industrial Revolution on a Brechtian, vermin-infested London. The indictment was conveyed through the tale of a half-mad barber (Len Cariou) who returns home after escaping from an unjust imprisonment to take vengeance on the judge who sentenced him, then ravished his wife, and now plans to marry his daughter. But Sweeney doesn't limit himself to one victim; he turns his indiscriminate rage against everyone in London by systematically slitting the throats of his customers, whose corpses are then made into meat pies by Todd's enterprising accomplice, Mrs. Lovett (Angela Lansbury). At the end, of course, all the bad ones are properly and gruesomely punished.

First shown on the London stage in 1847 as *A String of Pearls, or The Fiend of Fleet Street,* by George Dibdin Pitt, the Grand Guignol story has been presented in many versions since then, most recently Christopher Bond's 1973 London play, *Sweeney Todd,* on which Hugh Wheeler based his libretto. The fifth and most uncompromising collaboration between composer-lyricist Stephen Sondheim and director Harold Prince, the production was also noted for its towering setting (by Eugene and Franne Lee) made from an iron foundry. During the run at the Uris Theatre (now the Gershwin, on 51st west of Broadway), Miss Lansbury was succeeded by Dorothy Loudon, Mr. Cariou by George Hearn. In 1984, the musical entered the repertory of the New York City Opera; in 1989, it was revived Off-Broadway with Bob Gunton and Beth Fowler.
RCA OC/ Dodd, Mead (1979)/ MTI.

# PETER PAN

**Music:** Mark Charlap; Jule Styne
**Lyrics:** Carolyn Leigh; Betty Comden & Adolph Green
**Play:** James M. Barrie
**Producers:** Zev Bufman & James Nederlander
**Director-choreographer:** Rob Iscove
**Cast:** Sandy Duncan, George Rose, Beth Fowler, Arnold Soboloff, Marsha Kramer
**Songs:** Same as original production
**New York run:** Lunt-Fontanne Theatre, September 6, 1979; 551 p.

(See page 163.)

# EVITA

**Music:** Andrew Lloyd Webber
**Lyrics:** Tim Rice
**Producer:** Robert Stigwood
**Director:** Harold Prince
**Choreographer:** Larry Fuller
**Cast:** Patti LuPone, Mandy Patinkin, Bob Gunton, Mark Syers, Jane Ohringer
**Songs:** "On This Night of a Thousand Stars"; "Buenos Aires"; "I'd Be Surprisingly Good for You"; "Another Suitcase in Another Hall"; "A New Argentina"; "Don't Cry for Me, Argentina"; "High Flying Adored"; "Rainbow Tour"; "The Actress Hasn't Learned"; "And the Money Kept Rolling In"; "Dice Are Rolling"
**New York run:** Broadway Theatre, September 25, 1979; 1,567 p.

Because of its huge success in London (where it opened in 1978 and ran 2,900 performances), *Evita* was such a pre-sold hit in New York that it was able to surmount a mixed critical reception and remain on Broadway for three years nine months. Based on events in the life of Argentina's notorious Eva Peron, the musical —with Patti LuPone as Eva — begins in 1934 when Eva Duarte is 15, takes her from her hometown to Buenos Aires where she becomes a model, film actress, and the wife of Gen. Juan Peron (Bob Gunton). When Peron is elected president, Eva becomes the most powerful woman in South America, and though she does little to improve the conditions of her people, is regarded as a saint when she dies of cancer at the age of 33. Another character in the musical, the slightly misplaced Che Guevera (Mandy Patinkin), serves as narrator, observer, and conscience.

Though the plot is told entirely through song and dance (there is no credit for librettist) and the work had originated as a record project, the highly theatrical concept devised by authors Andrew Lloyd Webber and Tim Rice and director Harold Prince — as well as the popularity of "Don't Cry for Me, Argentina" — helped turn *Evita* into an internationally acclaimed musical. During the Broadway run, six actresses took over the title role from Miss LuPone: Terri Klausner, Nancy Opel, and Pamela Blake (matinees), and Derin Altay, Loni Ackerman, and Florence Lacey (evenings). The show's three touring companies traveled a total of three and one-half years.
MCA OC/ MTI.

# SUGAR BABIES

**Music:** Jimmy McHugh, etc.
**Lyrics:** Dorothy Fields, etc.
**Conception:** Ralph G. Allen & Harry Rigby
**Sketches:** Ralph G. Allen
**Producers:** Terry Allen Kramer & Harry Rigby
**Directors:** Ernest Flatt, Rudy Tronto
**Choreographer:** Ernest Flatt
**Cast:** Mickey Rooney, Ann Miller, Sid Stone, Jack Fletcher, Ann Jillian, Bob Williams, Scot Stewart
**Songs:** "A Good Old Burlesque Show" (lyric: Arthur Malvin); "I Feel a Song Comin' On"; "Don't Blame Me"; "Mr. Banjo Man" (music & lyric: Malvin); "I'm Keeping Myself Available for You" (lyric: Malvin); "Warm and Willing" (lyric: Jay Livingston & Ray Evans); "Exactly Like You"; "I Can't Give You Anything but Love"; "I'm Shooting High" (lyric: Ted Koehler); "On the Sunny Side of the Street"; "You Can't Blame Your Uncle Sammy" (lyric: Al Dubin & Irwin Dash).
**New York run:** Mark Hellinger Theatre, October 8, 1979; 1,208 p.

Like *Star and Garter, Wine, Women and Song,* and *Michael Todd's Peep Show* of an earlier era, *Sugar Babies* was an idealized version of a burlesque show. According to sketch writer Ralph G. Allen, who conceived the entertainment with co-producer Harry Rigby, the show was a celebration of American variety entertainment from 1905 to 1930 and the aim was to recreate as authentically as possible some of the classic low-comedy sketches and routines of that period. Making his Broadway debut top banana Mickey Rooney appeared in such traditional roles as the lascivious judge in a manic courtroom scene, as the naughty little boy in "The Little Red Schoolhouse," and as Countess Francine, complete with cotton-candy wig and exaggerated bosoms, leading her troupe of female minstrels. Also memorable, if hardly authentic, was the session at the grand piano with Mickey and Ann Miller going through Jimmy McHugh standards. Rooney was followed on Broadway by Joey Bishop, Rip Taylor, and Eddie Bracken, then headed the touring company with the leg-flashing Miss Miller. The show was on the road for almost three and a half years.
B'way Entertainment OC/ Samuel French (1983)*/ SF.

# OKLAHOMA!

**Music:** Richard Rodgers
**Lyrics & book:** Oscar Hammerstein II
**Producers:** Zev Bufman & James Nederlander
**Director:** William Hammerstein
**Choreographer:** Agnes de Mille recreated by Gemze de Lappe
**Cast:** Laurence Guittard, Christine Andreas, Mary Wickes, Christine Ebersole, Martin Vidnovic, Harry Groener, Bruce Adler
**Songs:** Same as original production
**New York run:** Palace Theatre, December 13, 1979; 293 p.

(See page 119.)

# BARNUM

**Music:** Cy Coleman
**Lyrics:** Michael Stewart
**Book:** Mark Bramble
**Producers:** Judy Gordon, Cy Coleman, Maurice & Lois Rosenfield
**Director-choreographer:** Joe Layton
**Cast:** Jim Dale, Glenn Close, Marianne Tatum, Terri White, Leonard John Crofoot, William C. Witter
**Songs:** "There Is a Sucker Born Ev'ry Minute"; "The Colors of My Life"; "One Brick at a Time"; "Bigger Isn't Better"; "Come Follow the Band"; "Black and White"; "The Prince of Humbug"; "Join the Circus"
**New York run:** St. James Theatre, April 30, 1980; 854 p.

The story of America's "Prince of Humbug," Phineas Taylor Barnum, had long attracted producers and writers as a fitting subject for a musical, but it was not until Cy Coleman, Michael Stewart, and Mark Bramble got together with director-choreographer Joe Layton that a way was found to depict the colorful impresario's life on stage. Their solution: don't bother too much with characterization or biographical detail, simply offer the show as a total circus concept with the entire cast constantly in motion tumbling, clowning, marching, twirling, and flying through the air. Best of all, give the title role to Jim Dale, an actor who can dance, juggle, leap off a trampoline, and sing and walk a tightrope at the same time.

The musical offers a guided tour of the highlights of Barnum's career from 1835 to 1880, when the showman joins James A. Bailey (William C. Witter) in creating "The Greatest Show on Earth." Along the way, we are treated to such legendary sucker-bait attractions as Joice Heth (Terri White), George Washington's alleged 160-year-old nurse, the midget Tom Thumb (Leonard John Crofoot), Jumbo the elephant, the Swedish Nightingale Jenny Lind (Marianne Tatum), and — finally — the three-ring circus. What conflict there is is supplied by the unfulfilled desire of Barnum's wife Chairy (Glenn Close) to settle down to a more prosaic life. During the run, Dale was succeeded by Tony Orlando and Mike Burstyn. For other show-business biographies, see *Annie Get Your Gun*, page 130. Columbia OC/ Doubleday (1980)/ TW.

**Barnum.** Jim Dale and Glenn Close. (Martha Swope)

**42nd Street.** Jerry Orbach and
Wanda Richert. (Martha Swope)

# 42nd STREET
**Music:** Harry Warren
**Lyrics:** Al Dubin
**Book:** Michael Stewart & Mark Bramble
**Producer:** David Merrick
**Director-choreographer:** Gower Champion
**Cast:** Jerry Orbach, Tammy Grimes, Wanda Richert, Lee Roy Reams, Joseph
Bova, Carole Cook
**Songs:** "Young and Healthy"; "Shadow Waltz"; "Go Into Your Dance"; "You're
Getting to Be a Habit With Me"; "Dames"; "We're in the Money"; "Lulla-
by of Broadway"; "About a Quarter to Nine"; "Shuffle Off to Buffalo";
"Forty-Second Street"
**New York run:** Winter Garden, August 25, 1980; 3,486 p.

Re-creating the classic 1933 backstage movie musical of the same name, *42nd
Street* followed its cliché-riddled model with a minimum of camp but with a maxi-
mum of high-powered, ingenious choreography devised by Gower Champion
(who died the day the musical opened on Broadway). Once again the simple-
minded saga relates the tale of stage-struck chorus girl Peggy Sawyer (Wanda
Richert) from Allentown, Pennsylvania, who gets her big chance when Dorothy
Brock (Tammy Grimes), the star of *Pretty Lady,* breaks her ankle during the
show's tryout, and Peggy goes on to triumph on "naughty, bawdy, gaudy, sporty
42nd Street." Among changes from the movie: the ending now indicated a possible romance between Peggy and the hard-driving director Julian Marsh (Jerry
Orbach) rather than juvenile lead Billy Lawlor (Lee Roy Reams), and nine more
Harry Warren songs (seven of which also written with Al Dubin) were added to the
four Warren-Dubin numbers that were retained.

The musical, which opened with a new top ticket price of $30, had two
Broadway antecedents. A sketch in the *Ziegfeld Follies of 1936* offered Fanny
Brice and Bob Hope in a takeoff on the film, which was also spoofed in the 1968
Off-Broadway hit *Dames at Sea.* During the run, the part of Dorothy was also
played by Millicent Martin, Elizabeth Allen, Anne Rogers, and Dolores Gray; Jul-
ian by Barry Nelson and Jamie Ross. The first touring company was originally
headed by Nelson and Miss Gray, the second by Jon Cypher and Miss Martin.
RCA OC/ TW.

**The Pirates of Penzance.** Kevin Kline, Rex Smith, and pirates. © Martha Swope.

# THE PIRATES OF PENZANCE

**Music:** Arthur Sullivan
**Lyrics & book:** William S. Gilbert
**Producer:** Joseph Papp for the New York Shakespeare Festival
**Director:** Wilford Leach
**Choreographer:** Graciela Daniele
**Cast:** Kevin Kline, Estelle Parsons, Linda Ronstadt, George Rose, Rex Smith, Tony Azito
**Songs:** "Oh, Better Far to Live and Die"; "Oh, Is There Not One Maiden Breast?"; "Poor Wandering One"; "I Am the Very Model of a Modern Major-General"; "When the Foeman Bares His Steel"; "When a Felon's Not Engaged in His Employment"; "With Cat-Like Tread"
**New York run:** Uris Theatre, January 8, 1981; 772 p.

When, on December 31, 1879, *The Pirates of Penzance* opened in New York at the 5th Avenue Theatre, it marked the only occasion that a Gilbert and Sullivan comic opera had its première in a city other than London. When, 101 years later, it opened in New York at the Uris Theatre, it marked the only occasion — so far — that a Gilbert and Sullivan comic opera had a commercial Broadway run. With its modern orchestrations, bravura performances, and slightly campy approach, this version had been acclaimed when it was presented the previous summer in Central Park, where it played 42 free performances as part of Joseph Papp's New York Shakespeare Festival. (When moved to Broadway, the only major cast change was Estelle Parsons for Patricia Routledge as Ruth.) The operetta's ardent arias and duets and sprightly patter songs are mated to a charmingly inane tale of poor Frederic (Rex Smith), who after accidentally being apprenticed to a pirate (Kevin Kline), falls in love with Mabel (Linda Ronstadt), one of the eight daughters of a very model of a modern Major- General (George Rose).

Among those who appeared in the Broadway production after the original cast were Treat Williams (Pirate King); Kaye Ballard (Ruth); Maureen McGovern, Kathryn Morath, and Pam Dawber (Mabel); George S. Irving (Major-General); and Robby Benson, Patrick Cassidy, and Peter Noone (Frederic). The road company was initially headed by Barry Bostwick, Jo Anne Worley, Pam Dawber, Clive Revill, and Andy Gibb. The original Broadway cast — except for the substitution of Angela Lansbury for Miss Parsons — appeared in the 1983 film version. Elektra OC/ MTI.

**Sophisticated Ladies.** The "Caravan" number led by Gregg Burge. (Kenn Duncan)

# SOPHISTICATED LADIES

**Music:** Duke Ellington
**Lyrics:** Miscellaneous writers
**Conception:** Donald McKayle
**Producers:** Roger Berlind, Manheim Fox, Sondra Gilman, Burton Litwin, Louise Westergaard
**Director:** Michael Smuin
**Choreographers:** Donald McKayle, Michael Smuin, Henry LeTang
**Cast:** Gregory Hines, Judith Jamison, Phyllis Hyman, P. J. Benjamin, Hinton Battle, Terri Klausner, Gregg Burge, Mercedes Ellington, Priscilla Baskerville
**Songs:** 36 from the Duke Ellington catalogue
**New York run:** Lunt-Fontanne Theatre, March 1, 1981; 767 p.

Though different in concept, *Sophisticated Ladies* followed the lead of *Ain't Misbehavin'* and *Eubie!* by being an entertainment built around the catalogue of a single composer. Here the celebration of the music of Duke Ellington was far more of an elaborate, brassy nightclub floor show than its predecessors, with a 21-piece on-stage orchestra (led by Ellington's son Mercer Ellington) and a castful of such highpowered steppers as Gregory Hines, Judith Jamison, Hinton Battle, and Gregg Burge. The show's Broadway success was totally unexpected. Its opening-night tryout in Washington had gone so badly that director Donald McKayle, who had conceived the production, was replaced by ballet choreographer Michael Smuin. Despite his inexperience in the world of Broadway, Smuin turned things around by adding nine songs, rearranging the sequence of the 36 numbers, introducing new dance routines, and dropping all existing dialogue.

During the Broadway run, Gregory Hines was succeeded by his brother, Maurice Hines, and P. J. Benjamin by Don Correia. The first of two road companies was headed by Harold Nicholas, Paula Kelly, and Freda Payne. RCA OC/ R&H.

# WOMAN OF THE YEAR

**Music:** John Kander
**Lyrics:** Fred Ebb
**Book:** Peter Stone
**Producers:** Lawrence Kasha, David Landay, James Nederlander, etc.
**Director:** Robert Moore
**Choreographer:** Tony Charmoli
**Cast:** Lauren Bacall, Harry Guardino, Roderick Cook, Marilyn Cooper, Eivind Harum, Grace Keagy, Rex Everhart, Jamie Ross
**Songs:** "Woman of the Year"; "One of the Boys"; "The Grass Is Always Greener"; "We're Gonna Work It Out"
**New York run:** Palace Theatre, March 29, 1981; 770 p.

Updating the 1942 movie, *Woman of the Year* told a battle-of-the-sexes story with Lauren Bacall as Tess Harding, a Barbara Walters-type television personality, and Harry Guardino as Sam Craig, a satirical cartoonish suggesting Garry Trudeau. Angered by some television comments made by Tess about "funnies," Sam retaliates by putting her in his strip as a character named "Tessie Cat." The two meet, explode, marry, continue to explode, and eventually decide to try to work things out. *Woman of the Year* had certain points of similarity with Miss Bacall's previous musical, *Applause.* Both shows were told in flashback, and both involved a strong-willed public personality trying to solve the problem of juggling a career and marriage. During the musical's run, Miss Bacall was succeeded by Raquel Welch, Debbie Reynolds, and Louise Troy.
Arista OC/ Samuel French (1984)*/ SF.


# JOSEPH AND THE AMAZING TECHNICOLOR DREAMCOAT

**Music:** Andrew Lloyd Webber
**Lyrics:** Tim Rice
**Producers:** Zev Bufman & Susan Rose
**Director-choreographer:** Tony Tanner
**Cast:** Bill Hutton, Laurie Beechman, David Ardeo, Tom Carder
**Songs:** "Joseph's Coat"; "One More Angel in Heaven"; "Go, Go, Go Joseph"; "Pharaoh's Story"; "Those Canaan Days"; "Benjamin Calypso"; "Any Dream Will Do"
**New York run:** Entermedia Theatre, November 18, 1981; 824 p.

*Joseph and the Amazing Technicolor Dreamcoat,* the first collaboration of Andrew Lloyd Webber and Tim Rice, lasted all of 15 minutes when it was initially presented in a London school in 1968. Five years later, by now expanded to 40 minutes, the work was offered on the West End and then expanded again to almost 90 minutes. In 1976, *Joseph* had its first New York showing at the Brooklyn Academy of Music. The 1981 production, which ran 77 performances in an East Village theatre, moved to the Royale on January 27, 1982, where it remained for 747 performances. Told entirely in song, this biblical cantata — actually an eclectic grabbag of rock, country, vaudeville song-and-dance, French ballad, and calypso — relates the Old Testament tale of Joseph (Bill Hutton), Jacob's favorite of 12 sons, to whom papa gives a resplendent coat of many colors. Joseph's jealous brothers thereupon sell him into slavery and he is taken to Egypt where he interprets the dream of an Elvis Presley-type Pharaoh (Tom Carder). His wise prophecy so impresses the Pharaoh that he becomes Egypt's Number Two man and saves the country from famine. During the Broadway run, Andy Gibb and David Cassidy were two of the four actors who succeeded Bill Hutton.
Chrysalis OC/ Holt, Rinehart (1982)/ MTI.

# DREAMGIRLS

**Music:** Henry Krieger
**Lyrics & book:** Tom Eyen
**Producers:** Michael Bennett, Bob Avian, Geffen Records
**Director:** Michael Bennett
**Choreographers:** Michael Bennett, Michael Peters
**Cast:** Obba Babatunde, Cleavant Derricks, Loretta Devine, Ben Harney, Jennifer Holliday, Sheryl Lee Ralph, Deborah Burrell
**Songs:** "Fake Your Way to the Top"; "Cadillac Car"; "Steppin' to the Bad Side"; "Dreamgirls"; "And I Am Telling You I'm Not Going"; "I Am Changing"; "When I First Saw You"; "Hard to Say Goodbye, My Love"
**New York run:** Imperial Theatre, December 20, 1981; 1,522 p.

With *Dreamgirls,* Michael Bennett returned to the heartbreak world of show business that he had explored in *A Chorus Line* to create another high-voltage concept musical. Tom Eyen's tough-tender book about the corruption of innocence was primarily based on the story of the Supremes. The success of the black vocal trio of the 1960s was maneuvered by Motown Records chief Berry Gordy at the price of dropping lead singer Florence Ballard in favor of Diana Ross because Ballard didn't present the right image (she drifted into obscurity and died at the age of 32). In the musical, it is Effie Melody White (Jennifer Holliday), the heavyset lead singer of a rhythm and blues trio (the other two: Sheryl Lee Ralph and Loretta Devine), who is sacrificed because a slick manager (Ben Harney) feels that the singers — whom he names the Dreams — must offer a more glamorous appearance to enable them to cross over to the more lucrative pop mainstream. Unlike Florence Ballard, however Effie surmounts a difficult period and goes on to win fame on her own.

To keep his glitzy, glittery show in constant fluid motion through some 20 scenes — beginning in 1962 on the stage of the Harlem Apollo and ending ten years later in Hollywood — Bennett was aided by set designer Robin Wagner, costume designer Theoni V. Aldredge, and lighting designer Tharon Musser (all of whom had worked on *A Chorus Line*). Also contributing to the production's close weave was Henry Krieger's Motown-influenced score with over 30 musical numbers used both for specialties and as dramatic dialogue. Impressive newcomer Jennifer Holliday repeated her role in the touring company. A new touring production of *Dreamgirls* returned to Broadway in 1987.
Geffen OC.

**Dreamgirls.** Loretta Devine, Jennifer Holliday, Sheryl Lee Ralph, and Cleavant Derricks. (Martha Swope)

# NINE

**Music & lyrics:** Maury Yeston
**Book:** Arthur Kopit, Mario Fratti
**Producers:** Michel Stuart, Harvey Klaris, Roger Berlind, etc.
**Director:** Tommy Tune
**Choreographers:** Tommy Tune, Thommie Walsh
**Cast:** Raul Julia, Karen Akers, Shelly Burch, Taina Elg, Lilianne Montevecchi, Anita Morris, Kathi Moss
**Songs:** "My Husband Makes Movies"; "A Call from the Vatican"; "Only With You"; "Folies Bergères"; "Nine"; "Be Italian"; "Unusual Way"; "The Grand Canal"; "Simple"; "Be on Your Own"
**New York run:** 46th Street Theatre, May 9, 1982; 732 p.

The influence of the director-choreographer was emphasized again with Tommy Tune's highly stylized, visually striking production of *Nine.* The musical evolved from composer-lyricist Maury Yeston's fascination with Federico Fellini's semi-autobiographical 1963 film *8½,* and — appropriately — it took nine years for it to make it to Broadway. During the show's creation, disagreements arose over the libretto by Mario Fratti, prompting his replacement by Arthur Kopit, and Tune's decision to have a cast of 21 women and only one adult male. The story spotlights Guido Contini (Raul Julia), a celebrated but tormented director who has come to a Venetian spa for a rest, and his relationships with his wife (Karen Akers), his mistress (Anita Morris), his protégé (Shelly Burch), his producer (Lilianne Montevecchi), and his mother (Taina Elg). The production, which flashes back to Guido's youth and also takes place in his imagination, offers such inventive touches as an "overture" in which Guido conducts his women as if they were instruments, and an impressionistic version of the Folies Bergères. During the Broadway run, Julia was succeeded by Bert Convy and Sergio Franchi. CBS OC/ Doubleday (1983)/ SF.

# LITTLE SHOP OF HORRORS

**Music:** Alan Menken
**Lyrics & book:** Howard Ashman
**Producers:** WPA Theatre, David Geffen, Cameron Mackintosh
**Director:** Howard Ashman
**Choreographer:** Edie Cowan
**Cast:** Ellen Greene, Lee Wilkof, Hy Anzell, Franc Luz, Leilani Jones
**Songs:** "Little Shop of Horrors"; "Skid Row"; "Grow for Me"; "Somewhere That's Green"; "Suddenly Seymour"
**New York run:** Orpheum Theatre, July 27, 1982; 2,209 p.

A campy musical about a man-eating Venus's-flytrap with all the principals dead by the end of the show would seem far riskier than the usual theatrical enterprise, but *Little Shop of Horrors* won over a majority of the critics to its offbeat humor, and remained for over 2,000 performances at its Lower East Side theatre. Based on the low-budget 1960 Roger Corman movie, the musical is set in a flower shop inconveniently located on Skid Row where meek Seymour Krelbourn (Lee Wilkof) breeds a tiny plant that he names Audrey II out of love for salesgirl Audrey (Ellen Greene). Since the mysterious plant needs blood to live, Seymour, in a Faustian pact, agrees to feed it in return for a guarantee that it will attract publicity to make him rich and famous. Soon this unlikely Sweeney Todd has found a way to do in anyone he wants, and when last seen the monstrous mutant is about to devour the audience. A film version was released in 1986. Geffen OC/ Doubleday (1982)/ SF.

# CATS

**Music:** Andrew Lloyd Webber
**Lyrics:** Based on T.S. Eliot
**Producers:** Cameron Mackintosh, Really Useful Co., Ltd., David Geffen
**Directors:** Trevor Nunn, Gillian Lynne
**Choreographer:** Gillian Lynne
**Cast:** Betty Buckley, Rene Clemente, Harry Groener, Stephen Hanan, Reed Jones, Christine Langner, Terrence V. Mann, Anna McNeely, Ken Page, Timothy Scott
**Songs:** "Jellicle Songs for Jellicle Cats"; "The Old Gumbie Cat"; "The Rum Tum Tugger"; "Old Deuteronomy"; "The Jellicle Ball"; "Grizabella"; "Macavity"; "Mr. Mistoffelees"; "Memory"
**New York run:** Winter Garden, October 7, 1982; (still running 11/1/89)

At this writing, *Cats* is still running in London (where it opened May 11, 1981) and in New York. Charged with incredible energy, flare, and imagination, the feline fantasy has been staged in its Broadway version as even more of an environmental experience than it was in its West End original. With the entire Winter Garden auditorium transformed into an enormous junkyard, a theatregoer is confronted by such sights as outsized garbagy objects spilling into the audience, a stage area without a proscenium arch, and a ceiling that has been lowered and turned into a twinkling canopy suggesting both cats' eyes and stars.

Composer Andrew Lloyd Webber began setting music to T.S. Eliot's poems in *Old Possum's Book of Practical Cats* in 1977. Later, he arranged the music for concerts, and still later — now in collaboration with director Trevor Nunn — he reworked the concept into a dramatic structure. In the song-and-dance spectacle, which has only the barest thread of a story line and no spoken dialogue, are such whimsically named characters as Jennyanydots (Anna McNeely), the Old Gumbie Cat who sits all day and becomes active only at night; the never satisfied Rum Tum Tugger (Terrence V. Mann); Bustopher Jones (Stephen Hanan), the well-fed, elegant cat about town; Mungojerrie and Rumpleteazer (Rene Clemente and Christine Langner), those two knockabout clowns and cat burglars; the patriarchal Old Deuteronomy (Ken Page); Skimpleshanks the Railway Cat (Reed Jones); and the mysterious Mr. Mistoffelees (Timothy Scott). The musical's song hit, "Memory," is sung by Grizabella (Betty Buckley), the faded Glamour Cat who, at the evening's end, ascends to the cats' heaven known as the Heaviside Layer. During the Broadway run (which saw ticket prices ascend from $40 to $55), Miss Buckley was succeeded by Laurie Beechman and Loni Ackerman. The first of three touring companies began traveling in December 1983.
Geffen OC/ Faber & Faber, London (1981).

**Cats.** "The Jellicle Ball" number. (Martha Swope)

# ON YOUR TOES

**Music:** Richard Rodgers
**Lyrics:** Lorenz Hart
**Book:** Richard Rodgers, Lorenz Hart & George Abbott
**Producers:** Alfred de Liagre Jr., Roger L. Stevens, John Mauceri, Donald Seawell, Andre Pastoria
**Director:** George Abbott
**Choreographers:** George Balanchine, Donald Saddler, Peter Martins
**Cast:** Natalia Makarova, George S. Irving, Dina Merrill, George de la Peña, Christine Andreas, Lara Teeter, Betty Ann Grove, Peter Slutsker, Michael Vita
**Songs:** Same as original production
**New York run:** Virginia Theatre, March 6, 1983; 505 p.

(See page 94.)

# MY ONE AND ONLY

**Music:** George Gershwin
**Lyrics:** Ira Gershwin
**Book:** Peter Stone, Timothy S. Meyer
**Producers:** Paramount Theatres (Dan Sherkow), Lester Allen, Francine LeFrak, Kenneth Greenblatt, Mark Schwartz
**Director-choreographers:**Thommie Walsh & Tommy Tune (Mike Nichols, Michael Bennett uncredited)
**Cast:** Twiggy, Tommy Tune, Charles "Honi" Coles, Bruce McGill, Denny Dillon, Roscoe Lee Browne
**Songs:** "I Can't Be Bothered Now"; "Blah, Blah, Blah"; "Boy Wanted"; "Soon"; "High Hat"; "Sweet and Low-Down"; "He Loves and She Loves"; " 'S Wonderful"; "Strike Up the Band"; "Nice Work If You Can Get It"; "My One and Only"; "Funny Face"; "Kickin' the Clouds Away" (lyric with B.G. DeSylva); "How Long Has This Been Going On?"
**New York run:** St. James Theatre, May 1, 1983; 767 p.

Within a week after the Broadway première of *Nine,* which he had directed, Tommy Tune was in rehearsal with Twiggy for what was originally announced as a revival of the Gershwins' 1927 musical *Funny Face.* By the time the show opened in New York, however, it had a completely new story, at least four directors, a score with only six of the original 12 songs (augmented by 11 other Gershwin standards), and it was now called *My One and Only.* Initially, the director and librettist were to have been Peter Sellars and Timothy Meyer, but after disagreements Sellars was replaced first by Mike Nichols then by Tune and Thommie Walsh, and Meyer by Peter Stone. The resulting book, still set in 1927, was an often anachronistic framework for the imaginatively staged song-and-dance numbers which found Tune playing a barnstorming aviator and Twiggy a champion swimmer who incongruously get involved with a bootlegging Harlem minister (Roscoe Lee Browne), an enigmatical tap-dancing philosopher (Charles "Honi" Coles), and a blackmailing Russian spy (Bruce McGill). Twiggy and Tune were succeeded on Broadway by Sandy Duncan and Don Correia. For the tour, Tune was co-starred with Miss Duncan.
Atlantic OC.

**On Your Toes.** George de la Peña and Natalia Makarova in the "Princess Zenobia" ballet. (Martha Swope)

**My One and Only.** Tommy Tune and Charles "Honi" Coles dancing to the title song. (Kenn Duncan)

# LA CAGE AUX FOLLES

**Music & lyrics:** Jerry Herman
**Book:** Harvey Fierstein
**Producer:** Allan Carr
**Director:** Arthur Laurents
**Choreographer:** Scott Salmon
**Cast:** George Hearn, Gene Barry, Jay Garner, John Weiner, Elizabeth Parrish, Leslie Stevens, William Thomas Jr., Merle Louise
**Songs:** "A Little More Mascara"; "With You on My Arm"; "Song on the Sand"; "La Cage aux Folles"; "I Am What I Am"; "Masculinity"; "The Best of Times"
**New York run:** Palace Theatre, August 21, 1983; 1,176 p.

French author Jean Poiret's successful play and film about the relationship between the owner of a St. Tropez drag-queen nightclub and his star attraction provided Broadway with its first homosexual musical. In the story, the flamboyant Albin (George Hearn) — known on the stage as Zaza — and the more conservative Georges (Gene Barry) are middle-aged lovers who have been together for over 20 years. Their domestic peace is shattered, however, when Jean-Michel (John Weiner), Georges' son as a result of a youthful indiscretion, advises his father that he plans to wed the daughter of Edouard Dindon (Jay Garner), a local morals crusader. In order that Georges appear to his future in-laws as an upstanding citizen, he agrees that Albin must somehow be put back into the closet. Though hurt and defiant ("I Am What I Am"), Albin swallows his pride and aids the deception by dressing up as Georges' wife. After inadvertently revealing that he is what he is, Albin is not above a little blackmail to force Dindon to permit the marriage to take place.

Except for the homosexual angle, *La Cage aux Folles* (the name of Georges' nightclub) was in the tradition of the big, splashy Broadway book musical, complete with a glamorous chorus line (which even has two female dancers among the Cagelles). And though it was originally to have been put together by a different team of collaborators (when it was known as *The Queen of Basin Street*), the musical was a predestined smash by the time of its Boston tryout. The show marked Jerry Herman's tenth score (as well as his first hit since *Mame*) and playwright Harvey Fierstein's first experience as a librettist. George Hearn, who scored a notable hit as Albin, was succeeded by Walter Charles and Keene Curtis; Gene Barry was followed by Jamie Ross, Keith Michell, Van Johnson, Steeve Arlen, and Peter Marshall. The show's two road companies were headed by, respectively, Michell (replaced by Barry) and Charles, and by Marshall and Curtis. *La Cage aux Folles* was the first musical to charge $47.50 for orchestra seats.

Male actors appearing in drag have long been part of the Broadway musical scene. In the late 19th Century, Tony Hart made a specialty of performing women's roles in Harrigan and Hart shows, and other early female impersonators were Julian Eltinge (the most celebrated of all) and Bert Savoy (of the team of Savoy and Brennan). Later actors who donned feminine attire — usually as a transvestite sight gag — included Ole Olsen in *Hellzapoppin,* Bobby Clark in *Mexican Hayride, Sweethearts,* and *As the Girls Go,* Ray Bolger in *Where's Charley?,* Myron McCormick in *South Pacific,* Bert Lahr (as Queen Victoria) in *Two on the Aisle,* Jack Gilford in *A Funny Thing Happened on the Way to the Forum,* Robert Morse and Tony Roberts in *Sugar,* Mickey Rooney in *Sugar Babies,* and James Coco in the revival of *Little Me.* Actual homosexual — or at least effeminate — characters have been portrayed by Bobbie Watson in *Irene,* Danny Kaye in *Lady in the Dark,* Ray Bolger in *By Jupiter,* Joel Grey in *Cabaret,* Rene Auberjonois in *Coco,* Lee Roy Reams in *Applause,* Tommy Tune in *Seesaw,* and Michel Stuart and Sammy Williams in *A Chorus Line.*
RCA OC/ Samuel French (1987)*/ SF.

**La Cage aux Folles.** Les Cagelles. (Martha Swope)

**La Cage aux Folles.** The "Masculinity" number with Gene Barry and George Hearn. (Martha Swope)

**Zorba.** Anthony Quinn in the title role. (Martha Swope)

# ZORBA

**Music:** John Kander
**Lyrics:** Fred Ebb
**Book:** Joseph Stein
**Producers:** Barry & Fran Weissler, Kenneth Greenblatt & John Pomerantz
**Director:** Michael Cacoyannis
**Choreographer:** Graciela Daniele
**Cast:** Anthony Quinn, Lila Kedrova, Robert Westenberg, Debbie Shapiro
**Songs:** Same as original production, plus "Mine Song" and "Woman"
**New York run:** Broadway Theatre, October 16, 1983; 362 p.

(See page 225.)

# THE TAP DANCE KID

**Music:** Henry Krieger
**Lyrics:** Robert Lorick
**Book:** Charles Blackwell
**Producers:** Stanley White, Evelyn Barron, Harvey Klaris, Michel Stuart
**Director:** Vivian Matalon
**Choreographer:** Danny Daniels
**Cast:** Hinton Battle, Samuel E. Wright, Hattie Winston, Alfonso Ribeiro, Alan Weeks, Martine Allard, Jackie Lowe
**Songs:** "Dancing Is Everything"; "Fabulous Feet"; "Class Act"; "I Remember How It Was"; "Dance If It Makes You Happy"
**New York run:** Broadhurst Theatre, December 21, 1983; 669 p.

The methods by which ambitious young blacks have been able to box or sing their way out of the ghetto have been documented in such musicals as *Golden Boy* and *Dreamgirls,* but *The Tap Dance Kid* offered the unaccustomed situation of an upper middle-class family in which a successful lawyer (Samuel E. Wright) tries to stifle the dreams of his ten-year-old son Willie (Alfonso Ribeiro) to follow the profession of his Uncle Dipsey (Hinton Battle) and become a dancer. Featuring Battle's exciting footwork, the show surmounted a divided press to chalk up a surprisingly long Broadway run. The musical's origin was a television play (in which librettist Charles Blackwell played the father) that had been based on a novel, *Nobody's Family Is Going to Change,* by Louise Fitzhugh.
Polydor OC/ Samuel French (1988)*/ SF.

# SUNDAY IN THE PARK WITH GEORGE

**Music & lyrics:** Stephen Sondheim
**Book:** James Lapine
**Producers:** Shubert Organization & Emanuel Azenberg
**Director:** James Lapine
**Cast:** Mandy Patinkin, Bernadette Peters, Charles Kimbrough, Barbara Bryne, Dana Ivey, William Parry, Robert Westenberg
**Songs:** "Sunday in the Park With George"; "Finishing the Hat"; "We Do Not Belong Together"; "Beautiful"; "Sunday"; "Children and Art"; "Move On"
**New York run:** Booth Theatre, May 2, 1984; 604 p.

After six productions in a row with director Harold Prince, Stephen Sondheim joined with director-librettist James Lapine for an especially challenging and personal work. *Sunday in the Park With George* reveals what the authors feel about art, the creative process, the artist's sacrifice of human emotions, and the need to avoid being influenced by what is currently trendy and faddish. To express these feelings, Sondheim and Lapine concentrated on the creation of one painting, Georges Seurat's "A Sunday Afternoon on the Island of La Grande Jatte."

In the first act, which takes place on the island in 1884, George (Mandy Patinkin) is busily painting the Parisians who are enjoying a day off strolling through a park on the Seine. We get to know the people and their relationships with one another, and in particular we get to know George and his relationship with Dot (Bernadette Peters), his model and mistress. The artist's preoccupation with his work, however, makes theirs a doomed romance, and the model, who is pregnant, accepts a baker's offer of marriage. The second act jumps to the present in New York, where the painter's great-grandson, a multi-media sculptor also named George, is at a creative impasse after completing his seventh "Chromolume." His confidence is restored, however, when he visits La Grande Jatte and is urged by the ghost of his great-grandmother to stop worrying about where he is going and what others think and "just keep moving on."

*Sunday in the Park With George,* which was first staged as a Playwrights Horizons workshop production in July 1983, was awarded the 1985 Pulitzer Prize for drama. During its run, Patinkin was spelled by Robert Westenberg and Harry Groener, and Miss Peters was succeeded by Betsy Joslyn and Maryann Plunkett.
RCA OC/ Dodd, Mead (1986).

**Sunday in the Park With George.** Mandy Patinkin and Bernadette Peters. (Martha Swope)

# BIG RIVER

**Music & lyrics:** Roger Miller
**Book:** William Hauptman
**Producers:** Rocco Landesman, Heidi Landesman, Rick Steiner, M. Anthony Fisher, Dodger Productions
**Director:** Des McAnuff
**Choreographer:** Janet Watson
**Cast:** Rene Auberjonois, Reathal Bean, Susan Browning, Patti Cohenour, Gordon Connell, Bob Gunton, Daniel H. Jenkins, Ron Richardson
**Songs:** "Guv'ment"; "Muddy Water"; "River in the Rain"; "Waiting for the Light to Shine"; "Worlds Apart"; "You Ought to Be Here With Me"; "Leaving's Not the Only Way to Go"
**New York run:** Eugene O'Neill Theatre, April 25, 1985; 1,005 p.

Producers Rocco and Heidi Landesman came up with the idea of a musical version of Mark Twain's *Adventures of Huckleberry Finn* primarily because they were anxious to find the right property that would best introduce Broadway to the talents of country music songwriter Roger Miller. *Big River* was tried out at the American Repertory Theatre (ART) in Cambridge, Massachusetts, early in 1984, and then at the La Jolla Playhouse in California before those connected with the show felt that it was ready for New York. Set in 1849, with the action taking place both on the Mississippi River and in various locations along its banks (thanks to Heidi Landesman's atmospheric settings), the imaginative and faithfully conceived adaptation of the picaresque novel is concerned primarily with the relationship between Huck Finn and the runaway slave Jim (Daniel H. Jenkins and Ron Richardson) as they enjoy the untethered life traveling on a raft down the Mississippi from Hannibal, Missouri, to Hillsboro, Arkansas. In 1957, a previous musical based on Mark Twain's Mississippi River stories was offered Off Broadway under the title *Livin' the Life.*
MCA OC/ Grove Press (1986)/ R&H.

**Big River.** Ron Richardson and Daniel H. Jenkins. (Martha Swope)

# SONG AND DANCE

**Music:** Andrew Lloyd Webber
**Lyrics:** Don Black, Richard Maltby Jr.
**Adaptation:** Richard Maltby Jr.
**Producers:** Cameron Mackintosh, Shubert Organization, FWM Producing Group
**Director:** Richard Maltby Jr.
**Choreographer:** Peter Martins
**Cast:** Bernadette Peters, Christopher d'Amboise, Gregg Burge, Charlotte d'Amboise, Cynthia Onrubia, Scott Wise
**Songs:** "Capped Teeth and Caesar Salad"; "So Much to Do in New York"; "Unexpected Song"; "Come Back With the Same Look in Your Eyes"; "Tell Me on a Sunday"
**New York run:** Royale Theatre, September 18, 1985; 474 p.

The "Dance" of the title originated in 1979 when Andrew Lloyd Webber composed a set of variations on Paganini's A-Minor Caprice that seemed perfect for a ballet; the "Song" originated a year later with a one-woman television show, *Tell Me on a Sunday,* consisting entirely of musical pieces. Two years after that both works were presented together in London as a full evening's entertainment. In New York, this unconventional package won praise for Bernadette Peters, whose task in Act I was to create, without dialogue, the character of a free-spirited English girl who has dalliances in America with four men. The second act offered a choreographic self-examination of one of the men (Christopher d'Amboise) and the two halves were joined when girl and boy were reunited. After a year on Broadway, Miss Peters was succeeded by Betty Buckley. RCA OC/ R&H.

# THE MYSTERY OF EDWIN DROOD

**Music, lyrics & book:** Rupert Holmes
**Producer:** Joseph Papp for the New York Shakespeare Festival
**Director:** Wilford Leach
**Choreographer:** Graciela Daniele
**Cast:** George Rose, Cleo Laine, Betty Buckley, Howard McGillin, Patti Cohenour, Jana Schneider, John Herrera, Jerome Dempsey
**Songs:** "Moonfall"; "The Wages Of Sin"; "No Good Can Come from Bad"; "Ceylon"; "Perfect Strangers"; "Both Sides of the Coin"; "Off to the Races"; "Don't Quit While You're Ahead"
**New York run:** Imperial Theatre, December 2, 1985; 608 p.

The *Mystery of Edwin Drood* came to Broadway after being initially presented the previous summer in a series of free performances sponsored by the New York Shakespeare Festival at the Delacorte Theatre in Central Park. It was the first stage work of composer-lyricist-librettist Rupert Holmes, whose lifelong fascination with Charles Dickens' unfinished novel had been the catalyst for the project. Since there were no clues as to Drood's murderer or even if a murder had been committed, Holmes decided to let the audience provide the show's ending by voting how it turns out. The writer's second major decision was to offer the musical as if it were being performed by an acting company at London's Music Hall Royale in 1873, complete with such conventions as a Chairman (George Rose) to comment on the action and a woman (Betty Buckley) to play the part of Edwin Drood. During the run, Miss Buckley was replaced by Donna Murphy, and Cleo Laine (as the mysterious Princess Puffer) by Loretta Swit and Karen Morrow. On November 13, 1986, in an attempt to attract more theatre-goers, the musical's title was officially changed to *Drood.* Polydor OC/ Doubleday (1986)/ TW.

# SWEET CHARITY

**Music:** Cy Coleman
**Lyrics:** Dorothy Fields
**Book:** Neil Simon
**Producers:** Jerome Minskoff, James Nederlander, Arthur Rubin, Joseph Harris
**Director-choreographer:** Bob Fosse
**Cast:**   Debbie Allen, Michael Rupert, Bebe Neuwirth, Allison Williams, Lee
          Wilkof, Mark Jacoby, Irving Allen Lee
**Songs:** Same as original production
**New York run:** Minskoff Theatre, April 27, 1986; 368 p.

(See page 216.)

**Me and My Girl.** Robert Lindsay and Maryann Plunkett dancing to the title song.
(Alan Berliner)

# ME AND MY GIRL

**Music:** Noel Gay
**Lyrics:** Douglas Furber, etc.
**Book:** L. Arthur Rose & Douglas Furber; revised by Stephen Fry
**Producers:** Richard Armitage, Terry Allen Kramer, James Nederlander, Stage Promotions Ltd.
**Director:** Mike Ockrent
**Choreographer:** Gillian Gregory
**Cast:** Robert Lindsay, Maryann Plunkett, George S. Irving, Jane Connell, Jane Summerhays, Nick Ullett, Timothy Jerome, Thomas Toner, Justine Johnston, Elizabeth Larner
**Songs:** "Thinking of No-One But Me"; "The Family Solicitor"; "Me and My Girl"; "Hold My Hand" (music with Maurice Elwin; lyric: Harry Graham); "Once You Lose Your Heart" (lyric: Noel Gay); "The Lambeth Walk"; "The Sun Has Got His Hat On" (lyric: Frank Butler); "Take It on the Chin"; "Love Makes the World Go Round" (lyric: Gay); "Leaning on a Lamppost" (lyric: Gay)
**New York run:** Marquis Theatre, August 10, 1986; (still running 11/1/89)

One of the most unlikely Broadway hits of 1986 was an almost fifty-year-old London musical comedy that, despite its near record-breaking run of 1,646 performances, had always been deemed too "English" to be considered for a New York showing before. Yet, followed by a successful West End reincarnation in 1985, *Me and My Girl* became an instant smash upon being offered as the premiere attraction at the newly built Marquis Theatre (located in the Marriott Marquis Hotel on Broadway between 45th and 46th Streets). Part of the reason had to do with the imaginative staging, Noel Gay's simple, catchy melodies, and the show's general spirit of eager-to-please innocent merriment. But most of the show's popularity surely was due to the protean talents of Robert Lindsay, the original star of the London revival who made his Broadway debut in the musical. (Lindsay was subsequently succeeded by Jim Dale and James Brennan.) The road company, which began touring in 1987, was initially headed by Tim Curry.

It was producer Richard Armitage, the son of the composer (Gay's real name was Reginald Armitage), who first saw the potential in bringing back *Me and My Girl*. The younger Armitage devoted years to tracking down the original score and script, then signed playwright Stephen Fry to do the text revisions with an assist from director Mike Ockrent. The book was still about a pugnacious Cockney, Bill Snibson (Lindsay), who turns up as the long-lost heir to the Earldom of Hareford. Complications arise over Bill's devotion to his Lambeth sweetie, Sally Smith (Maryann Plunkett), and the efforts of the Hareford clan (led by George S. Irving and Jane Connell) to send her back where she belongs. But the bluebloods —who even join in the high-strutting, thumb-cocking dance known as "The Lambeth Walk"—eventually give their consent and Bill ends up with both his inheritance and his girl (who has been miraculously transformed, *Pygmalion* fashion, into an elegant lady).

The character of Bill Snibson was originated in 1935 by the diminutive clown Lupino Lane in *Twenty to One,* a race-track yarn in which Bill tilts with the stuffy killjoys of the Anti-Gambling League. Lane became so attached to the part that two years later he had the show's librettists fashion a new musical for him about Bill's tilting with the stuffy members of the aristocracy. *Me and My Girl* was such a personal triumph that Lane toured in it extensively and brought it back to London in 1941, 1945, and 1949.

MCA OC/ Samuel French, London (1954)*/ SF.

**Les Misérables.** Colm Wilkinson, Michael Maguire and David Bryant manning the barricade. (Michael Le Poer Trench/Bob Marshak)

# ANYTHING GOES

**Music & lyrics:** Cole Porter
**Book:** Timothy Crouse & John Weidman based on original by P. G. Wodehouse & Guy Bolton, Howard Lindsay & Russel Crouse
**Producer:** Lincoln Center Theatre (Gregory Mosher, Bernard Gersten)
**Director:** Jerry Zaks
**Choreographer:** Michael Smuin
**Cast:** Patti LuPone, Howard McGillin, Bill McCutcheon, Rex Everhart, Anne Francine, Linda Hart, Anthony Heald, Kathleen Mahony-Bennett
**Songs:** Same as original production plus "No Cure Like Travel"; "Easy to Love"; "I Want to Row on the Crew"; "Friendship"; "It's De-Lovely"; "Goodbye, Little Dream, Goodbye"
**New York run:** Vivian Beaumont Theatre, October 13, 1987; 804 p.

(See page 88.)


# INTO THE WOODS

**Music & lyrics:** Stephen Sondheim
**Book:** James Lapine
**Producers:** Heidi Landesman, Rocco Landesman, Rick Steiner, M. Anthony Fisher, Frederic Mayerson, Jujamcyn Theatres
**Director:** James Lapine
**Cast:** Bernadette Peters, Joanna Gleason, Chip Zien, Tom Aldredge, Robert Westenberg, Barbara Bryne, Kim Crosby, Danielle Ferland, Merle Louise, Ben Wright, Joy Franz, Edmund Lyndeck, Kay McClelland, Lauren Mitchell
**Songs:** "Into the Woods"; "Hello, Little Girl"; "I Know Things Now"; "Giants in the Sky"; "Agony"; "It Takes Two"; "Stay With Me"; "Any Moment"; "Last Midnight"; "No More"; "No One Is Alone"; "Children Will Listen"
**New York run:** Martin Beck Theatre, November 5, 1987; 764 p.

First tried out at the Old Globe Theatre in San Diego in December 1986, *Into the Woods* took a look at the darker—or grimmer—side of fairy tales in dealing with the themes of communal responsibility, the importance of showing consideration to others, and the values we pass on to our children. The story brings together such familiar characters as Cinderella and her Prince, Jack the Giant Killer, Little Red Ridinghood and the Wolf, Rapunzel, Snow White, and Sleeping Beauty, plus two original characters, a Baker and his wife, and puts them in a plotty tale that gets somewhat burdened down by the allegorical references. This was Stephen Sondheim's second musical with librettist-director James Lapine, the first being *Sunday in the Park With George.* It also involved the same costar (Bernadette Peters), set designer (Tony Straiges), costume designer (Patricia Zipprodt), lighting designer (Richard Nelson), and music director (Paul Gemignani). During the run, Miss Peters was followed by Phylicia Rashad, Betsy Joslyn, Nancy Dussault, and Ellen Foley. In the summer of 1988, Dick Cavett took over the part of the Narrator for two months. The road company, which toured for 10 months, was headed by Cleo Laine (Witch), Mary Gordon Murray (Cinderella), and Charlotte Rae (Jack's Mother).
RCA OC/ Theatre Comm. Group (1987)/ TW.

# THE PHANTOM OF THE OPERA

**Music:** Andrew Lloyd Webber
**Lyrics:** Charles Hart, Richard Stilgoe
**Book:** Richard Stilgoe & Andrew Lloyd Webber
**Producer:** Cameron Mackintosh & The Really Useful Theatre Co.
**Director:** Harold Prince
**Choreographer:** Gillian Lynne
**Cast:** Michael Crawford, Sarah Brightman, Steve Barton, Judy Kaye, Cris Groenendaal, Nicholas Wyman, Leila Martin, David Romano, Elisa Heinsohn, George Lee Andrews
**Songs:** "Think of Me"; "Angel of Music"; "The Phantom of the Opera"; "The Music of the Night"; "Prima Donna"; "All I Ask of You"; "Masquerade"; "Wishing You Were Somehow Here Again"; "The Point of No Return
**New York run:** Majestic Theatre, January 26, 1988; (still running 11/1/89)

Turn-of-the-century French novelist Gaston Leroux wrote *Le Fantôme de l'Opéra* after visiting the subterranean depths of the Paris Opera House—including its man-made lake. Though not a success when published in 1911, the ghoulish tale of the mad, disfigured Phantom who lives in the bowels of the theatre and does away with those who would thwart the operatic career of his beloved Christine, became internationally celebrated in 1925 when it served as a movie vehicle for Lon Chaney. (Subsequent film versions were made in 1943 with Claude Rains, in 1962 with Herbert Lom, in 1989 with Robert Englund, and—for television—in 1982 with Maximilian Schell.)

In 1984 a stage adaptation, using excerpts from public-domain operas by Verdi, Gounod, and Offenbach, was written and directed by Ken Hill and produced by Joan Littlewood at an East London fringe theatre. Andrew Lloyd Webber thought it might be developed into a campy West End musical—something along the lines of *The Rocky Horror Show*—that he would co-produce with Cameron Mackintosh. After reading the Leroux novel, however, Lloyd Webber realized that far from being a penny dreadful, Leroux's work was a genuinely romantic and moving tale, and he decided to write the score himself. His lyricist and co-adapter was Richard Stilgoe and his director was Harold Prince. After a tryout of the first act at a summer festival at his home in Sydmonton (with Colm Wilkinson as the Phantom and Lloyd Webber's wife Sarah Brightman as Christine), the composer felt that there was need for a more romantic approach in the lyrics and, after first trying to enlist Alan Jay Lerner and then Tim Rice, he settled on the relatively inexperienced Charles Hart to augment Stilgoe's work.

*The Phantom of the Opera* opened in London in 1986 with Michael Crawford and Miss Brightman. It won a resoundingly affirmative reception for its cast, staging, and scenic effects, including a chandelier that descends from the auditorium ceiling and crashes on stage. At this writing, the musical is still running at Her Majesty's Theatre. Basically the same production was transferred to Broadway, with Crawford, Miss Brightman, and Steve Barton (as The Phantom's romantic rival) repeating their roles. A presold hit with an $18 million advance, the show made Andrew Lloyd Webber the first composer to have three musicals running simultaneously in London and New York. (The other two: *Cats,* and *Starlight Express.)*

So far during the Broadway run, Crawford has been succeeded by Timothy Nolen and Cris Groenendaal; Miss Brightman by Patti Cohenour and Rebecca Luker; Barton by Kevin Gray; and Judy Kaye by Marilyn Caskey. Two road companies opened in 1989: the first, in Los Angeles, had a cast headed by Crawford, Dale Kristien, Reece Holland, and Leigh Munro; the second, in Toronto, featured Colm Wilkinson, Rebecca Caine, Byron Nease, and Lyse Guerin. Polydor OC/ Henry Holt (1987).

**The Phantom of the Opera.** Michael Crawford and Sarah Brightman. (Clive Barda)

# JEROME ROBBINS' BROADWAY

**Music & lyrics:** Miscellaneous writers
**Producers:** The Shubert Organization, Roger Berlind, Suntory Intl. Corp., Byron Goldman, Emanuel Azenberg
**Director-choreographer:** Jerome Robbins
**Cast:** Jason Alexander, Charlotte d'Amboise, Susann Fletcher, Susan Kikuchi, Michael Kubala, Robert LaFosse, Jane Lanier, Joey McKneely, Luis Perez, Faith Prince, Debbie Shapiro, Scott Wise
**Songs:** "New York, New York" (Leonard Bernstein-Betty Comden, Adolph Green); "Charleston" (Morton Gould); "Comedy Tonight" (Stephen Sondheim); "West Side Story" dances (Bernstein); "The Small House of Uncle Thomas" (Richard Rodgers-Oscar Hammerstein II); "You Gotta Have a Gimmick" (Styne-Sondheim); "I'm Flying" (Mark Charlap-Carolyn Leigh); "On a Sunday by the Sea" ballet (Styne); "Mr. Monotony" (Irving Berlin); "Fiddler on the Roof" scenes (Jerry Bock-Sheldon Harnick)
**New York run:** Imperial Theatre, February 26, 1989; (still running 11/1/89)

The stage equivalent of MGM's *That's Entertainment* series, *Jerome Robbins' Broadway* is a sampling of highlights from Robbins' 21-year career—from *On the Town* in 1944 to *Fiddler on the Roof* in 1964. Featured in this well-organized *déjà vu* revue (which cost $8.8 million and utilizes a cast of 62) are sequences from nine of the 15 productions for which Robbins' served as choreographer or director-choreographer, plus one number, "Comedy Tonight" from *A Funny Thing Happened on the Way to the Forum,* which he had been called in to stage during the show's tryout and for which he received no program credit. Another piece, Irving Berlin's "Mr. Monotony," makes its Broadway debut in this production since it had been cut out of both *Miss Liberty* and *Call Me Madam.* The show established a new top ticket price of $55, subsequenlty raised to $60. So far during the run, Jason Alexander has been succeeded by Terrence Mann, and Debbie Shapiro by Karen Mason.
RCA OC.

# Indexes

# Show Index

# Composer/Lyricist Index

**Henderson, Ray**
Flying High, 71
Follow Thru, 67
George White's Scandals, 52 & 76
Good News!, 56
Hold Everything!, 65

**Heneker, David**
Half a Sixpence, 211
Irma la Douce, 190

**Herbert, Victor**
Babes in Toyland, 8
Fortune Teller, The, 6
Mlle. Modiste, 10
Naughty Marietta, 17
Red Mill, The, 13 & 128
Sweethearts, 19 & 134

**Herman, Jerry**
Hello, Dolly!, 204
La Cage aux Folles, 266
Mame, 217
Milk and Honey, 195

**Hester, Hal**
Your Own Thing, 222

**Heyward, DuBose**
Porgy and Bess, 91 & 156

**Hirsch, Louis A.**
Ziegfeld Follies, 20 & 38

**Holmes, Rupert**
Mystery of Edwin Drood, The, 271

**Hooker, Brian**
Vagabond King, The, 48

**Horwitt, Arnold B.**
Make Mine Manhattan, 137
Plain and Fancy, 166

**Hoschna, Karl**
Madame Sherry, 17

**Hoyt, Charles H.**
Trip to Chinatown, A, 5

**Hughes, Langston**
Street Scene, 132

**Jacobs, Jim**
Grease, 234

**James, Paul**
Fine and Dandy, 72

**Jones, Stephen**
Poppy, 40

**Jones, Tom**
Fantasticks, The, 189
I Do! I Do!, 220
110 in the Shade, 203

**Kahn, Gus**
Whoopee, 66

**Kalman, Emmerich**
Countess Maritza, 53

**Kander, John**
Cabaret, 219
Chicago, 244
Happy Time, Tho, 222
Woman of the Year, 260
Zorba, 225 & 268

**Kern, Jerome**
Cat and the Fiddle, The, 77
Girl from Utah, The, 19
Leave It to Jane, 26
Music in the Air, 81
Oh, Boy!, 24
Oh, Lady! Lady!!, 26
Roberta, 84
Sally, 33
Show Boat, 60 & 128
Sunny, 50
Sweet Adeline, 68
Very Good Eddie, 23

**Kleban, Edward**
Chorus Line, A, 243

**Kretzmer, Herbert**
Les Misérables, 275

**Krieger, Henry**
Dreamgirls, 261
Tap Dance Kid, The, 268

**Lane, Burton**
Earl Carroll Vanities, 76
Finian's Rainbow, 133
On A Clear Day You Can See Forever, 213

## Composer/Lyricist Index

# Librettist Index

## Abbott, George
Boys from Syracuse, The, 107
Damn Yankees, 167
Fiorello!, 186
High Button Shoes, 136
New Girl in Town, 173
On Your Toes, 94 & 264
Pajama Game, The, 161
Pal Joey, 112 & 153
Tree Grows in Brooklyn, A, 152
Where's Charley?, 138

## Anderson, Maxwell
Knickerbocker Holiday, 104
Lost in the Stars, 144

## Appell, Don
Milk and Honey, 195

## Ashman, Howard
Little Shop of Horrors, 262

## Atteridge, Harold
Sinbad, 29

## Barer, Marshall
Once Upon a Mattress, 181

## Barras, Charles M.
Black Crook, The, 3

## Barrett, James Lee
Shenandoah, 242

## Bart, Lionel
Oliver!, 201

## Bartholomae, Philip
Very Good Eddie, 23

## Baum, L. Frank
Wizard of Oz, The, 8

## Behrman, S. N.
Fanny, 164

## Besoyan, Rick
Little Mary Sunshine, 186

## Bissell, Richard
Damn Yankees, 167
Pajama Game, The, 161

## Blackwell, Charles
Tap Dance Kid, The, 268

## Blitzstein, Marc
Cradle Will Rock, The, 101
Threepenny Opera, The, 159

## Blossom, Henry
Mlle. Modiste, 10
Red Mill, The, 13

## Bock, Jerry
Apple Tree, The, 218

## Bolton, Guy
Anything Goes, 88
Follow the Girls, 124
Girl Crazy, 72
Lady, Be Good!, 44
Leave It to Jane, 26
Oh, Boy!, 24
Oh, Kay!, 53
Oh, Lady! Lady!!, 26
Rio Rita, 55
Rosalie, 62
Sally, 33
Tip-Toes, 52
Very Good Eddie, 23

## Bontemps, Arna
St. Louis Woman, 129

## Bramble, Mark
Barnum, 256
42nd Street, 257

## Bricusse, Leslie
Roar of the Greasepaint—The
  Smell of the Crowd, The, 212
Stop the World—I Want to Get
  Off, 199

## Brown, Lew
Flying High, 71

**Nemiroff, Robert**
Raisin, 239

**Newley, Anthony**
Roar of the Greasepaint—The
Smell of the Crowd, The, 212
Stop the World—I Want to Get
Off, 199

**Norman, Monty**
Irma la Douce, 190

**O'Hara, John**
Pal Joey, 112 & 153

**Odets, Clifford**
Golden Boy, 210

**Panama, Norman**
Li'l Abner, 171

**Pascal, Fran**
George M!, 223

**Pascal, John**
George M!, 223

**Perelman, S. J.**
One Touch of Venus, 120

**Post, W. H.**
Vagabond King, The, 48

**Rado, James**
Hair, 224

**Ragni, Gerome**
Hair, 224

**Randall, Bob**
Magic Show, The, 240

**Rice, Elmer**
Street Scene, 132

**Rigby, Harry**
Irene, 238

**Roberts, Ben**
Merry Widow, The, 120

**Rodgers, Richard**
Babes in Arms, 98
By Jupiter, 116
I Married an Angel, 102
On Your Toes, 94 & 264

**Roos, William**
As the Girls Go, 139

**Root, Lynn**
Cabin in the Sky, 111

**Rose, L. Arthur**
Me and My Girl, 273

**Rose, Philip**
Purlie, 228
Shenandoah, 242

**Russell, Robert**
Take Me Along, 183

**Ryskind, Morrie**
Cocoanuts, The, 51
Louisiana Purchase, 110
Of Thee I Sing, 78
Strike Up the Band, 70

**Saidy, Fred**
Bloomer Girl, 125
Finian's Rainbow, 133
Jamaica, 176

**Samuels, Lesser**
Greenwillow, 187

**Schulberg, Budd**
What Makes Sammy Run?, 206

**Schulberg, Stuart**
What Makes Sammy Run?, 206

**Schwab, Laurence**
Follow Thru, 67
Good News!, 56
New Moon, The, 64
Take a Chance, 82

**Shapiro, Mel**
Two Gentlemen of Verona, 234

**Shaw, David**
Redhead, 179

**Sheldon, Sidney**
Merry Widow, The, 120
Redhead, 179

# Director Index

**Caird, John**
Les Misérables, 275

**Capalbo, Carmen**
Threepenny Opera, The, 159

**Carroll, Earl**
Earl Carroll Vanities, 76

**Carroll, Vinnette**
Don't Bother Me, I Can't Cope, 235

**Champion, Gower**
Bye Bye Birdie, 188
Carnival, 195
42nd Street, 257
Happy Time, The, 222
Hello, Dolly!, 204
High Spirits, 208
I Do! I Do!, 220
Irene, 238
Lend an Ear, 139
Sugar, 235

**Charlot, Andre**
Andre Charlot's Revue of 1924, 42

**Charnin, Martin**
Annie, 247

**Coe, Peter**
Oliver!, 201

**Cohan, George M.**
Forty-five Minutes from
Broadway, 13
Little Johnny Jones, 10

**Coini, Jacques**
Naughty Marietta, 17

**Collier, William**
Music Box Revue, 37

**Colvan, Zeke**
Show Boat, 60

**Connolly, Bobby**
Ziegfeld Follies, 85

**Coward, Noël**
Bitter Sweet, 68
High Spirits, 208

**Da Costa, Morton**
Music Man, The, 177
Plain and Fancy, 166

**Dale, Grover**
Magic Show, The, 240

**Delmar, Harry**
Follow the Girls, 124

**de Mille, Agnes**
Allegro, 136

**Dexter, John**
Do I Hear a Waltz?, 210

**Dickey, Paul**
Rose-Marie, 43

**Dietz, Howard**
Flying Colors, 80

**Dixon, Harry**
Robin Hood, 5

**Donehue, Vincent J.**
Sound of Music, The, 184

**Donnelly, Dorothy**
Poppy, 40

**Dowling, Edward Duryea**
Hellzapoppin, 103

**Driver, Donald**
Your Own Thing, 222

**Eagle, Oscar**
Cocoanuts, The, 51

**Edouin, Willie**
Florodora, 6

**Edwardes, Felix**
Lady, Be Good!, 44

**Errol, Leon**
Ziegfeld Follies, 20

**Feuer, Cy**
Boy Friend, The, 162
Little Me, 200
Silk Stockings, 166

# Choreographer Index

# Choreographer Index

**Charmoli, Tony**
Woman of the Year, 260

**Cole, Jack**
Funny Thing Happened on the
Way to the Forum, A, 198
Jamaica, 176
Kismet, 158
Man of La Mancha, 215

**Connolly, Bobby**
Desert Song, The, 54
Flying High, 71
Follow Thru, 67
Funny Face, 59
Good News!, 56
New Moon, The, 64
Take a Chance, 82
Ziegfeld Follies, 85

**Costa, David**
Black Crook, The, 3

**Cowan, Edie**
Little Shop of Horrors, 262

**Dale, Grover**
Magic Show, The, 240

**Daniele, Graciela**
Mystery of Edwin Drood, The,
271
Pirates of Penzance, The, 258
Zorba, 268

**Daniels, Danny**
High Spirits, 208
Little Show, The, 67
Sweet Adeline, 68
Tap Dance Kid, The, 268

**Deas, Lawrence**
Shuffle Along, 34

**de Mille, Agnes**
Allegro, 136
Bloomer Girl, 125
Brigadoon, 134
Carousel, 127
Gentlemen Prefer Blondes, 146
Hooray For What!, 100
Oklahoma!, 119 & 255
110 in the Shade, 203
One Touch of Venus, 120
Paint Your Wagon, 152

**Denby, Edwin**
Knickerbocker Holiday, 104

**Erdman, Jean**
Two Gentlemen of Verona, 234

**Faison, George**
Don't Bother Me, I Can't Cope, 235
Wiz, The, 241

**Faria, Arthur**
Ain't Misbehavin', 251

**Felix, Seymour**
Hit the Deck!, 56
Peggy-Ann, 54
Rosalie, 62
Whoopee, 66

**Field, Ron**
Applause, 228
Cabaret, 219
Zorba, 225

**Fields, Herbert**
Garrick Gaieties, The, 46

**Flatt, Ernest**
Sugar Babies, 255

**Flatt, Kate**
Les Misérables, 275

**Fokine, Michel**
Rosalie, 62
Ziegfeld Follies, 38

**Fosse, Bob**
Bells Are Ringing, 171
Chicago, 244
Damn Yankees, 167
Dancin', 250
How to Succeed in Business
Without Really Trying, 196
Little Me, 200
New Girl in Town, 173
Pajama Game, The, 161
Pippin, 236
Redhead, 179
Sweet Charity, 216 & 272

**Foster, Allan K.**
Jumbo, 93
Maytime, 24

# Major Cast Members Index

**(Includes only major cast members of opening night Broadway performances.)**

## Major Cast Members Index

**Bernard, Sam**
Music Box Revue, 37

**Bernardi, Herschel**
Zorba, 225

**Berry, Eric**
Boy Friend, The, 162
Pippin, 236

**Beruh, Joseph**
Threepenny Opera, The, 159

**Bettis, Valerie**
Inside U.S.A., 137

**Bickel, George**
Follies of 1907, 14

**Bigley, Isabel**
Guys and Dolls, 148
Me and Juliet, 157

**Bikel, Theodore**
Sound of Music, The, 184

**Binney, Constance**
Oh, Lady! Lady!!, 26

**Birch, Peter**
Carousel, 127

**Bishop, Kelly**
Chorus Line, A, 243

**Blaine, Vivian**
Guys and Dolls, 148

**Blair, Betsy**
Panama Hattie, 111

**Blair, Pamela**
Best Little Whorehouse in Texas,
The, 250
Chorus Line, A, 243
Sugar, 235

**Blaisdell, J. W.**
Black Crook, The, 3

**Blake, Eubie**
Shuffle Along, 34

**Blane, Ralph**
Hooray For What!, 100
Louisiana Purchase, 110

**Bledsoe, Jules**
Show Boat, 60

**Bliss, Helena**
Song of Norway, 124

**Blitzstein, Marc**
Cradle Will Rock, The, 101

**Blore, Eric**
Gay Divorce, 82

**Blyden, Larry**
Apple Tree, The, 218
Flower Drum Song, 178
Wish You Were Here, 154

**Boland, Mary**
Face the Music, 79
Jubilee, 92

**Boles, John**
One Touch of Venus, 120

**Boley, May**
Fortune Teller, The, 6
Jubilee, 92

**Bolger, Ray**
By Jupiter, 116
George White's Scandals, 76
Life Begins at 8:40, 87
On Your Toes, 94
Where's Charley?, 138

**Bolin, Shannon**
Damn Yankees, 167
Golden Apple, The, 160

**Bond, Ruth**
One Touch of Venus, 120

**Bond, Sheila**
Make Mine Manhattan, 137
Street Scene, 132
Wish You Were Here, 154

**Bonfanti, Marie**
Black Crook, The, 3

**Carradine, John**
Funny Thing Happened on the
Way to the Forum, A, 198

**Carrington, Katherine**
Face the Music, 79
Music in the Air, 81

**Carroll, Barbara**
Me and Juliet, 157

**Carroll, Diahann**
House of Flowers, 165
No Strings, 197

**Carroll, Joan**
Panama Hattie, 111

**Carroll, June**
New Faces of 1952, 154

**Carroll, Marie**
Oh, Boy!, 24

**Carson, Doris**
Cat and the Fiddle, The, 77
On Your Toes, 94
Strike Up the Band, 70

**Carter, Nell**
Ain't Misbehavin', 251

**Carter, Ralph**
Raisin, 239

**Carus, Emma**
Follies of 1907, 14

**Case, Allen**
Once Upon a Mattress, 181

**Cassidy, Jack**
Inside U.S.A., 137
She Loves Me, 202
Wish You Were Here, 154

**Castle, Irene**
Watch Your Step, 20

**Castle, Vernon**
Watch Your Step, 20

**Casto, Jean**
Pal Joey, 112

**Catlett, Walter**
Lady, Be Good!, 44
Sally, 33

**Cavanaugh, Hobart**
As the Girls Go, 139
Irene, 32

**Cawthorn, Joseph**
Fortune Teller, The, 6
Girl from Utah, The, 19
Sunny, 50

**Ceballos, Rene**
Dancin', 250

**Chadman, Christopher**
Dancin', 250

**Chandler, Jamie Beth**
Starlight Express, 276

**Channing, Carol**
Gentlemen Prefer Blondes, 146
Hello, Dolly!, 204
Lend an Ear, 139

**Channing, Stockard**
Two Gentlemen of Verona, 234

**Chaplin, Sydney**
Bells Are Ringing, 171
Funny Girl, 207

**Chapman, William**
Greenwillow, 187

**Charnin, Martin**
West Side Story, 175

**Chasen, Dave**
Fine and Dandy, 72

**Chastain, Don**
No Strings, 197

**Ching, William**
Allegro, 136

**Chisholm, Robert**
Sweet Adeline, 68

**Choi, Hye-Young**
King and I, The, 248

**Christie, Audrey**
I Married an Angel, 102

**Christmas, David**
Dames at Sea, 226

## Major Cast Members Index

**Harrigan, Edward**
Mulligan Guard Ball, The, 4

**Harrington, Pat**
Call Me Madam, 147
Panama Hattie, 111

**Harrington, Robert**
Peter Pan, 163

**Harris, Barbara**
Apple Tree, The, 218
On a Clear Day You Can See
Forever, 213

**Harrison, Ray**
Make Mine Manhattan, 137

**Harrison, Rex**
My Fair Lady, 168

**Harrold, Orville**
Naughty Marietta, 17

**Hart, Linda**
Anything Goes, 277

**Hart, Teddy**
Boys from Syracuse, The, 107
One Touch of Venus, 120

**Hart, Tony**
Mulligan Guard Ball, The, 4

**Hart, Vivian**
Countess Maritza, 53

**Hartman, David**
Hello, Dolly!, 204

**Hartman, Grace**
Red, Hot and Blue!, 96

**Hartman, Paul**
Red, Hot and Blue!, 96

**Harum, Eivind**
Woman of the Year, 260

**Harvey, Georgette**
Porgy and Bess, 91

**Haskell, David**
Godspell, 233

**Hassell, George**
Countess Maritza, 53
Student Prince in Heidelberg,
The, 45

**Havoc, June**
Mexican Hayride, 122
Pal Joey, 112

**Hawkins, June**
Carmen Jones, 122
St. Louis Woman, 129

**Haworth, Jill**
Cabaret, 219

**Hay, Mary**
Sally, 33
Sunny, 50

**Hayes, Bill**
Me and Juliet, 157

**Haynes, Tiger**
Wiz, The, 241

**Hazzard, John E.**
Very Good Eddie, 23

**Heald, Anthony**
Anything Goes, 277

**Hearn, George**
La Cage aux Folles, 266

**Heatherton, Joey**
Sound of Music, The, 184

**Heatherton, Ray**
Babes in Arms, 98

**Hecht, Paul**
Rothschilds, The, 230
1776, 227

**Heffernan, John**
Purlie, 228

**Heinsohn, Elisa**
Phantom of the Opera, The,
278

**Hemsley, Sherman**
Purlie, 228

**Henderson, Florence**
Fanny, 164
Wish You Were Here, 154

**Henning, Doug**
Magic Show, The, 240

**Herbert, Evelyn**
New Moon, The, 64

# Major Cast Members Index

# Major Cast Members Index

# Major Cast Members Index

**Whiting, Jack**
Golden Apple, The, 160
Hold Everything!, 65
Hooray For What!, 100
Take a Chance, 82
Ziegfeld Follies, 38

**Whittell, Josephine**
No, No, Nanette, 47

**Wickes, Mary**
Oklahoma!, 255

**Wilkerson, Arnold**
Don't Bother Me, I Can't Cope, 235

**Wilkinson, Colm**
Les Misérables, 275

**Wilkof, Lee**
Little Shop of Horrors, 262
Sweet Charity, 272

**Willard, John**
Very Good Eddie, 23

**Williams, Allison**
Sweet Charity, 272

**Williams, Ann**
Applause, 228

**Williams, Bert**
Ziegfeld Follies, 20 & 31

**Williams, Bob**
Sugar Babies, 255

**Williams, Derek**
Jubilee, 92

**Williams, Frances**
Cocoanuts, The, 51
George White's Scandals, 52
Life Begins at 8:40, 87
New Yorkers, The, 74

**Williams, Herb**
At Home Abroad, 89

**Willams, Hope**
New Yorkers, The, 74

**Williams, Jack**
Let's Face It!, 115

**Williams, Ralph**
She Loves Me, 202

**Williams, Sammy**
Chorus Line, A, 243

**Wills Jr., Lou**
One Touch of Venus, 120
Tree Grows in Brooklyn, A, 152

**Wilson, Billy**
Jamaica, 176

**Wilson, Dooley**
Bloomer Girl, 125
Cabin in the Sky, 111

**Wilson, Edwin**
Sweethearts, 19

**Wilson, Lloyd**
Trip to Chinatown, A, 5

**Wilson, Patricia**
Fiorello!, 186

**Winninger, Charles**
No, No, Nanette, 47
Show Boat, 60

**Winston, Hattie**
Tap Dance Kid, The, 268

**Winter, David**
West Side Story, 175

**Winter, Edward**
Cabaret, 219
Promises, Promises, 226

**Winters, Lawrence**
Call Me Mister, 129

**Wise, Scott**
Jerome Robbins' Broadway, 279
Song and Dance, 271

**Withee, Mabel**
Cocoanuts, The, 51
Sinbad, 29

**Witter, William C.**
Barnum, 256

**Wolfington, Iggie**
Music Man, The, 177

**Wolfson, Martin**
South Pacific, 143

# Theatre Index